GALATIANS

Sacra Pagina Series

Volume 9

Galatians

Frank J. Matera

Daniel J. Harrington, S.J.
Editor

A Michael Glazier Book
THE LITURGICAL PRESS
Collegeville, Minnesota

Illustration reproduced with the permission of the Universitätsbibliothek Graz, Austria, Cod. 143, fol. 501b (13th c. Breviarium Benedictinum), from a microfilm in the Hill Monastic Manuscript Library, Collegeville, Minnesota.

A Michael Glazier Book published by The Liturgical Press.

1   2   3   4   5   6   7   8   9

Library of Congress Cataloging-in-Publication Data

Matera, Frank J.
    Galatians / Frank J. Matera ; Daniel J. Harrington, editor.
       p. cm. — (Sacra pagina series ; v. 9)
    "A Michael Glazier book."
    Includes bibliographical references and index.
    ISBN 0-8146-5811-3
    1. Bible. N.T. Galatians—Commentaries. I. Harrington, Daniel
J. II. Bible. N.T. Galatians. English. Matera. 1992.
III. Title. IV. Series: Sacra pagina series ; 9.
BS2685.3.M38   1992
227'.4077—dc20   92-12400
                                                 CIP

CONTENTS

v

EDITOR'S PREFACE

Sacra Pagina is a multi-volume commentary on the books of the New Testament. The expression *Sacra Pagina* ("Sacred Page") originally referred to the text of Scripture. In the Middle Ages it also described the study of Scripture to which the interpreter brought the tools of grammar, rhetoric, dialectic, and philosophy. Thus *Sacra Pagina* encompasses both the text to be studied and the activity of interpretation.

This series presents fresh translations and modern expositions of all the books of the New Testament. Written by an international team of Catholic biblical scholars, it is intended for biblical professionals, graduate students, theologians, clergy, and religious educators. The volumes present basic introductory information and close exposition. They self-consciously adopt specific methodological perspectives, but maintain a focus on the issues raised by the New Testament compositions themselves. The goal of *Sacra Pagina* is to provide sound critical analysis without any loss of sensitivity to religious meaning. This series is therefore catholic in two senses of the word: inclusive in its methods and perspectives, and shaped by the context of the Catholic tradition.

The Second Vatican Council described the study of "the sacred page" as the "very soul of sacred theology" (*Dei Verbum* 24). The volumes in this series illustrate how Catholic scholars contribute to the council's call to provide access to Sacred Scripture for all the Christian faithful. Rather than pretending to say the final word on any text, these volumes seek to open up the riches of the New Testament and to invite as many people as possible to study seriously the "sacred page."

DANIEL J. HARRINGTON, S.J.

PREFACE

The writing of a commentary involves many skills, not the least of which is patience. It takes time to listen to the text, and it takes time to learn what others have said. The writing of this commentary has been time-consuming and, at times, all-consuming. It is my hope that this time has not been spent in vain, and that this commentary will be of assistance to the community of faith.

Those acquainted with Galatians know that in recent years there has been a veritable information explosion about this letter. Moreover, several excellent commentaries have been produced. I think especially of those written by Cousar, Bruce, Betz, Fung, Mussner, and most recently that of Longenecker. And of course, there are the venerable commentaries of Lightfoot, Burton, Lagrange, and Schlier. Why, then, yet another commentary?

One can argue, and argue very well, that the market is saturated. However, although American Catholics have been active in Pauline studies, only a few (Fitzmyer, Osiek, Quesnell) have produced commentaries on Galatians. Their commentaries were either constrained by the space allotted to them, or they were more popular in intent. This commentary is more extensive and has had the luxury of investigating the letter in greater detail.

Every commentator inevitably makes a number of decisions that he or she must sustain. In the case of this commentary, reviewers will soon discover that I have argued for the subjective genitive when interpreting *pistis Iēsou Christou* (2:16). Thus, I believe that Paul was talking about the faith of Jesus Christ. Likewise, I have argued that the expression, "works of the Law" (2:16), refers primarily to circumcision, dietary regulations, and Sabbath observance rather than to the several prescriptions of the Torah. In my view Paul was not arguing against legalists who required righteousness by works so much as he sought to integrate Gentiles and Jews by pointing to the Christ event as the fulfillment of God's promises. Finally, it is my conviction that the often neglected parenesis in the final chapters of Galatians is an integral part of the argument that the Apostle develops and not a mere appendage to the letter.

The translation of Galatians is, of course, my own. For the most part, it tends to be rather literal. Where possible, I have employed gender-inclusive language. When quoting texts other than Galatians, however, I have made use of the NRSV. The exegetical notes provide a commentary which deals with technical and philological matters, while the commentary proper gives the reader a more synthetic view of the letter.

I wish to express my gratitude to Daniel Harrington who read the manuscript of this work and made many helpful suggestions. Finally, this book is dedicated to the memory fo the Most Reverend John F. Whealon, Archbishop of Hartford from 1969 to 1991. A pastor and a man of learning, Archbishop Whealon was a pioneering member of the Catholic Biblical Association and an important voice among his fellow bishops on behalf of biblical scholarship. It is my hope that this commentary will honor his memory.

FRANK J. MATERA
Department of Theology
The Catholic University of America

ABBREVIATIONS

Biblical Books and Apocrypha

Gen	Nah	1-2-3-4 Kgdms	John
Exod	Hab	Add Esth	Acts
Lev	Zeph	Bar	Rom
Num	Hag	Bel	1-2 Cor
Deut	Zech	1-2 Esdr	Gal
Josh	Mal	4 Ezra	Eph
Judg	Ps (*pl.*: Pss)	Jdt	Phil
1-2 Sam	Job	Ep Jer	Col
1-2 Kgs	Prov	1-2-3-4 Macc	1-2 Thess
Isa	Ruth	Pr Azar	1-2 Tim
Jer	Cant	Pr Man	Titus
Ezek	Eccl (*or* Qoh)	Sir	Phlm
Hos	Lam	Sus	Heb
Joel	Esth	Tob	Jas
Amos	Dan	Wis	1-2 Pet
Obad	Ezra	Matt	1-2-3 John
Jonah	Neh	Mark	Jude
Mic	1-2 Chr	Luke	Rev

Periodicals, Reference Works, and Serials

AnBib	Analecta biblica
AnGreg	Analecta Gregoriana
ANRW	Aufstieg und Niedergang der römischen Welt
AusBR	Australian Biblical Review
BAG	W. Bauer, W. F. Arndt, F. W. Gingrich, and F. W. Danker, *Greek-English Lexicon of the NT*
BDF	F. Blass, A. Debrunner, and R. W. Funk, *A Greek Grammar of the NT*
BETL	Bibliotheca ephemeridum theologicarum lovananiensium

Bib	Biblica
BibKir	Bibel und Kirche
BJRL	Bulletin of the John Rylands University Library of Manchester
BSac	Bibliotheca Sacra
BZNW	Beihefte zur ZNW
CBQ	Catholic Biblical Quarterly
CNT	Commentaire du Nouveau Testament
CurTM	Currents in Theology and Mission
EstBib	Estudios biblicos
ETR	Études théologiques et religieuses
EvQ	Evangelical Quarterly
ExpTim	Expository Times
HeyJ	Heythrop Journal
HR	History of Religions
HTKNT	Herders theologischer Kommentar zum Neuen Testament
HTR	Harvard Theological Review
ICC	International Critical Commentary
Int	Interpretation
ITQ	Irish Theological Quarterly
JAAR	Journal of the American Academy of Religion
JB	Jerusalem Bible
JBL	Journal of Biblical Literature
JETS	Journal of the Evangelical Theological Society
JSNT	Journal for the Study of the New Testament
JSNTSup	Journal for the Study of the New Testament — Supplement Series
KJV	King James Version
LD	Lectio Divina
LS	Louvain Studies
LumVie	Lumière et vie
LXX	Septuagint
MT	Masoretic Text
NAB	New American Bible
NCB	New Century Bible
NEB	New English Bible
NICNT	New International Commentary on the New Testament
NIGTC	New International Greek Testament Commentary
NIV	New International Version
NJB	New Jerusalem Bible
NJBC	New Jerome Biblical Commentary
NovT	Novum Testamentum
NovTSup	Novum Testamentum, Supplements
NRSV	New Revised Standard Version
NT	New Testament
NTM	New Testament Message
NTS	New Testament Studies
OT	Old Testament

RB	Revue biblique
REB	Revised English Version
RSR	Recherches de science religieuse
RSV	Revised Standard Version
SBLDS	SBL Dissertation Series
SE	Studia Evangelica
SEA°	Svensk exegetisk arsbok
SJT	Scottish Journal of Theology
SNTSMS	Society for New Testament Studies Monograph Series
Str-B	H. Strack and P. Billerbeck, Kommentar zum Neuen Testament
TDNT	G. Kittel and G. Friedrich (eds). *Theological Dictionary of the New Testament*
THKNT	Theologischer Handkommentar zum Neuen Testament
TrinJour	Trinity Journal
TToday	Theology Today
USQR	Union Seminary Quarterly Review
WBC	Word Biblical Commentary
WTJ	Westminster Theological Journal
ZAW	Zeitschrift für die alttestamentliche Wissenschaft
ZNW	Zeitschrift für die neutestamentliche Wissenschaft
WMANT	Wissenschaftliche Monographien zum Alten und Neuen Testament

INTRODUCTION

I. The Crisis at Galatia

Although commentators disagree about the precise circumstances which occasioned Paul's letter to the Galatians, all agree that the Apostle wrote to the Galatians in response to a severe crisis. From the very outset of the letter, when Paul affirms his apostleship and rebukes the Galatians for abandoning the one who called them, it is clear that Paul is responding to a situation which threatens "the truth of the Gospel" (1:6).

Paul is a passionate writer and no other letter, except Second Corinthians, is so emotional and passionate in tone as is Galatians. At one moment the Apostle rebukes his audience for abandoning the gospel (1:6-9), at another moment he recalls their former friendship and compares himself to a mother in the pangs of childbirth, until Christ be formed in the community once more (4:12-20). Angered by the intrusion of others who have, in his view, perverted the gospel of Christ (1:7), Paul's language even descends to the level of bad taste when he calls for the self-castration of those who are disturbing his congregation (5:12). Paul's tone is emotional and passionate because the crisis at Galatia threatens the very foundation of the Torah-free gospel which he preaches. What then was the crisis that occasioned Paul's letter to the Galatians?

There is a general agreement among commentators that Paul is responding to a group of teachers or missionaries who are urging the Galatians to be circumcised. But here the agreement ceases. Who are these advocates of circumcision? Where did they come from? Why are they proposing that the Galatians be circumcised? Why is their message of circumcision so appealing to the Galatians who, after all, are Gentiles?

The search for the identity, origin, and message of those who advocate circumcision has generated a veritable library of articles and monographs, but not a consensus. Moreover, whereas scholars formerly labeled the advocates of circumcision "Judaizers," or "Paul's opponents," the development of new hypotheses has resulted in revised labels which are intended to identify the circumcisers more accurately and less tenden-

1

tiously. Thus R. Jewett ("The Agitators") prefers the term "agitators" (the term employed in this commentary), whereas J.L. Martyn ("A Law Observant Mission") advocates the label "teachers." Others, however, continue to refer to the circumcisers as "Judaizers," or as "Paul's opponents." Given the limited data about the situation at Galatia, there will probably never be a consensus about the identity of the agitators and the content of their message. Nevertheless, by reviewing the evidence at hand and the methodology that scholars have employed, it is possible to judge some proposals as more or less probable. Therefore, after reviewing some of the major solutions which have been set forth, this commentary will propose a scenario of the circumstances which led to the crisis at Galatia.

A Brief History of Research

Most hypotheses about the identity of the agitators and the content of their message can be placed into one of the following categories: (1) The agitators were Jewish Christians from Jerusalem. Their relationship to the Church at Jerusalem, their attitude toward Paul, and their message, however, are all matters of dispute. (2) The agitators were Gentile Christians, or Jewish Christians, but from Galatia. (3) The agitators were Gnostics, or sycretistic Jewish Christians, their place of origin not being of primary importance. (4) The agitators consist of two groups, legalists and pneumatics of a libertine tendency. While the former group probably originated in Jerusalem, the latter arose within the Galatian congregation.

F. C. Baur (*Die Christuspartei in der korinthischen Gemeinde*, 1831) is credited with giving rise to the classical expression of the first position: the agitators were Jewish Christians from Jerusalem. Basing himself upon data found in Paul's Corinthian correspondence, Baur concluded that the early Church was characterized by a fierce opposition between Paulinists and Petrinists, i.e., Judaizers. It was the latter, laying great stress upon circumcision, their Jewish heritage, and their relationship to the Jerusalem apostles, who attacked Paul's apostolic authority and dogged him on his Gentile mission, not only at Corinth but at Philippi and Galatia as well.

Although not all agreed with his interpretation of early Christianity, Baur's characterization of the agitators as Judaizers from Jerusalem held sway until the beginning of this century. In 1919, however, W. Lütgert (*Gesetz und Geist*), followed later by J. H. Ropes (*The Singular Problem of the Epistle to the Galatians*, 1929), argued that Paul was actually fighting two sets of opponents at Galatia: Judaizing Christians from Jerusalem and a radical party of spiritualists who opposed both Paul and the Judaizers. Because of the libertine tendencies of these spiritualists Paul altered his argument in the final chapters of Galatians, according to Lütgert, cautioning the Galatians not to abuse their freedom (5:13). Ropes modified Lütgert's hypothesis slightly, suggesting that the Judaizers were of Gentile origin and from Galatia, but he also insisted that in addition to Judaizers, a spiritualist party confronted Paul at Galatia.

Further challenges to Baur's hypothesis came from J. Munck (*Paul and the Salvation of Mankind*, 1954) and a number of authors who have followed his lead. Pointing to 6:13, Munck contended that the present participle in that verse, *peritemnomenoi*, should be construed as a middle voice ("those who receive circumcision") so that the participle refers not to the agitators but to the Galatians: "For even those among you who receive circumcision (*peritemnomenoi*) do not themselves keep the law." In other words, the Judaizers were not outsiders at all. Rather, they were Gentile members of the Galatian community: "they supposed from their reading of the Old Testament that God required of his people that they should be circumcised and observe everything that he had commanded in His Law" (*Paul and the Salvation*, 132). Others have followed Munck's lead. Thus J. Tyson ("Paul's Opponents in Galatia," 1968) advocated that the Judaizers were Jewish Christians, native to Galatia, who, after their conversion, raised questions about the non-circumcised Gentile members of the church. By contrast, A.E. Harvey, ("The Opposition to Paul," 1968) argued that those troubling the Galatians were Gentiles who had only recently become Jewish converts, or were contemplating doing so, and that they were promoting circumcision as a way of avoiding persecution and discrimination. Following a similar line, G. Wagner ("Les motifs de la rédaction de l'épître aux Galates," 1990) has recently proposed that the agitators were newly converted Gentiles who advocated circumcision as a way of attaching themselves to Judaism because it was a religion acknowledged and protected by Roman authority. Though these authors diverge in their interpretation of the evidence, their hypotheses share a common denominator: the agitators did not come to Galatia from Jerusalem.

W. Schmithals ("Die Häretiker in Galatien," 1956) raised yet another challenge against Baur's position. Complaining that the traditional understanding of the agitators was a presupposition of the exegesis of Galatians rather than a result of it, he proposed that the agitators were Gnostics. In his argument, Schmithals relied heavily upon two texts: 5:3 and 6:13. In the first, Paul tells the Galatians that anyone who accepts circumcision must keep the whole Law, and in the second he says that even the circumcised do not keep the Law. In Schmithals's view, both texts indicate that the agitators were neither interested in, nor required, strict observance of the Law. Rather, they advocated circumcision as a kind of mystical rite which would bring the Galatians to a higher state of perfection, whether or not they practiced all of the prescriptions of the Law.

Such an understanding of circumcision and Law suggests to Schmithals that the agitators were Gnostics.

Despite the ingenuity of their theories, Lütgert, Ropes, Munck, Schmithals, and others have not convinced the majority of scholars. First, there is no real indication that Paul is opposing two distinct groups at Galatia: legalists and spiritualists. As this commentary will show, the final chapters of Galatians are not directed at a second front but are a continuation of Paul's argument against accepting the Law. Second, Paul regularly distinguishes between the Galatians and those who are disturbing them (1:7; 3:1; 5:7; 6:12-13), indicating that the agitators have come from outside of the community. It is unlikely, then, that Paul is dealing with a purely internal problem at Galatia. Finally, there is even less likelihood that the agitators were Gnostics. Paul's remarks in 5:3 and 6:13 need not mean that the agitators did not take the Law seriously. In 5:3, Paul is simply reminding the Galatians of something they should already know: circumcision demands fulfillment of the Law. And in 6:13, his remark is basically polemical and *ad hominem*: the agitators do not observe the Law that they preach. Moreover, Paul's argument about Abraham's descendants in chapters 3-4 shows that the Mosaic Law was an integral part of the agitators' message to the Galatians.

Despite the challenges from Lütgert, Ropes, Munck, and Schmithals, it appears that the agitators were Jewish Christians from Jerusalem who espoused circumcision and Law observance. But what was their relationship to the Church at Jerusalem? Did they have the full backing of the Jerusalem apostles, or were they acting independently? Again, how did they view Paul, as a partner or as an enemy? Why did they embark upon a "judaizing" mission? All of these questions have received a variety of answers.

Concerning the relationship of the agitators to the Church at Jerusalem, F.F. Bruce ("Galatian Problems," 1971) argued: "The simplest interpretation of Galatians, on the basis of its internal evidence, agrees remarkably with the statement in Acts xv. 1 that, some time after the extension of the gospel to Asia Minor . . . 'certain persons who had come down from Judaea began to teach the brotherhood that those who were not circumcised in accordance with Mosaic practice could not be saved' " (270). According to this scenario, the agitators did not have the full backing of the Jerusalem Church, as the rest of Acts 15 makes clear. Rather, the Jerusalem apostles supported Paul. Others have been even more specific in their identification of the agitators. For example, G. Luedemann, (*Opposition to Paul*, 1983) contends that "the opponents of Paul are identical with the so-called false brethren who were not able to execute their demand at the Jerusalem Conference that Titus be circumcised and who obviously had not participated in the agreement that was worked out there"

(101). Viewing the situation somewhat differently, however, F. Watson (*Paul, Judaism and the Gentiles*, 1986), identifies the agitators as the "men from James" (Gal 2:12) who defeated Paul at Antioch. According to Watson, "hearing that Paul had founded new churches in Galatia, they too [the men from James] went there in order to put into practice the policies which had already been successful at Antioch" (60).

Concerning the relationship of the agitators to Paul, there is further disagreement. H.D. Betz (*An Anti-Pauline Fragment?*, 1973), for example, argued that experiences such as the incident at Antioch led the agitators to develop a theology which was diametrically opposed to that of Paul, a theology which, Betz contends, can be found in 2 Cor 6:14–7:1. In contrast to Betz, G. Howard (*Crisis in Galatia*, 1979) maintains that although Paul treats the agitators with contempt, they did not view him with similar hostility. They did not oppose Paul but insisted that he, like them, preached circumcision (5:11). Galatians responds to this allegation of the agitators.

Finally, why did the agitators embark upon their mission? Two important responses have been given by R. Jewett and J. L. Martyn. According to Jewett, ("The Agitators," 1971), during the late forties and fifties Jewish zealots persecuted fellow Jews who had close contacts with Gentiles, or who did not maintain the purity of Israel. The agitators at Galatia were Jewish Christians from Judea who reacted to this zealot pressure by embarking upon a campaign of circumcision and Law observance among Gentile Christians such as Paul's converts. The motivation of the agitators, therefore, was to avoid the persecution of Zealots (6:12) by proving their loyalty to the Law. According to Martyn ("A Law Observant Mission," 1985), the agitators were evangelists who are more properly called "teachers." They "are embarked on an ecumenical mission under the genuine conviction that, through the law of his Messiah, God is now reaching out for the Gentiles and thus the whole of humankind" (315). Moreover, the teachers are essentially benevolent to Paul; it is he, not they, who are reacting.

To summarize, there is a general consensus that the agitators were Jewish Christians from Judea who advocated circumcision and Law observance. But there is no consensus about their relationship to the leadership of the Jerusalem Church, their view of Paul, and the precise motives for their mission. While some see the agitators as hostile to Paul, others argue that they viewed themselves as completing or complementing Paul's mission. Therefore, these commentators argue that it is best to call them "teachers" or "evangelists," terms which do not suggest an inherent opposition to Paul. Finally, a variety of answers have been offered, not all of which are catalogued here, to explain why the "teachers," "agitators," "judaizers" undertook their mission, e.g., to avoid persecution, to make the Gentiles Law-observant now that the Messiah has come, etc. All of these questions must now be investigated in light of the text.

A Question of Methodology

After this brief review, the reader is undoubtedly in despair of discovering anything about the identity of the agitators. How is one to distinguish fact from fiction, truth from fancy? Given the complicated and somewhat frustrating quest for "the historical agitators," no commentator can realistically hope to propose a solution which will generate a scholarly consensus. What commentators can do, however, is to bring some methodological clarity to the problem so that the reader can understand how particular commentators have arrived at their conclusion about Paul's opponents. This question of method has been addressed by J. Barclay ("Mirror Reading a Polemical Letter") and G. W. Hansen (*Abraham in Galatians*), and what follows is indebted, in part, to their work.

First, it is important to distinguish between the real agitators at Galatia who lived in the first century and the portrayal of them found in Paul's letter to the Galatians. Since the real agitators are necessarily mediated by what Paul says in his letter, the twentieth-century reader will never come into direct and immediate contact with them. For good or for ill, contemporary readers are destined to know the real agitators through Paul's portrait of them. Consequently, it is salutary to launch a quest for the real agitators with a sense of limitation and humility. Interpreters can then proceed in two stages. In the first stage, they must provide an accurate portrait of what Paul does say about the agitators, realizing that his portrait may or may not correspond to the real historical situation. In the second, on the basis of that portrait and other indications within the text, interpreters can attempt to extrapolate an historical portrait of the agitators from this Pauline portrait, conscious that their reconstruction will never fully correspond to the real agitators.

Second, the primary source for developing a portrait of the agitators is Paul's letter to the Galatians. Thus interpreters must begin with what is found in Galatians and endeavor to describe the crisis at Galatia on the basis of data in the letter. Other sources of information, e.g., Paul's other correspondence, the Acts of the Apostles, second-century sources, etc., may prove helpful, but they are not primary sources for solving the questions raised by the crisis at Galatia. Thus commentators should refrain from too quickly identifying Paul's opponents at Galatia with his opponents at Corinth, Philippi, etc. Moreover, when interpreters fill in the "gaps" found in Galatians with information from Acts, they should clearly and honestly acknowledge this.

Third, a portrait of the agitators should make sense of as much of the data in Galatians as is possible. Theories which are built upon individual verses (5:3; 6:12; 6:13), or which only focus upon one portion of the letter are always suspect. For a hypothesis to be convincing, it must be constructed upon the several texts and themes of Galatians.

Fourth, in order to reconstruct the situation which occasioned Paul's letter to the Galatians, one must deduce and infer the problems Paul faced from the answers that he provides. In effect, interpreters must read the text as if looking into a mirror, moving from answer to question, solution to problem. In doing so, however, they must be careful that their "mirror reading" does not result in an over-reading of the text. For example, not every strong affirmation made by Paul is necessarily a response to a charge made by the agitators. Paul's strong affirmation in 1:1, for instance, that his apostleship does not derive from human beings may mean that the agitators questioned his apostolic credentials, but it does not necessarily mean this. Reading 1:1 as a defense of Paul's apostolic credentials is one possible reading of the text, but it is not the only one (see, G. Lyons, *Pauline Autobiography*).

In reconstructing the situation that occasioned Galatians, then, interpreters should give special attention to those themes and motifs which are repeatedly emphasized and are clearly central to Paul's argument. For example, Paul spends a great deal of time discussing his relationship with the Church at Jerusalem. Likewise, the person of Abraham, as well as terms such as "faith" and "works of the Law" occur again and again. Finally, the last two chapters of Galatians provide an extended moral exhortation in which Paul encourages his converts to walk by the Spirit. Why? Given the important role that these themes and texts play in the letter, it is probable that this material is a response, at least in part, to the teaching of the agitators.

Fifth, attention should be paid to scriptural texts or stories employed by Paul which, on face value, do not appear to support his position. For example, why does Paul employ the allegory of Sarah and Hagar (4:21-31) when the literal meaning of the story does not support his argument? Could it be that the agitators were the first to use this story and that Paul is reinterpreting it for the Galatians? If interpreters keep these criteria in mind, they will be able to offer a tentative description of the agitators.

The Agitators and Their Gospel

There are five texts in which Paul directly refers to the agitators: 1:7; 3:1; 4:17; 5:7-12; and 6:12-13.

> 1:7. There is no other gospel, but some (*tines*) are disturbing (*tarassontes*) you and want to pervert the gospel of Christ.

3:1. O foolish Galatians! Who (*tis*) bewitched you, before whose eyes Jesus Christ was publicly portrayed as crucified?

4:17. They court your favor, not in a way which is commendable, but they want to isolate you in order that you might court their favor.

5:7, 10, 12. You were running so well. Who (*tis*) hindered you from obeying the truth? . . . the one disturbing you (*ho tarassōn*) you will bear the judgment, whoever he (*hos tis ean*) is. . . . Would that those disturbing (*hoi anastatountes*) you might make eunuchs of themselves!

6:12-13. Those (*hosoi*) who want to make a good showing in the flesh, these (*houtoi*) are trying to compel you to be circumcised, only that they might not be persecuted for the cross of Christ. Not even those who are circumcised keep the Law, but they want you to be circumcised so that they can boast in your flesh.

Whether or not the portrait of the agitators found in these texts corresponds to the real agitators, there is little doubt about how Paul perceives them. First, they are outsiders who have disturbed (*tarassontes, anastatountes*) the equilibrium of the Galatians. Thus the term "agitators" is an apt description of these people, at least from Paul's point of view. Second, this disturbance has endangered the gospel message which Paul preached to the Galatians. Thus Paul accuses the agitators of perverting the gospel of Christ; that is, they are misconstruing what God has done in Christ. Third, Paul views the agitators as cunning, deceptive, and hypocritical. Previous to their arrival, the Galatians were making progress in the Christian life as preached by Paul. The agitators, however, have mesmerized the Galatians to the point of bewitching them. As a result, the progress of the Galatians in the gospel has been seriously impeded. Moreover, while the agitators are presently courting the favor of the Galatians, Paul argues that the real motive of the agitators is to isolate them so that they will be totally dependent upon them. Fourth, circumcision and Law observance are central to the message of the agitators. But from Paul's point of view, the agitators are hypocritical since they seek to escape persecution and do not observe the Law which they preach.

Given the rebuking nature of these remarks, it should be clear that Paul's depiction of the agitators is less than objective. Moreover, it is probable that the Galatians were taken aback by Paul's description of the agitators; otherwise there would have been no need for Paul to describe them in such harsh terms. Despite the tendentious nature of Paul's remarks, however, it is still possible to extrapolate some important information about the real agitators: namely, they require the Galatians to be circumcised and to observe the Mosaic Law. Whether or not the agitators were as hostile to Paul as he was to them, however, it is impossible to say on the basis of these remarks alone.

The texts listed above are the only places in which Paul directly refers to his opponents. In addition to these texts, however, some of the arguments which he makes in Galatians offer clues to the "other gospel" that the agitators proclaimed. A first clue is found in 3:6-29, the centerpiece of Paul's argument that the Galatians are Abraham's descendants because they are "in Christ." While this argument is ingenious, it is hardly convincing given Genesis 17 in which God tells Abraham: "Any uncircumcised male who is not circumcised in the flesh of his foreskin shall be cut off from his people; he has broken my covenant" (Gen 17:14). Given the importance of circumcision in the Abraham narrative, one wonders if Paul would have appealed to the Abraham story if the agitators had not already done so. Paul's use of the Abraham narrative becomes even more problematic when one considers the Sarah-Hagar allegory in 4:21-31. The plain meaning of the story is that the Gentiles are the descendants of Hagar, but Paul argues that his Galatian converts are the descendants of Isaac, even though they are not circumcised! In addition to this exegesis, Paul spends a great deal of time drawing a wedge between the promise made to Abraham and the Law given through the mediation of angels (3:15-25) to Moses. Here, Paul's interpretation of the Law again runs counter to traditional Jewish exegesis, suggesting that he is responding to the teaching of the agitators. On the basis of the material found in chapters 3–4, it appears that the agitators came to Galatia with a message something like the following.

> Paul has told you that Jesus is the long awaited Messiah of Israel. However, you will only enjoy the full benefit of Israel's Messiah if you become Abraham's descendants. God made an eternal covenant of circumcision with Abraham (Gen 17:19) and required that all of his descendants be circumcised. Furthermore, God gave the Law to Moses, warning that those who do not do all that is written in the Book of the Law will be cursed (Deut 27:26, see Gal 3:10), and promising that those who do the Law will live (Lev 18:5, see Gal 3:12). Therefore, if you want to participate in the full benefit of Israel's Messiah, you must do the "works of the Law"; that is, you must accept circumcision, abstain from unclean food, and respect the days and festivals required by Torah.

A second clue to the message of the agitators is found in Paul's extended autobiographical statement in the first two chapters of this letter. In those chapters, Paul is intent upon establishing the divine origin of his Torah-free gospel and his independent, but respectful, relationship to the Church at Jerusalem. Thus he asserts that he did not receive the Torah-free gospel that he preaches from other human beings, nor was he taught it. Rather, it came from God, through a revelation of Jesus Christ (1:11-12). To substantiate this Paul recalls his former life as a persecutor of the Church and two visits which he made to Jerusalem. The first of these visits was a private meeting with Cephas, three years after Paul's call, for the sake of consultation. A second meeting followed fourteen years later (2:1) at which Paul defended the truth of the gospel. At that meeting the pillar apostles acknowledged his gospel despite the protestations of certain false brethren who urged that Titus (and so all Gentile converts) be circumcised. Finally, at Antioch Paul withstood Peter to his face because Peter betrayed the truth of the gospel by withdrawing from table fellowship.

This material, of course, is open to many diverse interpretations. Nevertheless, it is clear from chapters 1–2 that Paul found it necessary to explain the origin of his Torah-free gospel and his relationship to Jerusalem. Thus the agitators may have come to Galatia with claims such as these.

> We have a special relationship to Jerusalem. Indeed, Jerusalem is our mother. Therefore, you must heed our gospel which is rooted in the authentic gospel preached at Jerusalem. That gospel, unlike the gospel proclaimed by Paul, requires Torah and circumcision. If you heed our gospel, you will do what the pillar apostles require of all Gentiles, for at Antioch even Peter, Barnabas, and other Jewish believers refused to share table fellowship with Gentile believers until they practiced "works of the Law."

A third clue to the message of the agitators is found in the final chapters of this letter (5:13–6:10) where Paul provides an extended moral exhortation. In that parenesis the Apostle warns the Galatians to avoid community strife (5:15, 26), and tells them that if they walk by the Spirit they will overcome the desires of the flesh (5:16). Furthermore, he instructs the Galatians that the Law is fulfilled in the love commandment (5:14). Thus, if they serve one another in love (5:13), and bear each other's burdens, they will fulfill the Law of Christ (6:2). These remarks suggest that the Galatians were in need of moral guidance. Their community was torn by community strife and jealousy. In such a situation, the Galatians may have questioned the value of a Law-free gospel. Thus the agitators may have argued in the following way.

> The Law provides moral guidance; Paul's Torah-free gospel does not. Therefore, if you want to live a life in accordance with the teaching of the Messiah, you must follow the precepts of the Law. Paul's Torah-free gospel is not sufficient; it does not teach you what is right and what is wrong. It does not enable you to overcome the desires of the flesh.

By way of summary, the agitators probably came from Jerusalem with claims of support from some faction of the Jerusalem apostles. Exactly what faction, however, it is impossible to say. Claiming the support of Jerusalem, they criticized Paul and said that his Torah-free gospel was not sufficient. The core of their own message centered upon the person of Abraham and the importance of becoming his descendant. Thus they told the Galatians that they could only enjoy the full benefits of the Jewish Messiah if they accepted circumcision and did the "works of the Law." The Law, they said, is not opposed to faith in the Messiah. Rather, it brings this faith to completion (3:3). Moreover, the Law provides a way of overcoming the desires of the flesh.

The problem at Galatia, then, was primarily social in nature: how are Gentile Christians to interact with Christians who are Jewish by birth? Must they accept the customs, practices, and culture of Jewish believers, or may they become members of the commonwealth of Israel solely on the basis of what God has done in Jesus Christ? The agitators espoused a doctrine which might anachronistically be called cultural imperialism: one cannot become a descendant of Abraham apart from those nomistic (legal) works which traditionally identify Jews as Jews: circumcision; food regulations, Sabbath and festival observances.

The Letter to Galatians is not so much about legalism, righteousness by works, and personal salvation as it is about doing the right works of the Law and proper cultural behavior in order to become a full member of the commonwealth of Israel.

II. *Paul's Response to the Crisis at Galatia*

Paul's response to the crisis at Galatia is, of course, his letter to the Galatians. In terms of rhetorical criticism, this letter is a sustained exercise in deliberative rhetoric; that is, Paul tries to persuade the Galatians not to accept the agitators' gospel of circumcision. To be sure, Paul employs other rhetorical strategies as well. Thus there are moments when the Apostle rebukes the Galatians for having gone astray and appeals to them to change their present course of action. Moreover, there are sections in which Paul clearly defends the divine origin of his Torah-free gospel. But, taken as a whole, Galatians is primarily an example of deliberative rhetoric. Paul's concern is to persuade the Galatians that they will embark upon the wrong path if they submit to circumcision as the agitators demand. Put most simply, Paul's response to the crisis at Galatia is to persuade his audience that they do not need to be circumcised.

But what is Paul's rhetorical strategy? What does he do in order to persuade his Gentile converts that they should not be circumcised? The detailed answer to these questions, of course, is found in the pages of this commentary. Commentaries, however, are rarely read from cover to cover. Those who read them are usually interested in particular passages or sections. As a result, the reader often fails to grasp the broader movement of the work's argument. The purpose of this section, therefore, is to provide the readers of this commentary with an overview of what is found in this commentary: a summary or synopsis of Paul's response to the crisis at Galatia.

The Structure of Galatians

The manner in which authors present their material is the single, most important factor in the rhetoric of argumentation. Evidence alone does not persuade. Effective lawyers and persuasive public speakers know that how they present their evidence, and the manner in which they arrange their arguments, are as important as the evidence which they present. Legions of lawyers and public speakers have failed to persuade their audiences, not because the evidence was against them, but because they did not order and arrange their argument in a persuasive manner. This is not to say that style is more important than substance, or that rhetoric is simply a manner of manipulation. Rather it is an affirmation that all speech is to one degree or another rhetorical, and that all arguments, even the least effective, are structured. The more carefully structured the argument is, however, the more likely it is to persuade.

Paul carefully structured and arranged his own letters in order to persuade the congregations which heard them to adopt his point of view. For example, in Romans, in order to persuade the members of that community that everybody, Jew as well as Greek, is in need of God's justifying grace, the Apostle describes the universal sinfulness of humanity (Rom 1:18-3:20). As a result, those who hear or read Romans find themselves in a rhetorical maze with a single exit: since all have sinned, all are in need of God's righteousness (Rom 3:21-26).

Paul's letter to the Galatians is no exception to this rule of rhetoric. In Galatians, Paul is intent upon showing his Gentile converts the utter folly of accepting circumcision. In order to persuade them to adopt his point of view, he arranges his arguments in such a way that by the end of the letter the Galatians find themselves in a rhetorical maze with only one exit: they must refuse to be circumcised because Gentiles who accept circumcision are cut off from Christ; circumcision will relegate them to the realm of the Law. Paul structures his letter in the following way.

THE GREETING 1:1-5

A STATEMENT OF ASTONISHMENT 1:6-10

I. *The Truth of the Gospel 1:11–2:21*

1:11-12   Paul's gospel is not of human origin.
1:13-17   Paul received his gospel through a revelation of Jesus Christ.

Greeting and Rebuke (1:1-10)

Paul begins his rhetorical task in the greeting of his letter (1:1-5) by emphasizing his apostolic credentials. He did not receive his apostleship from a human being or through a human being, but directly through Jesus Christ and the God who raised Jesus from the dead. Moreover, Paul signals what will be a central theme of his argument: the saving death of Jesus Christ who gave himself for our sins in order to deliver us from the present evil age. From the outset of the letter, therefore, Paul establishes his apostolic credentials and alludes to the content of the gospel which he preaches.

The most startling aspect of Paul's introductory remarks, however, is the absence of a thanksgiving formula after the greeting. Instead of a prayer on behalf of the community, Paul begins with a sharp rebuke, a statement of astonishment (1:6-10). From the very outset, the Galatians are put off guard as Paul seizes the rhetorical high ground. He accuses the Galatians of abandoning the God who called them and of turning to another gospel which Paul immediately identifies as a perversion of the gospel of Christ. Before Paul has even begun the main body of the letter, therefore, he has put the Galatians in a defensive posture. It is not he who needs to defend himself; it is the Galatians! They are in the process of abandoning the one who called them by turning to a false gospel.

The Truth of the Gospel (1:11-2:21)

The first part of Galatians (1:11-2:21) consists of an extended autobiographical statement which begins with Paul's life as a persecutor of the Church and concludes with the incident at Antioch. The manner in which Paul narrates these events signals that the autobiographical information of this section is not purely informational. The Galatians undoubtedly knew many of the events of Paul's life which are narrated in this section. What they did not know, however, was Paul's perspective on them. Therefore, he recounts his call to preach the gospel to the Gentiles, his visits to Jerusalem, and the incident at Antioch in order to persuade the Galatians (1) that his Torah-free gospel was divinely revealed, (2) that even the pillar apostles (James, Cephas, and John) acknowledged that he was entrusted with the gospel to the Gentiles, and (3) that his behavior corresponds to the gospel which he preaches.

Paul was not taught the gospel that he preaches, nor did he receive it from another human being. Rather God, who had set aside Paul from his mother's womb, revealed his Son to him so that Paul could preach the gospel to the Gentiles. It was in that moment of revelation that the Torah-free gospel was born for Paul, even if its many details were hammered out later in the midst of controversy such as that at Galatia. Because Paul understood the meaning of that revelation, he immediately went to Arabia where he presumably began to preach to Gentiles. When he did go to Jerusalem three years later, it was only to visit privately with Cephas, and only for a fortnight. It was not an official meeting at which Paul was deputized or instructed about the revelation he had received three years earlier.

A more official meeting occurred fourteen years after the first visit to Jerusalem. At this second meeting two things happened. First, Paul defended the truth of the gospel for his Gentile converts by refusing to submit to certain false brethren who urged him to circumcise Titus. Second, even the pillar apostles acknowledged his apostolate among the uncircumcised, and by implication among the Galatians. What Paul already knew from his revelation of Jesus Christ, Jerusalem acknowledged: there is no need for Gentiles such as the Galatians to be circumcised.

The meeting at Jerusalem, however, did not settle all issues. Certain partisans of James came to Antioch and persuaded Peter, Barnabas, and other Jewish Christians to withdraw from table fellowship with Gentile Christians. But whereas Peter betrayed the truth of the gospel at Antioch by withdrawing, Paul withstood the partisans of James, just as he withstood the false brethren at Jerusalem, just as the Galatians should withstand the agitators.

At the end of this section (2:15-21) Paul lays out the content of the gospel that he preaches. No one stands acquitted before God on the basis of nomistic service ("works of the Law"). Those outward works that distinguish Jews from Gentiles (circumcision, food regulations, Sabbath observance) do not justify a person. Rather, we are put in the correct and proper relationship to God on the basis of the faithfulness of Jesus Christ in whom we believe. The faith of Jesus Christ, not the works of the Law, acquit us. This faith is Christ's faithfulness to God which he manifested by handing himself over for us to deliver us from the present evil age. On the basis of this faith, we believe in Jesus Christ.

By the close of this autobiographical section, Paul has maneuvered his audience to a position which is favorable to his point of view: the Torah-free gospel is the result of a revelation of Jesus Christ; the pillar apostles acknowledged the grace of Paul's mission to the uncircumcised; and Paul's own behavior corresponds to the gospel which he preaches. The Galatians should be well disposed to hear the rest of Paul's argument.

The Children of the Promise (3:1–5:12)

Having explained the divine origin of his Torah-free gospel and his relationship to Jerusalem, in the second part of Galatians (3:1–5:12) Paul explains why it is not necessary for the Galatians to accept circumcision: they are already Abraham's seed because they are in Christ who is Abraham's singular descendant. This line of argumentation is necessary because the agitators have told the Galatians that unless they are circumcised they will not be numbered among the descendants of Abraham.

To persuade the Galatians that nomistic service will not be of any value to them, Paul points to the experience of the Galatians: they already enjoy the eschatological gift of the Spirit (3:1-6). The Galatians received that gift, however, long before they thought of adopting the legal works advocated by the agitators; they received the Spirit when they believed in the message of faith, the message of the crucified Christ which Paul preached to them. If they have already received the eschatological gift of the Spirit, what do they hope to attain by nomistic service?

The heart of Paul's argument, however, is found in 3:7-29. Here, he begins by telling the Galatians that people of faith (*hoi ek pisteōs*) are Abraham's children (3:7), and he concludes by proclaiming that if the Galatians are in Christ they are Abraham's seed (3:29). Between these two verses, Paul employs a series of complicated arguments which focus upon the relationship of the promise made to Abraham and the Law given by Moses. Whereas the agitators interpreted the promise made to Abraham in light of the Mosaic Law, Paul vigorously argues that the Law is subordinated to the promise. Now that the heir of the promise, the Christ, has come, the Law's role is concluded.

To persuade the Galatians of this, Paul develops a complicated exegetical argument in 3:7-14 intended, perhaps, to counter an argument made by the agitators. Thus, whereas the agitators may have contended that those who do not do the Law are cursed (Deut 27:26) and every one who does the Law will live (Lev 18:5), Paul counters that Christ came to free us from the curse of the Law (Deut 21:23) and that the righteous will live by faith (Hab 2:4).

Next (3:15-20) he argues that the Law is subordinate to the promise and cannot alter God's promise made to Abraham. The Law came 430 years after the promise and was given through the mediation of angels. By contrast, God spoke directly to Abraham. The heart of Paul's argument is that God's promise to Abraham had a singular offspring in view: the Christ. Consequently, all who have been incorporated into Christ through baptism are Abraham's seed, even if they have not been circumcised.

But what about the Law? Is it opposed to the promise? Here Paul's answer departs from the traditional way of understanding Torah. In his view, the role of the Law was temporary. The Law was like a Greek slave, the *paidagōgos*, charged with the discipline and training of a youth. The Law made people aware that they were transgressing God's will, but it did not give life, otherwise justification would have been through the Law. That Christ died upon the cross proves that righteousness does not come from the Law. Otherwise, why did God send his Son? No, the Law only had a temporary function which is concluded now that Abraham's singular offspring has come. The Galatians are not under the Law so long as they are in Christ.

Having shown the Galatians that they are Abraham's offspring because they are in Christ, in 4:1–5:12 Paul's argument takes a rhetorical turn. First, in 4:1-11 he rebukes the Galatians for returning to the period of their religious infancy. Before receiving the gospel, they were in bondage to the elemental principles of religion (*ta stoicheia*), worshipping things that by their very nature were not gods. Having been set free from these elementary principles, they are returning to them by a different route by placing themselves under the Law, another form of rudimentary religion (*ta stoicheia tou kosmou*). Paul wonders if he has labored in vain.

Second, in 4:12-20 Paul makes a personal appeal to the Galatians, asking them to become as he is, free from the Law. He recalls that when he first came to them, they received him as if he were an angel from God. But now that the agitators have arrived, the Galatians view him as their enemy, and only because he has told them the truth. The Apostle likens himself to a mother suffering the pangs of childbirth until Christ be formed in the community once more.

Third, the theme of childbirth provides a transition to the allegory of Hagar and Sarah in 4:21-31, some form of which the Galatians must have heard from the agitators. But whereas the agitators probably used the story to argue that Abraham's descendants, through Isaac, observe the everlasting covenant of circumcision (Gen 17), Paul allegorizes the story and places the agitators in the line of descent that issues from Hagar. Hagar was a slave and her descendants are associated with Mount Sinai. Mount Sinai corresponds to Jerusalem because both are associated with the Law. It is the agitators, then, who are the real descendants of Hagar. Consequently, those who are free of the Law, Paul's own Gentile converts, are the descendants of the free woman, even if they have not been circumcised. There is only one thing to do. Throw out the descendants of the slave woman, throw out the agitators!

Although circumcision is the central issue at Galatia, Paul has not yet mentioned the word. But in the final unit (5:1-12) of this section, he finally does. Since Christ has set the Galatians free, they should not take on a yoke of slavery again by submitting to circumcision. If they do submit to circumcision, they will be responsible for the whole Law; they will be cut off from Christ; and they will fall from grace. This section ends with a crude and even vulgar remark: if the agitators are so intent upon circumcision, let them go all the way. Let them castrate themselves.

By the conclusion of part two, it should be clear to the Galatians that there is no need for circumcision. The Galatians already have what is important: the Spirit. Moreover, they are already Abraham's seed because they are in Christ. But one problem remains. If there is no need for circumcision, and if they are not under the Law, how can they fulfill the Law? How can they live a life which is pleasing to God?

Living by the Spirit (5:13–6:10)

In the third and final part of Galatians (5:13–6:10), Paul responds to the questions raised above. His first answer is that the Galatians will fulfill the Law if they serve one another in love (5:13-15), for the whole Law is fulfilled in a single commandment: love your neighbor as yourself. Consequently, if the Galatians bear one another's burdens they will fulfill the Law of Christ (6:2). This Law of Christ is not another Law above and beyond the Mosaic Law, but the Mosaic Law as lived by Christ. Those who live by the commandment of love, spending themselves for others, will fulfill the Mosaic Law as Christ did.

But how is this possible? In 5:16-26 Paul provides the answer. If the Galatians walk by the Spirit, if they are led by the Spirit, if they follow the Spirit, they will not carry out the desires of the flesh or do the works of the flesh. Instead, the Spirit will produce its fruit within them. In effect, Paul proposes a vision of the moral life in which the believer is guided by the Spirit. Those who are in the realm of the Spirit will live by the Spirit. Far from being an appendix which is loosely related to the main argument, the moral exhortation of these chapters is a continuation of Paul's deliberative rhetoric. There is no need for the Galatians to accept circumcision because they can fulfill the Law through the love commandment. Most importantly, if they walk by the Spirit, the craving of the flesh will have no power over them.

The Conclusion (6:11-18)

Just as the introductory remarks to this letter allowed Paul an opportunity to signal some of the major themes of the letter, so the letter closing provides him with an occasion to summarize what he views as most important. Thus in 6:11-18, Paul once more warns the Galatians about the agitators. Those who are trying to force circumcision upon them are operating from impure motives. They know that if they preach a Torah-free gospel, as Paul does, they will suffer persecution. In God's view, neither circumcision nor the lack of it means anything because in Christ all has been created anew. The death of Christ has effected a new creation which has broken down the wall of separation between Jew and Gentile, slave and free, male and female. How foolish, then, for the Galatians to submit to circumcision. If they adhere to the gospel of the agitators they will remove themselves from the new creation; they will no longer be the Israel of God.

What then is Paul's response to the Galatian crisis? From one point of view, despite his many complicated arguments, it is simple. The Galatians need not be circumcised because they are in Christ. Because they are in Christ, they are already Abraham's offspring. In Christ, they share the gift of the Spirit which allows them to overcome the desires of the flesh. In Christ, they are a new creation so that the distinction between circumcision and the lack of it is abolished. In effect, Paul has put the

Galatians in a rhetorical maze which has only one exit: an absolute and resolute refusal to be circumcised. Should the Galatians refuse to accept this conclusion, they will no longer be in Christ.

III. *The Identity of the Galatians*

Paul addresses this letter *tais ekklesiais tēs Galatias* ("to the churches of Galatia"). From the outset, therefore, it is clear that the Apostle is not writing to a single community but to a number of congregations in Galatia. Moreover, since Paul's purpose is to dissuade the Galatians from accepting circumcision, it would appear that the membership of these churches was composed predominantly, if not exclusively, of Gentiles. But who were the Galatians, and where were their congregations located?

Why There Is A Problem

The identity of the Galatians is a problem because, when Paul wrote to the Galatians, the term "Galatia" could be understood in two different ways. Originally, Galatia referred to a small territory bounded on the north by Bithynia and Paphlagonia, on the east by Pontus, on the south by Cappadocia and Lycaonia, and on the west by Phrygia. This territory was inhabited by a people who were, by race, Celtic. Defeated in 230 B.C. by Attalus I, the king of Pergamum, these Celtic tribes were confined to the area described above which included the cities of Ancyra, Tavium, and Pessinus. After the death of the Galatian King Amyntas in 25 B.C., Augustus formed Galatia into a Roman province which, in addition to the old territory of Galatia, extended further south to include portions of Lycaonia, Pisidia, and Phrygia. As a result, the province of Galatia was larger than the old territory of Galatia and included people who were not ethnically Galatians (Celts). Rather, they were called Galatians because they lived in the Roman province of Galatia. Among these "new Galatians" were the inhabitants of Antioch in Pisidia, Lystra, Iconium, and Derbe, cities in which Paul established Christian communities on his first missionary journey according to Acts 13–14.

These historical and geographical facts lead to the question, "who were the Galatians?" Was Paul writing to the ethnic Galatians, the old Celtic tribes who inhabited the territory to the north, in and around the cities of Ancyra, Tavium, and Pessinus? Or, was he addressing the churches in the southern part of the Roman province of Galatia which he established on his first missionary journey? The answers to these questions have resulted in two theories: the North Galatian hypothesis and the South Galatian hypothesis. Those who support the North Galatian hypothesis argue that Paul was writing to the ethnic Galatians in the old territory to the north, while those who advocate the South Galatian hypothesis contend that he was addressing the churches in the southern portion of the Roman province which he evangelized, according to Luke, on his first missionary journey.

While this question has been strongly contested in scholarly circles, its resolution has more direct importance for Pauline chronology and history than it does for exegesis. Those who espouse one hypothesis or the other are not necessarily committed to interpret the text of Galatians in a particular way. But a decision about this question significantly affects the dating of this letter and the historical reconstruction of the events which surround the crisis at Galatia. For example, the South Galatian hypothesis permits one to assign an early date to the composition of Galatians. Thus F. F. Bruce, a modern commentator who espouses the South Galatian hypothesis, argues that this letter is the earliest of the Pauline letters that we possess. By contrast, the North Galatian hypothesis usually commits a commentator to a later dating of the letter, e.g., the mid-fifties.

The South Galatian hypothesis, however, need not be identified with an early dating of Galatians any more than the North Galatian hypothesis should be associated with a later dating of the same. H. D. Betz (*Galatians*, 5, 12), for example, espouses the North Galatian hypothesis but an early dating of the letter, while R. Fuller (*A Critical Introduction to the New Testament*, 26) favors the South Galatian hypothesis and a later dating of the letter. If readers keep this word of caution in mind, they will find the following summary of assistance.

> *North Galatian hypothesis:* The letter is addressed to the territory to the north inhabited by the old Celtic tribes; this "usually" results in a later dating of the letter, the mid-fifties, because it presupposes further (unattested) missionary activity by Paul.
>
> *South Galatian hypothesis:* The letter is addressed to the province of Galatia which Paul visited on his first missionary journey; this "usually" results in an early dating of the letter, e.g. the late forties or early fifties, because it fits the evidence in Acts.

Why The Problem Is So Difficult To Solve

There are at least two reasons why it is so difficult, if not impossible, to arrive at a consensus about the identity of the Galatians. First, there is only a limited amount of data in the letter which is relevant to this question, and this data is open to different interpretations. The data is as follows.

(1) In 1:1 Paul addresses his letter to "the churches of Galatia," and in 3:1, he rebukes his readers, "O foolish Galatians!" Those who espouse the North Galatian hypothesis argue that Paul would never have called the inhabitants in the southern portion of the Roman Province "Galatians." Those who espouse the South Galatian hypothesis, however, contend that Paul usually employed Roman provincial terminology, e.g., Macedonia and Achaia. Moreover, they argue that "Galatians" would have been the only all-embracing term available to Paul by which to address the inhabitants of a province that included such diverse populations as the inhabitants of Antioch in Pisidia, and the Lycaonian cities of Iconium, Lystra, and Derbe.

(2) In 4:13-15, Paul recalls the circumstances involving his arrival at Galatia. His Galatian ministry was completely fortuitous. Because of a sickness, the exact nature of which he does not disclose, he found it necessary to stay at Galatia. Despite his ailment, the Galatians received him as if he were an angel of God; and so he preached the gospel to them. While this passage informs us about the circumstances of Paul's visit, it does not reveal the location of the Galatian churches. Those who espouse the North Galatian hypothesis, however, point out that in Luke's description of Paul's first missionary journey through South Galatia, there is no indication that Paul suffered any illness as described here, a point against the South Galatian hypothesis.

(3) In 4:20 Paul vents his frustration at the sudden change in the behavior of the Galatians, and he expresses a wish that he could visit them. But for reasons that he does not explain, Paul cannot come to Galatia at this time. While it is impossible to determine exactly why Paul cannot travel to Galatia, many suggest that his preoccupation with the Corinthian crisis would have made such a visit impossible. If this is so, Paul is writing from Ephesus, in the mid-fifties, a point which could be construed as favorable to the North Galatian hypothesis, as traditionally stated.

The second reason it is so difficult to solve this question arises from the complex and subtle relationship between the data of Galatians and the Acts of the Apostles. Acts presents a wealth of information about Paul's missionary activity, but there is no consensus about how that information should be coordinated with what Paul says in Galatians. For example, is the apostolic conference described by Luke in Acts 15 to be identified with the meeting related by Paul in Galatians 2? If it is, how are the differences to be explained, e.g., the absence of an apostolic decree from Gal 2? Again, Acts reports that Paul undertook three great missionary journeys: a first journey before the conference of Acts 15, and two journeys, to Asia Minor and Greece, after the conference. While there is substantial agreement that Paul did, in fact, undertake such journeys, questions have been raised about the Lucan order of the journeys. Thus some authors contend that all of these missionary journeys occurred after the apostolic conference.

Finally, it should be noted that there is a widespread perception that those who espouse the South Galatian hypothesis are conservative scholars whose real purpose is to defend the historical veracity of Luke's account. Conversely, those who favor the North Galatian hypothesis are often perceived as liberal scholars, essentially skeptical about the information found in Acts, and it is thought that their real purpose is to preserve a later dating for Galatians. While there is some truth that conservative scholars have favored the South Galatian hypothesis and more liberal scholars the North Galatian hypothesis, this characterization is precisely that and nothing more. The South Galatian hypothesis does not require one to be a "true believer" in the historical reliability of Acts any more than the North Galatian hypothesis demands that one be a skeptic about Luke's account.

The Solutions Proposed to Solve the Problem

The commentaries of W. M. Ramsay (1900), E. De Witt Burton (1920), and F. F. Bruce (1982), present the classical expression of the South Galatian hypothesis, while the classical description and defense of the North Galatian hypothesis is found in the commentary of J. B. Lightfoot (1910) and J. Moffat's *Introduction to the New Testament* (1915). Moreover, readers will find a critical summary of both hypotheses in the recent commentary of R. N. Longenecker (1990). The purpose of this section, therefore, is not to review all of the arguments once more but to explain why scholars gravitate to one position or the other. As will be seen, a good part of the controversy revolves around the text of Acts, especially 16:6 and 18:23.

For the proponents of the South Galatian hypothesis much of the argument depends upon the information found in Acts 13:4–14:28, Luke's description of Paul's first missionary journey. In this section, Luke gives an extended account of the mission undertaken by Paul and Barnabas, first on the Island of Cyprus, and then in the cities of the Roman province of Galatia: Antioch in Pisidia, Iconium, Lystra, and Derbe. Those who espouse the South Galatian hypothesis urge that since Acts speaks of Paul's missionary activity in the southern part of the province of Galatia, his letter to the Galatians is addressed to the churches of this area.

The proponents of the North Galatian hypothesis, on the other hand, focusing upon the texts of Acts 16:6 and 18:23, argue that there is evidence in Acts that Paul evangelized the old Celtic tribes in the north. The first of these texts occurs at the beginning of Paul's second missionary journey. After his dispute with Barnabas (Acts 15:36-41), Paul visits the churches which he and Barnabas founded on their first missionary journey. Then in 16:6 Luke writes: "They went through the region of Phrygia and Galatia" (*Diēlthon de tēn Phrygian kai Galatikēn chōran*). This translation suggests that after leaving Derbe, Lystra and Iconium, Paul went north through Phrygia and then through the old *territory* of Galatia.

Next, proponents of the North Galatian hypothesis point to Acts 18:23 which occurs at the beginning of Paul's third missionary journey. In 18:22 Luke describes Paul's visits to Jerusalem and Antioch in Syria, and then in 18:23 he writes: "After spending some time there [Antioch in Syria] he departed and went from place to place through the region of Galatia and Phrygia [*dierchomenos kathexēs tēn Galatikēn chōran kai Phrygian*), strengthening all the disciples." Thus, it is supposed that on his third missionary journey, Paul returned to the churches of North Galatia (18:23) that he established on his second missionary journey (16:6). On the basis of Acts 16:6 and 18:23, proponents of the North Galatian hypothesis contend that Paul evangelized the Celtic tribes in the territory of Galatia on his second and third missionary journeys. Moreover, some maintain that there is indirect evidence for this in Gal 4:13 where Paul says that it was on account of an infirmity that he visited the Galatians *to proteron*, "on the former occasion," which implies that there were two visits.

There are, however, difficulties with both of these positions. On the one hand, North Galatianists have pointed out that Luke never calls the area which Paul and Barnabas visited on their first missionary journey "Galatia." Thus in Acts 13:14 Luke describes Antioch as "Antioch in Pisidia," and in 14:6 he identifies Lystra and Derbe as Lycaonian cities. In other words, Luke does describe these cities in relationship to the Roman province of Galatia but by popular terminology. If Luke did not think of this area as Galatia, perhaps Paul did not either.

On the other hand, the South Galatianists note that Acts 16:6 and 18:23 do not necessarily mean that Paul evangelized the territory of North Galatia. First, although 18:23 says that Paul "strengthened" the disciples, neither 16:6 nor 18:23 relates any activity of evangelization on Paul's part. Rather, they imply that Paul simply traveled through the area. Second, the Greek of 16:6 (*tēn Phrygian kai Galatikēn chōran*) can be construed in two ways. While the North Galatianists interpret it to mean two different areas, Phrygia and Galatia, the South Galatianists argue that it refers to a single region and should be translated: "They traveled through the Phrygian and Galatian region." This would be the region of Phrygia that was in the *province* of Galatia; that is, Galactic Phrygia. Thus Paul never visited the territory of North Galatia.

As the reader can see, both positions are characterized by weaknesses as well as strengths. Given the data available, therefore, it is unlikely that there will be a consensus among scholars. At the present time, however, the majority of scholars lean in the direction of the North Galatian hypothesis, in part, one suspects, because it usually results in a later dating of the letter. The South Galatian hypothesis, however, has much to commend it. First, Acts does describe an extensive Pauline mission in the province of Galatia, even though Luke never calls this area Galatia. Second, even if Acts 16:6 and 18:23 refer to North Galatia, which is questionable, they do not describe any evangelistic activity in this region. The balance of probability, therefore, weighs ever so slightly in favor of the South Galatian hypothesis. Paul is writing to the churches which he founded on his first missionary journey.

An Hypothesis: The Date of the Letter and the Order of Events

Let the reader beware! What follows is an hypothesis which, on the basis of data from Acts and Galatians, attempts to reconstruct the events surrounding the crisis at Galatia and to assign a date to the composition of this letter. This hypothesis employs the following presuppositions.

(1) Galatians 1–2 provides the basic framework for reconstructing the events.

(2) Galatians 2 and Acts 15 relate essentially the same event. Since Paul knows nothing about the apostolic decree, however, the meeting described in Acts 15 probably includes information from another conference at which Paul was not present. In other words, Luke may have telescoped two or more meetings into a single meeting which he narrates in Acts 15.

(3) Paul's first missionary journey occurred after the apostolic conference described in Galatians 2 and Acts 15 and the incident at Antioch. The present order in Acts (first journey—apostolic conference—second and third journeys) is a Lucan ordering of the events in order to prepare for the Jerusalem conference. If this is so, the first missionary journey (Acts 13:4–14:28) is a doublet of the beginning of Paul's second missionary journey (Acts 16:1-5).

Using the outline provided by Paul's autobiographical statement in Gal 1–2 as a framework, this commentary makes the following proposal about the events surrounding the Galatian crisis.

(1) Shortly after his call/conversion, Paul went to the Nabataean kingdom of Arabia where he began his preaching of the gospel; he then returned to Damascus. This initial preaching activity lasted about three years. See Gal 1:17-18.

(2) Three years after his call/conversion, Paul went to Jerusalem for the first time, and there he met privately with Cephas (Peter). See Gal 1:18-20.

(3) After his call, Paul returned to the regions of Syria and Cilicia. Since the Church of Antioch was located in Syria, Paul probably worked in and with that community. And since Paul's birth place was in Tarsus of Cilicia, he probably returned to the regions of his homeland. It does not appear that Paul undertook the missionary journey described in Acts 13–14 during this period. See Gal 1:21-24.

(4) While Paul was at Antioch, "false brethren" came to that city in order to spy on the freedom enjoyed by the Church of Antioch. This is suggested by the side remark of Gal 2:4-5 which makes more sense if Paul is alluding to something that happened prior to the Jerusalem conference rather than during it.

(5) Because of the problems caused by these false brethren, Paul and Barnabas went to Jerusalem, taking along the uncircumcised Titus. This visit occurred fourteen years after Paul's first visit to Jerusalem, or 14 years after his call/conversion; the language of 2:1 is ambiguous. At this meeting the pillar apostles recognized that Paul had been entrusted with the gospel to the uncircumcised and extended the right hand of fellowship to him and Barnabas. See Gal 2:1-10.

(6) Paul returned to Antioch, and shortly after this the "Antioch Incident" took place. Although Jerusalem recognized Paul's ministry to the uncircumcised, the question of food laws and table fellowship with Gentiles was not settled. When certain men from James came to Antioch, therefore, they were offended that Jewish and Gentile Christians shared table fellowship. Therefore, they pressured Peter and other Jewish Christians to withdraw from table fellowship with Gentiles. Peter withdrew, and even Barnabas was taken in by the "hypocrisy." See Gal 2:11-14.

At this point, the framework provided by Galatians 1–2 ends, and this construction become more hypothetical and open to error.

(7) After the Antioch incident, an incident which probably marked a bitter defeat for Paul, Paul undertook an extended missionary journey which brought him to the cities of South Galatia. From there he eventually went to Macedonia and Achaia, making Corinth his base of operations. Luke describes this journey in two phases: a first journey before the Jerusalem conference (Acts 13:4–14:28) and a second journey after the conference (15:36–18:21). As noted above, the first journey is an extended doublet of the first part of the second journey (16:1-5).

(8) Paul visited the churches of Galatia a second time (Acts 18:23), and from there he went to Ephesus. During his Ephesian ministry, the Corinthian crisis broke out. It was during this period that Paul wrote 1 Corinthians. The remark in 1 Cor 16:1 ("Now concerning the collection for the saints: you should follow the directions I gave to the churches of Galatia") suggests that Paul was still on good terms with the Galatians when

he wrote 1 Corinthians, and that he instructed the Galatians about the collection, perhaps at the time of his second visit.

(9) Because of the victory of the partisans of James, agitators came to Paul's new mission field in Galatia with the purpose of "Judaizing" his new converts. The agitators probably had some relationship with the "false brethren" and the partisans of James.

(10) At Ephesus, Paul heard about the problems at Galatia, but he was unable to visit the churches there (Gal 4:20) because of the severe difficulties he was experiencing with the Corinthian congregation. Therefore, Paul writes a letter to the Galatians from Ephesus.

(11) The letter to the Galatians was probably written in the mid-fifties, after 1 Corinthians, but sometime before, or during the period that Paul wrote 2 Corinthians.

Many scholars will immediately ask, "But what about Barnabas?" According to Acts, he was Paul's companion on the Apostle's first missionary journey, but according to this reconstruction, Barnabas does not appear to accompany Paul on his missionary journey to the churches of Galatia. This is a serious objection, but not necessarily a fatal one. If the missionary journey of Acts 13:4–14:28 is an extended doublet of the first part of the second journey (Acts 16:1-5), then it is possible that Barnabas never accompanied Paul as Luke narrates. Or, if Barnabas did accompany Paul, then he and Paul parted company after evangelizing the Galatians as Luke narrates in Acts 15:36-41. In this case, Acts would preserve a valuable piece of historical information.

The advantage of this hypothesis is that it combines the attractive elements of the North and South Galatian theories. On one hand, Paul wrote to the churches in the province of Galatia. On the other, Galatians is dated later, during the period of Paul's Ephesian ministry.

IV. *Galatians Today*

Although it consists of only six chapters, Paul's letter to the Galatians has been, and remains, one of the most influential documents of the New Testament. Indeed, one could say that after Romans it holds a certain pride of place since it and Romans provide the most extensive expositions of Paul's doctrine of justification by faith apart from the Law. Thus Romans and Galatians played an important role both in Augustine's controversy with Pelagius and in the great Reformation debates of the sixteenth century. Both the Reformers and the Council Fathers of Trent appealed to these and other Pauline letters as they formulated their doctrines of justification.

As a result of the great debates of the sixteenth century, Catholic and Protestant commentators inevitably read Paul's letters, especially Romans and Galatians, either through the prism of the Reformation or of the Council of Trent. For example, Lutherans are especially concerned to emphasize the forensic nature of justification (the imputation of a righteousness which is received by faith) in order "to safeguard the unconditional character of God's promises in Christ" (*Justification by Faith: Lutherans and Catholics in Dialogue VII*, 50). Catholics, on the other hand, emphasize that this forensic act of acquittal, called justification, effects what it proclaims, namely the sanctification of the sinner. Consequently, Protestants perceive Catholics as unwilling to rely totally upon the grace of Jesus Christ, and Catholics view Protestants as denying the importance of the ethical life.

Fortunately, the ecumenical dialogue begun by the Second Vatican Council and the dedicated work of historians, systematicians, and biblical specialists has resulted in a new atmosphere of understanding. In the United States, for example, in 1985 Lutherans and Catholics issued a common statement on justification by faith in which they proclaimed:

> our entire hope of justification and salvation rests on Christ Jesus and on the gospel whereby the good news of God's merciful action in Christ is made known: we do not place our ultimate trust in anything other than God's promise and saving work in Christ.
>
> (*Justification by Faith: Lutherans and Catholics in Dialogue VII*, 16)

In a sense, then, many of the old debates which characterized the sixteenth century have been bypassed by new and better highways constructed by historians, systematicians, and biblicists. While no commentator can, or should, disregard his or her religious tradition, it is now possible to read old texts without the blinders imposed by the polemical debates of a particular, albeit important, moment in the life of the Church. For example, Catholics can and do readily affirm the forensic nature of justification, and Protestants can acknowledge that in this forensic act of justification God's Word effects what it proclaims. In a word, today exegetes are more apt to disagree with each other about the interpretation of biblical texts on the grounds of historical and linguistic data than on the basis of Church creeds.

At this point, the reader might be inclined to think that a certain calm has come upon the Galatian sea and that the major issues have been settled because the debates of the sixteenth century no longer rage as once they did. The waters, however, are not so tranquil. All to the contrary, a new storm has broken upon the Galatian sea, a storm so powerful that it is tossing both Tridentine and Reformation ships, ladened with their traditional exegesis of Galatians, to and fro.

The Traditional Understanding of Galatians

What is this traditional exegesis of Galatians? What follows is a characterization, but like all characterizations it is not without foundation. When drawing characterizations, artists choose certain features which they judge to be most significant, and then they highlight them. The following description of the traditional understanding of justification should be read in light of this artistic genre.

According to the traditional understanding of Galatians, Paul was opposed by, and opposed, Judaizers who were basically legalists at heart. These Judaizers insisted that the Galatians be circumcised and perform "works of the Law," by which the Judaizers meant the ethical prescripts of the Mosaic Law, in order to be saved. Thus, although the Judaizers believed in Christ they were also proponents of obtaining righteousness by works; they maintained that salvation is earned by doing the works of the Law. In contrast to the Judaizers, Paul stands forth as the champion of justification by faith. Human beings are not saved by what they do but by their faith in Jesus Christ. Thus the essential argument of Galatians concerns salvation. How is a person saved? How does one find a gracious God? The answer of the Judaizers is faith in Jesus Christ *and* doing the works of the Law. The counter-response of Paul is faith, and faith alone. To insist upon the works of the Law is to undermine the work of God in Christ and to maintain the fiction that human beings can merit their salvation.

What then is the purpose of the Law? According to the traditional interpretation of Galatians, the purpose of the Law is to make people aware of their utter sinfulness so that they will rely entirely upon the grace of Jesus Christ. The Law is not a means of meriting salvation but of driving the sinner to rely totally and utterly upon faith in Christ. According to the traditional view, therefore, Paul's letter to the Galatians is a profound statement about the nature of salvation. It proclaims that faith in Jesus Christ, not the accumulation of good works, is the only way to righteousness. One could say that Paul's real enemy in Galatians is the religious person! While the historical Judaizers were Jewish Christians, the Judaizer today is the religious person who tries to assure personal salvation by doing good works. Thus, during the period of the Reformation, it was natural for the Reformers to see in Paul's opponents the religious leadership of the Roman Church.

A New Understanding of Galatians

This traditional understanding of Galatians has held sway in both Protestant and Catholic circles and has deeply influenced the religious imagination of believers within both communions. Moreover, while Catholics once thought of justification by faith as primarily a Protestant byword, the renewal of Catholic Moral Theology has made them more aware of the dangers of legalism. Thus it is no coincidence that the pioneering work of the Catholic Moral Theologian Bernard Häring was entitled *The Law of Christ,* a phrase taken from Gal 6:2. Häring was one of many Catholic moralists who cautioned against the legalism which characterized so much of the moral theology found in the Catholic manuals of an earlier generation. The Pauline doctrine of justification by faith could now become a rallying cry for Catholics who insisted upon the spirit of the Law and the primacy of love.

The pioneering essay of K. Stendahl ("The Apostle Paul and the Introspective Conscience of the West," *Paul Among Jews and Gentiles*), the works of E. P. Sanders (*Paul and Palestinian Judaism,* and *Paul, The Law, and The Jewish People*), and J. D. G. Dunn (*Jesus, Paul and the Law*), and most recently F. Watson (*Paul, Judaism and The Gentiles*) have called into question the traditional understanding outlined above. In the words of Sanders (*Paul, The Law,* 18), "The subject of Galatians is not whether or not humans, abstractly conceived, can by good deeds earn enough merit to be declared righteous at the judgment; it is the condition on which Gentiles enter the people of God."

Galatians is "about the condition on which Gentiles enter the people of God"; that is, what are the entrance requirements for Gentile Christians who want to be recognized as full members of that portion of Israel which believes in Jesus the Messiah? Must they adopt the cultural practices of Jews in order to enter the congregation of Israel's Messiah, the Church? Must they accept circumcision, practice specific dietary regulations, and follow the Jewish religious calendar? Or is it possible to be accepted as a full member of the Church on the basis of faith in Christ, apart from doing these works of the Mosaic Law?

Seen in this perspective, Galatians is not primarily a letter about individual salvation. Galatians may have provided an answer to Luther and the Reformers as they struggled to find a gracious God and to sooth anxious consciences. But for Paul it was first and foremost a defense of the rights of Gentiles to enter the Church on the basis of their faith in Jesus Christ without adopting the cultural practices of Jewish Christians. Thus K. Stendahl (*Paul Among Jews and Gentles,* 2) maintains that the Pauline doctrine of justification by faith "was hammered out by Paul for the very specific and limited purpose of defending the rights of Gentile converts to be full and genuine heirs to the promises of God to Israel."

Again, seen in the light of this new interpretation, Galatians is a letter about legalism of a special kind. While the traditional interpretation views Paul as combatting a righteousness by works that seek to assure one's own salvation, this view of Galatians argues that the legalism which Paul opposes is a cultural hegemony rather than a legalistic morality. To put it anachronistically, the Judaizers or agitators have come to Galatia and have said, "In order to become a Christian, you must first become a Jew." Thus the Gentiles must surrender the customs and practices of their culture and adopt those of Judaism in order to be counted as full members of the Church.

This new view of Galatians has arisen because contemporary biblicists have reread this letter in terms of the historical occasion which necessitated it and with a more sympathetic understanding of the Judaism during the period when the New Testament was written. In the past and even now, Christian scholars have often viewed the Judaism of the New Testament period as a legalistic religion which encouraged the accumulation of merit through works of the Law in order to obtain righteousness before God. To be sure, Judaism, like every religion, has its legalistic side. But in recent years, it has become apparent that the picture of first century Judaism as a religion of righteousness by works has more to do with the theories of Christian theologians than with objective historical research. The Judaism of the New Testament period was centered upon the gracious aspect of God's covenant with Israel. And the "works of the Law" were not a means assuring personal salvation but of maintaining one's status within the covenant people of God. Salvation was and remains God's gracious gift to the covenant people.

With this renewed appreciation of first century Judaism, the historical circumstances surrounding the letter to the Galatians become clearer, and the theological stance of the agitators more understandable. Thus the agitators would have reasoned that if God has finally sent the Messiah to his covenant people, it is reasonable to expect Gentile converts to do those works of the Law which assure their entrance into the covenant people of God and the maintenance of that covenant relationship e.g., circumcision, food laws, Sabbath observance, etc. The recovery of this historical situation, and this appreciation of first century Judaism as a covenant religion, have led to a rethinking of the Pauline doctrine of justification and to the interpretation of Galatians.

Reading Galatians Anew

At this point the reader, especially those charged with preaching the gospel, may be asking, "If such is the new interpretation of Galatians, what theological value does this letter have?" The question is well put. If Paul was primarily responding to a social problem, the integration of Jews and Gentiles, and if the Reformation understanding of Galatians has missed the mark, at least partially, then what is the theological value of this letter? Does this mean that Galatians is merely the remnant of an historical and social debate which has long since been settled? What is the preacher and teacher to do? What comfort and sustenance can the believer hope to attain from a letter which responds to a crisis long since settled in favor of Paul's Gentile converts? The detailed answer to these questions is found in the exegesis of the text. But by way of anticipation the following theses are proposed.

(1) *The doctrine of justification by faith needs to be understood anew, not abandoned.* Indeed, many will find that this new understanding of Galatians will help them to make sense of a doctrine that is often only associated with the intricacies of Reformation and Tridentine theology. Since Paul hammered out this doctrine in the context of an ecumenical controversy, his understanding of justification has social and ecumenical dimensions for today. Paul argued against the cultural hegemony of a Jewish Christianity which sought to impose its customs and practices upon a minority of Gentile Christians. Today, of course, that controversy has long since been settled in favor of Gentiles. The minority has become a powerful majority which often seeks to impose its customs and practices upon new minorities. To take one example, Hispanic Catholics are often encouraged, if not coerced, to become americanized in order to enjoy full membership in the Catholic Church in the United States. But is such cultural assimilation a necessary condition of the gospel? Paul's answer, of course, is clear. What God has done in Christ is sufficient. The faith of Jesus Christ and faith in Christ is essential for full membership in the Church whereas cultural and national differences are a matter of indifference.

(2) *The social dimension of justification does not eliminate the personal dimension of justification.* Although Paul's primary concern was to defend the rights of Gentiles, his doctrine of justification has important ramifications for the life of the individual believer and, in this regard, the Fathers of Trent and the Reformers understood Paul correctly. Thus in Galatians, Paul proclaims that he has been crucified with Christ and that he now lives by the faith of the Son of God "who loves *me* and handed himself over for *me*" (2:19-20). This makes it clear that Christ's death upon the cross has important theological implications for the individual as well as for the social relationship between Gentiles and Jews. Something, then, has happened to the individual which leads to a new relationship between communities of people once at odds with each other. Because Christ has died on behalf of our sins (1:4), all are equal before God.

(3) *Justification means to be "in Christ."* In his struggle against the agitators, Paul argues that the Gentiles are Abraham's seed (3:29) because they belong to Christ who is Abraham's singular descendant (3:16). This

incorporation into Christ occurred at baptism when the Galatians con-
fessed their faith in the crucified Christ. Because the Galatians are in
Christ, circumcision or the lack of it means absolutely nothing. There is
neither Gentile nor Jew, slave nor free person, male and female (3:28),
for in Christ the Galatians have been created anew (6:15). Justification,
therefore, entails a transferal from the realm of the Law to the sphere
of Christ which is characterized by life in the Spirit. To be justified is to
be "in Christ," and it is this aspect of being "in Christ" which brings
about the essential equality of Gentile and Jew making cultural differences a matter of indifference.

(4) *The justified walk according to the Spirit.* Because Paul is not combatting "work righteousness" or "legalism," as is often thought, it should
be clear that there is no contradiction between justification by faith and
living a moral and ethical life. Paul is not an antinomian. Rather, he argues that the believer fulfills the Law through the love commandment
(5:14). Paul expects his Gentile converts to live moral and ethical lives;
he certainly does not excuse them from the moral demands of the Mosaic
Law. The difference between Paul and his opponents is the point of depar-
ture. Whereas the agitators ask the Galatians to place themselves in the
sphere of the Law, Paul tells his converts to walk by the Spirit. In the
sphere of the Spirit, in Christ, the Galatians will be able to fulfill the Law
through the love commandment. The legalism against which Paul argues
is a legalism that would force Gentiles to adopt the cultural patterns and
practices of Jewish Christian believers.

(5) *Paul's argument in Galatians is against fellow Jewish Christians.* Again
and again, readers of Galatians must remind themselves that Paul was
a Jewish Christian and that he is contending with fellow Jewish Christians, not against Judaism as such. To be sure, Paul believes that the
majority of his kinsfolk have gone astray because they have not accepted
Jesus as the Messiah (Romans 9–11); nevertheless, in Galatians he is not
contending against Jews as such. Rather, his disagreement is with the
judaizing tactics of fellow Christians who are Jews. If modern readers
remember this and recall that Paul's audience is predominantly, if not
exclusively Gentile, they will be less inclined to view Galatians as a polemic against Judaism.

Paul's letter to the Galatians is a response to a specific situation, a conflict between Gentile and Jewish Christians; it is an intra-Christian debate. Nonetheless, the answers provided here can still nourish the Church
if it is prepared to hear the Word of God anew.

V. *Bibliography*

A. *Commentaries*

Betz, H. D. *Galatians: A Commentary on Paul's Letter to the Churches in Galatia.* Hermeneia; Philadelphia: Fortress, 1979.

Bonnard, P. *L'Épître de Saint Paul aux Galates.* 2nd ed. CNT; Neuchâtel and Paris: Delachaux & Niestle, 1972.

Bruce, F. F. *The Epistle to the Galatians: A Commentary on the Greek Text.* NIGTC; Grand Rapids: Eerdmans, 1982.

Burton, E. de Witt. *A Critical And Exegetical Commentary on The Epistle to the Galatians.* ICC; Edinburgh: T. & T. Clark, 1921.

Calvin, J. *The Epistles of Paul the Apostle to the Galatians, Ephesians, Philippians and Colossians.* Calvin's New Testament Commentaries; Grand Rapids: Eerdmans, 1965.

Chrysostom, John. *Commentary on the Epistle to the Galatians and Homilies on the Epistle to the Ephesians.* A Library of Fathers of the Holy Catholic Church Anterior to the Division of the East and West; Oxford: John Henry Parker, 1840.

Cousar, C. B. *Galatians.* Interpretation: A Bible Commentary for Teaching and Preaching; Atlanta: John Knox Press, 1982.

Ebeling, G. *The Truth of the Gospel: An Exposition of Galatians.* Philadelphia: Fortress, 1985.

Erasmus of Rotterdam. *The Paraphrase on the Epistle of Paul the Apostle to the Galatians. Collected Works of Erasmus,* R. D. Sider ed. University of Toronto Press, 1984.

Fitzmyer, J. A. "The Letter to the Galatians." *The New Jerome Biblical Commentary.* R. E. Brown, J. A. Fitzmyer, R. E. Murphy, eds. Englewood Cliffs, N.J.: Prentice Hall, 1990.

Fung, R. Y. K. *The Epistle to the Galatians.* NICNT; Grand Rapids: Eerdmans, 1988.

Guthrie, D. *Galatians.* NCB; Grand Rapids: Eerdmans, 1973.

Lagrange, M.-J. *Saint Paul Épître aux Galates.* 5th ed. EBib; Paris: Librairie Lecoffre, 1942.

Lightfoot, J. B. *Saint Paul's Epistle to the Galatians: A Revised Text with Introduction, Notes, and Dissertations.* London: Macmillan, 1910.

Longenecker, R. N. *Galatians.* WBC; 41; Dallas: Word Books, 1990.

Luther, M. *Lectures on Galatians 1535 Chapters 1-4.* Luther's Works 26; Saint Louis: Concordia, 1963.

Mussner, F. *Der Galaterbrief.* 5th ed. HTKNT; Freiburg: Herder, 1988.

Oepke, A. *Der Brief des Paulus an die Galater.* J. Rohde, ed. THKNT 9; Berlin: Evangelische Verlagsanstalt, 1973.

Osiek, C. *Galatians.* NTM 12; Wilmington, Del.: Michael Glazier, 1980.

Ramsay, W. M. *A Historical Commentary on St. Paul's Epistle to the Galatians.* New York: G. P. Putnams's Sons, 1900.

Schlier, H. *Der Brief an die Galater.* 12 ed. Kritisch-Exegetischer Kommentar Über Das Neue Testament; Göttingen: Vandenhoeck & Ruprecht, 1962.

B. Selected Books and Articles

(The following bibliography consists of seminal works for a study of Galatians. There are additional bibliographical references after each section of this commentary.)

Anderson, H. G. *et al*, ed. *Justification by Faith: Lutherans and Catholics in Dialogue VII*. Minneapolis: Augsburg, 1985.

Barclay, J. M. G. "Mirror-Reading a Polemical Letter: Galatians as a Test Case." *JSNT* 31 (1987) 73–93.

Barclay, J. M. G. *Obeying the Truth: A Study of Paul's Ethics in Galatians*. Edinburgh: T & T Clark, 1988.

Barrett, C. K. *Freedom and Obligation: A Study of the Epistle to the Galatians*. Philadelphia: Westminster, 1985.

Barth, M. " 'The Faith of the Messiah.' " *HeyJ* 10 (1969) 63–70.

Bassler, J. A., ed. *Pauline Theology I: Thessalonians, Philippians, Galatians, Philemon*. Minneapolis: Fortress, 1991.

Bellville, L. " 'Under Law': Structural Analysis and the Pauline Concept of Law in Galatians 3:21–4:11." *JSNT* 26 (1986) 53–78.

Betz, H. D. "In Defense of the Spirit: Paul's Letter to the Galatians as a Document of Early Christian Apologetics." *Aspects of Religious Propaganda in Judaism and Early Christianity*. E. Schussler Fiorenza, ed. University of Notre Dame, 1976, 99–114.

Betz, H. D. "Spirit, Freedom, and Law: Paul's Message to the Galatian Churches." *SEA°* 39 (1974) 145–160.

Betz, H. D. "The Literary Composition and Function of Paul's Letter to the Galatians." *NTS* 21 (1975) 353–379.

Betz, H. D. "2 Cor 6:14–7:1: An Anti-Pauline Fragment?" *JBL* 92 (1973) 88–107.

Bligh, J. *Galatians in Greek: A Structural Analysis of St. Paul's Epistle to the Galatians with Notes on the Greek*. University of Detroit Press, 1966.

Brinsmead, B. H. *Galatians—Dialogical Response to Opponents*. SBLDS 65; Chico, CA: Scholars Press, 1982.

Bruce, F. F. "Galatian Problem 3. The 'Other' Gospel." *BJRL* 53 (1971) 253–271.

Cosgrove, C. H. "Justification in Paul: A Linguistic and Theological Reflection." *JBL* 106 (1987) 653–670.

Cosgrove, C. H. "The Law Has Given Sarah No Children (Gal 4:21-30)." *NovT* 29 (1987) 219–235.

Cosgrove, C. H. *The Cross and the Spirit: A Study in the Argument and Theology of Galatians*. Macon, GA: Mercer, 1988.

Cosgrove, C. H. "Arguing Like a Mere Human Being: Galatians 3:15-18 in Rhetorical Perspective." *NTS* 34 (1988) 536–549.

Cosgrove, C. H. "The Mosaic Law Preaches Faith: A Study of Galatians 3." *WTS* 41 (1978-79) 146–164.

Crownfield, F. R. "The Singular Problem of the Dual Galatians." *JBL* 64 (1945) 491–500.

Dunn, J. D. G. "The New Perspective on Paul." *BJRL* 65 (1983) 95–122.

Dunn, J. D. G. *Jesus, Paul and the Law: Studies in Mark and Galatians.* Louisville: Westminster/John Knox, 1990.

Dunn, J. D. G. " 'A Light to the Gentiles', or 'The End of the Law'? The Significance of the Damascus Road Christophany for Paul." *Jesus, Paul and the Law,* 89–107.

Dunn, J. D. G. "The Relationship between Paul and Jerusalem according to Galatians 1 and 2." *NTS* 28 (1982) 461–478.

Dunn, J. D. G. "The Theology of Galatians." *Jesus, Paul and the Law,* 242–264.

Dunn, J. D. G. "The Incident at Antioch (Gal 2:11-18)." *JSNT* 18 (1983) 95–122.

Dunn, J. D. G. "Works of the Law and the Curse of the Law (Galatians 3:10-14)." *NTS* 31 (1985) 523–542.

Fitzmyer, J. A. *Paul and His Theology: A Brief Sketch.* 2nd ed. Englewood Cliffs, N.J.: Prentice Hall, 1989.

Gaston, L. *Paul and the Torah.* Vancouver: University of British Columbia, 1987.

Gaventa, B. R. "Galatians 1 and 2: Autobiography as Paradigm." *NovT* 28 (1986) 309–326.

Gordon, T. D. "The Problem at Galatia." *Int* 41 (1987) 32–43.

Hansen, G. W. *Abraham in Galatians: Epistolary and Rhetorical Contexts.* JSNTSup 29; Sheffield: JSOT Press, 1989.

Harvey, A. E. "The Opposition to Paul." *SE* 4 (1968) 319–332.

Hays, R. B. "Christology and Ethics in Galatians: The Law of Christ." *CBQ* 49 (1987) 268–290.

Hays, R. B. *The Faith of Jesus Christ: An Investigation of the Narrative Substructure of Galatians 3:1–4:11.* SBLDS 56; Chico, CA.: Scholars Press, 1983.

Hooker, M. D. "PISTIS CHRISTOU." *NTS* 35 (1989) 321–342.

Howard, G. *Paul: Crisis in Galatia: A Study in Early Christian Theology.* 2nd ed. SNTSMS 35; Cambridge University Press, 1990.

Howard, G. "The 'Faith of Christ.' " *ExpTim* 85 (1974) 212–215.

Howard, G. "Notes and Observations on the 'Faith of Christ.' " *HTR* 60 (1967) 459–484.

Hübner, H. *Law in Paul's Thought.* Edinburgh: T. & T. Clark, 1984.

Hultgren, A. J. "The PISTIS CHRISTOU Formulation in Paul." *NovT* 22 (1980) 248–263.

Jewett, R. *A Chronology of Paul's Life.* Philadelphia: Fortress, 1979.

Jewett, R. "The Agitators and the Galatian Congregation." *NTS* 17 (1971) 198–212.

Kieffer, R. *Foi et Justification à Antioche: Interprétation d'un conflit (Ga 2, 14-21).* LD 111; Paris: Cerf, 1982.

Kim, S. *The Origin of Paul's Gospel.* Grand Rapids: Eerdmans, 1981.

Lategan, B. C. "Is Paul Defending His Apostleship in Galatians?" *NTS* 34 (1988) 411–430.

Luedemann, G. *Paul Apostle to the Gentiles: Studies in Chronology.* Philadelphia: Fortress, 1984.

Luedemann, G. *Opposition to Paul in Jewish Christianity.* Minneapolis: Fortress, 1989.

Lull, D. J. *The Spirit in Galatia: Paul's Interpretation of Pneuma as Divine Power.* SBLDS 49; Chico, CA: Scholars Press, 1989.

Lyons, G. *Pauline Autobiography: Toward a New Understanding.* SBLDS 73; Atlanta: Scholars Press, 1985.

Martin, B. L. *Christ and the Law in Paul*. NovTSup 62; Leiden: Brill, 1989.

Martyn, J. L. "A Law-Observant Mission to the Gentiles: The Background of Galatians." *SJT* 38 (1985) 307–324.

Martyn, J. L. "Apocalyptic Antinomies in Paul's Letter to the Galatians." *NTS* 31 (1985) 410–424.

Martyn, J. L. "Paul and His Jewish Christian Interpreters." *USQR* 42 (1988) 1–16.

Martyn, J. L. "The Covenants of Hagar and Sarah." *Faith and History. Essays in Honor of Paul W. Meyer*. J. T. Carroll *et al*, eds. Atlanta: Scholars Press, 1990, 160–192.

Mitchell, S. "Population and the Land in Roman Galatia." *ANRW* 7:2. 1053–1081."

Munck, J. "The Judaizing Gentile Christians: Studies in Galatians." *Paul and the Salvation of Mankind*. Atlanta: John Knox, 1959.

Räisänen, H. *Paul and the Law*. Philadelphia: Fortress, 1983.

Refoulé, F. "Approches de l'Épître aux Galates." *LumVie* 38 (1989) 15–28.

Refoulé, F. "Date de L'Épître aux Galates." *RB* 95 (1988) 161–183.

Reumann, J. *Righteousness in the New Testament*. Philadelphia: Fortress, 1982.

Robinson, D. W. B. " 'Faith of Jesus Christ'—a New Testament Debate." *The Reformed Theological Review* 29 (1970) 71–81.

Ropes, J. H. *The Singular Problem of the Epistle to the Galatians*. HTS 14; Cambridge: Harvard University Press, 1929.

Russell, W. "Who Were Paul's Opponents in Galatians?" *BSac* 147 (1990) 329–350.

Sanders, E. P. *Paul, the Law, and the Jewish People*. Philadelphia: Fortress, 1983.

Schmithals, W. "Häretiker in Galatien." *ZNW* 47 (1956) 25–67.

Schütz, J. H. *Paul and the Anatomy of Apostolic Authority*. SNTSMS 26; Cambridge, 1975.

Smit, J. "The Letter of Paul to the Galatians: a Deliberative Speech." *NTS* 35 (1989) 1–26.

Stendahl, K. *Paul Among Jews and Gentiles*. Philadelphia: Fortress, 1976.

Suhl, A. von. "Der Galaterbrief—Situation und Argumentation." *ANRW* II 25.4: 3067–3144.

Taylor, G. M. "The Function of *PISTIS CHRISTOU* in Galatians." *JBL* 85 (1966) 58–76.

Thielman, F. *From Plight to Solution: A Jewish Framework for Understanding Paul's View of the Law in Galatians and Romans*. NovTSup 61; Leiden: Brill, 1989.

Tyson, J. B. " 'Works of Law' in Galatians." *JBL* 92 (73) 423–431.

Tyson, J. B. "Paul's Opponents in Galatia." *NovT* 10 (1968) 241–254.

Watson, F. *Paul, Judaism, and the Gentiles*. SNTSMS, 56; Cambridge University Press, 1986.

Williams, S. K. "The Hearing of Faith: *AKOĒ PISTEŌS* in Galatians 3." *NTS* 35 (1989) 82–93.

Williams, S. K. "Again Pistis Christou." *CBQ* 49 (1987) 431–447.

Williams, S. K. "*Promise* in Galatians: A Reading of Paul's Reading of Scripture." *JBL* 107 (1988) 709–720.

Williams, S. "Justification and the Spirit in Galatians." *JSNT* 29 (1987) 91–100.

Wilson, R. McL. "Gnostics—in Galatians?" *SE* 4 (1968) 358–367.

Yates, R. "Saint Paul and the Law in Galatians." *ITQ* 51 (1985) 105–124.

Young, N. H. "*Paidagōgos*: The Social Setting of a Pauline Metaphor." *NovT* 29 (1987) 150–176.

TRANSLATION, NOTES, INTERPRETATION

INTRODUCTION:
GREETING AND STATEMENT OF ASTONISHMENT (1:1-10)

The Greeting (1:1-5)

1. Paul, an apostle, not from human beings nor through a human being, but through Jesus Christ and God the Father who raised him from the dead, 2. and all the brethren with me to the churches of Galatia, 3. grace and peace to you from God our Father and the Lord Jesus Christ 4. who gave himself for our sins so that he might deliver us from the present evil age in accordance with the will of our God and Father, 5. to whom be the glory for ever and ever. Amen.

NOTES

1. *Paul*: According to Luke, Paul's Jewish surname was "Saul," and this is how the Evangelist identifies him until Acts 13:9, at which point Luke employs the Roman name "Paul." *Paulos* is the Greek form of a well known Roman family name *Paulus* (Fitzmyer, *Paul and His Theology*, 2). Paul's name was not changed at the time of his call. It is more likely that "Paul" was his given name and that "Saul" was added for use in Jewish circles. The Apostle always refers to himself as "Paul" and never employs "Saul."

an apostle: In the NT an apostle is someone sent with full authority. In this regard, an apostle is akin to the Jewish institution of the *shaliaḥ,* a delegate or messenger commissioned by a congregation for a specific purpose. Such delegates represented those who sent them and spoke, not with their own authority, but with the authority of the one who commissioned them. Paul, however, did not view his apostleship as originating from any congregation or human commission but directly from God, as the following phrase will show.

Among the Synoptic Evangelists, Luke especially identifies the group of twelve chosen by Jesus as apostles (6:13; see Matt 10:2). In Acts 14:4, 14, he calls Paul and Barnabas apostles, but otherwise reserves the title for the Twelve. Paul, by contrast, views the circle of apostles as broader than the circle of the Twelve (see 1 Cor 15:5, 7). He is an apostle because he has seen the Lord (1 Cor 9:1) and been directly commissioned by God (Gal 1:15-16). Thus Paul identifies himself as an apostle in the salutations of Romans, and 1 & 2 Corinthians. The title also occurs in the salutations of Ephesians, Colossians, 1 & 2 Timothy, and Titus, writings which are probably Deutero-Pauline. Paul and his interpreters understood his apostleship in terms of his mission to the Gentiles (Rom 11:13; Eph 3:1-2). Not all Christians, however, were so willing to grant Paul the title of apostle in the full sense that he claimed it (see 1 Cor 9:1; 2 Cor 11:5; 12:11-12).

not from human beings nor through a human being: Paul employs two prepositions, each preceded by a negative. His apostleship did not originate from humans (*ouk ap'*) nor was it mediated by anyone (*oude di'*). His apostleship does not derive from community authority, nor was it mediated by another individual, e.g., one of the Twelve.

but through Jesus Christ and God the Father: The preposition *dia* ("through") governs both Jesus Christ and God. Thus Jesus is accorded the honor of being associated with God. It also stands in contrast with the same preposition in the phrase above and emphasizes that Paul's apostleship comes directly from God and Jesus.

who raised him from the dead: The final phrase defines the relationship between Jesus and the Father and specifies the God in whom Christians believe: the God who raised Jesus from the dead.

2. *and all the brethren with me*: In other letters, Paul names those associated with him: 1 Corinthians (Sosthenes); 2 Corinthians (Timothy); Philippians (Timothy); 1 Thessalonians (Silvanus, Timothy); Philemon (Timothy). In Romans, the letter salutation lists no one else except Paul. Galatians is unique in mentioning the *adelphoi* ("brethren") without identifying them. The reference to them, however, shows that Paul writes with the support and encouragement of others. His apostleship is from God and Jesus, but he does not work in isolation from others.

to the churches of Galatia: The plural *ekklēsiais* ("churches") indicates that this is a circular letter meant to be read at several Galatian congregations. See the introduction to this commentary for a discussion of which Galatian churches are intended.

3. *grace and peace to you*: This is the standard greeting in all of Paul's letters. *Charis* ("grace") and *eirēnē* ("peace") refer to God's covenant favor toward his people. See Num 6:24-26, "The Lord bless you and keep you; the Lord make his face to shine upon you, and be *gracious* to you; the Lord lift up his countenance upon you, and give you *peace*." Paul extends this covenant favor, once reserved exclusively for Israel, to his Gentile congregations.

from God our Father and the Lord Jesus Christ: Some manuscripts (P46, B, D, F, G, H) change the word order to read "from God the Father *and our Lord* Jesus Christ." The word order of the text, however, reflects Pauline usage in Rom 1:7; 1 Cor 1:3; 2 Cor 1:2; Phil 1:2; Phlm 3 and is to be preferred. The text was probably altered by copyists who sought to associate the possessive pronoun more closely with "Lord Jesus Christ" (Metzger, *Textual Commentary*, 589).

4. *who gave himself for our sins*: Some manuscripts (P46vid, S*, A, D, F, G) read *peri* ("for") instead of *hyper* ("for"). While Paul does employ *peri* (Rom 8:3), he uses *hyper* more regularly. The preposition functions as a technical term when the Apostle speaks of Christ's death on our behalf (Rom 5:6, 7, 8; 14:15; 1 Cor 1:13; 15:3; 2 Cor 5:14, 15). Paul employs *hyper* two more times in Galatians (2:20; 3:13) when speaking of Christ's death on our behalf. The emphasis on Christ dying on behalf of our sins indicates the salvific dimension of Christ's death which plays a major role in the rest of the letter.

so that he might deliver us from the present evil age: This is the only occurrence of the verb *exaireō* in the Pauline writings. Used in the middle voice, it has the sense of setting free, delivering, rescuing. See Acts 7:10, 34; 12:11; 23:27; 26:17. Likewise, this is the only time that Paul employs the adjective *ponēros* ("evil") to describe the present age. In the rest of his correspondence, he speaks of *ho aiōn houtos* ("this age"), but always in a negative sense (Rom 12:2; 1 Cor 1:20; 2:6, 8; 3:18; 2 Cor 4:4). The terminology, "this age," points to the apocalyptic dimension of Paul's thought which distinguishes between two aeons: the present age, evil and corrupt; and the age to come in which God will be victorious. The believer stands between these ages (1 Cor 10:11, "on whom the end of the ages has come"). The old aeon has run its course, and the new age of God's grace has begun.

in accordance with the will of our God and Father: This is the only reference to God's will in Galatians, but the expression *thelēma tou theou* ("will of God") does occur frequently in Paul's writings (Rom 1:10; 12:2; 1 Cor 1:1; 2 Cor 1:1; 8:5; 1 Thess 4:3; 5:18). "God's will" qualifies all that precedes it in v. 4, namely, the Son's self-surrender in order to rescue humanity from the present evil age. This is the third time that Paul has referred to God as "Father" in this greeting, see vv. 1, 3.

5. *to whom be the glory for ever and ever: Amen*. To whom is the final doxology applied? To Christ who gave himself on behalf of our sins? To God the Father? Or to both? Although "our God and Father" occurs in the clause governed by *kata* ("according to the will of our God and Father"), it comes immediately before the doxology making it the nearest antecedent. Moreover, the theocentric dimension of Paul's thought makes it more probable that the object of the doxology is God the Father.

INTERPRETATION

The opening verses of this letter follow the traditional form for ancient letters: the sender identifies himself and those to whom he is writing, and then extends a greeting to them. While this form is generally very simple in personal letters ("Aquila to Sarapion, greetings"), in Paul's letters, especially Romans and Galatians, this greeting is highly developed. Nonetheless the basic structure of the letter opening remains intact: Paul, to the Galatians, grace and peace.

Employing this structure as a scaffold, Paul constructs an elaborate salutation which differs from most of his other letter openings in significant ways and which signals many of the issues and concerns that dominate this letter. Among these distinguishing elements are (1) the manner in which Paul identifies himself, those with him, and the Galatians; (2) the extended description of Jesus' salvific work; (3) and the closing doxology. Among the themes which are announced here are Paul's apostleship, the identity of Jesus, and Jesus' salvific work.

Form and Greeting. As in the greetings of Romans, 1 & 2 Corinthians, and the Deutero-Pauline letters Ephesians, Colossians, 1 & 2 Timothy, Titus, Paul identifies himself as an apostle. By contrast, in Philippians, he calls himself the slave of Jesus Christ, and in 1 & 2 Thessalonians he is simply identified as "Paul." In each of the instances that Paul identifies himself as an apostle, he emphasizes either his call and/or God's will: "called to be an apostle" (Romans); "called to be an apostle of Christ Jesus by the will of God" (1 Corinthians); "an apostle of Christ Jesus by the will of God" (2 Corinthians). This emphasis upon Paul's call is also found in Galatians, but here it is underlined more strongly than in any other Pauline letter. Paul insists that his apostleship did not originate with human beings (*ouk ap' anthrōpōn*), nor was it mediated by human beings (*oude di' anthrōpou*). Standing in contrast to these negative statements is Paul's assertion that his apostleship has its origin in Jesus Christ and God (*dia Iēsou Christou kai Theou patros*). While the preposition *dia* usually points to mediation, the fact that it governs both God and Jesus indicates that mediation is not the controlling notion here. Paul's apostleship originates with God and Jesus; no human being commissioned Paul to be an apostle.

The contrast between these two negative assertions and this strong positive statement has led many commentators (Burton, Bonnard, Mussner, and Bruce) to conclude that already, in the letter opening, Paul is responding to attacks upon his apostleship by his opponents. According to this "mirror reading" of the text, Paul's opponents have questioned his apostolic credentials and told the Galatians that he was commissioned an apostle by others; he did not receive a direct apostolic commission from the Lord as did the Jerusalem apostles.

This scenario which can only be inferred, not proven, from the text, cannot be ruled out of court, given the attacks that were launched against

Paul's apostolic credentials at Corinth (see especially 2 Corinthians). The situation at Corinth, however, should not be transferred to Galatia. The question of Paul's apostolic credentials is not an issue in the rest of this letter, not even in the autobiographical section which follows. Instead, Paul's primary concern is the gospel. He proclaims the divine origin of his apostleship in order to establish the divine origin of the Torah-free gospel that he preaches among the Gentiles. As the delegate (*shaliah*) of Jesus Christ he does not represent himself, nor is his authority his own. He represents the one who sent him; his authority is the authority of the one who commissioned him. In other words, the emphasis upon Paul's apostleship has the rhetorical function of grounding the Torah-free gospel in God and Jesus rather than of defending Paul from the attacks of opponents.

In addition to identifying himself as an apostle, Paul refers to those associated with him in a manner different from his other correspondence. In 1 Corinthians, Paul writes in conjunction with Sosthenes, in 2 Corinthians, Philippians, Colossians, and Philemon with Timothy, and in 1 & 2 Thessalonians with Silvanus and Timothy. (In Romans Paul does not list any co-authors.) In Galatians, however, the Apostle refers to those with him (*hoi syn emoi pantes adelphoi* ["all the brethren with me"]). The members of this group are left unnamed, and it is difficult to determine to whom the group refers: Paul's fellow missionaries (Burton, *Galatians*, 8); the members of the community where he happens to be (Bonnard, *Galates*, 20); or the united Christian fellowship which Paul represents (Schlier, *Galaterbrief*, 29). Paul's use of a similar phrase in Phil 4:21 (*hoi syn emoi adelphoi*), which refers to a group distinct from *hoi hagioi* ("the saints") at Philippi (Phil 4:22), argues against interpreting this phrase as a reference to the Christians of the community where Paul happens to be. It is more likely that he intends his missionary companions who, at this critical moment, form a united front with him. Given the extreme crisis, it is not sufficient for Paul to include one or two co-workers in the salutation of this letter. Paul wants the Galatians to understand that the entire Pauline circle stands with him on the question of the Torah-free gospel.

In addition to identifying himself and his co-workers in a distinctive fashion in this letter, Paul addresses the recipients in an unusual manner. In other correspondence, the recipients are addressed in the following ways: "To all God's beloved in Rome"; "to the Church of God that is in Corinth, to those who are sanctified in Christ Jesus, called to be saints, together with all those who in every place call on the name of our Lord Jesus Christ"; "to the Church of God that is in Corinth, including all the saints throughout Achaia"; "to all the saints in Christ Jesus who are in Philippi, with the bishops and deacons"; "to the Church of the Thessalonians in God the Father and the Lord Jesus Christ"; "to Philemon our dear friend and co-worker, to Apphia our sister, to Archippus our fellow soldier, and to the Church in your house." As these greetings show, in each case the recipients are identified in some way which highlights their dignity as believers or their relationship to Paul. But in Galatians there is only the simple address, "to the churches of Galatia," without further elaboration. Paul may have abbreviated this portion of the greeting because the rest of the salutation is unusually long, but it is more likely that the curt address reflects the strained relationship between him and the Galatians. Because they have begun to desert the one who called them (1:6), Paul makes no mention of their Christian dignity.

The reference to the churches of Galatia, indicates that the letter is not addressed to a single congregation but to several churches in Galatia (for what Paul intends by Galatia see the introduction to this commentary). The letter, therefore, is a circular letter intended to be read at several congregations. Despite this curt address, Paul wishes the Galatians *charis* ("grace") and *eirēnē* ("peace"). This greeting of grace and peace is a distinctive aspect of his letters and it may have originated with the Apostle himself. While the simple greeting *chaire* ("hail") is found in most Hellenistic letters, and while Jewish literature spoke of peace and mercy (*eleos*), Paul's letters employ the double greeting of *charis* and *eirēnē*. The first refers to God's gracious activity in Christ, while the second indicates the effect of that activity: peace between God and humanity (Rom 5:1).

In addition to the ways in which Paul identifies himself, his co-workers, and the Galatians, the letter opening of Galatians is distinctive because of its emphasis upon Christ's salvific work and its closing doxology. No other Pauline letter, including the Deutero-Paulines, has a section which concludes with a doxology as does this letter: "to whom be the glory forever and ever. Amen." Doxologies are found in Paul's letters and those attributed to him (Rom 11:36; Eph 3:20-21; Phil 4:20; 1 Tim 1:17). These doxologies, however, occur within the body of the letter, after the Apostle has developed, in some fashion, the theme of God's salvific work. The presence of a doxology here, at the end of the greeting, is probably explained in a similar fashion. Having described Jesus' salvific work in v. 4, Paul concludes with a doxology which, in effect, highlights that work. In addition, it is possible that the Apostle introduced a doxology here because he omits the traditional letter of thanksgiving (see below). This second explanation, however, is less satisfying than the first.

To summarize, Paul maintains the basic structure of the Hellenistic letter greeting (sender to receiver: greeting) and then builds upon it in several ways (how he identifies himself, his co-workers, his audience; the addition of the doxology). Because the structure has been modified, the opening of Galatians alerts the audience to several important points:

the origin of Paul's apostleship; his strained relationship with the Galatians; and the nature of Christ's salvific work.

Theological themes. Except for the salutation of Romans, no other Pauline letter opening is so rich in theology as is Galatians. In v. 1 Paul employs the preposition *dia* ("though") to govern a phrase which includes both Jesus and God the Father who raised Jesus from the dead. As a result, when Paul describes the origin of his apostolic commission, he accords Jesus a godly status. Likewise, in v. 3, God and Jesus are described as the source of the grace and peace which Paul extends to the Galatians. Although one should not impose a later trinitarian theology upon Paul's thought, it is clear that in Paul's eyes Jesus enjoys a unique and privileged status before God. It is precisely this status which allows Paul to make Jesus the sole mediator between God and the Galatians, eliminating the need for the Law.

Finally, in v. 4, Paul provides a remarkable statement about Jesus' salvific work: Jesus Christ gave himself for (*hyper*) our sins, to deliver us from the present evil age, in accordance with God's will. The Synoptic Gospels regularly employ the verb *paradidomi* (to hand over, to deliver) with reference to Jesus, e.g., Jesus prophesies that the Son of Man will be handed over (Mark 9:31; 10:33; 14:21, 41). Paul also employs *paradidomi* to speak of Jesus being handed over (Rom 4:25; 8:32; 1 Cor 11:23). But here, and in 2:20, he emphasizes Jesus' initiative in handing himself over, a theme which is also found in Eph 5:2, 25; 1 Tim 2:6; Titus 2:14. The purpose of this initiative is explained by the preposition *hyper* ("for," "on behalf of") which underscores that Christ died *for* our sins. The only other instance in which Paul says that Christ died for our sins is 1 Cor 15:3 which probably represents a pre-Pauline tradition. In other places Paul writes that Christ died *for* the ungodly (Rom 5:6), *for* us (Rom 5:8), was crucified *for* us (1 Cor 1:13), and died *for* all (2 Cor 5:14, 15). In Galatians, Paul employs two formulas found nowhere else: "the Son of God, who loved me and gave himself *for* me" (2:20); "Christ redeemed us from the curse of the Law by becoming a curse *for* us" (3:13).

Christ's purpose in handing himself over for our sins was to deliver us from the present evil age (*aiōnos tou enestōtos ponērou*). This present evil age, as Jerome, Augustine, Aquinas, and Calvin were quick to point out in their commentaries on Galatians, does not mean that the world, understood as God's creation, is evil. Rather, it is "the corruption which is in the world" (Calvin), "on account of the evils which are in it" (Aquinas), "on account of evil men" (Augustine), "because of the evil things which are done in this age" (Jerome). The use of this expression ("the present evil age") implies another aeon, free from all evil, and points to the apocalyptic nature of Paul's thought. Gal 4:3 suggests that the present evil age is under the power of the *stoicheia tou kosmou* ("elements" or "rudiments of the world"). The Jews lived under the power of the *stoicheia* inasmuch as they were under the Law, while the Gentiles lived under the *stoicheia* by serving things that appeared to be gods (4:8) but in fact were not (4:9). It is this evil age to which humanity must not conform itself (Rom 12:2) because the form of this world is passing away (1 Cor 7:31), and because the ends of the ages have come upon those who believe in Christ.

Christ's salvific work, to free us from sin in order to deliver us from the present evil age, is not merely the act of one who heroically sacrificed his life for another. For Paul, Christ's death was *kata to thelēma tou theou,* according to God's will. Thus it is Christ's submission to God's will which makes this deed salvific.

From a rhetorical standpoint, the salutation of this letter clarifies Paul's apostolic authority before the Galatian community and provides the necessary foundation for his Torah-free gospel. Because he received his commission directly from Jesus Christ and God, Paul speaks as their messenger and with their authority. Because Christ freely surrendered his life in accordance with God's will, the one necessary act of salvation has been completed. This death was in vain if righteousness comes from the Law rather than through Christ (2:21). By stating the soteriological value of Christ's death at the outset of this letter, Paul shows that there is no other means of salvation.

FOR REFERENCE AND FURTHER STUDY

Doty, W. G. *Letters in Primitive Christianity.* Philadelphia: Fortress, 1973.

Fitzmyer, J. A. "Introduction to the New Testament Epistles," and "Paul," in *The New Jerome Biblical Commentary.* R. E. Brown, J. A. Fitzmyer, R. E. Murphy, eds. Englewood Cliffs, N.J.: Prentice Hall, 1990.

Francis, F. O. and Sampley, J. P. *Pauline Parallels,* 2nd ed. Philadelphia: Fortress, 1984.

Stowers, S. K. *Letter Writing in Greco-Roman Christianity.* Philadelphia: Westminster, 1986.

White, J. L. "Saint Paul and the Apostolic Letter Tradition." *CBQ* 45 (1983) 433–444.

A Statement of Astonishment (1:6-10)

6. I am amazed that you are so quickly turning away, from the one who called you by [the] grace [of Christ], to a different gospel. 7. There is no other, but some are disturbing you and want to pervert the gospel

of Christ. 8. But even if we or an angel from heaven should preach [to you] contrary to what we preached to you, let such a one be cursed! 9. As we have already said, and now I say again, if someone preaches to you contrary to what you have received, let such a one be cursed! 10. Am I now currying favor with human beings, or with God? Or am I seeking to please human beings? If I were still striving to please human beings, I would not be Christ's slave.

NOTES

6. *I am amazed that you are so quickly turning away*: A few manuscripts (F, G) omit *houtōs* ("so"). The main verb, *metatithesthe* ("turning away"), when used in the middle voice, has the sense of desert or turn apostate as in 2 Macc 7:24: "Antiochus not only appealed to him in words, but promised with oaths that he would make him rich and enviable if he would turn away (*metathemenon*) from the ways of his ancestors." The present tense of the verb suggests that the "apostasy" in the Galatian churches is in progress but not a *fait accompli*.

from the one who called you by [the] grace [of Christ]: The reading "by the grace of Christ" is supported by P51, S, A, B, whereas the simpler reading "by grace" is supported by P46, a third century papyrus codex with a somewhat free text. Still other texts (D) read "by the grace of Jesus Christ," and others (327) "by the grace of God." Although the first reading has strong external witnesses, the shorter reading of P46 is to be preferred. The addition of *Christou* "of Christ," however, makes explicit what is implicit in the text. The text does not specify who called the Galatians: God, Christ, Paul? The last possibility, of course, is excluded if one reads "by the grace of Christ." Similar problems regarding the one who calls arise in 5:8 and 5:13. In all of these instances, however, it is more probable that the one calling is God since God is the subject of the verb (*kalein*) in most other instances that Paul employs it (Rom 4:17; 8:30; 9:12,24; 1 Cor 1:9; 7:15,17; 1 Thess 2:12; 4:7; 5:24). *En chariti* is translated "by grace" rather than "in grace" since the NT does use *en* in place of the instrumental dative (Zerwick, *Biblical Greek*, 40) and the context suggests the instrumental usage here. Grace is a central concept in Paul's writings and expresses his understanding of the salvation event (*TDNT*, IX, 393). One does not have a claim upon God; rather one is called (1:15) by God and given grace (2:9). This same grace, however, can be rejected (2:21), especially by seeking one's own justification on the basis of the Law (5:4).

to a different gospel: The use of *heteron* ("different") suggests that Paul is speaking of something more than another version of the same gospel. The message to which the Galatians are succumbing is different in kind from the gospel that Paul preaches. Note how *heteros* is employed in Rom 7:23 and 1 Cor 15:40. Thus there is no similarity between this gospel and what Paul preaches. A similar phrase is found in 2 Cor 11:4 where Paul complains that the Corinthians submit too easily to a "different gospel" from the one they received. When Paul speaks of the gospel (*euaggelion*) he is not referring to a written record but to the proclamation of what God has done in Jesus Christ, more specifically, the salvific event of Christ's death and resurrection. On several occasions, he employs the absolute expression "the gospel" (Rom 10:16; 11:28; 1 Cor 4:15; 9:14, 18), suggesting that his audience readily understands its content. At other times he offers a fuller description of the gospel as "the gospel of God" (Rom 1:1; 15:16; 2 Cor 11:7), "the gospel of Christ" (Rom 15:19; 1 Cor 9:12; 2 Cor 2:12; 9:13; 10:14; Phil 1:27; 1 Thess 3:2), or "the gospel of his Son" (Rom 1:9). While the first phrase refers to the origin of the gospel (God), the last two point to its content (God's Son, Jesus Christ). Although Paul can speak of "my gospel" (Rom 2:16; 16:25) and "our gospel" (2 Cor 4:3), he insists that there is only one gospel (Gal 1:7). In Galatians he speaks of "the gospel of Christ" (1:7), "the gospel" (1:11; 2:2), "the truth of the gospel" (2:5,14), "the gospel to the circumcised," and "the gospel to the uncircumcised" (2:7). This letter clearly shows that the gospel, when preached to Gentiles, is "Torah-free," a sign of God's graciousness.

7. *There is no other*: Paul changes adjectives (*allo,* "other"), but the thought remains the same; there is no other gospel, different in kind, from that which he preached to the Galatians. See Burton, *Galatians,* 23–24.

but some are disturbing you: In this translation "but" translates *ei mē* ("except"). See Zerwick, *Biblical Greek,* 158. This is the first mention of the agitators. The verb *tarassein* refers to "mental and spiritual agitation and confusion" (BAG). Paul employs the same verb in 5:10 in reference to any individual who might unsettle the Galatians by compelling them to accept circumcision. In Acts 15:24 Luke uses the verb in reference to those who unsettled the Antioch Church by saying, "unless you are circumcised . . . you cannot be saved" (Acts 15:1).

and want to pervert the gospel of Christ: The verb *metastrephein* means to change or alter something, often to its opposite, e.g., Sir 11:31, "for they lie in wait, *turning* good into evil"; Jas 4:9, "Let your laughter *be turned* into mourning." In Paul's view, the agitators have distorted the essential meaning of the gospel. "The gospel of Christ" may be construed as a subjective genitive (the gospel preached by Christ) or as an objective genitive (the gospel whose content is Christ). The latter is preferable; the agitators are perverting the gospel about Christ. One must keep in mind, however, that this gospel also originates with Christ (1:11-12).

8. *But even if we or an angel from heaven should preach [to you] contrary to what we preached to you*: This is the first part of a conditional sentence which expresses an eventual condition, but one which is improbable. The scenario described in the opening clause is possible, but not probable. Thus the conditional clause functions as a rhetorical device to highlight the singular message of the gospel. In 3:19 Paul refers to the mediation of angels to indicate the inferiority of the Mosaic Law, and in 4:14 he reminds the Galatians that they received him as an angel (*aggelos*) of God when he first visited them. *Euaggelizein* ("to preach") is the verbal counterpart of *euaggelion* ("gospel"). Thus to preach is to proclaim the gospel, i.e., what God has done in Christ. Of the nineteen occurrences of the verb in the undisputed Pauline correspondence, seven appear in Galatians, six of these in this chapter (1:8 [twice], 9, 11, 16, 23; 4:13).

The words "to you" are found in the texts of D and L but are missing from several important manuscripts (S*). Later copyists may have omitted the words because they could be interpreted too narrowly, i.e., Paul is *only* speaking to the Galatians. By omitting the words, the text clearly refers to all believers.

let such a one be cursed: Anathema can refer to something dedicated or consecrated to God, or something delivered up to divine wrath (*TDNT*, I, 354). In Paul, the word always denotes the object of a curse (Rom 9:3; 1 Cor 12:3; 16:22; Gal 1:8,9).

9. *As we have already said, and now I say again*: In an attempt to avoid the difficulty caused by the change of subject, the text of S* reads "As I have already said." The use of "we," however, may be Paul's way of including the brethren mentioned in v. 1. It is not only Paul who imposes this curse but his coworkers as well. Similar phrases can be found in 2 Cor 13:2; 1 Thess 3:4; 4:6. The text can be interpreted in two ways: either Paul is referring to something he said to the Galatians when he first visited them, or he is alluding to what he has just said in v. 8. The presence of *arti* ("now") suggests that a period of time has elapsed and seems to indicate that Paul is referring to an earlier visit.

If someone preaches to you contrary to what you received, let such a one be cursed: Since *euaggelizetai* ("preaches") includes the notion of the gospel, one may translate it, "If someone preaches a gospel . . . ." "Received" translates *parelabete*, a technical word employed in reference to the tradition or the gospel message (1 Cor 11:23; 15:1,3; Phil 4:9; 1 Thess 2:13; 4:1). While Paul hands on the gospel to others, he did not receive it from another human being (Gal 1:12).

10. *Am I now currying favor with human beings, or with God?*: The translation does not adequately reproduce the Greek which contains the particle *gar* ("for"), the force of which is to relate this verse to the preceding verses. Therefore, while Nestle-Aland, *Novum Testamentum Graece*, begins a new paragraph here, I have kept this verse as part of the previous paragraph. The opening phrase is notoriously difficult to translate; the difficulty is twofold. First, how should the verb *peithein* be translated? While it ordinarily means "to persuade" or "to appeal to" (in either a positive or negative sense), it can also mean "to strive to please," or "to curry favor with someone." Second, how should the particle *ē* ("or") be construed? Is it disjunctive, implying a contrast in Paul's behavior toward God and human beings, or is it copulative, implying the same behavior before God and human beings? If *peithein* is construed as "persuade," and if *ē* is interpreted as a copulative, then Paul is asking, "am I trying to persuade human beings and God by my rhetoric?" The implied answer is that he is not trying to persuade either. But if *peithein* is construed as "curry favor with," and if *ē* is interpreted disjunctively, then Paul is asking, "who am I trying to please? God, or human beings?" The implied answer is "God." The first position is espoused by Betz (*Galatians*, 54–56), the second by G. Lyons (*Pauline Autobiography*, 136–146). This commentary takes Paul's question in the second sense because, as Lyons shows, the letter plays

on the basic contrast between God and human beings. Moreover, this interpretation best fits the immediate context: having pronounced his anathemas, it is clear that Paul's real purpose is to please God, not human beings. Thus he asks a question which expects the answer, "your primary concern is to please God, not human beings."

Or am I seeking to please human beings?: While the sense of this question is clear, one would expect a more balanced formula, e.g., Am I seeking to please God, or am I seeking to please human beings? Thus in 1 Thess 2:4, "even so we speak, not to please mortals, but to please God."

If I were still striving to please human beings, I would not be Christ's slave: Some manuscripts (D²) have *gar*, "*For* if I were . . . ." giving the phrase the sense of a conclusion. The imperfect tense of the verb *ēreskon* ("striving to please") has a conative sense, while *eti* (still) emphasizes that the period of pleasing human beings has come to a close in Paul's life. Paul identifies himself as Christ's slave (*doulos*) in Rom 1:1; Phil 1:1. See Titus 1:1. In Paul's theology, one is a slave either to sin or to the obedience which leads to righteousness (Rom 6:16). As Christ's slave, Paul is completely subservient to his master, and yet he has found a freedom which only obedience to Christ can bring.

INTERPRETATION

In Paul's other correspondence, and in Hellenistic letters generally, the opening salutation is followed by a brief thanksgiving or blessing. For example, after greeting the Corinthians, Paul writes:

> I give thanks to my God always for you because of the grace of God that has been given you in Christ Jesus, for in every way you have been enriched in him, in speech and knowledge of every kind—just as the testimony of Christ has been strengthened among you—so that you are not lacking in any spiritual gift as you wait for the revealing of our Lord Jesus Christ. He will also strengthen you to the end, so that you may be blameless on the day of our Lord Jesus Christ. God is faithful; by him you were called into the fellowship of his Son, Jesus Christ our Lord (1 Cor 1:4-9).

For other examples of the thanksgiving see Rom 1:8-15; 2 Cor 1:3-11; Phil 1:3-11; 1 Thess 1:2-10; Phlm 4-6. While these thanksgivings and blessings vary in length and style, they tend to express gratitude for the faith of the community, to pray that such faith will continue, to signal themes that will be developed in the rest of the letter, and to strengthen the rapport between Paul and the community. Thus in Romans, Paul thanks God for the faith of the community which is now proclaimed in all the world (1:8), prays that he may come to Rome for the mutual strengthening of faith (1:9-12), and explains that he has often tried to come to Rome but has been prevented from doing so (1:13-15). Galatians, however, does not have a thanksgiving or blessing, setting it apart from Paul's other correspondence.

The omission of a thanksgiving derives, in part, from the situation which Paul faced at Galatia. Because the Galatians were in the process of abandoning the God who called them and were embracing a different gospel, there was little reason for Paul to commend their faith. Moreover, the strong bond which previously joined Paul and the community (4:14-15) was in the process of disintegrating (4:16). In place of the traditional thanksgiving, therefore, Paul inserts a strong statement of indignation and amazement in which he argues that there is only one gospel.

From a rhetorical point of view, the omission of the thanksgiving and its replacement by a statement of astonishment alerts the audience that the situation has reached crisis proportions. Paul does not bypass the thanksgiving in order to insult the Galatians but to signal that this is not an ordinary letter. The bond of communion between him and the Galatians is in danger of dissolving if they do not alter their ways. Nonetheless, this section does function like a letter of thanksgiving in one respect: it signals a major theme of this letter, the singularity of the gospel.

The statement of astonishment builds upon what Paul has already said in the salutation, especially v. 4. There he stated that Christ gave himself for our sins in order to deliver us from the present evil age. Here he accuses the Galatians of turning from the God who called them to a different gospel. By doing so, the Galatians will, in fact, return to the present evil age from which Christ has delivered them. The major theme of this paragraph, the singularity of the gospel, will be substantiated by Paul's autobiographical statement in the following sections.

This is the first time that Paul makes any reference to those disturbing the Galatian congregations. Since there is no need to identify the agitators to the Galatians, the agitators are simply described as those who are disturbing (*tarassontes*) the Galatians and perverting (*metastrepsai*) the gospel of Jesus Christ. *Tarassein* is the same verb that Paul employs when speaking of the agitators in 5:10, and that Luke uses in Acts 15:24 ("Since we have learned that certain persons who have gone out from us, though with no instruction from us, have said things to disturb [*etaraxan*] you and have unsettled your minds [*anaskeuazontes tas psychas hymōn*], . . ."). According to Acts 15:1, the Church at Antioch was disturbed because "certain individuals came down from Judea and were teaching the brothers, 'Unless you are circumcised according to the custom of Moses, you cannot be saved.'" As will become clearer later, circumcision was the main issue at Galatia (5:2-12).

From Paul's perspective, the requirement that the Galatians submit to circumcision was a perversion of the gospel since it undercut the work of Christ who gave himself for our sins (1:4). If righteousness comes through the Law, then there was no need for Christ to die (2:21). Paul clearly understood something about Christ's redemptive work that neither the Galatians nor his fellow Jewish believers realized: the sufficiency of the Christ event for salvation. Because Christ died to deliver humanity from the present evil age, it is no longer necessary for those who believe in him to rely upon "works of the Law" (2:16).

Paul's language in v. 6 indicates that the Galatians have begun the process of changing their allegiance from Paul's Torah-free gospel to a version of the gospel proclaimed by the agitators: a gospel which required the Galatians to be circumcised. Consequently, he accuses the Galatians of "turning away" from the one who called them, that is, from God. The verb which Paul employs, *metatithēmi*, is strong and to the Galatians it must have seemed an overstatement since it has the sense of deserting or apostatizing. The Galatians undoubtedly thought that by accepting circumcision and other works of the Law they were completing and perfecting the conversion they began at Paul's preaching. But in Paul's view circumcision implied that Christ's death upon the cross was insufficient for salvation.

Paul's response to the Galatians is that there is only one gospel. Here, gospel (*euaggelion*) does not refer to a written document, or even to an oral tradition. The gospel, which Paul sometimes calls "the gospel of God," "the gospel of Christ," or "the gospel of his Son" is the proclamation of an event: the death and resurrection of Christ. Although Paul also speaks of the gospel to the uncircumcised and the gospel to the circumcised (2:7), he does not imply that there are two different versions of the gospel. At the heart of his argument is the conviction that there is a single gospel for Jew and Gentile which was revealed to him by a revelation of Jesus Christ (1:11). The nature of that revelation will be discussed in the next section, but suffice it to say that God revealed his Son to Paul and commissioned him as the Apostle to the Gentiles.

From Paul's point of view, then, he cannot alter the Torah-free gospel, which he has already preached to the Galatians, to include circumcision. As J. H. Schütz notes, "Paul can preach only what he has already preached, and the community can receive only what it has already received. The gospel is thus a double-sided norm—for preaching and for receiving" (*Paul and the Anatomy of Apostolic Authority*, 123). Paul's authority is not found in himself but in the gospel that he preaches, and the Galatians owe their obedience not to Paul but to the gospel that he preaches. Because the agitators preach a version of the gospel at variance with the gospel that Paul received from Christ, Paul denies that they preach the gospel of Christ.

To establish his point, Paul pronounces a double curse and places himself, as well as any heavenly messenger, under it. Because he received the gospel, he is also subservient to it. Not even he has the power to alter it. The reference to an "angel from heaven" emphasizes the point. This text should be read in conjunction with 3:19 where Paul says that the Law was ordained by angels. Although angels may have had a role in the promulgation of the Mosaic Law, they have, in Paul's view, no role in the promulgation of the gospel. Like Paul, they are subservient to it.

When repeating the curse a second time (1:9), Paul says, "As I have already said and now I say again." Exactly what he intends here is not clear. The Apostle may simply be emphasizing what he has already said in the previous verse. However, the adverb "now" suggests a lapse of time. At one point in the past, Paul made a similar statement to the Galatians. But even if this second interpretation is correct, it is not possible to identify to which occasion in the past Paul is referring (cf. Gal 4:13 and Acts 16:6; 18:22).

The final verse of this section presents a number of problems which are explained in the exegetical notes. While several commentators (Bonnard, Bruce, Burton, Schlier) treat v. 10 as the conclusion of this section, Mussner sees it as the beginning of a new section while Betz extends the section to include v. 11. Verse 11, with its formula of disclosure ("I want you to know"), however, begins a new section, whereas v. 10 is the natural conclusion to what Paul has just said. Having stated that the gospel is one and cannot be altered, either by himself or by an angel from heaven, Paul asks a series of rhetorical questions in v. 10. Paul is not trying to please human beings; his one concern is to please God. By threatening a curse upon anyone who preaches a different gospel, he demonstrates that he has no intention of simply pleasing others by telling them what they want to hear.

The rhetorical questions of v. 10, however, raise another issue: was Paul responding to charges laid against him by the agitators at Galatia? Did the agitators accuse him of making the gospel easy so that the Galatians would be more readily attracted to it? Bonnard (*Galates*, 25) and Mussner (*Galaterbrief*, 63) suggest such a scenario, but in the view of this commentary they read too much into the text. Paul employs the questions of v. 10 for rhetorical purposes in order to establish his integrity as the slave of Jesus Christ; he presents himself as a model for the Galatians to emulate. Just as he has given whole-hearted service to the singular gospel of Jesus Christ, so the Galatians must devote themselves wholeheartedly to the Torah-free gospel, no matter what others may think.

While the title of this section is "A Statement of Astonishment," it now becomes clear that the main theme is "the singular gospel of Jesus Christ"; it is from this gospel that Paul derives his authority.

FOR REFERENCE AND FURTHER STUDY

Lategan, B. "Is Paul Defending his Apostleship in Galatians?" *NTS* 34 (1988) 411–430.

Lyons, G. *Pauline Autobiography: Toward a New Understanding.* SBLDS 73; Atlanta: Scholars Press, 1985.

Schütz, J. H. *Paul and the Anatomy of Apostolic Authority.* SNTSMS 26; Cambridge University Press, 1975.

Smit, J. "The Letter to the Galatians: A Deliberative Speech." *NTS* 35 (1989) 1–26.

I: THE TRUTH OF THE GOSPEL (1:11–2:21)

Paul's Gospel Is Not of Human Origin (1:11-12)

11. For I want you to know, brethren, that the gospel preached by me is not a human affair, 12. for I did not receive it from a human, nor was I taught it, but it came through a revelation of Jesus Christ.

NOTES

11. *For I want you to know, brethren*: Some manuscripts (P46, S*) replace *gar* ("for") with *de* ("and," "but") providing a closer connection with the previous verse, but *gar* is attested by S¹, B, D*, F, G, 33. *Gnōrizō* ("I want you to know") functions as a disclosure formula and indicates the beginning of a new section. See 1 Cor 12:3; 15:1; 2 Cor 8:1 for similar formulas. The statement does not necessarily mean that the Galatians are ignorant of the events that Paul will now narrate, for in v. 13 he writes, "You have heard of my former way of life in Judaism. . . ." Undoubtedly they knew something of his past life, but now Paul will put those events into proper perspective and interpret them.

that the gospel preached by me is not a human affair: "Human affair" is a translation of *kata anthrōpon* ("according to man"). The same expression occurs in 3:15 where Paul speaks to the Galatians "in a human fashion," or "from the point of view of a human being." The point is that the gospel he preaches was not devised by any human being; its origin is in God. For "gospel" see the notes for 1:6.

12. *for I did not receive it from a human, nor was I taught it*: Some manuscripts (S, A, D*, F, G, P) replace *oute* ("nor") with *oude* in order to balance the first

oude. The text of P46, B, and D¹, followed here, is to be preferred. See the note on v. 9 for Paul's use of *paralambanein* ("receive"). While Paul insists that he did not "receive" the gospel from a human being, he does acknowledge that he "received" traditions from others (1 Cor 15:3, and perhaps 11:23). Teaching (*didaskein*) presupposes the context of the Church, e.g., 1 Cor 14:6,26; Rom 12:7. Paul denies that any other member of the Church taught him the gospel which he now preaches.

but it came through a revelation of Jesus Christ: The "revelation of Jesus Christ" can be understood as either a subjective genitive (a revelation which originated from Jesus Christ) or an objective genitive (a revelation, the content of which was Jesus Christ). The descriptions of Paul's call in Acts 9, 22, 26 are Christophanies and would suggest a subjective genitive, but vv. 15–16 favor an objective genitive: God revealed his Son to Paul.

INTERPRETATION

This unit is the beginning of a major section that begins with 1:11 and concludes with 2:21. In this section (1:11-2:21) Paul employs autobiographical material to persuade the Galatians that the gospel he preaches is not *kata anthrōpon;* that is, it is not a human affair, it does not have a human origin.

The autobiographical material of this section (1:11–2:21) has always been of great interest to NT scholars. Because it represents the most extended autobiographical section of any Pauline letter, exegetes have studied it in their attempts to reconstruct the chronology and course of Paul's life. However, the endeavor to arrive at a satisfactory chronology has rarely been successful. As detailed as this section is, it raises as many questions as it settles. For example, where and why did Paul persecute the Church? By what authority did he persecute the Church? What was the nature of the revelation of Jesus Christ? Was Paul called or converted? In addition to these questions raised by the text of Galatians, others are occasioned by Luke's account in the Acts of the Apostles. While Luke and Paul corroborate each other on some points, there are other instances in which they stand in tension with each other. How then is the data of Galatians and Acts to be employed? While all agree that Paul's own writings are primary sources and Luke's secondary, there is also a recognition that Paul's narration of these events is selective. Because he finds himself in a defensive posture, he presents the events in a way that will best support the argument which he intends to make. In light of this, commentators should not simply dismiss the data of Acts when it does not perfectly agree with Paul's account.

In addition to these questions, there are more fundamental issues concerning the nature of the autobiographical material. Why did Paul recount these events? What relationship does this material have to the rest of the letter? Until recently, most commentators answered that Paul developed this autobiographical section to defend himself from charges leveled against him by the agitators at Galatia. According to one scenario, Paul defends himself against charges that he is *dependent upon Jerusalem* for his gospel and apostolic credentials. In a word, Paul is subservient to the Jerusalem Church. Thus he insists that his apostleship and gospel are not of human origin (1:1; 1:11-12), and he employs autobiographical material to support this contention.

According to another scenario, the agitators at Galatia charged Paul of acting *independently of Jerusalem*. They complained that in his effort to win converts among the Galatians, he preached a watered-down version of the gospel which dispensed with circumcision. In a word, he was accused of trying to please human beings (1:10). Thus it is supposed that Paul marshals autobiographical material to answer the charges of opponents concerning his Torah-free gospel.

In both instances, those who espouse these positions assume that Paul is responding to charges made by opponents: Paul is dependent upon Jerusalem for his apostolic commission, or he preaches his gospel independently of Jerusalem. In both instances the methodology employed is that of "mirror reading" the text. It is assumed that when Paul makes a strong assertion, for example, that his gospel did not come from human beings, the "mirror image" (that Paul received his gospel from human beings) is the charge leveled against him by his opponents. Most recently, however, G. Lyons (*Pauline Autobiography*), has shown the weakness of this approach. After studying the use of autobiography in the Greco-Roman world, Lyons argues: "A frequent concern of ancient autobiographies was to demonstrate the consistency between one's theory and practice, often in contrast to the inconsistency of his rivals" (67). Thus autobiography was employed as a rhetorical device to show that an author's behavior corresponded to the doctrine or philosophy that he or she espoused.

Lyons's investigation has an important bearing upon the interpretation of Paul's autobiographical section. It suggests that Paul employs autobiography to demonstrate the consistency between his own behavior and the gospel he preaches, not to defend himself from the charges of opponents. More specifically, Paul employs autobiography in the service of the gospel. He recounts certain events from his life to demonstrate that the gospel is not of human origin and that his own life is lived in conformity with the gospel that he preaches.

It is the contention of this commentary that the autobiographical material found in 1:13–2:14 has a rhetorical function intended to persuade the Galatians that the gospel is not of human origin (1:11-12), rather than an apologetic function of defending Paul from the accusations of opponents. This, in turn, leads to a further point. Since the autobiographical material is employed to demonstrate the non-human origin of the gospel, its primary focus is to substantiate Paul's Torah-free gospel and not to construct a chronology of his life. Therefore, while readers will find helpful biographical information in this section, they must remember that it is not Paul's primary purpose to recount the course of his life. The material in this section is structured in the following manner.

1:11-12   The theme announced: the gospel is not of human origin.
1:13-17   First proof: Paul received his gospel through a revelation of Jesus Christ.
1:18-20   Second proof: The Jerusalem Church did not commission Paul.
1:21-24   Third proof: Those in Judea glorified God because of Paul.
2:1-10   Fourth proof: Paul defended the truth of the gospel at Jerusalem.
2:11-14   Fifth proof: Paul defended the truth of the gospel at Antioch.
2:15-21   Paul's gospel: We are justified by the faith of Jesus Christ.

The gospel is not of human origin (Gal 1:11-12). The opening words of these verses, *gnōrizō gar hymin* ("I want you to know") function as a disclosure formula and indicate that Paul is beginning a new section. These verses, however, are not part of the autobiographical material (1:13–2:14) proper. Rather, they announce the theme which that material will illustrate in a concrete manner: the gospel is not of human origin (*kata anthrōpon*). This theme, the divine origin of the gospel, is foundational for everything that Paul will say in this letter. Because the gospel originates with God, what seemed utterly impossible has taken place: God has accepted the Gentiles into the commonwealth of Israel on the basis of faith rather than on the basis of works of the Law. Furthermore, these verses announce the fundamental argument that Paul will employ in this letter. Since Paul's Torah-free gospel originates with God, the Galatians should refuse all efforts by others to make them adopt the works of the Law. Inasmuch as these verses announce the fundamental theme and argument of the letter, they are similar to Rom 1:16-17 which proclaims the theme of that letter: the gospel is the power of God for salvation for everyone who believes because the righteousness of God is revealed in it.

Paul's statement that the gospel is not *kata anthrōpon* is reinforced by two other statements: he did not receive (*paralebon*) it, and he was not taught (*edidaxthēn*) it. After these qualifications, Paul announces his theme: his gospel came through a revelation of Jesus Christ (*apokalypseōs Iēsou Christou*). These verses clearly echo what Paul has already said in v. 1 concerning his apostleship; it did not come from or through a human being but through Jesus Christ and God the Father. Thus Paul establishes a link between the gospel he preaches and his apostleship. Both have their origin with God, neither can be accounted for by a human commission.

Negatively stated, Paul's gospel is not *kata anthrōpon* because he did not receive it from, nor was he taught it by, another human being. When Paul says that he did not receive the gospel from human beings, he is not excluding all human tradition. In 1 Cor 15:3-7, for example, he relates a tradition about the resurrection which he received ("For I handed on to you as of first importance what I in turn had received . . ."). And in 1 Cor 11:23-26 he narrates a Eucharistic tradition ("For I received from the Lord what I also handed on to you, . . ."). Furthermore, it is reasonable to assume that when Paul visited Peter for the first time (1:18), Peter communicated some of the Jesus traditions to Paul. Likewise, Paul was undoubtedly taught some things by the early Christian communities of Jerusalem, Damascus, and Antioch. Indeed, the very fact that Paul received Eucharistic and resurrection traditions from them means that he was instructed by them. Furthermore, Paul's description in 1 Cor 14:26-32 of how worship should take place indicates that he profited from teachers within the worshipping assembly. But while others may have learned the gospel from the preaching of others, this was not the case with Paul. For him the gospel came as "a revelation of Jesus Christ." The phrase could mean a revelation *from* Jesus Christ, a revelation whose *object* was Jesus Christ, or even a revelation from Christ the object of which is Jesus Christ. But Paul's statement in 1:15, that God revealed his Son to him, shows that this *apokalypsis Iēsou Christou* should be taken as an objective genitive. Paul received a revelation from God, the content and object of which was Jesus Christ.

While most authors identify this revelation with Paul's Damascus road experience, described by Luke in narrative form (Acts 9, 22, 26), a few commentators do not. Bonnard argues that the revelation of Jesus Christ refers principally to all that the Spirit revealed to Paul, during his first days as a Christian, concerning the meaning of Christ's death and resurrection for the Gentiles (*Galates*, 30). Paul's further description of this revelation, however, which seems to have taken place in and around Damascus (1:16-17), indicates that he is referring to his call/conversion. One must, however, resist the temptation to interpret this phrase purely in terms of Luke's narrative.

For Paul, *apokalypsis* ("revelation") can refer to a charismatic or mystical experience (1 Cor 14:6, 26, 30; 2 Cor 12:1, 7; Gal 2:2; Phil 3:15), experiences which he clearly enjoyed. But *apokalypsis* also has an eschatological dimension, denoting what will be revealed at the end of time (Rom 2:5; 8:18-19; 1 Cor 1:7; 3:13). Paul's "revelation of Jesus Christ," mentioned here, is clearly foundational. Through it God revealed his Son to Paul, and from this Paul derived the basic shape of his gospel. Although Ephesians was probably not written by Paul, the author of that letter provides what is perhaps the earliest and best commentary on the revelation made to Paul: "for surely you have already heard of the commission of God's grace that was given me for you, and how the mystery was made known to me by revelation . . . that is, the Gentiles have become fellow heirs, members of the same body, and sharers in the promise in Christ Jesus through the gospel" (Eph 3:1-7).

To summarize, these verses are the foundation for all that Paul will argue in the rest of the letter. His gospel, which proclaims that God has justified the Gentiles on the basis of faith, not on the basis of works of the Law, came directly from God, without human mediation. Because this Torah-free gospel came from a revelation of Jesus Christ, Paul cannot alter it, nor should the Galatians swerve from it. Anyone who tampers with it violates the truth of the gospel (Gal 2:5, 14).

For Reference and Further Study

Barclay, J. M. G. "Mirror-Reading a Polemical Letter: Galatians as a Test Case." *JSNT* 31 (1987) 73-93.

Gaventa, B. R. "Galatians 1 and 2: Autobiography as Paradigm." *NovT* 28 (1986) 309-326.

Lategan, B. "Is Paul Defending His Apostleship in Galatians?" *NTS* (1988) 411-430.

Lyons, G. *Pauline Autobiography: Toward a New Understanding.* SBLDS 73; Atlanta, GA: Scholars Press, 1985.

Paul Received His Gospel through a Revelation (1:13-17)

13. You have heard of my former way of life in Judaism, that I persecuted God's Church to an extraordinary degree and was trying to annihilate it. 14. I was advancing in Judaism beyond many of my contemporaries among my race, being far more a zealot for the traditions of my ancestors. 15. But when [God], who set me apart from my mother's womb, and called me through his grace, was pleased 16. to reveal his Son in me, in order that I might preach him among the nations, I did not immediately consult with flesh and blood, 17. nor did I go up to Jerusalem to those who were apostles before me, but I went to Arabia and again I returned to Damascus.

Notes

13. *You have heard of my former way of life in Judaism:* "Way of life" translates *anastrophēn* of which this is the only occurrence in the undisputed Pauline letters. The word occurs twice in the Deutero-Paulines (Eph 4:22; 1 Tim 4:12)

and six times in 1 Peter with an emphasis upon behavior or the ethical aspect of conduct (1:15, 18; 2:12; 3:1, 2, 16). "Way of life" is appropriate here. Although Paul now judges his former conduct negatively, from his perspective as a Christian, he did not lead an unethical life before his call. As to righteousness under the Law, he was blameless (Phil 3:6). For a different view of Paul's former life see 1 Tim 1:13. "Former" is a translation of *pote*. This same word occurs twice in v. 23 forming an inclusion (vv. 13-23) with this verse which focuses upon Paul's former life and his call. For similar uses of *pote* see Rom 7:9; 11:30. Gal 1:13,14 are the only occurrences of *Ioudaismos* in the NT. Except for 2 Macc 2:21; 8:1; 14:38; 4 Macc 4:26, "Judaism" does not occur in the Greek OT, the Apocrypha, Pseudepigrapha, Philo, or Josephus. The Maccabean revolt was a struggle against Hellenization and an attempt to preserve the distinguishing marks of being Jewish: circumcision and food laws. It is against this background that "Judaism" is to be understood. The translations of the NEB and the REB ("when I was still a practicing Jew") suggest that Paul is no longer a practicing Jew. While Paul probably did not observe the legal requirements of Torah concerning food laws when he was in the company of Gentiles (Gal 4:12; 1 Cor 9:21), he certainly did not apostatize from his former faith (see Rom 9-11).

that I persecuted God's Church to an extraordinary degree: Paul describes himself as a persecutor in 1 Cor 15:9 and Phil 3:6. In the Lucan accounts of Paul's call, the recurring question of the Risen Lord is, "Saul, Saul, why do you persecute me?" (Acts 9:4; 22:7; 26:14). In this letter, the verb *diōkoun* occurs in 1:23; 4:29; 5:11; and 6:12. Its occurrence in 1:23 forms, along with *pote*, the inclusion noted above (vv. 13–23), and its use in chs. 4–6 are part of an important theme which will be explained below. Paul speaks of the Church of God in 1 Cor 1:2; 15:9; 2 Cor 1:1, and of the churches of God in 1 Cor 11:16 and 1 Thess 2:14. The expression is rooted in the OT designation of Israel as the *qahal Yahweh* ("the congregation of Yahweh"); see Deut 23:2-3. The description of the Church as God's congregation pits Paul the Pharisee, zealous for the Law, against God.

and was trying to annihilate it: Luke employs the same verb *eporthein* ("annihilate") in his description of Paul in Acts 9:21. The imperfect tense has a connative sense. The verb occurs again in v. 23 as part of the inclusion noted above. A few manuscripts (F, G) replace *eporthoun* with *epolemoun* ("warred upon, fought against"). The same variant occurs in v. 23.

14. *I was advancing in Judaism*: The imperfect *proekopton* ("advancing") focuses upon Paul's on-going progress in Judaism. The same verb is applied to Jesus "who increased in wisdom and in stature" (Luke 2:52). The only other use of the verb by Paul is found in Rom 13:12.

beyond many of my contemporaries among my race: The comparison with contemporaries (*synēlikiōtas*), people of his own age, suggests Paul's extreme zealousness for the Law. Among my race (*en tō genei mou*) refers to the people of Israel, as it does in 2 Cor 11:26 and Phil 3:5.

being far more a zealot: The ideal of zeal is deeply rooted in the OT (Num 25:11, 13; 1 Kgs 19:10, 14; Sir 45:23; 48:2) and is exemplified by several OT figures:

Phinehas (Numbers 25), Elijah (1 Kgs 18–19), Simeon and Levi (Genesis 34). Zeal came to a special prominence during the Maccabean period (1 Macc 2:24, 26, 27, 50; 2 Macc 4:2). Such zeal was more than a commitment to the Law; it included a willingness to use violence against all, Jew or Gentile, who opposed the Law. See T. Donaldson, "Zealot and Convert." In Acts 21:20, James points to the thousands of believers who are zealous for the Law, and in Acts 22:3 Paul describes himself as "being zealous for God." A person's zealousness, however, can be misdirected. In Acts 5:17; 13:45; 17:5, Luke explains that the Jews persecuted the Church because they were zealous, and in Phil 3:6 Paul says that his zeal was expressed in his persecution of the Church. The fact that Paul's zealousness for the Law led him to persecute God's Church is an essential part of the paradox that he establishes here. One who persecuted the Church should never have been called to preach the gospel.

for the traditions of my ancestors: While *patrikōn* ("of my ancestors") could denote the traditions of his father's house, Paul's concern for the Law suggests the whole body of the Law and the oral tradition associated with the sect of the Pharisees (cf. Mark 7:1-5).

15. *But when [God]*: "God" is not found in the manuscripts of P46, B, F, G; it is present in S, A, D. It is more likely that it was introduced to make the subject of the verb explicit than that it was purposely or accidentally omitted.

who set me apart from my mother's womb: The participle *aphorisas* ("set me apart") has the sense of setting aside for service, separating clean from unclean, consecrating for service (Exod 13:12; 19:12, 23; Lev 13:4, 5; Ezek 45:1, 4). In Rom 1:1 Paul says that he has been set aside (*aphorismenos*) for the gospel of God, and in Acts 13:2 the Holy Spirit asks the Church to set aside (*aphorisate*) Saul and Barnabas for the work the Spirit has prepared for them. The phrase "from my mother's womb" alludes to the call narratives of Isa 49:1; Jer 1:5 (LXX).

and called me: The entire phrase is missing from P46. Its absence results in a smoother reading which suggests that it may have been omitted for this reason. The theme of being called by God plays an important role in this letter (see 1:6; 5:8, 13). For Paul the Christian life is a call from God (1 Thess 2:12; 4:7; 5:24). This gracious aspect of God's call (*dia tēs charitos autou*) is also mentioned by Paul in 1 Cor 15:10: "By the grace of God I am what I am, and his grace toward me has not been in vain." For other references to the grace given to Paul, see Rom 12:3; 15:15; 1 Cor 3:10. For references to God's grace in this letter, see 1:3, 6, 15; 2:9, 21; 5:4; 6:18.

was pleased: Although this verb (*eudokēsen*) comes at the end of the English sentence, it stands toward the beginning of the Greek sentence highlighting the divine initiative. See 1 Cor 1:21; 10:5 for other instances where God is the subject of this verb.

16. *to reveal his Son*: This phrase suggests that "the revelation of Jesus Christ" in verse 12 is to be interpreted as an objective genitive: God revealed his Son to Paul. For other references to Jesus as the Son in the undisputed Pauline letters, see Rom 1:3, 9; 5:10; 8:3, 29, 32; 1 Cor 1:9; 2 Cor 1:19; Gal 2:20; 4:4, 6; 1 Thess 1:10. The precise meaning of the title "Son" is difficult to define.

In the Hellenistic world, philosophers, mythical heroes and those endowed with divine power could be viewed as sons of God. In Jewish literature the title is predicated of angels (Gen 6:2; Job 1:6), the people of Israel (Exod 4:22; Hos 2:1), the king (2 Sam 7:4; Ps 2:7), and the righteous person (Wis 2:18; 5:5). The early Church clearly identified the Messiah as the Son of God (Mark 14:61), but it is doubtful that this identification was made before the NT period in Jewish literature. The manner in which Paul views Jesus in his writings, e.g. the Christ hymn (Phil 2:5-11), and the salvific dimension which he attributes to Christ's death (Gal 1:4; 2:20-21), show that the title describes a unique relationship between Jesus and God which others can only share, in an analogous fashion, by incorporation into Christ. Thus, believers can call God "Father" (*Abba*) because God has sent the Spirit of his Son into their hearts (Gal 4:4), but Jesus' relationship to God is unique. While Paul's thought is not framed in the formulas of the Church's creeds, those creeds can be seen as the development of a process begun by Paul and other NT writers. See J. Fitzmyer, "Pauline Theology," *NJBC*, 1393-94.

in me: the phrase, *en emoi*, can be translated "to me" or "in me." While the former suggests a more external revelation such as that described in Acts 9, 22, 26, the latter denotes an interior experience, e.g., 2 Cor 4:6 ("For it is the God who said, 'Let light shine out of darkness,' who has shone in our hearts to give the light of the knowledge of the glory of God in the face of Jesus Christ"). This distinction, however, between external and internal experience should not be pressed. Neither phrase absolutely excludes the dimension highlighted by the other. In Galatians Paul simply does not describe his Damascus road experience in detail as does Luke in Acts.

in order that I might preach him among the nations: This clause expresses the purpose for which God revealed his Son to Paul. Grammatically it is the most important phrase in vv. 15-16. "Among the nations" refers to Paul's ministry to the Gentiles (see 2:2, 7, 8, 9). That Paul was the Apostle to the Gentiles is an important theme in the Deutero-Pauline correspondence (Eph 3:1, 8; 1 Tim 2:7; 3:16; 2 Tim 4:7). His call to be an apostle to the Gentiles echoes the call of the servant in Isa 49:1-6, especially v. 6 ("I will give you as a *light to the nations*, that my salvation may reach to the end of the earth").

I did not immediately consult: The verb *prosanethemēn* ("consult with") means to refer a matter for consideration. Dunn ("The Relationship between Paul and Jerusalem according to Galatians 1 and 2," in *Jesus, Paul and the Law*, 110) writes that *prosanethemēn* means "consult in order to be given a skilled or authoritative interpretation." That Paul did not consult with others shows that the revelation was immediately clear and that he did not need anyone to interpret it. Compare Acts 9:10-19 and 22:12-16; in the second of these accounts Ananias explains the significance of the Damascus road event to Paul.

flesh and blood: The expression is a Semitism for what is human, a human being. See 1 Cor 15:50; Eph 6:12; Matt 16:17.

17. *nor did I go up to Jerusalem to those who were apostles before me*: Several manuscripts (P51, B, D, G) read *apēlthon* ("go away," "go") in place of *anēlthon* ("go up"), the reading of S, A^vid. P46 simply has *ēlthon* ("go," "went"). Those who

were apostles before Paul probably refers to a group broader than the Twelve. See 1 Cor 15:5-7 where Paul distinguishes between "the Twelve" and "all the apostles." The Twelve, however, were closely associated with the Jerusalem Church according to the Acts of the Apostles.

but I went to Arabia: While "Arabia" usually refers to the vast desert peninsula between Iraq and the Persian Gulf on the east, the Indian Ocean on the south, and the Red Sea on the West, the name can also denote the area east of Jerusalem. Here, Paul is probably referring to a small settlement east of Damascus, in the kingdom of the Nabateans. See 2 Cor 11:32 where he recounts how the governor of Damascus, under orders from King Aretas (Aretas IV, 9BC-AD40), tried to seize him at Damascus. Perhaps Paul's activity "in Arabia," i.e., the Nabatean kingdom of Aretas, was the occasion for this. In 4:35 Paul refers to Arabia in a more general sense.

and again I returned to Damascus. Damascus is located in Syria, to the north of Palestine. In 85 BC the Romans made it the capital of the Nabatean kingdom. When Paul came to Damascus, Aretas IV was in charge. While Acts 9:3 says that the revelation occurred as Paul approached Damascus, this is the first time that Paul localizes the event of his call. Josephus's accounts of the massacre of the Jews at Damascus (*War* 2:561; 7:368) indicate that there was a sizable Jewish population there.

INTERPRETATION

The Revelation of Jesus Christ (1:13-17). This unit begins a section in which autobiographical material plays an important role. As mentioned above, the purpose of this material is to substantiate Paul's claim that the Torah-free gospel he preaches among the Gentiles is not of human origin, and to show that his life and behavior correspond with the gospel that he preaches.

This unit can be divided into two subsections. In the first (vv. 13–14), Paul recalls his former life as a persecutor. In the second (vv. 15–17), he describes his conversion/call and his commission to preach the gospel to the Gentiles. The fact that these two phases of his life are so diametrically opposed constitutes Paul's first argument that the gospel which he preaches is not of human origin. From a purely human point of view (*kata anthrōpon*), it is inconceivable that one so zealous for the Law and so ardent a persecutor of the Church should now preach a Torah-free gospel to Gentiles. One might concede that Paul could be converted to the new way. One might even concede that as a convert he would preach to Gentiles. But it is inconceivable that a converted Paul would preach a Torah-free gospel to Gentile or Jew. That Paul preaches such a gospel is an indication that he received a divine commission. He did not decide to exempt the Galatians, or other Gentiles, from observance of the Torah. He was not taught to do this, nor did he receive it from any tradition; the Torah-free gospel came from Paul's *apokalypsis Iēsou Christou*.

Paul begins the first subsection (vv. 13–14) by reminding the Galatians of what they already know: he persecuted the Church of God and was excessively zealous for his ancestral traditions. This aspect of Paul's life is corroborated by what he says of himself elsewhere (1 Cor 15:9; Phil 3:4-6), as well as by other writings of the NT (Acts 8:3; 9:1-2; 22:4-5; 26:9-11; 1 Tim 1:13). Paul's past as a persecutor, therefore, was not unknown to the Galatians, and one can suppose that the Apostle made use of it when he preached to the Galatians. Now, however, he employs this autobiographical material to persuade the Galatians that the gospel he preaches is not *kata anthrōpon* since it is hardly the message that a zealot and former persecutor would devise. Beyond the general statement that he was zealous for the Law and persecuted the Church, Paul does not offer any other details about the nature of his activity as a persecutor, e.g., his motivation, the people whom he persecuted, where they resided, etc. In terms of Paul's argument all of this is irrelevant.

In the second subsection (vv. 15–17) Paul speaks of his conversion/call and what resulted. These three verses form a single, rather complex sentence in Greek. The primary purpose of this sentence is not to describe what is traditionally referred to as Paul's conversion but to explain the outcome of that experience: he did not consult with others, nor did he go to the Jerusalem Apostles; rather he went to Arabia and then returned to Damascus. The reference to Damascus is the first indication of where these events took place and suggests that Paul is describing the Damascus road event narrated in Acts 9, 22, 26.

The exact nature of Paul's experience has been disputed, especially since the publication of K. Stendahl's influential essay, "Paul among Jews and Gentiles." While this experience has been traditionally referred to as Paul's "conversion," the term is anachronistic since Judaism and Christianity did not yet exist as two distinct faiths. Thus, Paul and other Jewish believers in Christ did not think of themselves as moving from one religion to another. Moreover, here Paul's language clearly refers to the prophetic calls of the Servant in Isa 49 and the prophet Jeremiah. Consequently, Stendahl and those following him insist upon the term "call" rather than "conversion."

Stendahl's essay provides an important corrective, but Alan Segal (*Paul the Convert*) has recently insisted upon the language of conversion. Granted that Paul did not convert from one religion to another, it is undeniable that the course of his life was inextricably altered by the revelation that he received in or near Damascus. Segal is not far from the truth when he argues that Paul was converted from Pharisaic Judaism to an apocalyptic form of Christianity. It seems prudent, therefore, to retain the language of conversion while acknowledging that Paul describes this conversion in the language of a prophetic call. Thus this commentary employs the somewhat awkward expression call/conversion.

In the light of his call/conversion, Paul now understands that the whole course of his life has been divinely determined. The God who called him set him apart from the moment of his conception for the Torah-free gospel that he now proclaims. The choice of *aphorizein* (''to set apart'') is significant because it is often used in the OT in reference to someone or something set aside for consecrated service. Moreover, it is the same verb which Paul employs in Rom 1:1 when he writes, ''Paul, a servant of Jesus Christ, called to be an apostle, *set apart* for the gospel of God.''

Because he was set apart from his mother's womb, the circumstances of Paul's call were similar to those of Jeremiah and the Servant of Isa 49, both of whom were called before their births, and both of whom were called to bring their message to the nations.

> Before I formed you *in the womb* I knew you, and *before you were born* I consecrated you; I appointed you a prophet *to the nations* (Jer 1:5).
>
> The Lord *called me before I was born*, while I was *in my mother's womb* he named me. . . . I will give you as a *light to the nations*, that my salvation may reach to the end of the earth (Isa 49:1, 6).

Since Paul's mission to the Gentiles was determined before he was born, there can be no doubt that his Torah-free gospel was divinely ordained.

Not only did God determine that Paul would bring the gospel to the Gentiles; it was God who determined *when* He would reveal his Son to Paul (*hote de eudokēsen ho Theos*). Paul did not and could not choose the time and place. Only when the time was fulfilled could the revelation occur. J. H. Schütz (*Paul and the Anatomy of Apostolic Authority*, 134) incisively notes that Paul's description of himself, as set apart from conception, intimates that the whole of his life—persecutor and preacher of the gospel—falls under the sovereignty of God's will. Just as the Law had a role to play in the economy of salvation and then was surpassed by Christ, so Paul's life as a persecutor of God's Church played a necessary role only to give way to his life as the Apostle to the Gentiles.

When the time arrived, God revealed his Son to Paul (*en emoi*) in order that he might preach the gospel to the Gentiles. The exact meaning of these words is disputed. What kind of a revelation did Paul experience and what did he learn from it? In Acts 9, 22, 26, his experience is described as a Christophany which could be attested to, at least in part, by his travelling companions. Thus, although those with Paul did not see the Lord, they heard the voice speaking to him. In 1 Cor 9:1, Paul asks, ''Have I not seen (*heoraka*) our Lord?'' And in 1 Cor 15:8 he says, ''he appeared (*ōphthē*) also to me,'' suggesting a revelation with some objective value.

However, in 2 Cor 4:6 he writes, "for it is the God who said, 'Let light shine out of darkness,' who has shone in our hearts to give the knowledge of the glory of God in the face of Jesus Christ." This points to a more subjective experience. Likewise, Paul's description of his visions and revelations (optasias kai apokalypseis) in 2 Cor 12:1-10 can best be described as ecstatic experiences. On balance then, the experience described here seems to be a resurrection appearance (1 Cor 9:1; 15:8), an experience more subjective in nature than that portrayed by Luke in Acts.

It is clear that Christ was the object and content of this experience. Through this revelation God disclosed to Paul that the one whom Paul was persecuting was none other than God's Son. However, it is apparent from what follows that the purpose of this revelation was more embracing than a simple Christological disclosure. God revealed his Son in order that Paul might preach the gospel to the Gentiles. Paul learned that the final age had begun, and that the time had come to incorporate the Gentiles into the community of Israel.

The most surprising aspect of this unit is Paul's description of what he did not do. He did not seek an authoritative interpretation of what happened (ou prosanethemen sarki kai haimati); and he did not go up to Jerusalem. Instead he went to Arabia and then returned to Damascus. While these events may seem secondary to the description of Paul's call/conversion, they are, in fact, essential to the argument. If Paul sought an authoritative interpretation from anyone, then it would be apparent that his gospel was mediated by a human being. And if he went directly to Jerusalem, then one might conjecture that he had been commissioned by one of the original apostles. But the meaning of the revelation was clear to Paul: God was sending him to the Gentiles. Consequently, there was no need for Paul to consult with others. Instead, he went directly to Arabia, the Nabatean kingdom of Aretas IV, and most likely began his preaching to Gentiles. In a word, Paul's behavior reflected a perfect correspondence with the gospel he received: immediately after God revealed his Son to Paul, he preached the gospel to Gentiles.

Paul's activity in Arabia lasted at least three years (1:18), after which he returned to Damascus. Since there was a community of believers at Damascus, one can suppose that Paul participated in it, learning new traditions about Jesus. Paul's Torah-free gospel, however, came from God.

FOR REFERENCE AND FURTHER STUDY

Bruce, F. F. Paul: Apostle of the Heart Set Free. Grand Rapids: Eerdmans, 1977.
Cerfaux, L. "St. Paul's Vocation," in The Christian in the Theology of St. Paul. New York: Herder and Herder, 1967.

Collins, R. F. "Paul's Damascus Experience: Reflections on the Lukan Account." *LS* 11 (1986) 99–118.

Dietzfelbinger, C. *Die Berufung des Paulus als Ursprung seiner Theologie.* WMANT 58; Neukirchen-Vluyn: Neukirchener Verlag, 1985.

Donaldson, T. L. "Zealot and Convert: The Origin of Paul's Christ-Torah Antithesis." *CBQ* 51 (1989) 655–682.

Dunn, J. D. G. " 'A Light to the Gentiles', or 'The End of the Law'? The Significance of the Damascus Road Christophany for Paul," in *Jesus, Paul and the Law: Studies in Mark and Galatians.* Louisville: Westminster/John Knox, 1990.

Gaventa, B. R. *From Darkness to Light: Aspects of Conversion in the New Testament.* Philadelphia: Fortress, 1986.

Kim, S. *The Origin of Paul's Gospel.* Grand Rapids: Eerdmans, 1982.

Munck, J. "The Call," in *Paul and the Salvation of Mankind.* Atlanta: John Knox, 1959.

Räisänen, H. "Paul's Conversion and the Development of His View of the Law." *NTS* 33 (1987) 404–419.

Segal, A. *Paul the Convert.* New Haven: Yale University Press, 1990.

Stendahl, K. "Call Rather than Conversion," in *Paul Among Gentiles and Jews.* Philadelphia: Fortress, 1976.

The Jerusalem Church Did Not Commission Paul (1:18-20)

18. Then after three years I went up to Jerusalem to visit Cephas, and I stayed with him fifteen days. 19. And I did not see any of the other apostles except James, the brother of the Lord. 20. What I am writing to you, I swear before God that I am not lying.

Those in Judea Glorified God because of Paul (1:21-24)

21. Then I went into the regions of Syria and Cilicia; 22. I was unknown by sight to the churches of Judea which are in Christ. 23. They only heard that "the one who formerly persecuted us is now preaching the faith which he formerly tried to annihilate." 24. And they glorified God because of me.

Notes

18. *Then after three years I went up to Jerusalem*: This is the first use of *epeita* ("then") by Paul to mark off an important series of events which occurred after his

call (1:18, 21; 2:1). His first visit to Jerusalem occurs three years after his call. Since the ancients often reckoned even part of a year as a year, the period mentioned here may be less than three full years. Grammatically *epeita* can refer to Paul's return to Damascus or to his revelation. In the first instance, his visit would have occurred three years after his return to Damascus. In the second, it would have occurred three years after his call. If one chooses the first option, it is impossible to tell how long Paul spent in Arabia. If one chooses the second, it would seem that he spent about three years in Arabia. Here, the second option (three years after the revelation) has been chosen since it makes better sense of the chronology, and because the revelation is the main event with which Paul is concerned.

to visit Cephas: The verb *historein* ("to visit") implies more than a friendly visit. It has the sense of visiting someone for the purpose of gaining information. See J. Dunn, "The Relationship between Paul and Jerusalem according to Galatians 1 and 2." If Paul obtained information about the life and ministry of Jesus, however, it is not reflected in his extant correspondence. It is possible, however, that he received some of the Church's traditions which are reflected in his letters, e.g., 1 Cor 11:23; 15:3. "Cephas" is Aramaic for "rock" and, except for Gal 2:7,8, it is the way by which Paul usually identifies Peter (1 Cor 1:12; 3:22; 9:5; 15:5; Gal 1:18; 2:9, 11, 14). Some manuscripts (S², D, F, G) substitute "Peter" for "Cephas."

and I stayed with him fifteen days: The brevity of the visit and the fact that it was private are important for Paul's argument. This was not an official visit to the Jerusalem apostles.

19. *And I did not see any of the other apostles except James*: The text may be construed in two ways. First, Paul did not see any of the apostles, but he did see James (who is not an apostle). Second, Paul did not see any of the apostles except James (who is also numbered among the apostles). The later interpretation is to be preferred on the basis of 1 Cor 15:7 which seems to identify James as an apostle because he saw the Lord. The NT speaks of several persons named James: (1) James the son of Zebedee, one of the Twelve (Matt 10:2), executed by Herod Agrippa I (Acts 12:2); (2) James the son of Alphaeus, one of the Twelve (Matt 10:3); (3) James the son of Mary (Matt 27:56) perhaps identical with the James mentioned in number two; (4) James the father of the apostle Judas (Luke 6:16a); (5) James the brother of the Lord (Matt 13:55; Mark 6:3; Acts 12:17; 15:13; 21:18; 1 Cor 15:7; Gal 1:19; 2:9,12; Jas 1:1; Jude 1; also Josephus, *AJ* 20:200). This James, the brother of the Lord, was a powerful figure within the Jerusalem Church and a strong advocate of Jewish Christianity: he is the James referred to here.

the brother of the Lord: Matt 13:55 and Mark 6:3 speak of James as one of the Lord's *adelphoi* (Joseph/Joses, Simon, and Judas being the others). In Acts, James eventually becomes the leader of the Jerusalem Church (Acts 12:17; 15:13; 21:18), but he is not one of the Twelve, and Luke never refers to him as an apostle or as the Lord's brother. That he does not refer to him as the Lord's brother may be Luke's way of ascribing perpetual virginity to Mary.

20. *What I am writing to you, I swear before God that I am not lying*: The words ''I swear'' do not occur in the Greek text; they have been introduced to clarify the Greek which literally translated is, ''behold, before God I am not lying.'' *Ou pseudomai* functions as a formula of affirmation in Rom 9:1; 2 Cor 11:31; 1 Tim 2:7. In the present instance, it affirms that the facts about Paul's first visit to Jerusalem, as recounted here, are accurate.

21. *Then I went into the regions of Syria and Cilicia*: Paul uses *epeita* (''then'') a second time, marking off this event from the visit he has just narrated. In Acts 9:30 Luke seems to allude to the same event. However, according to Acts, Paul left Jerusalem because the Hellenists sought to kill him (9:30). Nothing of such troubles is intimated here. Syria became a Roman Province in 64 BC and was governed by a Roman legate. Bounded on the north by the Taurus mountains, on the east by the Euphrates, on the south by Palestine, and on the west by the Mediterranean, its capital was Antioch, the center of a vibrant Gentile Church according to Acts. Cilicia, the eastern portion, was part of the same province. Located in the southwestern corner of Asia Minor, its capital was Tarsus, the birthplace of Paul according to Acts 21:39; 22:3. According to Acts 15:41, after the Jerusalem conference, Paul ''went through Syria and Cilicia, strengthening the churches.'' The text of Acts 15:41 is curiously similar to this text of Galatians. See Acts 15:23 where Syria and Cilicia are also paired.

22. *I was unknown by sight to the churches of Judea which are in Christ*: Judea is the southern part of Palestine in contrast to Samaria, Galilee, Peraea, and Idumaea. In a broader sense it can refer to the region occupied by the Jewish nation (Luke 1:5; 4:44; 6:17; 7:17; 23:5; Acts 10:37). When this letter was written, ''the Roman province of Judaea included Galilee as well as Judaea (in the narrower sense) and Samaria . . . 'Judaea' may then denote the whole of Palestine'' (Bruce, *Galatians*, 103). A similar phrase is found in 1 Thess 2:14 (''the churches of God in Christ Jesus that are in Judea''). In Rom 15:31 Paul asks for prayers in order to ''be rescued from the unbelievers in Judea.'' The description of these churches as ''in Christ'' (*en Christō*) describes their relationship to Christ; they belong to him. Thus the phrase is translated ''the Christian congregations in Judea'' by the REB, and ''Christ's congregations'' by the NEB. Luke's description of what seems to be similar events in Acts 9:28-29 differs from Paul's. According to Acts, Paul was well known by other Christians in Jerusalem.

23. *They only heard that ''the one who formerly persecuted us is now preaching the faith which he formerly tried to annihilate''*: A few manuscripts (F, G) replace *eporthei* (''annihilate'') with *epolemei* (''wage war''). See note on v. 13. Whereas Paul usually speaks of faith as the trusting attitude of the believer, here he employs it in a more objective sense: the message which is proclaimed and believed. Thus faith is almost equivalent to the gospel. For other instances where Paul describes himself as a persecutor, see 1 Cor 15:9; Phil 3:6. For other references to persecution in Galatians, see 1:13, 23; 4:29; 5:11; 6:12. References to Paul's preaching (*euaggelizomai*) have occurred several times in this chapter (vv. 8, 9, 11, 16, 23).

24. *And they glorified God because of me*: The phrase *en emoi* can be translated in several ways: "because of me" (RSV, NAB); "to me" (REB); "for me" (NEB, NJB). Here it is rendered in a causal sense: Paul's call becomes the occasion for those he once persecuted to praise God.

INTERPRETATION

This section consists of two units (18-20, 21-24) which support Paul's claim, made in vv. 11-12, that his gospel is not of human origin. Each unit begins with *epeita* ("then"), and the final unit concludes with a reference to Paul's activity as a persecutor ("the one who formerly *persecuted* us . . . he formerly tried to *annihilate*") thereby forming an inclusion with v. 13 ("I *persecuted* God's Church . . . and was trying to *annihilate* it"). In the first of these units, Paul argues that the purpose of his initial visit to Jerusalem was to meet Cephas, not to be commissioned as an apostle or to be taught the gospel. In the second, he shows that his call/conversion became an occasion for the churches of Judea to praise God, even though they did not know him personally. Thus they implicitly approved of his gospel which he clearly did not receive from them.

Jerusalem did not commission Paul (1:18-20). This is the first of three units which are marked off by the adverb *epeita* ("then"). See 1:21; 2:1. Paul's use of the adverb gives the impression that he is providing a careful chronology of the events. As the notes of this commentary explain, however, his use of *epeita* is open to more than one interpretation (three years after his revelation, or three years after his return to Damascus). Since Paul's revelatory experience is the central event, *epeita* is best interpreted in reference to it; three years after his call/conversion Paul made his first visit to Jerusalem. This rendering of the chronology suggests that Paul spent two to three years preaching in Arabia, the Nabatean kingdom.

Paul's description of this visit is presented in a manner intended to minimize its importance. His purpose was to visit (*historēsai*) Cephas. The visit only lasted fourteen days. Paul did not see any of the other apostles except James. Paul concludes with an oath, testifying before God, that what he writes is the truth. What then was the purpose of the visit? And why does Paul feel that it is necessary to describe it in this fashion?

The verb *historein* indicates that the purpose of the visit was more than a social call. The basic meaning of the verb is "to inquire into, about, or from." Thus Paul went to Jerusalem to visit Peter for the sake of inquiring. But about what? Everything that Paul has said thus far excludes any need for guidance about his revelation. Paul had already gone to Arabia and preached there for three years on the basis of that revelation. The more likely explanation, therefore, is that he went to inquire about Jesus from Peter. At this point in his career, Paul clearly understood the importance of the Jerusalem Church and the one who was its acknowledged leader. It is not surprising, then, that he went to the holy city to consult with Peter. And it would be most surprising if Peter did not communicate something of the earthly Jesus and the Church's growing traditions to Paul.

Paul's careful description of this visit, however, indicates that it was not an official visit before the whole of the Jerusalem Church; it was a private affair. Some commentators, however, interpret this to mean that Paul is responding to accusations made by his adversaries that he owes his apostleship to the Church of Jerusalem and so is subservient to the Jerusalem apostles. As noted earlier, G. Lyons has argued that such mirror reading misconstrues the rhetorical use of the autobiographical material in this section. The question here concerns Paul's gospel which was announced in vv. 11–12, and only secondarily his apostolic credentials.

By describing this first visit as he does, Paul avoids any misunderstanding that he received his gospel from the Jerusalem Church. He consulted (*historein*), but he did not receive (*paralabein*), nor was he taught (*didaskein*) the gospel. Except for James, Paul did not see the other apostles. Consequently, he could not have received the gospel from them, nor could he have been taught it by them. Since Paul did not receive the gospel from Jerusalem, it follows that he was not commissioned by the Jerusalem Church. He received his gospel and the commission to preach it directly from God.

But why the oath? Why does Paul find it necessary to swear to what he is saying? Clearly Paul's visit to Jerusalem was known to others, and one cannot exclude the possibility that it was used against him by the agitators at Galatia. Thus Paul assures the Galatians that no matter what they have heard, this was a purely private consultation with Cephas. Paul may also be using the oath to avoid a possible misunderstanding of his activity in Syria and Cilicia which is described in the next unit. By swearing to the private nature of this visit, Paul forestalls any suggestion that Peter, or the Jerusalem Church, sent him on mission to these regions. Just as Paul went to Arabia after his revelatory experience to preach the gospel, so he went to Syria and Cilicia, on his own initiative, to preach the gospel.

Paul's recounting of his initial visit to Jerusalem after his call/conversion emphasizes its private nature in order to show that he did not receive the gospel from Peter or the other apostles. In fact, the narrative implies that Peter treated Paul as one who had seen the Lord and received his gospel directly from Christ.

Those in Judea glorified God (1:21-24). This unit also begins with the adverb *epeita* ("then"), but in this instance there is no ambiguity about its meaning. Having consulted with Cephas, Paul went to the regions of Syria and Cilicia. As in the case of his sojourn to Arabia, Paul does not say what he did, but the natural assumption is that he continued to preach to the Gentiles on the basis of the revelation and commission he received (1:15-16). Tarsus, the capital of Cilicia, was the birthplace of Paul according to Acts (22:3), and Syria the home of the Antioch Church was a center of Gentile missionary activity (Acts 13:1-3).

Once more, the purpose of this unit is to establish Paul's claim that the gospel is not of human origin (1:11-12). Although the churches of Judea did not know Paul personally (*tō prosōpō*), they glorified God on account of him because now he preached the faith that he formerly persecuted. This statement about the reversal in Paul's life recalls the opening of this section which described how God revealed his Son to the persecutor (1:13). Thus the Judean churches affirm Paul's dramatic call/conversion. If Paul had been known personally to the churches of Judea, one might suppose that he had been instructed and commissioned by them. But the astonishment exhibited by these congregations indicates that they cannot point to any human reason to explain the reversal that took place in Paul's life. The gospel he preaches, therefore, derives directly from God.

Paul's choice of words, that he now preaches the faith (*nyn euaggelizetai tēn pistin*) he once persecuted, is significant. As the exegetical notes indicate, here faith almost functions as a substitute for gospel. However, Paul may have chosen *pistis* instead of *euaggelion* since faith is the central aspect of the gospel that he preaches. Formerly Paul persecuted the Church because it seemed, to him, to replace Torah with faith in the Crucified One. Now it is precisely that faith, a Torah-free gospel, that Paul preaches. This faith allows Gentiles to associate themselves with Israel, apart from circumcision and the attendant demands of the Law.

FOR REFERENCE AND FURTHER STUDY

Bornkamm, G. *Paul*. New York: Harper & Row, 1971.
Dunn, J. D. G. "The Relationship between Paul and Jerusalem according to Galatians 1 and 2." *NTS* 28 (1982) 461-478 = *Jesus, Paul and the Law*, 108-128.
Jewett, R. *A Chronology of Paul's Life*. Philadelphia: Fortress, 1979.
Luedemann, G. *Paul Apostle to the Gentiles: Studies in Chronology*. Philadelphia: Fortress, 1984.

Paul Defended the Truth of the Gospel at Jerusalem (2:1-10)

1. Then after fourteen years, I again went up to Jerusalem with Barnabas, taking along Titus. 2. I went up in accord with a revelation, and I set before them the gospel which I preach among the Gentiles, privately, however, to those who were influential, lest somehow I might be running or had run in vain. 3. But not even Titus, who was with me, even though he was a Greek, was compelled to be circumcised. 4. But because of false brethren secretly brought in, who slipped in to spy on our freedom which we have in Christ Jesus in order to enslave us— 5. to whom we did not submit for a moment so that the truth of the gospel might be preserved for you. 6. And from those considered to be influential—what they once were makes no difference to me, God shows no partiality—those considered to be influential imposed nothing upon me. 7. Rather, seeing that I had been entrusted [with the gospel] to the uncircumcised just as Peter had with the gospel to the circumcised— 8. for the one who worked in Peter for apostleship to the circumcised also worked in me for the Gentiles— 9. and realizing the grace given to me, James and Cephas and John, those considered to be pillars, extended the right hand of fellowship to me and Barnabas, so that we might go to the Gentiles, and they to the circumcised. 10. They only asked that we should be mindful of the poor, which very thing I was eager to do.

Notes

1. *Then after fourteen years*: This is the third time that Paul uses the adverb *epeita* ("then") while narrating the events which occurred after his call (see 1:18, 21). Although *epeita* gives a sense of chronological precision, Paul's precise meaning here is not clear. Does *epeita* refer to the time of his call (vv. 15–16)? Or does it refer to his first visit to Jerusalem (vv. 18–20)? The judgment made at this point affects one's understanding of Pauline chronology. The fact that Paul says that he went to Jerusalem "again," however, suggests that he is dating this visit from the time of the first visit. Furthermore, Pauline usage (1 Cor 15:6, 7, 23, 48; 1 Thess 4:17) supports this interpretation. In 1 Cor 15:6, 7 Paul employs *epeita* while recounting a series of resurrection appearances, one following the other. Christ appeared to Peter, and then to the Twelve (1 Cor 15:5). *Then* he appeared to more than 500 (1 Cor 15:6). *Then* he appeared to James and all of the apostles (1 Cor 15:7). On the basis of this usage, it would appear that Paul means that fourteen years after his first visit *then* he went to Jerusalem for a second time. See Jewett, *A Chronology of Paul's Life*, 52–54. Recently, G. Luedemann has proposed a third alternative. He argues that "*Epeita* links up with what immediately precedes and introduces what follows" (*Paul: Apostle to the Gentiles*, 63). According to his interpretation, *epeita* in 1:18 "links up with the return to Damascus, and the 'three years' should be enumerated from the same return to Damascus" (63) rather than from the call. In a similar fashion, according to Luedemann, *epeita* in 2:1

separates the new trip to Jerusalem from what preceded, "the journey to the province of Syria and Cilicia" (63) not the first trip to Jerusalem or the call. Granted that there is an ambiguity in Paul's use of *epeita*, Luedemann's thesis weakens what is intended to be a forceful adverb. In 1:18 and 2:1 Paul is referring the reader to significant moments in narrative: the call and the first visit to Jerusalem.

I again went up to Jerusalem with Barnabas, taking along Titus: Paul's language indicates that Titus accompanied Paul and Barnabas as a subordinate. Thus, while Paul went with (*meta*) Barnabas, Paul took along (*symparalabōn*) Titus. The rest of the narrative suggests that Paul brought Titus in order to force the question of circumcision since he was a Greek, i.e., a Gentile like the Galatians. The name of Barnabas appears one other time in the undisputed Pauline correspondence. In 1 Cor 9:5-6 Paul says that he and Barnabas, unlike the rest of the apostles, traveled without wives. In Col 4:10 Mark is identified as the cousin of Barnabas. Barnabas appears most frequently in Acts (4:36; 9:27; 11:22, 30; 12:25; 13:1, 2, 7, 43, 46, 50; 14:12, 14, 20; 15:2, 12, 22, 25, 35, 36, 37, 39). A Levite who sold his farm and donated the proceeds to the Church, he became a prominent member of the Jerusalem Church and later of the Church of Antioch. It is he who, according to Acts, introduced Paul, after his call, to the apostles, and then brought him to Antioch after the apostle's stay in Tarsus. The Church of Antioch entrusted Barnabas and Paul with famine relief to the Church of Jerusalem, the first mission to the Gentiles, and made them delegates to the Jerusalem conference. Unlike Barnabas, Titus does not appear in Acts but does have a prominent role in 2 Corinthians (2:13; 7:6, 13, 14; 8:6, 16, 23; 12:18). He functioned as Paul's ambassador to the Corinthian community during the period of Paul's difficulties with that Church and played an important role in gathering the collection for Jerusalem. One of the Pastoral Epistles is addressed to Titus, but it is unlikely that Paul is its author or Titus its recipient.

2. *I went up in accord with a revelation.* What Paul means by a revelation (*apokalypsis*) can be determined by the manner in which he speaks of revelations elsewhere. In 2 Cor 12:1, 7 he defends himself to the Corinthians by boasting of visions and revelations of the Lord (*optasias kai apokalypseis kyriou*). The manner in which he speaks of these suggests that they were extraordinary events. In 1 Cor 14:6, 26, however, Paul writes of revelations which, he assumes, are part of the worship of the Corinthian community. In 1 Cor 14:6 revelation is associated with knowledge, prophecy and instruction which are gifts of the Spirit, and in 14:26 it is part of a list which includes psalms, instruction, tongues, and interpretation, which were elements of worship at Corinth. In the present instance, therefore, it would seem that Paul is not necessarily speaking of an extraordinary revelation such as is mentioned in 1:15-16, but of a revelation, perhaps experienced within in the worshipping assembly, that the time was ripe for another visit to Jerusalem. Whether Paul received this revelation directly, or whether it was made known to him by another, e.g., a prophet, he does not say.

and I set before them the gospel which I preach among the Gentiles: The verb *ane-themēn* ("I set before them"), when used in the middle, means declare, communicate, refer, with the added sense that the person to whom a matter is referred is asked for an opinion (BAG). The verb is found in Acts 25:14 where Festus refers the case of Paul to King Agrippa. Here, Paul sets his gospel before the Jerusalem Church, not for a judgment about its validity, but to insure that he is not laboring in vain. If Jerusalem did not acknowledge the divine origin of Paul's gospel, his mission among the Gentiles would be the more difficult. See Dunn, "The Relationship between Paul and Jerusalem according to Galatians 1 and 2." *Euaggelion* ("gospel") refers to Paul's preaching, not a narrative of the life and ministry of Jesus. This proclamation focuses upon the death and resurrection of Jesus and his imminent return as God's eschatological judge. In the letter opening of Romans, Paul summarizes his gospel as "the gospel concerning his Son who was descended from David according to the flesh and was declared to be Son of God with power according to the spirit of holiness by resurrection from the dead" (Rom 1:3-4). 1 Thess 1:9b-10 contains a summary of the message that Paul brought to the Thessalonians and other Gentiles: God has raised his Son from the dead and the Son will soon return to judge the world. Therefore, turn from idols to serve the living God if you wish to be saved from the coming wrath. In the context of Galatians it is clear that Paul's gospel is also Torah-free; it does not require Gentiles to be circumcised and follow the prescriptions of the Law. To whom did Paul present his gospel? *Autois* ("to them") could refer to the influential members of the church (*tois dokousin*), or to the general membership of the church. In the first instance, there would have been one meeting, a private meeting with the influential members of the church. In the second there would have been two meetings: a public meeting before the church and a private meeting with the influential members at which the matter was resolved.

privately, however, to those who were influential: Those who were influential (*tois dokousin*) are not identified. On the basis of v. 9, one could conclude that they are James, Cephas and John, but in v. 9 these three are also called pillars (*ho dokountes styloi einai*) which suggests that they formed an inner circle within the group of those considered to be influential. If this is the case, those of influence heard Paul's presentation of the gospel while James, Cephas, and John ratified the decision of those considered to be influential.

lest somehow I might be running or had run in vain: Given what Paul has already said about the divine origin of his gospel, the interpretation cannot be that he sought a judgment about the correctness of his gospel. Rather, his concern is with the unity of the Church. If the Jerusalem Church did not acknowledge his work among the Gentiles, then there would be an irrevocable division within the Church. Paul employs the athletic imagery of running to describe the Christian life in 1 Cor 9:24-27; Gal 5:7; and Phil 2:16. In the last text, he encourages the Philippians to hold fast to the word of life "that I can boast on the day of Christ that I did not run *in vain* or labor *in vain*." Paul does not doubt the truth of the gospel he preaches, but his preaching will have been in vain if the Philippians do not attain their goal. In Galatians, Paul is saying that his preaching will have been in vain if a barrier is erected between Jewish and Gentile believers.

3. *But not even Titus, who was with me, even though he was a Greek*: The phrase "who was with me" (*ho syn emoi*) appears repetitious in light of v. 1. Its purpose, however, is to reinforce that Paul brought Titus to make a point about circumcision. The description of Titus as a Greek means that he, like the Galatians, was an uncircumcised Gentile. According to Acts 16:1-3, Paul circumcised Timothy, but the case of Timothy was different: although his father was a Gentile, his mother was Jewish.

   was compelled to be circumcised: This is the first mention of circumcision in the letter. For other uses of the verb in Galatians see 5:2, 3; 6:12, 13; for uses of the noun see 2:7, 8, 9, 12; 5:6, 11; 6:15. In 6:12 there is a similar phrase ("It is those who want to make a good showing in the flesh that *try to compel you to be circumcised*") which might suggest a relationship between the false brethren mentioned in the next verse and those who are agitating the Galatians. Paul's choice of language here ("was not compelled") is somewhat ambiguous since it could mean that he did circumcise Titus for the sake of harmony within the Church, but the Church did not *compel* him to follow this course of action. Paul's strong statement in v. 5, however, militates against this interpretation. If Titus was eventually circumcised, it was not at the time of this visit. Paul's use of the verb "compel" (*ēnagkasthē*) has an ironic twist since the same verb is employed in v. 14. Here James, Cephas and John do not *compel* Titus to be circumcised; there Paul will accuse Cephas of trying to *compel* the Gentiles to live like Jews.

4. *But because of false brethren secretly brought in*: This and the next verse do not form a complete sentence. In order to provide a smoother translation, therefore, the REB begins the verse, "That course was urged only as a concession. . . ." This is the only occurrence of *pareisaktous* ("secretly brought in," "smuggled in,") in the NT. Although Paul speaks of the false brethren, he never identifies them nor explains when or where they infiltrated. They seem to have been Jewish Christians who argued that Gentile believers such as Titus should be circumcised (cf. Acts 15:1, 24). See 2 Cor 11:26 where Paul lists false brethren among the dangers he faced in his ministry. Here, Paul may be referring to an incident which happened earlier, perhaps at Antioch. Acts 15:1 does report that some brethren (*adelphoi*) came to Antioch from Jerusalem and taught that the Gentile members of the Church could not be saved unless there were circumcised.

   who slipped in to spy on our freedom which we have in Christ Jesus: Paul employs the verb *pareiserchomai* ("slip in") in Rom 5:20 in reference to the Law which entered, or slipped in, to increase trespasses. Its use here, as well as the infinitive *kataskopēsai* ("to spy"), points to the unworthy motives, in Paul's eyes, of the false brethren. Freedom (*eleutheria*) is an important theme in this letter (3:28; 4:22, 23, 26, 30, 31; 5:1, 13). It refers to freedom from the Mosaic Law which the Gentiles enjoy because of their faith in Christ. As chapters 5–6 will show, this freedom does not mean license. Rather, the Gentiles are free from the obligation of doing the works of the Mosaic Law: specifically, circumcision, Sabbath observance, and the observance of dietary regulations. Because this freedom derives from Christ's faith and faith in Christ, it is described as a freedom *en Christọ Iēsou* ("in Christ Jesus"). Paul indicates his solidarity with his Gentile converts by speaking of "our freedom which *we* have," showing that this freedom extends to Jews as well as Gentiles.

in order to enslave us: The false brethren would enslave (*katadoulōsousin*) Paul's Gentile converts by requiring them to become circumcised and observe the prescriptions of the Law. In 3:23–4:11, Paul describes the period of the Law as the time of humanity's infancy, a period of slavery. The use of "us" indicates Paul's solidarity with his Gentile converts. See 2 Cor 11:20 where Paul complains that the Corinthians too willingly accept enslavement from false apostles.

5. *to whom we did not submit for a moment*: There are two important variants at the beginning of this verse. The text of Marcion omits *ois* ("to whom"), doing away with the anacoluthon which plagues vv. 4–5. The text of D* omits *ois oude* ("to whom . . . not"), changing the meaning of the text: Paul *did* circumcise Titus in order to preserve the truth of the gospel. This change was probably made by scribes who had Paul's principle of accommodation (1 Cor 9:20-23), and the circumcision of Timothy (Acts 16:3), in mind. See, Metzger, *A Textual Commentary*, 591. Although neither variant is well attested, both testify to the difficulty of interpreting these verses. This is the only occurrence of the verb *eikein* ("to yield to someone") in the NT. Paul combines it with the noun *hypotagẹ* ("subjection," "submission") to emphasize that he did not accept the demands of the false brethren to circumcise Titus. For other uses of *hypotagẹ* see 2 Cor 9:12, 1 Tim 2:11; 3:4.

so that the truth of the gospel might be preserved for you: In v. 14 Paul accuses Peter of compromising the truth of the gospel by withdrawing from table fellowship with Gentiles. Here, the truth of the gospel concerns the matter of circumcision. If Titus had to be circumcised, then all Gentile believers would have to do the same. In that case, according to Paul's line of argument, Christ died in vain because salvation would come from the Law (2:21). The truth of the gospel is that God has provided a way of salvation for Gentile believers that does not require circumcision.

6. *And from those considered to be influential*: De is translated "and" rather than "but" because this sentence continues the thought of v. 3 which was interrupted by the remarks of vv. 4–5. Although Paul is showing his independence from the influential members of the church, he does not view himself in an adversarial relationship to them. His disagreement is with the false brethren, not with those of influence who did, in fact, support him. In v. 3 Paul spoke of *tois dokousin* ("to those who were influential"), here the expression is changed to *ton dokountōn einai ti* ("those considered to be influential," see Gal 6:3; Acts 5:36, 8:9). The introduction of the verb "to be" does not necessarily suggest a note of irony.

what they once were makes no difference to me, God shows no partiality: This parenthetical clause interrupts the main sentence, and its meaning is dependent upon the sense of *pote* ("once"). For other Pauline uses of *pote*, see Rom 7:9; 11:30; Gal 1:13, 23. The enclitic particle *pote* can be used after relative pronouns to give them an indefinite sense ("ever"), or to refer to past time ("once," "formerly"). In the first instance Paul would be saying, "It makes no difference to me what*ever* sort of people they were." In the second, "It makes no difference what they *once* were." If one chooses the second option, one must raise further questions. To what is Paul referring? The status of these people at the time of the meeting? The status of these people who once knew the earthly Jesus? Is the remark to be interpreted polemically? The remark that "God shows no partiality" indicates that Paul's concern is not the status of persons (their former relationship to Jesus, or their position within the community) but their actions. In point of fact, these people did support him at a crucial moment, even if they no longer do so. There seems to be a polemical note here, but polemics are not Paul's main concern. On the divine impartiality, see Deut 10:17; Sir 35:12; Rom 2:11.

those considered to be influential imposed nothing upon me: "Those who were influential" translates *ho dokountes* the same expression Paul uses in v. 2. Paul's assertion that nothing was imposed upon him has two implications. First, the Jerusalem apostles did not find fault with his gospel—nor did Paul expect that they would. Second, they could have imposed something upon him. Thus while Paul asserts his independence from Jerusalem, he implicitly acknowledges its authority.

7. *Rather, seeing that I had been entrusted with the gospel to the uncircumcised*: For other texts which speak of Paul being entrusted (*pepisteumai*) with the gospel, see 1 Thess 2:4; 1 Tim 1:11; Titus 1:3, also Eph 3:8; 1 Tim 2:7. Here the use of the passive suggests that God is the one who entrusted Paul with the gospel. This is the only instance of the expression *euaggelion tēs akrobystias* (literally, "gospel of uncircumcision"). The expression refers to a class of people, the uncircumcised, rather than to the content of the gospel.

just as Peter had with the gospel to the circumcised: Paul's normal usage is to refer to Peter as "Cephas." This and the following verse are the only times that he employs the name "Peter." According to Matt 16:18, the name "Peter" was given to the Apostle by Jesus. Although the text is translated, "the gospel to the circumcised," the Greek reads *tēs peritomēs* ("of circumcision"), "the gospel" being understood. The expression can be taken kerygmatically (the gospel which includes circumcision), geographically (the gospel limited to Palestine), or ethnically (the gospel to the circumcised). The last sense is adopted here.

8. *for the one who worked in Peter for apostleship to the circumcised*: The subject of *ho energēsas* ("the one who worked") is not expressed. In other instances (1 Cor 12:6; Phil 2:13, cf. Gal 3:5), the subject of this verb is God. The only other uses of *apostolē* ("apostleship") in the NT are Acts 1:25; Rom 1:5; and 1 Cor 9:2. In Rom 1:5 Paul speaks of the grace of apostleship he received to bring about the obedience of faith among the Gentiles.

also worked in me for the Gentiles: By repeating the verb *energein* ("to work"), Paul shows that the God at work in Peter's preaching to the Jews is also at work in his preaching to the Gentiles. The omission of "apostleship" here does not mean that Paul has an inferior position *vis à vis* Peter. Rather, there is a balance in the use of ellipsis in this and the preceding verse: Paul entrusted with *the gospel to the uncircumcised,* Peter *to the circumcised;* Peter entrusted with *apostleship to the circumcised,* Paul *to the uncircumcised.*

9. *and realizing the grace given to me*: The grace given to Paul refers to the revelation mentioned in 1:15-16: the call of Paul to preach the gospel to the Gentiles. See Rom 15:15-16, "because of the grace given me by God to be a minister of Christ Jesus to the Gentiles in the priestly service of the gospel of God."

James and Cephas and John: These three seem to form an inner circle within the group called "those of influence." In 1:18 Cephas is put in a position of primacy and James is only mentioned secondarily (1:19). Here James is named first leading to some confusion in the manuscript tradition. Codex A reads "James and John." P46 reads "James and Peter and John." D, F, G read "Peter and James and John." The reading of our text is preserved by S, B, C. The manuscripts seem concerned whether to place Peter first (D, F, G), to eliminate his name because it has already been mentioned (A), or to replace Cephas with Peter (P46). Overall, it seems best to maintain the order adopted here which highlights the influence of James in the Jerusalem Church as seen in the next episode (vv. 11-14). This is the first mention of John, and undoubtedly it refers to John, one of the Twelve.

those considered to be pillars: In 1 Tim 3:15 the Church is called the pillar and bulwark of the truth, and in Rev 3:13 the Risen Lord promises that he who conquers will be a pillar in the temple of God. In 1 Clem 5:2 the term is applied to apostles and other Church leaders. Here, Paul probably understands that James, Cephas, and John were considered to be pillars (*styloi*) of the Church. It does not appear that Paul is employing the expression in a sarcastic or negative manner. Were he doing so, it would be counterproductive since their recognition of his apostleship contributes to the case he is making.

extended the right hand of fellowship to me and Barnabas: For the Hebrew expression "to give the hand" see 2 Kings 10:15; Ezra 10:19; Ezek 17:16; 1 Chr 29:24; 2 Chr 30:8; Lam 5:6. Although the last three instances imply submission (Burton, *Galatians,* 95), that is not the case here since it is the pillar apostles who extend the handshake to Paul and Barnabas. Moreover, the handshake is described as the right hand of fellowship (*koinōnias*). This *koinōnia* points to an equality in the preaching of the gospel, see Phil 1:5.

so that we might go to the Gentiles, and they to the circumcised: The problem here is what kind of a division of labor is envisioned? Racial? Geographical? That is, were Paul and Barnabas to go only to Gentiles while Peter and the others preached only to Jews? Or, were they to limit their work to Gentile territory while Peter and the others remained within the confines of Palestine? From 1 Cor 9:20-21, it seems clear that Paul preached to Jews as well as Gentiles, but from his extant letters it would appear that he confined his missionary activity to Gentile lands. Thus, while Paul preached primarily to Gentiles, it would appear that the agreement was based on geographical rather than racial considerations. Burton (*Galatians,* 98) argues that the use of *eis ta ethnē* ("to" or "among the Gentiles"), rather than the simple dative, supports this position.

10. *They only asked that we should be mindful of the poor*: While the *ptōchos* ("poor") are those who are economically deprived, they are also those who have a special relationship to God. Deprived of human support, they are forced to rely upon God who will not disappoint them (Matt 5:3). The Jerusalem Church probably viewed itself as "the poor," those who relied upon God alone. In Rom 15:25 Paul says that he is going to Jerusalem with aid for the saints (*hagiois*), most likely "the poor" who are mentioned here.

which very thing I was eager to do: An important theme of Paul's letters is the Jerusalem collection (Rom 15:25-33; 2 Cor 8-9; cf. Acts 11:29; 24:17). More than economic relief, in Paul's view it was meant to establish a bond between his Gentile congregations and the mother Church of Jerusalem. See Rom 15:27, "for if the Gentiles have come to share in their spiritual blessings, they ought also to be of service to them in material blessings." In 1 Cor 16:1-4 Paul refers to the instructions he gave the Galatians concerning this collection.

INTERPRETATION

These verses continue Paul's exposition of the thesis statement in 1:11-12 that his gospel is not of human origin. Once more the Apostle employs autobiographical material to establish the divine origin of his Torah-free gospel. However, whereas 1:13-24 focuses upon the revelation by which God revealed his Son and called Paul to preach the gospel among the nations, the autobiographical material of 2:1-10 functions in a slightly different way. First, Paul's account of his second visit to Jerusalem demonstrates that the influential members of that Church acknowledged that God entrusted him with the gospel to the Gentiles and that the three pillar apostles extended the right hand of fellowship to him and Barnabas. Second, Paul recalls these events in order to show the Galatians how, in order to preserve the truth of the gospel for them, he refused to submit to the false brethren. Thus Paul provides two reasons why the Galatians should not accept circumcision: the Church at Jerusalem acknowledged his circumcision-free gospel; and in order to preserve the truth of the gospel, he refused to compromise it. The proper course of action for the Galatians is to do the same; for the sake of the truth of the gospel they must not submit to circumcision.

This section confronts the interpreter with a number of problems. First, there are a series of historical and literary questions concerning the relationship of this material to Luke's account of the apostolic conference related in Acts 15. Are Paul and Luke referring to the same meeting? If so, how does one reconcile the two accounts? A discussion of this is reserved until after the commentary on 2:15-21. Second, this section presents difficulties for the interpreter because of Paul's style at this point. In v. 4 Paul begins with a causal clause ("But because of false brethren . . ."). The would-be sentence extends through v. 5, but it is never completed. Thus the reader asks what happened "because of the false brethren?" In a similar fashion, in v. 6 Paul interrupts his thought to say "what they once were makes no difference to me, God shows no partiality," a remark whose meaning can be interpreted in several ways (see notes). Finally, after resuming his thought, Paul interrupts it again with a parenthetical remark (v. 8). Consequently, it is not surprising that readers find themselves confused by Paul's argument in this section. To appreciate the movement of Paul's thought one should read the text, placing vv. 4-5, 6b, and 8 in parentheses.

This section is divided into three parts. In the first, (vv. 1-3), Paul recounts his second visit to Jerusalem. During that visit, he explained the gospel that he preaches among the Gentiles. Most importantly, Titus, his Gentile companion, was not forced to be circumcised. In the second part (vv. 4-5), he relates how he withstood certain false brethren because of the truth of the gospel. Finally, in vv. 6-10, he resumes the thought of vv. 1-3. The Church of Jerusalem did not alter his gospel; on the contrary it affirmed that God commissioned him to preach to the Gentiles just as Peter was commissioned to preach to the circumcised.

Throughout this section, Paul carefully balances his respect for the Church of Jerusalem with his independence from it. On the one hand, he recognizes the importance of preaching the gospel in concert with the mother Church. Otherwise, why go to Jerusalem? Nonetheless, Paul clearly establishes a certain distance between himself and Jerusalem. If Jerusalem did not recognize his Torah-free gospel, his work would have been greatly crippled. Nevertheless, even if the Jerusalem Church did not recognize Paul's gospel, his preaching among the Gentiles would not have ended since he received his commission from a revelation of Jesus Christ, not from Jerusalem.

Paul's second visit to Jerusalem (2:1-3). Fourteen years after his visit (see notes), Paul returned to Jerusalem for the second time. This visit, unlike the first, was occasioned by a revelation (*apokalypsin*). Through prophetic utterance, or a vision, he learned that the time had come to explain to the Jerusalem Church the gospel that he had been proclaiming to the Gentiles for nearly seventeen years. The fact that he had been preaching this gospel for seventeen years suggests that he had no doubts about it. But for the sake of the Church, the time had come to explain this gospel to Jewish believers who undoubtedly heard about it, but not from Paul. One can probably suppose that the Galatians learned something about Paul's visit to Jerusalem from those who were agitating for circumcision. Paul's account, therefore, is carefully fashioned in order to show the Galatians the real significance of his visit: it was undertaken to protect the truth of the gospel for them.

Whereas Paul's first visit was a private consultation with Peter, this visit brought him into contact with a larger segment of the Jerusalem Church. Barnabas, Paul's missionary companion in Acts 13-14, accompanied him, as well as Titus. The presence of the uncircumcised Titus indicates that circumcision was a central issue and provided a concrete example of Paul's gospel. In effect, Titus represented all of Paul's Gentile converts. If the Jerusalem Church expected Titus to be circumcised, then it would also demand that Paul's other Gentile converts should be circumcised as well.

The nature of the meeting is difficult to determine. The Greek can be construed as referring to a public meeting before the entire church followed by a private meeting before the influential members of the congregation, or it can be construed as referring to a single private meeting before the influential members of the community (see notes). In either case, Paul presented the gospel that he preached among the Gentiles with a view to obtaining some sort of recognition from Jerusalem.

That Paul came to Jerusalem to lay his gospel before the church suggests a certain acknowledgment of Jerusalem's authority. But it does not necessarily mean that he sought Jerusalem's permission to continue his missionary practices among the Gentiles. The phrase "lest somehow I might be running or had run in vain" reveals Paul's real motivation. If the mother Church did not recognize the circumcision-free gospel, there would be no hope for unity between Jewish and Gentile believers. In a word, non-recognition would be disastrous for a mission intended to incorporate Gentiles into Israel. In a manner of speaking, Paul's work would be in vain. By bringing Titus to Jerusalem and presenting the circumcision-free gospel to the Church, Paul was raising the stakes and chancing a definitive break with Jerusalem. But from another point of view, he came to Jerusalem with supreme confidence because he had received his Torah-free gospel by a revelation of Jesus Christ. That Titus was not compelled (*ēnagkasthē*) to be circumcised was a victory for all of Paul's Gentile converts. The word "compel," however, indicates that the decision did not come without a struggle.

The False Brethren (2:4-5). These verses are the beginning of a sentence which is never concluded and which interrupts the train of thought introduced by the first three verses. Because of this, a few manuscripts alter the beginning of v. 5 to make these verses a complete sentence while others change their basic meaning (see notes). To complete the meaning of these verses, the reader must add a phrase, such as "the circumcision of Titus was urged," to either the beginning or the conclusion of v. 4. The abrupt manner in which these verses are introduced might suggest that the agitators had told the Galatians that the Jerusalem Church wanted Titus to be circumcised but that Paul refused to comply. If this is so, Paul's response is that this course of action was urged because of certain false brethren to whom he did not submit, nor did the influential members of the Jerusalem community agree with them.

Rhetorically, the section functions in two ways. First, it associates circumcision with the *pseudadelphoi* ("false brethren") who sought to enslave others. While these *pseudadelphoi* are not identified as the agitators, the implication is that the agitators are no different from the *pseudadelphoi* who opposed Paul at Jerusalem. Second, Paul employs this incident to point to the example of his own life. Because his life embodies the gospel that he preaches, he did not submit to the *pseudadelphoi* when confronted by their demands. In contrast to Paul, the Galatians are in the process of changing their allegiance (1:6). Thus whereas Paul fought to preserve the truth of the gospel for them, they are deserting the One (God) who called them to freedom.

There is no indication who the *pseudadelphoi* were. While Paul's designation, *pseudadelphoi*, casts them in a negative light, one must remember that the narrative is told from Paul's point of view, and what Paul interprets as a betrayal of the gospel, the *pseudadelphoi* may well have understood as essential if the Gentiles were to share in the full benefits of Israel. Thus the *pseudadelphoi* may have been Jewish Christians of a conservative stance who were willing to accept Gentile converts provided that they accepted the sign of the covenant: circumcision. That the influential members of the church and the acknowledged pillars of the church (James, Cephas, John) did not agree with the *pseudadelphoi* indicates that there were more moderate factions within the Jerusalem community.

The time and place of this incident are difficult to determine. Paul may mean that the *pseudadelphoi* slipped into his meeting with the influential members of the church and urged that Titus be circumcised. But it is also possible that Paul is referring to an earlier incident which took place elsewhere, either before or after the meeting in Jerusalem. Thus Bruce (*Galatians*, 116–117) thinks that Paul is recalling an event which occurred *after* the Jerusalem meeting when the *pseudadelphoi* infiltrated the Church at Antioch and tried to insist on circumcision. Schlier (*Galaterbrief*, 71), however, suggests that the incident happened at Antioch *before* the Jerusalem meeting. This last solution is attractive because it agrees with Luke's own narrative of the events (Acts 15:1), and seems more probable. Having recounted the Jerusalem meeting, Paul now recalls the incident which provoked the situation that led to his visit. Certain brethren had come to Antioch and urged the Gentile members of that church to be circumcised. When Paul brought the uncircumcised Titus to Jerusalem, therefore, he was forcing the issue.

Paul says that he did not submit for a moment, indicating that a struggle ensued between him and the *pseudadelphoi*. If the struggle began at Antioch, it undoubtedly continued in Jerusalem until the influential members of the community gave their support to Paul. One can surmise that although the *pseudadelphoi* lost this battle, they did not abandon their struggle against the Pauline position.

From Paul's perspective, the intentions of the *pseudadelphoi* were dishonorable from the start. They did not come as disinterested observers to Antioch (?) but slipped in secretly with the support of others for the purpose of spying upon (*kataskopēsai*) the freedom which the Torah-free gospel provided. This freedom can be understood from two vantage points. For Gentiles it was the freedom to enter the commonwealth of Israel apart from circumcision and other works of the Law, such as Sabbath observance and food laws. For Jews like Paul, who were already circumcised, it was a freedom from works of the Law which traditionally separated them from Gentiles, especially food laws which hindered table fellowship between Gentile and Jew. Consequently, Paul includes himself with his Gentile converts when he says that the *pseudadelphoi* spied on "our" freedom in order to enslave "us." Such enslavement would have come if the Gentiles were forced to be circumcised, the very work of the Law which the Galatians were about to undertake.

The truth of the gospel, therefore, is the right of Gentiles to share in the inheritance of Israel, apart from circumcision and other legal works. Concretely, it is the freedom of Jew and Gentile to live in community with each other on the basis of their faith in Christ rather than upon legal works such as circumcision, Sabbath observance, and food law. The truth of the gospel is the heart of the revelation that God granted to Paul when he revealed his Son to him. It was this truth of the gospel which the influential ones acknowledged when they did not require Titus to be circumcised.

The Results of the Jerusalem Meeting (2:6-10). After the digression of vv. 4–5, Paul turns his attention once more to the meeting at Jerusalem and, in a rather convoluted fashion, announces the results of his meeting with the influential members of the church (*hoi dokountes*). First, they did not add any new stipulation to the gospel that he preached. Second, the three pillar apostles, (James, Cephas, and John) extended the right hand of fellowship to Paul and Barnabas, thereby ratifying an agreement concerning future missionary activity. Third, the one thing Paul was asked to do was to remember the poor. In communicating the results of this meeting, it is clear that Paul has another purpose. He wants to show the Galatians that Jerusalem recognized the gospel which was entrusted to him (v. 7) and the grace of God given to him (v. 9). In effect, the Jerusalem

Church acknowledged Paul's God-given gospel to the Gentiles and so should the Galatians. This section is best understood if it is divided into its constituent parts:

6   They added nothing.
7-9a   They recognized Paul's gospel and the grace given him.
9b   They extended the right hand of fellowship.
9c   They agreed upon a division of labor.
10   They asked Paul to remember the poor.

The same influential members of the church to whom Paul spoke privately added nothing to his gospel. The parenthetical remark found in v. 6 need not be taken negatively (see notes). Paul is simply saying that while the influential apostles may carry more weight in other circles, e.g., Jerusalem, their prestige before others is of little importance to him, and of less to God. What really matters is not who they are, or were, but what they did: they did not alter the gospel that he preaches among the Gentiles. To the contrary, the influential members of the church recognized that the God who acted in Peter's mission to the circumcised acted in Paul's mission to the Gentiles. God entrusted the gospel of the uncircumcised to Paul and the gospel to the circumcised to Peter.

Because Jerusalem recognized the grace (*charis*) given to Paul, the pillar apostles (James, Cephas, and John) extended the right hand of fellowship to him and Barnabas. Paul and Barnabas would concentrate their missionary efforts in Gentile territory while the Jerusalem apostles would work among the Jews. Rhetorically, the disclosure of this division of labor shows the Galatians that they fall under Paul's sphere of influence. If Jewish Christian missionaries have come to Galatia, urging the Galatians to be circumcised, they are violating the agreement made between Paul and the pillar Apostles. The Galatians belong to Paul's sphere of influence, and they are bound by his circumcision-free gospel.

The one stipulation placed upon Paul did not affect the gospel that he preaches. The Jerusalem Church asked Paul to be mindful of the poor; that is, his Gentile congregations should help to support the Church of Jerusalem. When Paul says that he was eager to do this, he indicates more than his personal concern for the saints of Jerusalem. By bringing support from the Gentiles to the Church of Jerusalem, he was establishing a bond of unity between his Gentile congregations and the Jewish Church of Jerusalem. If Jerusalem accepted monetary support from Paul's circumcision-free churches, it would be a further acknowledgment of the legitimacy of his Torah-free gospel among the Gentiles. Conversely, if Jerusalem refused such support, it would be an indication that it did not accept Paul's gospel. More than monetary support, the great collection for Jerusalem was an external sign of the *koinōnia* ("community") Paul sought to establish between Jew and Gentile. Paul's instructions in 1 Cor 16:1-4 indicate that the collection had already begun in Galatia by the time that he was writing 1 Corinthians.

To summarize, the meeting at Jerusalem was a public recognition of Paul's gospel, and at Jerusalem Paul conducted himself in accord with the gospel he preaches. Rhetorically, the purpose of this section is to dissuade the Galatians from accepting circumcision.

For Reference and Further Study

Dunn, J. D. G. "The Relationship between Paul and Jerusalem according to Galatians 1 and 2." *NTS* 28 (1982) 461–478; reprinted in *Jesus, Paul and the Law*, 108–128.

Jewett, R. *A Chronology of Paul's Life.* Philadelphia: Fortress, 1979.

Knox, J. *Chapters in a Life of Paul.* Nashville: Abingdon, 1950.

Luedemann, G. *Paul, Apostle to the Gentiles: Studies in Chronology.* Philadelphia: Fortress, 1984.

McLean, B. H. "Galatians 2:7-9 and the Recognition of Paul's Apostolic Status at the Jerusalem Conference: A Critique of G. Luedemann's Solution." *NTS* 37 (1991) 67–76.

Schmidt, A. "Das historische Datum des Apostelkonzils," *ZNW* 81 (1990) 122–131.

Suhl, A. "Ein Konfliktlosungsmodell der Urkirche," *BibKir* 42 (1990) 80–86.

Peter Betrayed the Truth of the Gospel at Antioch (2:11-14)

11. When Cephas came to Antioch, I opposed him to his face because he stood condemned. 12. Before certain people from James came, he was accustomed to eat with the Gentiles, but when they came, he began to withdraw and separate himself fearing those who belong to the circumcision. 13. And even the rest of the Jews joined in the hypocrisy with him, so that even Barnabas was led away by their hypocrisy. 14. But when I saw that they were not straightforward about the truth of the gospel, I said to Cephas in front of everybody, "if you being a Jew live as a Gentile and not as a Jew, how can you force the Gentiles to live as Jews?"

Notes

11. *When Cephas came to Antioch*: Some manuscripts (D, F, G) replace Cephas with Peter, but the best manuscript tradition reads Cephas. Undoubtedly we are

to understand Antioch in Syria rather than Antioch in Pisidia (Acts 13:14). Syrian Antioch was located in the northwest corner of the province of Syria. The third largest city in the Empire, it was the capital of the province and a center of culture. Christianity was brought to Antioch by Hellenists about A.D. 40, and it was there that Hellenists from Cyprus and Cyrene converted Gentiles without demanding circumcision. According to Acts, Paul was a loyal member of this congregation. Paul makes no other mention of the city in the rest of his letters. There is no indication of when or why Peter came to Antioch. Perhaps he sought refuge there because of the persecution by Herod Agrippa mentioned in Acts 12:1-19.

I opposed him to his face because he stood condemned: Except for 1 John 3:20-21 this is the only use of *kataginoskein* ("to condemn") in the NT. The reason for Peter's condemnation, his hypocritical behavior, is explained below. Paul's bold behavior, described here, should be compared with the view of his adversaries reported in 2 Cor 10:1 that Paul is bold when at a distance but humble when face-to-face.

12. *Before certain people from James came*: P46 reads "before a certain one came from James." This is an interesting reading in light of 5:10 which could be interpreted as referring to an individual disturbing the Galatian community. The reading of P46, however, is not supported by any of the other important manuscripts, and it probably arose because of the well attested variant *ēlthen* (3rd sing.) in the same verse. See below. *Tinas apo Iakōbou* ("certain people from James") could be construed as a delegation sent by James to investigate the situation, or as people attached to James by bonds of allegiance but not sent by him. A decision can only be made within the context of the entire section. See commentary. Acts 12:17 suggests that James became the leader of the Jerusalem Church after Peter left Jerusalem because Herod Agrippa sought to destroy him. Perhaps Peter went to Antioch after Agrippa's persecution.

he was accustomed to eat with Gentiles: The imperfect *synēsthien* ("to eat") emphasizes Peter's customary behavior: he ate with Gentiles even though it was forbidden to share table fellowship with those who did not observe the dietary prescriptions of the Law. According to Acts 11:3, Peter was criticized by Jewish Christians when he associated with and ate with Gentiles, i.e., the members of Cornelius' household. But the point of the Cornelius story was to teach Peter that he should not call anyone "profane or unclean" (Acts 10:28). Gentile meals could be viewed as unclean (Ezek 4:13; Hos 9:3-4) for a variety of reasons: (1) the food had previously been offered to false gods (Exod 34:15; 1 Cor 10:28); (2) the food came from an unclean animal (Lev 11:1-20); (3) the food was not properly prepared (Exod 23:19). During the intertestamental period, stories of Daniel, Tobit, and Judith extolled these individuals for not eating Gentile food (Dan 1:8-16; Tob 1:10-13; Jdt 10:5; 12:1-20). Moreover, one of the purposes of the Maccabean revolt was to insure that Jews could observe their distinctive practices of circumcision, Sabbath observance, and ritual purity.

but when they came, he began to withdraw and separate himself fearing those who belong to the circumcision party: P46, S, B, D*, F, G, 33 read "but when he came." The reading may have been introduced in light of the textual variant noted above, "before *a certain one* came from James." Or, it may have in mind the beginning of v. 11, "When *Peter* came to Antioch . . . he ate with Gentiles, but when *he [Peter] came*." But this is an awkward reading. The plural, which refers to the people from James, is the preferred reading. The imperfect tense of the verbs *hypestellen* ("withdraw") and *aphōrizen* ("separate") indicates a gradual retreat on the part of Peter. By trying to separate himself from the Gentiles, Peter establishes the old boundaries between Jew and Gentile. In 1:15 Paul employed *aphōrizein* to describe how God set him aside for service to the gospel. See note on 1:15. "The circumcision party" translates *tous ek peritomēs*, literally, "those from the circumcision." These Jewish Christians refused to share table fellowship with Gentiles because the Gentiles did not observe the dietary prescriptions of the Law. In Col 4:11 Paul, or an author writing in his name, speaks of Justus as the only one from the circumcision among his co-workers. Titus 1:10 says "there are also many rebellious people, idle talkers and deceivers, especially those of the circumcision." This text, however, was not written by Paul, and probably reflects the situation toward the end of the first century rather than during the period of the Galatian controversy.

13. *And even the rest of the Jews joined in the hypocrisy with him*: P46 and B do not have *kai* ("even"). The rest of the Jews refers to other Jewish Christians who were at Antioch and shared table fellowship with the Gentiles before the arrival of the partisans of James. Perhaps they had accompanied Peter to Antioch. "Joined in the hypocrisy" translates a single verb *synypekrithēsan*, the sense of which is to play-act by masking one's true feelings. Paul intimates that Peter and the other Jewish Christians no longer believed in the validity of the dietary legislation but pretended to do so because they feared those associated with James.

so that even Barnabas was led away by their hypocrisy: Except for Rom 12:16, this is the only use of *synapagomai* ("to be led" or "carried away") in Paul's writings. See 2 Pet 3:17 for a similar usage. Paul suggests that Barnabas was taken in by their hypocrisy rather than that he acted hypocritically himself. As a result, whereas Paul and Barnabas once courageously opposed the false brethren, now Paul must stand alone.

14. *But when I saw that they were not straightforward about the truth of the gospel*: "He was not straightforward" translates the verb *orthopodousin* which only occurs here in the NT. An alternate translation is "they were not on the right road toward the truth of the gospel" (BAG). "The truth of the gospel," first mentioned in v. 5, is now defined in terms of table fellowship. To refuse table fellowship with Gentile believers because of legal restrictions is to deny the truth of the gospel.

I said to Cephas in front of everybody: Some manuscripts (D, F, G) read "Peter" instead of "Kephas." The fact that Peter is singled out indicates his importance. His hypocrisy is all the greater because he is one of the pillar apostles

(2:19). See 1 Tim 5:20, "As for those who persist in sin, rebuke them in the presence of all" (*enōpion pantōn*).

if you being a Jew live as a Gentile and not as a Jew: Peter lived like a Gentile (*ethnikōs*, the only occurrence in the NT) when he disregarded the dietary prescriptions of the Law. To live like a Jew (*Ioudaïkōs*, the only occurrence in the NT) is to observe the dietary laws of clean and unclean and to separate oneself from Gentiles who are unclean because they do not observe such laws.

how can you force the Gentiles to live as Jews? The verb *anagkazeis* ("force") is the same word employed in v. 3. At Jerusalem the pillar apostles did not force Titus to be circumcised, but now Peter is trying to force Gentiles to practice Jewish customs. The attempt to judaize the Gentiles is expressed by the verb *Ioudaïzein*, the only time the word occurs in the NT. Its basic sense is to adopt Jewish customs, to accept those external practices which mark one as a member of the covenant people: circumcision, food Laws, and Sabbath observance. Later, Paul will refer to these as "works of the Law." In his Epistle to the Magnesians (10:3), Ignatius employs the verb *ioudaïzein*: "It is monstrous to talk of Jesus Christ and to practice Judaism (*ioudaïzein*)."

INTERPRETATION

This is a complicated passage which never ceases to attract the attention of commentators because of the many historical questions that it raises, e.g., when did this incident take place? what were the issues? who were the participants? As important as these questions are, however, commentators must not allow the historical issues to distract them from focusing upon the rhetorical goal of this passage: to persuade the Galatians that Paul's gospel is not of human origin. Once more, Paul is employing autobiographical material to persuade his readers of the thesis statement made in 1:11-12: the divine origin of his gospel. In this instance, as in the preceding one, Paul's concern is to demonstrate the consistency between his behavior and the Torah-free gospel that he preaches. According to that gospel, Christ freed both Jew and Gentile from the demands of the Law. Consequently, Paul recalls his behavior at Antioch to show the Galatians that when the truth of the gospel was at stake, he did not shrink from confronting Peter, even though Paul was abandoned by Barnabas and other Jewish Christians. In such a situation one would have expected Paul to capitulate to the demands of the delegation from James, as did the others. But because Paul's gospel derives from a revelation of Jesus Christ, there was only one course of action open to him: to oppose Peter to his face.

This episode is clearly intended to be read in light of 2:1-10. During his second visit to Jerusalem, in order to preserve the truth of the gospel for the Galatians (2:5), Paul opposed those who urged the circumcision of Titus. Now he even confronts one of the pillar apostles who had previously approved his circumcision-free gospel and extended the right hand of fellowship to him and Barnabas. There is a clear message here; namely, how easy it is to fall from the truth of the gospel. James, Peter, and John had recently supported Paul in his defense of the gospel. But now Peter, at the instigation of partisans from James, shrinks from the truth of the gospel that he had so recently supported. If the pillar apostle Peter can fall from the truth of the gospel, how careful the Galatians must be not to do the same! The incident at Antioch, therefore, provides a striking contrast between two kinds of behavior: that of Peter and that of Paul. On the one hand, Peter turned from the truth of the gospel because of outside pressure. On the other, Paul stood firm in face of outside pressure. The Galatians who now find themselves under similar outside pressure must choose which example they will follow.

Whatever the historical circumstances surrounding this incident, its rhetorical goal is clear. Paul is subtly persuading the Galatians to resist the agitators at Galatia just as he stood firm against the partisans from James at Antioch. The Galatians must choose the truth of the gospel, even if it leaves them isolated and alone. The gospel Paul preached to them was not his own invention; he received it through a divine revelation.

While the majority of commentators date this incident shortly after the Jerusalem meeting, a few have argued that it occurred before the meeting at Jerusalem (H. M. Feret, André Méhat). For example, according to Méhat ("Quand Kèphas vint à Antioch. . . ."), Peter came to Antioch after the persecution of Herod Agrippa described in Acts 12. There he associated and ate with Gentiles. Shortly after this, because of Herod's persecution, partisans from James also fled to Antioch. The open table fellowship between Jewish and Gentile believers that they observed at Antioch scandalized them, and slowly they convinced Peter to withdraw from it. According to this scenario, then, the Antioch incident was the reason for the Jerusalem meeting narrated in Gal 2:1-10. Paul, however, has reversed the original order of events.

This theory helps to coordinate some of the material of Acts and Galatians. Moreover, it is noteworthy that after carefully delineating the other events of his autobiography with *epeita* ("then," 1:18, 21; 2:1), Paul begins this section *hote de* ("and when"), making no effort to date the incident. Nevertheless, dating the Antioch incident before the Jerusalem meeting raises as many issues as it solves. The meeting at Jerusalem, as described by Paul, was concerned with circumcision, but the incident at Antioch dealt with the question of table fellowship. Moreover, Paul's position at Antioch marks a step forward when compared to his stance at Jerusalem: not only are Gentiles free from circumcision, Jews as well as Gentiles are no longer under the obligation of dietary Laws which separate Gentile and Jew. On balance, therefore, it seem prudent to maintain Paul's chronology, even though he does not carefully delimit it. The Antioch incident occurred shortly *after* the Jerusalem meeting.

Peter's Behavior (2:11-13). Paul does not say when or why Peter came to Antioch, but the imperfect tense of the verb *synēsthien* ("he was accustomed to eat") suggests that he spent some time at Antioch and regularly joined in table fellowship with the Gentile members of that congregation. The precise nature of the meals is not disclosed. Schlier (*Galaterbrief*, 83) thinks that they were associated with the Eucharist since the Lord's Supper was, according to 1 Cor 11:20-21, in the context of a meal. But one cannot be sure that the Eucharist was celebrated in the same manner at Galatia and Corinth, especially since Paul seems to disapprove of the Corinthian practice. What is clear is that Peter did not experience any difficulty in joining with Gentiles in table fellowship.

The reference to certain people from James is equally ambiguous (see notes). Were they merely partisans of James or were they sent by him to investigate the situation at Antioch? Overall, the second opinion seems more plausible, otherwise why mention James at all? James sent certain members of the Jerusalem Church to survey the situation at Antioch. These delegates, however, should not be identified with the false brethren of 2:4 since James, Peter, and John did not agree with their position at the time of the Jerusalem meeting. Nor can one immediately suppose that the Jerusalem Church sent them specifically to investigate the question of table fellowship. Rather, having settled the question of circumcision, the church sent delegates to visit and observe the general situation at Antioch. When the delegation arrived, however, it was clearly disturbed by what it saw: Gentiles and Jews sharing table fellowship. Once more the precise nature of the offense is difficult to determine. Did the Antiochene Church disregard all food Laws? Or did the Church observe the minimal food regulations provided by the Noahic Law, e.g., to refrain from eating the flesh from living animals? Furthermore, why were the people from James scandalized? Did they object to the dietary habits of Gentile Christians, or to the fact that Jewish Christians were eating with them?

Given the importance of Jewish dietary regulations, and the fact that many Gentile Christians had previously been God-fearers, it seems unlikely that there was wholesale abandonment of dietary laws at Antioch. Rather, the Gentile Church probably practiced a level of table fellowship which fell within the Noahic Law. See Dunn, "The Incident at Antioch (Gal 2:11-18)." If this was the case, the real difficulty for the people from James was not the behavior of the Gentiles but the fact that Jewish Christians like Peter were no longer following all of the dietary prescriptions of the Law. They demanded that Peter and other Jewish Christians return to the full discipline of these prescriptions.

The use of the imperfect tense in the phrase *hypestellen kai aphōrizen* ("he began to withdraw and separate himself") indicates that Peter only gradually withdrew from such table fellowship. When he did, however, the consequences were momentous. Other Jewish Christians, including Barnabas, joined him. Henceforth, if the Gentiles wanted to share table fellowship with Peter, they would have to adapt themselves to the full discipline of the Torah regarding dietary Laws. The Noahic Laws would no longer be sufficient. In effect, there was a split within the community.

Paul identifies Peter's behavior as hypocrisy, pure and simple. But it is doubtful that Peter's motives can be explained so easily. In the period when the letter to the Galatians was written, there was a resurgence of Jewish nationalism and a concern for the marks of Jewish identity such as circumcision, Sabbath observance, and food Laws. One can imagine a scenario in which the people from James argued that Peter was endangering the unity of the Church by living like a Gentile. If Peter continued such behavior, he would discredit the Jerusalem Church in the eyes of faithful Jews. If the Church was to live as a viable community within Jerusalem, the Torah must be obeyed. Clearly, Paul did not see the situation in the same way. The unity of the Church was founded on the gospel that made no distinction between Jew and Gentile. To separate Gentile from Jew on the basis of food Laws was to undercut the truth of the gospel.

Paul's response (2:14). The extent of Paul's response to Peter is a matter of debate. While one could argue that the response concludes at the end of this chapter (2:21), many commentators limit Paul's response to this verse and understand vv. 15–21 as a more general statement addressed to the recipients of the letter. The scene, then, ends abruptly with no indication of its outcome, or of Peter's response to Paul. This abrupt ending has led many commentators to conclude that, despite his rebuke of Peter, Paul lost the battle at Antioch. Otherwise, why not tell the Galatians that Peter eventually agreed with him? While this may be the correct reading of the historical situation, it overlooks the rhetorical force of the present ending; namely, Peter is rendered silent. There is nothing he can say because Paul confronted him with the truth of the gospel. Consequently, even if Paul lost at Antioch, the manner in which he concludes this section makes it clear that his argument on behalf of the gospel is irrefutable.

The argument hinges upon the freedom granted by the gospel. If the gospel gives Peter the right to live like a Gentile (*ethnikōs*), that is, free from the Jewish laws concerning food, by what right can Peter impose (*anagkazeis*) those laws on the Gentiles, that is, judaize (*Ioudaïzein*) them? The argument, of course, presupposes that Christ freed Jewish believers from the Law as well as Gentile believers, something which Peter and other Jewish Christians had not yet understood. Moreover, it views Peter's retreat from table fellowship as a form of coercion. While this appears to overstate the case, it does highlight the practical result of Peter's action. Henceforth, Gentiles would be forced to observe Jewish food legislation if they wanted to enjoy table fellowship with Jewish Christians.

The significance of the Antioch incident. The incident at Antioch marks an important turning point in the life and thought of Paul. First, because of it, Paul appears to have reached a deeper understanding of the gospel revealed to him at Damascus. If he originally viewed that gospel in terms of the Gentiles and their freedom from the Law, now he clearly sees its importance for Jewish believers as well. Christ freed them as well as the Gentiles from the need to do legal works. The freedom from the Law which Christ brought extended to all.

Second, the incident at Antioch marked a turning point in Paul's relationship with the Church of Antioch. Previous to this incident, Paul carried out his missionary work as a member of the Church of Antioch. But if it is true that he failed to convince others at Antioch, then it is probable that this event marked a new phase in his missionary efforts. Henceforth, he undertook a number of independent missions in Asia Minor and Greece with co-workers who accepted his Torah-free gospel.

Finally, the incident at Antioch may have been one of the remote causes of the crisis at Galatia, especially if the Galatian churches were located in the region of Pisidian Antioch, Lystra, Iconium, and Derbe, and were founded after this incident (see introduction). In this case, sometime after this incident delegates were sent to these churches which Paul had evangelized in order to "judaize" them, i.e., require them to practice legal works, especially circumcision, food laws, and the observance of the Sabbath. This third point is, of course, hypothetical, but it does offer an explanation for the origins of Galatian crisis. Cf. Dunn, "The Incident at Antioch," in *Jesus, Paul, and the Law,* 161.

FOR REFERENCE AND FURTHER STUDY

Bottger, P. C. "Paul und Petrus in Antiochien. Zum Verständnis von Galater 2:11-21." *NTS* 37 (1991) 77-100.

Dippenaar, M. C. "Paul's Defense of the Gospel Against Peter in Antioch with Emphasis on Justification through Faith Alone: Galatians 2:11-21." *Theologica Viatorum* 18 (1990) 37-48.

Dunn, J. D. G. "The Incident at Antioch (Gal 2:11-18)." *JSNT* 18 (1983) 3-57; reprinted in *Jesus, Paul and the Law.*

Dupont, J. "Pierre et Paul à Antioch et à Jerusalem." *RSR* 45 (1957) 42-60.

Feret, H. M. *Pierre et Paul à Antioch et à Jerusalem.* Paris, 1955.

Kieffer, R. *Foi et Justification à Antioch: Interprétation d'un conflit (Gal 2, 14-21).* LD 111; Paris: Cerf, 1982.

Méhat, A. " 'Quand Kèphas vint à Antioch . . .' que s'est-il passé entre Pierre et Paul?" *LumVie* 38 (1989) 29–43.

Sanders, E. P. "Jewish Association with Gentiles and Galatians 2:11-12." *The Conversation Continues: Studies in Paul and John in Honor of J. Louis Martyn*. R. T. Fortna and B. R. Gaventa, eds. Nashville: Abingdon Press, 1990, 170–188.

We Are Justified by the Faith of Jesus Christ (2:15-21)

15. We who are Jews by birth and not sinners from among the Gentiles, 16. [but] knowing that a person is not justified by legal works but through the faith of Jesus Christ, even we have believed in Christ Jesus in order that we might be justified by the faith of Christ and not by legal works because by legal works no one will be justified. 17. But if in seeking to be justified in Christ, even we were found to be sinners, then has Christ become Sin's servant? Out of the question! 18. For if I build again those things which I tore down, I show myself to be a transgressor. 19. For through the Law I died to the Law in order that I might live to God. I am crucified with Christ. 20. It is no longer "I" who live, but Christ lives in me. The life I now live in the flesh, I live by the faith of the Son of God who loved me and handed himself over for me. 21. I have not nullified the grace of God, for if righteousness were through the Law, then Christ died in vain.

NOTES

15. *We*: Paul's reprimand to Peter becomes the statement of a theological position. "We" refers to Jews like Peter and Paul who have come to believe in Christ.

who are Jews by birth, and not sinners from among the Gentiles: "By birth" translates *physei* (literally, "by nature"). A similar usage is found in 4:8 and Rom 2:14. The expression emphasizes the racial aspect of being a Jew: one is born a Jew. Those who are born into the covenant people have the gift of the Law. By contrast, Gentiles are sinners by the fact that they stand outside of the covenant, deprived of the Law. See Eph 2:12 for a description of the Gentile situation prior to Christ. Sinner (*hamartolos*) is only used twice in Galatians (2:15, 17) and four times in Romans (3:7; 5:8, 19; 7:13). However, "sin" (*hamartia*) is a major concept in Romans where it occurs forty-eight times.

16. *[but] knowing that a person is not justified*: Some manuscripts, most notably P46, omit *de* ("but"). The *de* provides the translation with an adversative sense indicating that Jewish believers have come to a new understanding of justifi-

cation. This is the first use of the verb *dikaioun* ("to justify"). It occurs eight times in Galatians (2:16 [three times], 17; 3:8, 11, 24; 5:4), fifteen times in Romans (2:13; 3:4, 20, 24, 26, 28, 30; 4:2, 5; 5:1, 9; 6:7; 8:30 [twice], 33), twice in 1 Corinthians (4:4; 6:11) and twice in the Pastorals (1 Tim 3:16; Titus 3:7). The verb means (1) to show justice or do justice to someone; (2) to justify, vindicate or treat someone as just (see BAG). In the LXX *dikaioun* is primarily a forensic term, and it is the legal and forensic sense which Paul adopts: God acquits the sinner, God declares a person to be just. Whereas Protestants have traditionally emphasized the legal and forensic aspect of the verb (God declares that the sinner is upright), Catholics have stressed the results of God's justifying activity (God's declaration makes the sinner upright). This categorization of Protestant and Catholic positions, however, must be nuanced in light of recent ecumenical dialogue between Catholics and Protestants, see *Righteousness in the New Testament* by J. Reumann, and *Justification by Faith: Lutherans and Catholics in Dialogue VII*. While the primary sense of the verb *dikaioun* is forensic (God acquits humanity), Paul's statement that Christ lives in him (v. 20) indicates that this acquittal results in a new life for the believer.

by legal works: This translates *ex ergōn nomou*, literally "from/by works of Law." The instrumental sense of *ex* ("by") is more appropriate here. This phrase is usually interpreted in light of the Reformation debate between Protestants and Catholics concerning ethical works and their meritorious value. While Jerome understood the phrase to refer to circumcision, the Sabbath, and other ceremonial laws, Luther and Calvin insisted that Paul was speaking of the whole Law, not just its ceremonial aspects, and so do most modern commentators. Betz writes, it means "doing and fulfilling the ordinances of the Torah" (*Galatians*, 116). Bruce interprets it as "the actions prescribed by the Law" (*Galatians*, 137), and Reumann "the requirements of the Law" (*Righteousness in the New Testament*, 55). The context of this letter and the recent research of E. P. Sanders and J. Dunn, however, suggest that the expression primarily envisions circumcision, dietary laws, and the observance of Jewish feast days, all of which were viewed as identity markers that distinguished Jews from Gentiles. See T. R. Schreiner, "The Abolition and Fulfillment of the Law in Paul," and J. Dunn, "Works of the Law and the Curse of the Law." Thus *ex ergōn nomou* is a technical phrase akin to a code word and has a precise meaning for Paul and the Galatians. It also occurs in 3:2, 5, 10 and Rom 3:20, 28. In other places Paul simply speaks of "works" (Rom 4:2, 6; 9:12, 32; 11:6), and in Rom 2:15 he uses the expression "the work of the Law." J. B. Tyson ("Works of Law" in *Galatians*) suggests the translation "nomistic service" by which he means a particular kind of religious existence characteristic of the Jewish people that includes circumcision and the observance of food laws. Paul attacks this mode of existence, not works of righteousness.

but through the faith of Jesus Christ: A few manuscripts (A, B, 33) read "Christ Jesus" instead of "Jesus Christ." "Jesus Christ" occurs in 1:1, 3, 12; 3:1, 22; 6:14, 18. "Christ Jesus" is found in 2:4, 16; 3:14, 26, 28; 4:14. Except for 4:14 "Christ Jesus" is always introduced by the preposition *en* or *eis* ("in," "into") which suggests that the reading "Jesus Christ" is to be preferred here. *Dia pistēos Iēsou Christou* can be rendered either as an objective genitive ("through faith *in* Jesus Christ") or as a subjective genitive ("through the faith *of* Jesus Christ"). Since either interpretation is grammatically possible, the question can only be resolved by determining which translation makes better sense of the broader context. The majority of commentators and translators render the phrase as an objective genitive, arguing that the following phrase ("even we have believed *in* Christ Jesus") determines the meaning here. *Pistis Iēsou Christou*, or its equivalent, occurs seven times in Paul's undisputed writings (Rom 3:22, 26; Gal 2:16 [twice]; 2:20; 3:22; Phil 3:9), eight times if one accepts the reading of P46 for Gal 3:26. In the texts of Romans and Philippians the subjective genitive makes eminent sense and seems required by the broader context. See M. D. Hooker, *"PISTIS CHRISTOU."* For a contrary view, see A. J. Hultgren, "The *PISTIS CHRISTOU* Formulation in Paul." The reasons for adopting the subjective genitive here will be presented in the commentary on this passage, and in the commentary on chapter three. The subjective genitive does not oppose or do away with the concept of faith *in* Christ. Rather, it reestablishes priorities. One is justified by the faith of Jesus Christ manifested in his obedience to God by his death upon the cross. It is on the basis of that faith that one believes in Christ. *Pistis Christou*, therefore, could be rendered as "Christ-faith," the faith *of* Christ which grounds personal faith *in* Christ.

even we have believed in Christ Jesus: P46 has "Jesus Christ," but the use of the preposition *eis* suggests that "Christ Jesus" is the better reading. The emphatic *kai* emphasizes that even Jews by birth have come to this new understanding of justification. In this phrase Christ is clearly the object of belief. Having been saved by the faith of Jesus Christ, even Jewish Christians have put their faith in Christ. The verb "to believe" only occurs three other times in Galatians (2:7; 3:6, 22).

in order that we might be justified by the faith of Christ and not by legal works: The purpose clause explains why Paul and other ethnic Jews have believed in Christ: in order to be declared righteous by God *ek pisteōs Christou*. Once again, the phrase is best understood as a subjective genitive. *Ek pisteōs Christou* and *ex ergōn nomou* are mutually exclusive. The first is God's action manifested in the faith of Jesus Christ, the second is a series of boundary markers that identify one as a member of the covenant people: circumcision, dietary rules, Sabbath observance. Paul argues that because of the former there is no need for the latter.

because "by legal works no one will be justified": To support his argument, Paul quotes from Ps 143:2 (LXX 142). In the LXX, the Psalm reads, *hoti ou dikaiōthēsetai enōpion sou pas zōn* ("because before you no living thing will be justified"). Paul replaces *pas zōn* ("all living") with *pasa sarx* ("all flesh") and introduces *ex ergōn nomou* ("by works of the Law") substantially altering the meaning of the original psalm verse. In Rom 3:20 he quotes this Psalm in the same fashion and explains why no one is justified by legal works: "for through the Law comes the knowledge of sin."

17. *But if in seeking to be justified in Christ*: The preposition *en* has been translated in a locative sense ("in") rather than an instrumental sense ("by") because the divine acquittal involves more than an external judgment; it indicates a transfer of the sinner from one sphere (the Law) to another (Christ). This makes good sense considering Paul's statement in v. 20 that Christ lives in him.

even we were found to be sinners: Jewish Christians find themselves in the same situation as Gentiles: relying on Christ-faith, rather than legal works, they stand outside the boundaries of the Law; they are lawless!

then has Christ become Sin's servant?: This phrase is construed as a question because the Greek particle *ara* has a circumflex. A few manuscripts, however, have *ara* without the circumflex which makes the phrase declarative, "then Christ has becomes Sin's servant." The next phrase, however, suggests that a question is intended here. The expression "Sin's servant" translates *hamartias diakonos*. "Sin" is capitalized because in Gal 3:22 and Rom 5-8 Paul personifies it as a power. The phrase represents an objection to Paul's teaching on justification: faith in Christ results in ethnic Jews living as Gentile sinners because they no longer practice legal works such as the dietary laws. Consequently Christ has been turned into Sin's agent!

Out of the question: This translates *mē genoito*, literally, "let it not be!" The phrase is frequently used in Romans (3:4, 6, 31; 6:2, 15; 7:13; 9:14; 11:1, 11) after a question which Paul thinks absurd.

18. *For if I build again those things which I tore down*: The verse begins with *gar* ("for") and provides the first reason why Paul's teaching about righteousness does not make Christ Sin's servant. The context of this passage (the Antioch incident) suggests that what Paul tore down is the dietary legislation which separated Jew and Gentile by forbidding table fellowship.

I show myself to be a transgressor: Transgressor (*parabatēs*) like transgression (*parabasis*) is used in relationship to the Law. Thus, transgressors of the Law nullify their circumcision (Rom 2:25), and Gentiles who keep the Law will condemn Jews who are transgressors of it (Rom 2:27). If Paul were to reestablish the dietary laws, he would show that he is a transgressor of the Law since he no longer follows these laws, at least at Antioch.

19. *For through the Law I died to the Law*: This verse, like v. 18, begins with *gar* ("for"), providing a second reason why Paul's teaching on righteousness does not make Christ a servant of Sin: Paul has died to the Law. Paul uses the verb "to die" (*apothnēskein*) twice in Galatians: here in reference to himself, and in v. 21 in reference to Christ. His meaning here is clarified by what he says in Romans: by association with Christ's death through Baptism, Christians die to the Law. Thus Paul writes, "In the same way, my friends, *you have died to the Law* through the body of Christ" (Rom 7:4). This happened *dia nomou* ("through the Law") because Christ died under the Law (3:13).

in order that I might live to God: Of the nine times that the verb "to live" occurs in Galatians, five appear in vv. 19-20. The meaning here is defined by the previous phrase: dying to the Law. Paul views living to the Law and living to God as mutually exclusive realities. "In order that I might live to God" (*hina theō zēsō*) points to an eschatological reality. A similar concept is found in 4 Macc 7:19: "since they believe that they, like our patriarchs Abraham and Isaac and Jacob, do not die to God, but live to God (*zōsin tō theō*)." Also see Rom 6:10-11 and Luke 20:37-38.

I am crucified with Christ: The verb employed here, *systauroun*, is the same word used in the passion narratives (Matt 24:44, Mark 15:32; John 19:32) when speaking of those who were crucified *with* Christ. In Rom 6:6, in the context of baptism, Paul employs the verb in a sacramental sense ("We know that our old self was crucified with him"). Although Paul does not mention baptism here, it probably determines his thought. The use of the perfect tense suggests that he views his crucifixion with Christ as an enduring state. In 5:24 Paul exhorts the Galatians to crucify the flesh with its passions and desires, and in 6:14 he says that the world has been crucified to him, and he to the world. In these passages the meaning is to die to something: Paul has died to the world; the Galatians must die to their passions.

20. *It is no longer "I" who live, but Christ lives in me*: The Greek text emphasizes "I" and "Christ" by positioning them at the end of their respective phrases: "I live no longer *I*; but lives in me *Christ*." The phrase develops the thought of the preceding verse. When Paul was alive to the Law his self (*egō*) was the controlling factor of his life. But now that he is alive to God, Christ has replaced that self. See Romans 8:10. In Rom 7:9, 10, 14, 17, 20, 24, 25, where the problem is not the self but indwelling Sin (Rom 7:20), Paul refers to the "I" more positively. Here, in Galatians, Paul focuses upon the divine interchange: Christ in place of the "I."

The life I now live in the flesh: For "in the flesh" see 4:14 where Paul refers to his physical condition. While flesh (*sarx*) often has a negative sense in Paul's writings, here it refers to the physical sphere in which human beings live their lives.

I live by the faith of the Son of God: Some manuscripts (P46, B, D*, F, G) have "God and Christ" in place of "Son of God." However, Paul's more usual expression is Son of God (Rom 1:4; 5:10; 8:3, 29, 32; 1 Cor 1:9; 15:28; Gal 1:16; 4:4; 1 Thess 1:10). See Metzger, *Textual Commentary*, 593. The Greek *en pistei zō tē tou hyiou tou theou* can be rendered as an objective genitive ("I live by faith *in* the Son of God") or as a subjective genitive ("I live by the faith *of* the Son of God"). This commentary renders all such expressions as subjective genitives: Paul lives by the faith of the Son of God.

who loved me and handed himself over for me: This phrase is significant for several reasons. First, it is the only place where Paul speaks of Christ loving him, but cf. Rom 8:35. Second, whereas Rom 4:25 and 8:32 speak of God handing over Christ, here it is Christ who hands himself over to death. Third, the entire passage is highly personal. Fourth, the passage provides a vivid example of Christ's faith: he handed himself over for others.

21. *I have not nullified the grace of God*: The verb *athetein* ("to nullify") is also employed in 3:15: no one nullifies a legally ratified will. Here Paul uses the word

in reference to God's grace. Paul experienced this grace in his call to be an apostle to the Gentiles (1:15, 2:9). The Galatians are abandoning the one who called them by grace (1:15) and will be cut off from grace if they seek justification by the Law (5:4).

for if righteousness were through the Law: This is the first occurrence of *dikaiosynē* ("righteousness," "uprightness" or "justice") in Galatians. See 3:6, 21; 5:5 for other uses. The word represents a major Pauline concept found thirty-four times in Romans, once in 1 Corinthians, seven times in 2 Corinthians, and four times in Philippians. Whereas the verb *dikaioun* describes the activity of acquitting and is usually forensic in nature, the noun *dikaiosynē* describes the result of that activity for the human person. The believer is made upright by God's justice through God's justifying activity in Christ. Christ is "our righteousness, and sanctification and redemption" (1 Cor 1:30). Christ was made sin so that "we might become the righteousness of God" (2 Cor 5:21). Paul has counted all as loss in order to gain "the righteousness from God based on faith" (Phil 3:9). While these texts and others emphasize the present aspect of righteousness, Paul realizes that the gift is not complete, for in Gal 5:5 he writes, "we wait for the hope of righteousness." Narrowly defined, the Law (*nomos*) consists of the first five books of the Bible, the Pentateuch, the Torah. More broadly defined, it refers to the whole religious system of Judaism; it is the revelation of God's will. Before his call, Paul found a righteousness through the Law (Phil 3:6), but in light of the Christ event he considered this former righteousness as nothing (Phil 3:7). Christ, not the Law, leads to righteousness.

then Christ died in vain: If God's Son died for us, it was because the Law was incapable of bringing righteousness. A similar thought is expressed in 3:21. "In vain" translates *dōrean* which in Rom 3:24 and 2 Cor 11:7 means "undeserved," or "without payment."

INTERPRETATION

Thus far, Paul has employed a series of autobiographical episodes to demonstrate to the Galatians the divine origin of his gospel, the conformity of his behavior with the gospel that he preaches, and Jerusalem's recognition of that gospel. In effect, Paul has intimated that if the Galatians agree to circumcision they will be in conflict with the gospel that he has proclaimed to them, the gospel he received through a revelation of Jesus Christ. This passage (2:15-21) brings the first portion of Paul's letter (1:11–2:21) to a conclusion by summarizing the content of the Torah-free gospel of which Paul has been speaking.

From a literary point of view, this unit is a continuation of Paul's speech to Peter, but it is apparent that the speech now has a broader audience in view than Peter and those with him at Antioch. Just as Jesus' response to Nicodemus in John 3:10-21 becomes a discourse for the whole Johannine community, so Paul's rebuke of Peter is transformed into a theological statement of the gospel he preaches. It is not surprising, therefore, that most translations set this unit off as a separate paragraph, implying that Paul's rebuke of Peter concludes at 2:14. These words are more than an account of what Paul said to Peter at Antioch; they are a careful exposition of the truth of the gospel.

Rhetorically the unit functions like the *propositio* of an argument, recapitulating and foreshadowing Paul's argument. It recapitulates what Paul has said thus far in the following ways. First, in vv. 15–16 Paul summarizes the content of the gospel: justification on the basis of faith, apart from legal works. Second, in vv. 17–21 he deals with an objection to the consequences of his Torah-gospel, especially as that gospel was practiced in Antioch: the gospel turns Jewish believers into Gentile sinners and Christ into a servant of Sin. He affirms that he has not denied the grace of God which was given to him (1:15), implying that the Galatians who are abandoning their call (1:6) are about to do so. In addition to recapitulating what Paul has said, this unit introduces a number of important concepts and themes which will be developed in the following chapters.

> *Dikaiosynē* ("righteousness"): 2:21; 3:6, 21; 5:5
>
> *Dikaioō* ("to justify"): 2:16 (three times), 17; 3:8, 11, 24; 5:4
>
> *Nomos* ("Law"): 2:16 (three times), 19 (twice), 21; 3:2, 5, 10 (twice), 11, 12, 13, 17, 18, 19, 21 (three times), 23, 24; 4:4, 5, 21 (twice); 5:3, 4, 14, 18, 23; 6:2, 13
>
> *Ergon* ("work"): 2:16 (three times); 3:2, 5, 10; 5:19; 6:4
>
> *Pistis* ("faith"): 2:16 (twice), 20; 3:2, 5, 7, 8, 9, 11, 12, 14, 22, 23 (three times), 24, 25, 26: 5:5, 6, 22; 6:10
>
> *Zō* ("to live"): 2:14, 19, 20 (four times); 3:11, 12; 5:25

Of special interest is the contrast that Paul begins in this unit and develops in the following chapters, between *ex ergōn nomou* and *dia* or *ek pisteōs (Iēsou) Christou*. Paul proclaims that "legal works" and "the faith of Christ" or "faith in Christ" (see below) are mutually exclusive. In chapter three, by several references to Abraham and the Law, he explains why. The unit is structured in the following way.

> vv. 15–16   Paul recalls the common ground between himself and other Jewish Christians: justification comes *dia pisteōs Iēsou Christou*.
>
> v. 17   Paul raises an objection to his Torah-free gospel: it makes Christ a servant of Sin.
>
> vv. 18–21 The objection is false for three reasons:
>
> > v. 18   Reestablishing the Law would show that Paul is a transgressor.

vv. 19-20   Paul has died to the Law.
v. 21   The Law does not grant righteousness.

The common ground (vv. 15-16). Since the situation at Antioch is still very much in mind, the "we" which opens this section refers to Peter, Paul, and the other Jewish Christians. In effect, Paul makes the traditional distinction between Jew and Gentiles. Jews stand within the covenant which provides them with God's gracious gift of Torah. By obeying the precepts of the Law, they lead righteous lives and walk blamelessly in the Law of the Lord (Psalm 119). By contrast, Gentiles stand outside of the covenant, deprived of Torah. They are, *ipso facto*, sinners. Thus to be a Gentile is to be a sinner, as in 1 Macc 2:48 where the two are equated: "They rescued the Law out of the hands of the *Gentiles* and kings, and they never let the *sinner* gain the upper hand." In face of this distinction, Paul affirms what he and other Jewish Christians have come to realize: no one can be justified *ex ergōn nomou*. The careful and balanced structure of v. 16 highlights the basic opposition between *ex ergōn nomou* and *ek pisteōs Christou*. The precise meaning of the phrases will be explained below.

Knowing that a person is not justified   *ex ergōn nomou*
        but   *dia pisteōs Iēsou Christou*
even we have believed   *eis*   *Iēsou Christou*
in order that we might be justified   *ek pisteōs*   *Christou*
        and not   *ex ergōn nomou*
        because   *ex ergōn nomou*
        no one will be justified

Since the sixteenth century, this passage has been interpreted in light of the Reformation debate concerning the value of good works. Viewed within this context, it has been understood as a polemic against legalism: one is justified by trusting faith in Christ, not by the accomplishment of good works. While legalism is a danger to the Christian life, Paul is not arguing against legalism here. The immediate context of this unit, the Jerusalem conference and the incident at Antioch, as well as Paul's remarks in 4:10, suggest that by legal works (*ergōn nomou*) Paul means circumcision, dietary regulations, and the observance of certain Jewish festivals. Such "works" distinguished Jews from Gentiles, identifying the former as the covenant people and the latter as sinners; legal works were the proud signs of Jewish nationalism. When Paul says that he and other Jewish Christians acknowledge that they are not saved by legal works, therefore, he means that they have realized that the outward signs of being a Jew are not sufficient to place them in the proper relationship to God. As important as these are, Jewish Christians like Paul, in light

of the Christ event, have come to realize that something else is necessary. Consequently, they have believed *in* Christ in order to be justified
ek pisteōs Christou and not *ex ergōn nomou*. To support his position, Paul
quotes Ps 143:2, which he edits to make his argument more forceful (see
notes).

But what does Paul mean when he says that one is justified *dia* or *ek
pisteōs Christou?* The majority of commentators and translators render this
phrase as an objective genitive: faith *in* Christ. Thus they establish a contrast between legal works and one's faith in Christ. More recently, however, several authors have argued that the phrase should be taken as a
subjective genitive: the faith or faithfulness *of* Jesus Christ. Since both
translations are grammatically possible, the matter can only be settled
by determining which translation makes better sense within the broader
context of this letter and of Paul's other writings. This commentary espouses the view that Paul intends the subjective genitive, the faith of Jesus
Christ, for the following reasons.

First, Paul's understanding of justification in this passage argues for
the subjective genitive. In v. 17 he speaks of being "justified *en Christō*
("in Christ"), and in v. 20 he writes "Christ lives in me" (*zē en emoi
Christos*). These phrases suggest that justification entails participation in
Christ: Christ dwells in the believer and the believer is transferred to the
realm of Christ. In effect, believers are justified through (*dia*) and on the
basis (*ek*) of Christ's faith; they are justified by participation in the faith
of Jesus Christ.

Second, if Paul intended the phrases *dia pisteōs Iēsou Christou* and *ek
pisteōs Christou* to be taken as objective genitives, he has become unneces-
sarily verbose, if not redundant. Paul could have made his point more
clearly by writing *dia pisteōs* and *ek pisteōs* ("knowing that a person is not
justified by legal works but *through faith*, even we have believed in Christ
Jesus in order that we might be justified *by faith*"). That Paul adds "Jesus
Christ" and "Christ" suggests that he has the faith *of* Christ in view.
One believes *in* Christ in order to be justified *through* and *on the basis* of
Christ's faith.

Third, in this passage Paul establishes a contrast between *ex ergōn
nomou* and *ek pisteōs Christou*. To interpret the latter phrase as an objective genitive is to establish a contrast between a person's legal works and
a person's faith in Christ. While there is clearly an important difference
between the two, both are human actions: one active, the other passive.
The more powerful contrast is between a person's legal works and *the
work* of Christ, i.e., Christ's faithfulness in handing himself over for our
sins (1:4); Christ's faithfulness in accepting the curse of the cross (3:13);
Christ's faithfulness in fulfilling the mission entrusted to him by the Father
(4:4-5).

Fourth, in v. 20 Paul employs another phrase that can be interpreted as an objective or subjective genitive (*en pistei zō tȩ tou hyiou tou theou tou agapēsantos me kai paradontos heauton hyper emou*). Either Paul means that he lives by faith *in* the Son of God who loved him and handed himself over for him, or he means that he lives *by* the faith of the Son of God who loved him and handed himself over for him. If Paul intends the former (faith *in* the Son of God), then the last part of the phrase (who loved me and handed himself over for me) becomes a simple descriptive appendage. But if Paul intends the latter (by the faith *of* the Son of God), the final phrase becomes an explanation of Christ's faith: Christ's faith is embodied in the act of loving and handing himself over for others. Since the subjective genitive makes better sense of the phrase, it is to be preferred. And if this phrase is rendered as the faith of the Son of God, then Paul must intend the same for v. 16, the faith of Christ.

Fifth, in chapter three Paul personifies faith: "before the faith (*tēn pistin*) came, we were imprisoned under Law, confined for the sake of the faith destined to be revealed (*tēn mellousan pistin*)," (3:23) but "since the faith has come (*elthousēs de tēs pisteōs*), we are no longer under a custodian" (3:25). To what does "the faith" refer? The message of the gospel? The faith of believers? A more satisfying answer is provided in light of the subjective genitive under discussion here. This faith is *the* faith of Jesus Christ. Before the appearance of this faith, the Law imprisoned humanity, but with the appearance of Christ's faith humanity has been freed from its custodian.

Finally, the subjective genitive makes eminent sense in two other places that Paul employs this phrase. In Rom 3:22 he writes that the righteousness of God has been disclosed *dia pisteōs Christou* for all who believe. If the phrase is translated "through faith in Jesus Christ," the final phrase, "for all who believe" becomes redundant. It makes more sense to understand the revelation of God's righteousness through the faithfulness of Jesus Christ. Finally, in Rom 3:26 Paul writes, "it was to prove at the present time that he himself is righteous and that he justifies *ton ek pisteōs Iēsou*." This is the only place where Paul uses "Jesus" rather than "Jesus Christ" or "Christ" when speaking of faith. Read as an objective genitive, the phrase is translated "the one who has faith *in* (*ek*) Jesus," a strange translation for *ek*. It is more natural to render it, "the one who has the faith of [or from] Jesus." Not only does the translation make excellent sense, it prepares for Romans 4 where Paul considers the example of Abraham's faith. Moreover, in speaking of Abraham's faith Paul writes, *ek pisteōs Abraam* (4:16) which clearly parallels *ek pisteōs Iēsou*.

To summarize, there is substantial body of evidence that Paul means the faith of Christ when he writes *ek pisteōs Christou*. This interpretation does not dispense with or lessen the importance of faith in Christ, but it does reorient one's understanding of this important passage. The common ground between Paul and other Jewish Christians is the recognition that the outward signs of being a Jew (circumcision, foods laws, festivals) do not justify one before God. Justification comes from, and is based upon, the faith of Jesus Christ manifested upon the cross. That is why even Jewish Christians have believed *in* Christ. This faith embraces both the faith *of* Christ and faith *in* Christ and might well be called Christ-faith.

An objection (v. 17). Thus far Paul has established common ground between himself and Jewish Christians like Peter: all have come to realize that they are justified by the faith of Christ in whom they believe and not by legal works. On this point there is no dispute. But now Paul raises an objection to this common ground, an objection which the people from James may have posed to Paul and Peter in this fashion. "Granted that we are justified by the faith of Christ in whom we believe and not by legal works, we must continue to practice legal works, otherwise nothing will distinguish us from Gentiles; we will become like Gentile sinners. Making Christ's faith an excuse for no longer practicing legal works will only make Christ a servant of Sin. Therefore, while we acknowledge that we are justified by the faith of Christ in whom we believe, we insist upon the necessity of legal works."

Paul's first response to this objection is a vehement denial (*mē genoito*). The objection is absurd and unworthy of consideration. Any reasonable person will immediately rule it out of court. But since it has been raised, Paul deals with it. His response becomes highly personal, causing him to abandon the second person plural (vv. 15–17) in favor of the first person singular (18–21). One has the sense that Paul is speaking from deep, personal conviction. His response can be divided into three parts: v. 18; vv. 19–20; v. 21.

Responses (vv. 18–21). Paul's first line of argument (v. 18) is to shift the burden of blame from himself to those who would require legal works in addition to Christ's faith. He argues that if he reinstates legal works then he will show that he is a transgressor. In fact, this is precisely what Peter, Barnabas, and the Jewish Christians who withdrew from table fellowship with the Gentiles at Antioch have done. Before the arrival of the Jerusalem delegation, they ate with Gentiles; they did not observe one of the legal works: to eat only clean food. But when the people from James came, Peter and other Jewish Christians withdrew *as if* their previous behavior had been sinful. They, not Paul, made Christ a servant of Sin. If Paul reinstates legal works in addition to Christ-faith, he will be doing the same by implying that his past behavior among the Gentiles was sinful, when in fact it was not.

Paul's second response (vv. 19–20) is more developed and theological in nature. Justification by Christ-faith does not make Christ a servant of Sin because, through the Law, Paul has died to the Law in order to live to God (v. 19a). In effect, the Law has no more claim upon him because he has died to it. What Paul means by this is clarified by a series of statements in vv. 19b–20.

19a For through the Law I died to the Law
19b in order that I might live to God.
19c I am crucified with Christ.
20a It is no longer I who live *but*
20b Christ lives in me.
20c The life I now live in the flesh
20d I live by the faith of the Son of God
20e who loved me *and*
20f handed himself over for me.

Paul's statements in 19c ("I am crucified with Christ"), 20b ("Christ lives in me"), and 20d ("I live by the faith of the Son of God") explain what he means in 19a that he died to the Law. By associating himself with the crucified Christ, he has been transferred to the sphere of Christ. Even as Paul continues to live his carnal existence (*en sarki*), Christ lives in him, and he lives by participation in Christ's own faith.

But what does Paul mean when he says that he died to the Law *through the Law*? The answer is found in Paul's affirmation that he is crucified *with* Christ. In 4:4 Paul says that Christ was born under the Law, and in 3:13 he writes that Christ redeemed us from the curse of the Law by becoming a curse for us. In the last text Paul is referring to Deut 21:23 which proclaims a curse upon any one who hangs on a tree, i.e., is crucified. In effect, Paul views Christ as having been born under, and died under, the Law. But since the Law is binding only during a person's lifetime (Rom 7:1), Paul concludes that Christ and those *in* him are free from the Law because of Christ's death. By being baptized into Christ, one is baptized into his death (Rom 6:3); one is crucified *with* Christ. Paul has died to the Law *through* the Law by his co-crucifixion and with Christ. He is dead to the Law because he is alive to a new eschatological reality; he lives to God (4 Macc 7:19; Rom 6:10-11; Luke 20:37-38).

Paul's final response (v. 21) is his most direct and compelling answer. If it were possible to receive righteousness through the Law, then why did Christ die? The fact that God's Son loved "me" and gave himself for "me" suggests that his death did something that the Law could not. God sent his Son, born under the Law, to do something that the Law was powerless to do. Paul makes a similar statement in 3:21, "For if a Law had been given capable of providing life, righteousness would really have been from the Law." At this point, one suspects that Paul is breaking new ground, and that he no longer shares common ground with the Jewish Christians of Antioch. To say that a person is justified by Christ-faith, and not by legal works (understood as circumcision, food Laws, and festivals), is one thing, but to say that the Law (understood as the manifestation of God's will) does not give righteousness is quite another. Paul's reasons for saying this will be explained more fully in chapter three.

Once more Paul shifts the blame. It is not he who denies the grace of God but those who insist upon legal works: Peter, Barnabas, the people from James, and all Jewish Christians who take their side. Most importantly, the Galatians themselves will deny God's grace if they rely upon legal works rather than upon Christ-faith.

FOR REFERENCE AND FURTHER STUDY

Barth, M. "The Faith of the Messiah." *HeyJour* 10 (1969) 63–70.
Hays, R. B. *The Faith of Jesus Christ: An Investigation of the Narrative Structure of Galatians 3:1–4:11.* SBLDS 56; Scholars Press, 1983.
Hooker, M. D. "*PISTIS CHRISTOU.*" *NTS* 35 (1989) 321–342.
Howard, G. "Notes and Observations on the 'Faith of Christ.' " *HTR* 60 (1967) 459–484.
Howard, G. "The 'Faith of Christ' " *ExpTim* 85 (1974) 212–215.
Hultgren, A. J. "The *PISTIS CHRISTOU* formulation in Paul." *NovT* 22 (1980) 248–263.
Johnson, L. T. "Romans 3:21-26 and the Faith of Jesus." *CBQ* 44 (1982) 77–90.
Keck, L. " 'Jesus' in Romans." *JBL* 108 (1989) 443–460.
Lambrecht, J. "The Line of Thought in Gal 2.14b-21." *NTS* 24 (1978) 485–495.
Moo, D. J. " 'Law.' 'Works of the Law,' and Legalism in Paul." *WTJ* 45 (1983) 73–100.
Räisänen. H. "Galatians 2.16 and Paul's Break with Judaism." *NTS* 31 (1985) 543–553.
Robinson, D. W. B. 'Faith of Jesus Christ'—a New Testament Debate." *The Reformed Theological Review* 39 (1970) 71–81.
Taylor, G. M. "The Function of *PISTIS CHRISTOU* in Galatians." *JBL* 85 (1966) 58–76.
Tyson, J. B. " 'Works of Law' in Galatians." *JBL* 92 (73) 423–431.
Williams, S. K. "Again *Pistis Christou. CBQ* 49 (1987) 431–447.

EXCURSUS:
GALATIANS AND THE ACTS OF THE APOSTLES

This commentary has focused primarily upon the text of Galatians, paying special attention to the rhetorical function of Paul's autobiographical narration. Consequently, although there have been references to the Acts of the Apostles, there has been little effort to compare, contrast, or reconcile the accounts of Paul's life as narrated in Galatians and in Acts. Nor has the text of Galatians been interpreted through the text of Acts since the primary task of the commentator is to interpret the text on the basis of the text itself. Information gained outside of the text is important and necessary, but it is secondary to the text itself. Nonetheless, a commentary on Galatians should not bypass an important work such as Acts which parallels much of what Paul says in this letter. The purpose of this excursus, therefore, is to compare Galatians and Acts insofar as Acts parallels the events narrated in this section of Galatians. Such an undertaking, of course, could be the topic of an entire monograph. The goal here, however, is more modest. This comparison of Galatians and Acts intends to shed some light upon the perspective from which each document was written.

Paul the persecutor (Gal 1:13; Acts 8:3; 9:1-2; 22:4-5; 26:9-11). In Galatians Paul, without providing any details, recalls his former conduct as a persecutor of the Church of God. He simply says that he tried to destroy the Church, employing the same verb which Luke uses in Acts 9:21 (*porthein*). There is no indication of where Paul carried out this activity or by what authority he did it. In contrast to this, Luke is more specific. According to him, Paul persecuted the Church in Jerusalem (Acts 8:3; 26:10) and Damascus (Acts 9:2; 22:5; 26:10), and even pursued Christians to foreign cities (26:11). Luke says that Paul sought and received letters from the high priest to the synagogues at Damascus (9:1; 22:5; 26:10) in order to bring to Jerusalem those who adhered to the way. In Acts 26:10, Paul relates that when such believers were condemned to death, he had cast his vote against them. Overall, the Lucan picture presents Paul as someone who worked for and with the Jerusalem authorities. Given the tenor of Paul's argument in Galatians, it is somewhat surprising that he does not include this information in his autobiographical statement.

Paul's former way of life (Gal 1:14; Acts 22:3; 26:4-5). Paul's statement about his former way of life focuses upon his zeal for his ancestral traditions (Gal 1:14), but he is not more specific. Luke, however, states that although Paul was born in the Diaspora (Tarsus in Cilicia), he was educated in Jerusalem as a disciple of Gamaliel (Acts 22:3) and was an adherent of the Pharisees (26:5). This information comes from two defense speeches in Acts calculated to establish Paul's Jewish credentials. In Phil 3:6 Paul corroborates that he was a Pharisee, but never mentions that he was a student of Gamaliel or educated in Jerusalem.

Paul's call (Gal 1:15-16a; Acts 9:3-19a; 22:6-16; 26:12-18). Paul does not provide a detailed account of his conversion/call. He merely says that God revealed his Son to him (Gal 1:15-16a). By contrast, the accounts of Acts provide extensive narrative descriptions of Paul's Damascus road experience. The relationship between these three accounts has been the object of intense scholarly study, and there is no attempt to enter that debate here.

In Acts 9 Luke describes Paul's call as part of the sequence of his narrative whereas in Acts 22 and 26 the Lucan Paul recounts the events surrounding his call, first before the crowd at Jerusalem (Acts 22), and then before Agrippa, Bernice, and Festus (Acts 26). Both accounts belong to the genre of the defense speech and are intended to defend Paul against charges that he is an apostate from Judaism. The three accounts differ from each other in several minor details, nonetheless they agree in their major points. As Paul journeyed to Damascus, the Risen Jesus appeared to him, asking, "Saul, Saul, why do you persecute me?" Paul responds, "Who are you, Lord?" and the Lord answers, "I am Jesus whom you are persecuting." In the accounts of Acts 9 and 22, Paul is unable to see because of the light from the vision and is led to Damascus. There, Ananias plays a role, helping him regain his sight, explaining the significance of the vision, and leading him to baptism. Ananias does not appear in the account of Acts 26.

The three accounts of Acts are in the form of a Christophany whereas Galatians narrates a theophany in which God reveals his Son to Paul. Nonetheless, both Acts and Galatians employ the imagery of the prophetic call to describe Paul's experience and stress that he was called to preach the gospel to the Gentiles. Thus, although the accounts of Acts introduce several narrative elements not found in Galatians or Paul's other correspondence, the essential point made in Galatians can be found in the narratives of Acts: Paul was called to preach the gospel to the Gentiles.

Paul in Arabia and Damascus (Gal 1:16b-17; Acts 9:19b-25; 26:19-20). The events following Paul's call provide the first important difference in the chronologies of Paul and Luke. In Galatians, Paul insists that immediately after his call he did not consult with others, or go to Jerusalem. Instead he went to Arabia, and then, after approximately three years (Gal 1:18), returned to Damascus. This commentary has already suggested that the period in Arabia was the beginning of Paul's preaching to Gentiles.

By contrast, Luke says nothing of Paul's time in Arabia. Instead, he gives a detailed account of Paul's activities in Damascus following the call: he preached in the synagogues, the Jews plotted to kill him, disciples helped him to escape from the city (9:19b-25). Moreover, Luke gives the impression that Paul went to Jerusalem shortly after his stay in Damascus (Acts 9:26; 26:19-20). Either Luke did not know of, or passed over in silence, Paul's activity in Arabia. The absence of this incident, however, does allow Luke to bring Paul into contact with Jerusalem more quickly. On the other hand, the mention, in Galatians, of Paul's time in Arabia puts time and space between the Apostle's call and his first visit to Jerusalem.

First visit to Jerusalem (Gal 1:18-20; Acts 9:26-29; 22:17-21). According to Paul, his first visit to Jerusalem occurred three years after the call. It was a private visit with Peter, lasted only two weeks, and except for James, Paul did not see any of the other apostles. According to Luke, however, Paul's first visit to Jerusalem, after his call, was of a different nature (Acts 9:22-29). Paul tried to join the other disciples in Jerusalem but was prevented from doing so until Barnabas introduced him to the apostles. Thereafter, Paul preached boldly in Jerusalem and disputed with the Hellenists who eventually sought to kill him. In Acts 22:17-22, the Lucan Paul recounts that the Risen Lord appeared to him while he was praying in the temple and sent him off to the Gentiles.

It is obvious that there is no way to harmonize the accounts of Luke and Paul at this point. Paul's account is the primary evidence for this first visit while Luke's narrative is a later, literary development intended to highlight the close relationship between Paul and Jerusalem.

Paul in Syria and Cilicia (Gal 1:21; Acts 9:30; 11:25-26). At this point there is some agreement between Paul and Luke. According to Galatians, Paul went to Syria and Cilicia. Again, Paul does not say what he did, but one can suppose that he preached in these regions and eventually became active in the congregations of Antioch and Syria. This, at least, is how Luke constructs the events of this period. According to him, the plot of the Hellenists to kill Paul led some in Jerusalem to send Paul to Tarsus by way of Caesarea (9:30). Some time later, Barnabas brought Paul from Tarsus to Antioch (11:25-26). Luke does not say how long this period lasted, but Gal 2:1 suggests a period of about fifteen years.

Reaction to Paul's conversion (Gal 1:22-24; Acts 9:21, 27-29). Paul insists that he was still unknown to the churches of Judea during this period. Those churches simply heard of his conversion and glorified God because of it. This, of course, fits Paul's purpose in Galatians which is to establish distance between himself and the Jerusalem Church. By contrast, Luke gives the impression that Paul must have been known, at least in the

Jerusalem Church, before he preached in Jerusalem, and he reports that the Hellenists sought to kill Paul (9:27-29). But this also fits Luke's purpose which is to show Paul's solidarity with Jerusalem. The basic reaction to Paul's conversion, however, is the same in both Acts and Galatians: amazement that the persecutor is now preaching the gospel (Gal 1:23; Acts 9:21).

The conference at Jerusalem (Gal 2:1-10; Acts 11:30; 12:25; 15:1-29; 18:22). Nowhere is the relationship between Galatians and Acts more problematic than in the accounts of the Jerusalem conference (Gal 2:1-10; Acts 15). The content of both accounts, the question of circumcision, is clearly similar, and most scholars agree that Luke and Paul have the same event in mind. However, Luke's chronology does not agree with Paul's, and the two accounts of the conference have notable differences.

According to Paul, the conference was his second visit, after his call, to Jerusalem. According to Luke, it was Paul's third or fourth visit, depending upon the reading one adopts for 12:25, the first two being the visits of 9:26-30 and 11:29-30. In some manuscripts, Acts 12:25 is made the conclusion of the second visit (the visit to bring famine relief to Jerusalem), while in others it becomes a third visit. Acts 15:1-29, therefore, was Paul's third or fourth visit, followed by two other visits after the Apostle's second and third missionary journeys (18:22; 21:17).

> First visit after call (9:26-30)
> Second visit to bring famine relief (11:29-30)
> Conclusion of second visit or a third visit (12:25)
> Third or fourth visit (15:1-29)
> Visit after second missionary journey (18:22)
> Visit after third missionary journey (21:17)

How then does one reconcile Paul's insistence that the conference was his second visit with Luke's account which makes it his third or fourth visit? A variety of solutions have been offered to solve the problem.

For some, Galatians 2 should be equated with the famine relief visit of Acts 11, Acts 15 being the account of a second conference needed to resolve the problems left unresolved by the first conference. For others, Galatians 2 should be equated with Acts 15, the famine relief visit being viewed as a later, literary construction. For others, Galatians should be equated with Acts 18:22. According to this solution, Luke would have repositioned the conference from its original setting in 18:22 to chapter 15 in order to give the impression that Paul undertook his second and third missionary journeys after the conference and with the apostolic decree in hand (15:23-29).

In addition to the chronological problems noted above, there are important differences between Galatians 2 and Acts 15. According to Galatians, Paul went up to Jerusalem in accord with a revelation. The purpose of his visit was to explain the gospel that he preached. At this visit, Paul took Titus as a kind of test case. Despite pressure from false brethren, Titus was not compelled to be circumcised. Indeed, the pillar apostles (James, Cephas, and John) extended the right hand of fellowship to Paul and Barnabas, only asking them to remember the poor.

According to Acts 15, the Church at Antioch sent Paul and Barnabas to Jerusalem to resolve the question of circumcision because some brethren had come from Judea and said that unless the Gentiles were circumcised they could not be saved (15:1). Acts does not mention Titus. Moreover, according to Acts, Paul played a secondary role, the primary roles being reserved for Peter (15:6-11) and James (15:13-21). The conference decided that Gentiles need not be circumcised but did publish a letter regarding certain dietary restrictions (15:23-29), the apostolic decree of which Paul, in his letters, seems to be ignorant.

While the accounts of Galatians 2 and Acts 15 deal with the same basic issue, circumcision, it is clear that Acts 15 goes a step further by introducing a solution to resolve the question of table fellowship between Gentiles and Jews. This leads many scholars to view Acts 15 as a Lucan amalgamation of two meetings: one to resolve the question of circumcision, another to resolve the question of table fellowship.

What, then, can we say about the Lucan and Pauline accounts? First, Galatians 2 and Acts 15 undoubtedly refer to the same basic event. However, Acts 15 seems to incorporate the results of a further meeting at which the apostolic decree was issued, a meeting at which Paul was not present. For theological reasons, however, Luke has telescoped the two meetings into one. Thus Paul goes on his second and third missionary journeys after this great council at which the major problems of the Gentile mission were resolved. Second, the conference was Paul's second visit to Jerusalem after his call, the famine relief visit being a Lucan literary construction to show Paul's faithful service to Jerusalem on behalf of the Church of Antioch. Whether or not this conference actually occurred between Paul's first and second missionary journey (ch. 15), however, is another matter. The introduction to this commentary has proposed that Luke's arrangement of Paul's missionary journeys is artificial and that all of the Pauline missionary journeys narrated in Acts, including the journey of Acts 13-14, occurred after the conference of Acts 15 which recounts essentially the same event as is told in Gal 2.

The incident at Antioch (Gal 2:11-14; Acts 15:36-41). Luke does not recount any episode which can be compared with the incident at Antioch (Gal 2:11-14). Either Luke was unaware of this episode, or he chose to pass over it as being too harsh for the picture of the Church that he was trying to present. Luke does, however, recount a sharp disagreement between Paul and Barnabas which resulted in each going his own way (Acts 15:36-41). Like the incident at Antioch, this contention occurred after the Jerusalem conference. While some authors (most recently Luedemann) argue that the Antioch incident really occurred before the Jerusalem conference and precipitated it, it seems more prudent to follow the chronology which Paul has established. The incident at Antioch occurred shortly after the Jerusalem conference because the parties involved understood the agreement reached there differently. For Paul, the recognition of the gospel by Jerusalem meant that henceforth there should be table fellowship between Jews and Gentiles on the basis of their common faith in Jesus Christ. James and other Jewish Christians, however, clearly did not intend to permit such table fellowship even when they acknowledged the validity of Paul's circumcision-free gospel to the Gentiles. Setting aside the requirement for circumcision was one thing, setting aside the dietary prescriptions of the Law was another.

If the scenario described above is correct, then the Antioch incident precipitated the need for a second meeting at Jerusalem to settle the questions left unresolved by the first. Paul, however, was not present at this meeting, otherwise he would surely have recorded it. Or, the meeting may not have yet taken place at the time that he was writing Galatians. Luke, however, writing thirty years later, telescoped the two meetings into one, making it unnecessary to recount the disturbing incident at Antioch. In his presentation, all of the issues were settled at one harmonious conference (Acts 15) at which Paul was present.

Conclusion. Anyone who carefully compares Galatians and Acts sees that the two accounts present a frustrating mixture of episodes, some of which confirm each other, others of which are in tension with each other. Most will agree that the two narratives do not lend themselves to either simple or complex harmonizations. On balance, it seems best to recognize that Paul and Luke present the facts to suit their needs. Paul narrates in order to persuade the Galatians that his gospel did not originate from a human source. In doing so, he presents accurate information but narrates the facts in a way that is most helpful for his rhetorical goals. Luke, by contrast, writes at a time when the issues of circumcision and food laws have been settled in favor of the Gentiles, and when the Pauline position has won the day. His purpose is to show a new generation the close connection between Paul and the Jerusalem apostles. Consequently, for the sake of his narrative, Luke rearranges and telescopes events. When authors write with such different literary and theological purposes, it is not surprising that their narratives do not agree in every detail.

FOR REFERENCE AND FURTHER STUDY

Achtemeier, J. P. *The Quest for Unity in the New Testament Church: A Study in Paul and Acts.* Philadelphia: Fortress, 1987.
Krodel, G. *Acts.* Philadelphia: Fortress, 1981.
Mattill, A. J. "The Value of Acts as a Source for the Study of Paul." *Perspectives on Luke-Acts.* C. H. Talbert, ed. Edinburgh: T & T Clark, 1978.
Schmidt, A. "Das historische Datum des Apostelkonzils." *ZNW* 81 (1990) 122-131.

II: THE CHILDREN OF THE PROMISE (3:1-5:12)

The Spirit Did Not Come through Legal Works (3:1-6)

1. O foolish Galatians! Who bewitched you, before whose eyes Jesus Christ was publicly portrayed as crucified? 2. This alone I want to learn from you: did you receive the Spirit from legal works or from the message of faith? 3. Are you so foolish [as to think] that having begun with the Spirit you are now made perfect by the flesh? 4. Did you experience so many things in vain? If they really were in vain! 5. Therefore, does the One who is giving you the Spirit and working mighty deeds among you do so from legal works or from the message of faith? 6. In the same way, Abraham "believed God and it was counted to him as righteousness."

NOTES

1. *O foolish Galatians: Anoētoi* ("foolish") is also the Risen Lord's description of the two disciples on the road to Emmaus (Luke 24:25). The word is rendered by the NEB, REV, NAB, and NJB as "stupid." But in Rom 1:14 the same word is used in conjunction with "wise" (*sophros*) which suggests that its opposite is "foolish." Paul does not accuse the Galatians of lacking intelligence but of an inability or a refusal to recognize the real situation. For other uses of the word see 1 Tim 6:9; Titus 3:3.

Who bewitched you: After this phrase some manuscripts (C, D²) read "not to obey the truth." These words may have been added by scribes in light of a similar phrase in 5:7. Although Paul asks the Galatians who bewitched them, he is clearly referring to the same people mentioned in 1:7. This is the only occurrence of *baskainein* in the NT. It means to put someone under a spell, to bewitch someone as by an evil eye. See LXX Deut 28:54, 56 where the same word is used.

before whose eyes Jesus Christ was publicly portrayed as crucified: After *proegraphē* ("publicly portrayed") a few manuscripts (D, F, G) read "among you." The literal sense of *prographein* is "to write before," either in a temporal or spatial sense. See Rom 15:4; Eph 3:3; Jude 4. The phrase "before whose eyes" requires that the verb be translated in another sense: to proclaim publicly or to portray. Paul's preaching had the graphic effect of presenting the crucified Christ to the Galatians; his public proclamation served as a visual image of the crucified Messiah for them.

2. *This alone I want to learn from you*: Touto monon ("this alone") is placed at the beginning of the verse for emphasis. It suggests that the point of dispute between Paul and the Galatians will be settled if the Galatians honestly answer a single question. *Mathein* ("to learn") is often used in the sense of learn through instruction, or learn from someone. See Rom 16:17; 1 Cor 4:6; 14:31, 35. It is the verbal form of *mathētēs* ("disciple"). Here the sense is as in Acts 23:27, "to find out."

Did you receive the Spirit from legal works or from the message of faith: Paul opposes *ex ergōn nomou* ("from legal works") and *ex akoēs pisteōs* ("from the message of faith"). For the meaning of the first see the discussion of 2:16. The translation of the second expression is disputed since *akoē* and *pistis* can be rendered in different ways: *akoē* can mean hearing, or that which is heard, e.g., a message or report; *pistis* can mean the act of believing or that which is believed, e.g., the gospel. Thus the following four translations are possible: "from *hearing* with faith"; "from *hearing* the faith"; "from the *message* that results in believing"; "from the *message* of faith." The last translation has been adopted because the context suggests that Paul is opposing legal works and the gospel message of Christ's faithfulness to which he alludes in 3:1. This position is explained in the commentary. See the extended discussion S. Williams, "The Hearing of Faith: *AKOĒ PISTEŌS* in Galatians 3," and R. Hays, *The Faith of Jesus Christ*, 143–149, whose solution has been adopted here. Paul introduces the concept of *pneuma* ("spirit") for the first time. In Pauline thought, the Spirit is conceived of as "the miraculous divine power that stands in absolute contrast to all that is human." See Bultmann, *Theology of the New Testament*, vol 2, 153. The Spirit manifests itself in a person as mysterious and mighty, producing conduct which cannot be explained by merely human power. In Gal 4:6 the Spirit is identified as the Spirit of God's Son. It is the Spirit which enables the believer to live an ethical life. Thus believers are led by the Spirit (5:18) and walk by the Spirit (5:25), producing the fruit of the Spirit (5:22).

3. *Are you so foolish [as to think] that having begun with the Spirit you are now made perfect by the flesh*: Paul explains the reason for the Galatians' foolishness: having been brought into the eschatological realm of the Spirit, they seek perfection in the realm of the flesh. The verb *epiteleisthe* can be translated as a passive or middle. In the middle voice the sense is "are you now *ending* with the flesh" (NAB, NJB, RSV, NRSV). Construed as a passive, the sense is "do you now

look to the material *to make you perfect?"* (REV, NEB). The second translation has been chosen because the broader context of the letter suggests that the Galatians hope to gain something by circumcision: to perfect their faith. See Phil 1:6 where the same verbs, "begin" and "complete," are employed. Also, see 2 Cor 8:6. The phrase "as to think" has been added to render the Greek more clearly.

4. *Did you experience so many things in vain*: The verb *epathethe* can be translated either as "experience" or as "endure," depending upon how one interprets *tosauta* ("so many things"). If *tosauta* refers to persecutions, the translation would be "endure." But if it refers to the experiences of the Spirit, it is best translated "experience." Since Paul has been speaking of the Spirit, the latter translation has been chosen.

If they really were in vain: This is a literal translation of the Greek. The sense of the phrase is captured by the REB which translates the Greek as, "surely not!" The Galatians did not experience the Spirit in vain.

5. *Therefore, does the One who is giving you the Spirit and working mighty deeds among you do so from legal works or from the message of faith*: The One who supplies the Spirit and works mighty deeds is God. See 4:6 and 1 Thess 4:8 where God is the One who gives the Spirit. See 2:8 where the subject of *energēsas* ("working"), and 2 Cor 9:10 where the subject of *epichorēgōn* ("giving"), is God. The precise meaning of *dynameis* ("mighty deeds") is difficult to define. *En hymin* ("among you") suggests public manifestations of the Spirit which are probably to be understood as miraculous in nature. See Rom 15:19; 1 Cor 12:10, 28, 29 where the word is used in this sense. The present tense indicates that the granting of the Spirit is an ongoing experience in the life of the community.

6. *In the same way, Abraham*: There is disagreement about the placement of this verse. The *Novum Testamentum Graece*, RSV, NRSV, REV, and NJB make it the beginning of a new paragraph. The *Greek New Testament*, NEB, and NAB make it the conclusion of vv. 1-5. Here, *kathōs* is translated "in the same way" to indicate that Paul is making a comparison between the situation of the Galatians and that of Abraham. Thus this verse is viewed as the conclusion of vv. 1-5. While Abraham functions as an example of faith in Romans, in Galatians he is primarily viewed as the beneficiary of the promise. Outside of Romans and Galatians, the only reference to Abraham in Paul's writings is 2 Cor 11:22. Jewish tradition praised Abraham for his faithfulness to God's commandments (Gen 26:5; Sir 44:20; 1 Macc 2:52; Jub 21:2; Syr Bar 57:1-2), and James employs this text (Gen 15:6) to establish that a person is justified by works and not by faith alone (Jas 2:18-24). See G. W. Hansen, *Abraham in Galatians*, Appendix 2, "Abraham in Jewish Literature."

believed God and it was counted to him as righteousness: The quotation comes from Gen 15:6 and follows the LXX exactly. The verse belongs to a section in which God establishes a covenant with Abraham (Gen 15:1-7). Unlike the account of Genesis 17, however, circumcision does not play a role in this covenant, a point that Paul exploits in Romans 4, but not in Galatians. According to Gen 15:1-6, Abraham believed that his descendants would be as numerous as the stars, even though he was childless. *Logizomai* means to credit something to someone's account as in the case of wages credited to a worker. This is the only occurrence of the word in Galatians, but in Romans 4, where Paul also employs Gen 15:6, the word occurs eleven times. In Rom 4:4-12, Paul interprets the word to mean that when God "credited" righteousness to Abraham he granted it as a free gift, not as something earned. This is the second appearance of *dikaiosynē* ("righteousness," "justice," "uprightness") in Galatians. See 2:21. The noun expresses more than acquittal; it is the gift of God's justice.

INTERPRETATION

This unit (3:1-6) begins the second major portion of this letter (3:1–5:12). Having established the divine origin of his gospel and explained how he has remained faithful to the truth of the gospel (1:11–2:21), Paul draws out the consequences of the Torah-free gospel that he preaches. In this section (3:1–5:12) he provides the Galatians with specific reasons why they should not rely upon legal works such as circumcision. In 3:1-29, focusing upon the promise made to Abraham, Paul shows the Galatians that they are Abraham's true descendants because they already enjoy the Spirit and belong to Christ who is Abraham's promised seed. The Law does not supersede the promise made to Abraham nor was it intended to grant righteousness. Paul's exegesis of the Abraham story probably counters that of the agitators who have argued that only the circumcised are the true descendants of Abraham. Having made his counter-argument in 3:1-29, Paul employs a series of rebukes and appeals in 4:1–5:12 to dissuade the Galatians from adopting legal works. In 4:1-11 he warns them that they are in danger of returning to their minority by undertaking such works; in 4:12-20 he asks them to imitate his example; in 4:21-31, by means of an allegory, he urges them to cast out the agitators; and in 5:1-12 he warns them that if they are circumcised they will be cut off from Christ.

This unit consists of five rhetorical questions (vv. 1, 2, 3, 4, 5) and one verse (v. 6) which makes a comparison between the situation of Abraham and that of the Galatians. The correct answer to each question should be obvious to the Galatians, especially the question found in v. 2 and repeated in a slightly different form in v. 5: did the Galatians receive the Spirit *ex ergōn nomou* ("from legal works") or from *ex akoēs pisteōs* ("from the message of faith")? If the Galatians answer this question properly, they will recognize that there is no need for legal works, since they already have the Spirit *ex akoēs pisteōs*. The sharpness of Paul's opening statement is reminiscent of his rebuke in 1:6 ("I am astonished that you are so quickly turning . . . to a different gospel"). The Galatians have allowed themselves to fall under the spell of intruders who have promised them that they will attain a new level of perfection if they accept circumcision. In v. 3 Paul berates the Galatians for their foolishness. Not only have they *foolishly* fallen under the spell of the agitators; now they are so *foolish* as to think that having received the Spirit they can be perfected by the flesh, that is, the mark of circumcision.

Paul reprimands the Galatians for falling under the spell of the agitators, but the logic of the agitators' argument must have been compelling to them. Circumcision was the sign by which male Jews entered the covenant. Without it, one could not be a full member of the covenant people.

> This is my covenant which you shall keep, between me and you and your offspring after you: Every male among you shall be circumcised. . . . Any uncircumcised male who is not circumcised in the flesh of his foreskin shall be cut off from his people; he has broken my covenant (Gen 17:10-14).

Furthermore, Abraham was viewed as a model of Law observance, even though he lived before the Mosaic Law was promulgated.

> Abraham was the great father of a multitude of nations, and no one has been found like him in glory. *He kept the law of the Most High*, and entered into a covenant with him; *he certified the covenant in his flesh*, and when he was tested he proved faithful. Therefore the Lord assured him with an oath that the nations would be blessed through his offspring; that he would make him as numerous as the dust of the earth, and exalt his offspring like the stars, and give them an inheritance from sea to sea and from the Euphrates to the ends of the earth (Sir 44:19-21).

In light of these texts, one can understand why the Galatians were seduced by the agitators. Having become believers by accepting the gospel message, the Galatians viewed legal works as a means of full participation in the everlasting covenant God made with Abraham and as a way of perfecting their faith.

Paul's response is to remind the Galatians of his missionary preaching among them and its results. They were converted when he proclaimed the message of the crucified Christ ("'before whose eyes Christ Jesus was publicly portrayed as crucified"). The focus of this preaching was not legal works but the faithfulness of Jesus Christ who gave himself on behalf of their sins (1:4), who loved them and handed himself over for them (2:20), who became a curse for them (3:13), who was born under the Law and sent by God to redeem them from the Law (4:5-6). The result of this message, in which they put their trust, was a dramatic outpouring of the Spirit that was manifested within the Galatian community through miraculous deeds (*dynameis*). Paul's argument, therefore, is simple. How and when did the Galatians receive the Spirit: *ex ergōn nomou* or *ex akoēs pisteōs?* The answer, of course, is *ex akoēs pisteōs*. But what does this phrase mean?

The notes of this commentary indicate that *ex akoēs pisteōs* can be construed in at least four ways: from hearing with faith; from hearing the faith; from the message that results in faith; and from the message of faith. Most translations put the emphasis upon the act of believing: "*faith in what you heard*" (NAB); "*believing what you heard*" (NRSV); "*believing the gospel message*" (RSV). The effect of these translations is to draw a comparison between the faith of Abraham and the faith of the Galatians: just as Abraham believed and was declared righteous, so the Galatians believed and received the Spirit.

There is, of course, an important parallel between the faith of Abraham and that of the Galatians, but the opening verse of this unit, "before whose eyes Jesus Christ was publicly portrayed as crucified," suggests that Paul's primary focus is upon God's activity, proclaimed in the message of faith that Paul preached to the Galatians and in which they believed. It was Christ's faith, preached by Paul and believed by the Galatians, that resulted in the Spirit. Thus the contrast is not simply between two human activities, *doing* works and *believing* in Christ, but between the human and the divine: *doing* works and the *work* of Christ in whom the Galatians have believed. In other words, *ek akoēs pisteōs* should be read in light of *ex pisteōs Christou* (2:16). The message of faith in which the Galatians have believed is the report about the faithfulness of the Christ. See R. Hays, *The Faith of Jesus Christ*, 147.

Having reminded the Galatians that they received the Spirit from the message of faith in which they believed, Paul draws a comparison in v. 6 between their situation and that of Abraham. Just as Abraham was justified by the God in whom he believed, so the Galatians received the Spirit from the message of faith (the faith of Christ) in which they believed. Abraham was not declared righteous because of legal works, and the Galatians did not receive the Spirit because of legal works. In both instances the determining factor was the prior act of God. In the case of Abraham it was God's promise, in the case of the Galatians it was the message of the crucified Christ. In both instances there was the necessary response of faith.

> Abraham: God's Promise . . . Faith . . . Righteousness
> Galatians: Messsage of Faith . . . Faith . . . Spirit

When the Galatians received the Spirit, therefore, they were in a situation similar to that of Abraham. And just as righteousness was a free gift from the God in whom Abraham believed, so the Spirit was a free gift bestowed because of the message of faith in which the Galatians believed, apart from legal works.

For Reference and Further Study

Byrne, B. *'Sons of God'-'Seed of Abraham'*: A Study of the Idea of the Sonship of God of All Christians in Paul Against the Jewish Background. AnBib 83; Rome: Biblical Institute Press, 1979.

Cosgrove, C. H. *The Cross and the Spirit: A Study in the Argument and Theology of Galatians*. Macon: GA: Mercer University Press, 1988.

Elliott, J. H. "Paul, Galatians, and the Evil Eye." *CurrTheo/Miss* 17 (1990) 262–273.

Hays, R. B. *The Faith of Jesus Christ: An Investigation of the Narrative Structure of Galatians 3:1–4:11*. SBLDS 56; Chico: CA: Scholars Press, 1983.

Lull, D. J. *The Spirit in Galatia: Paul's Interpretation of Pneuma as Divine Power*. SBLDS 49; Scholars Press, 1980.

Neyrey, J. H. "Bewitched in Galatia: Paul and Cultural Anthropology," *CBQ* 50 (1988) 72–100.

Williams, S. "The Hearing of Faith: AKOĒ PISTEŌS," *NTS* 35 (1989) 82–93.

The People of Faith Are Abraham's Descendants (3:7-14)

7. Know, then, that people of faith, these are Abraham's sons. 8. Because Scripture foresaw that God would justify the Gentiles from faith, it proclaimed the gospel in advance to Abraham that "all the Gentiles will be blessed in you." 9. For this reason, people of faith are blessed with faithful Abraham. 10. All who rely on legal works are under a curse, for it is written, "Cursed be everyone who does not persevere in doing everything written in the Book of the Law." 11. It is clear that no one is justified before God by the Law because "the just one will live from faith." 12. But the Law is not based on faith, rather "the one who does them will live by them." 13. Christ redeemed us from the curse of the Law, becoming a curse on our behalf, for it is written, "cursed be everyone hanged on a tree," 14. in order that the blessing of Abraham might be extended to the Gentiles in Christ Jesus, and in order that we might receive the promised Spirit through the faith.

Notes

7. *Know, then, that people of faith, these are Abraham's sons*: "People of faith" renders *hoi ek pisteōs*, which literally translated is "the ones from faith." The only other place that the phrase occurs is in v. 9. In Rom 4:14 Paul uses a similar phrase in regard to the Law, *hoi ek nomou*. Most translators take the phrase as a description of people who believe: "those who have faith" (NAB); "those who believe" (NRSV, NIV); "those who have faith" (REB). While

the people who belong to this group are believers, the broader context of this letter suggests that *hoi ek pisteōs* are the ones from Christ-faith, that is, those who have been saved from and through the faith of Jesus Christ and so have believed in Jesus Christ (see 2:16). On this point consult the discussion on the faith of Jesus Christ in 2:15-21. When Paul employs the expressions *ek pisteōs* (3:8, 11, 12, 24; 5:5) and *dia pisteōs* (3:14, 26), they should be interpreted in light of the faith of Jesus Christ, without prejudice to the personal faith of the believer. *Hyioi Abraam* has been translated literally as "sons of Abraham" because the theme of sonship is so central to this section (3:7, 26; 4:4, 6, 7, 22, 30). It is clear from 3:26-29, however, that Paul's thought includes both men and women. The emphatic *houtoi* ("these") emphasizes this sonship, perhaps because the agitators taught that only the circumcised are Abraham's offspring.

8. *Because Scripture foresaw that God would justify the Gentiles from faith, it proclaimed the gospel in advance to Abraham*: *Hē graphē* refers to the Scriptures as a whole. Here and in 3:22, and perhaps 4:30, Scripture is personified. See Rom 4:3; 9:17. Just as David "foresaw" the Messiah's resurrection (Acts 2:31), so Scripture "foresaw" (*proïdousa*) that God would justify the Gentiles. The means by which God justifies is *ek pisteōs*, literally, "from faith." While this includes personal faith, the primary focus is upon the faith of Jesus Christ. See the discussion above. This is the only instance of *proeuaggelizomai* in the NT. In the rest of Galatians Paul employs *euaggelizein* when referring to the preaching of the gospel.

that "all the Gentiles will be blessed in you": The quotation is part of God's promise to Abraham in Gen 12:3. But whereas Gen 12:3 reads "*all the tribes of the earth* will be blessed in you," Paul writes *panta ta ethnē* ("all the nations") as in Gen 18:18 ("and through him all the nations of the earth will be blessed"). Here *ethnē* has been rendered as "Gentiles" because the nations are the Gentiles, and the Gentiles are Paul's primary concern. For other instances of the promise to Abraham see Gen 12:1-3, 7; 13:14-17; 15:5-6, 18; 17:4-8, 16; 18:18; 22:17-18.

9. *For this reason, people of faith are blessed with faithful Abraham*: The adjective *pistos* ("faithful") does not occur frequently in Paul's writings. It can refer to God (1 Cor 1:9; 10:13; 2 Cor 1:18; 1 Thess 5:24) or human beings (1 Cor 4:2,17; 2 Cor 6:15). This is the only time that it is used in Galatians, and the only time that it is applied to Abraham. As in v. 7, *hoi ek pisteōs* are those who have been justified by the faith of Jesus Christ and so believe in him.

10. *All who rely on legal works are under a curse*: "All who rely on the works of the Law" translates *hosoi ex ergōn nomou* (literally, "all from works of Law") and forms a contrast with *hoi ek pisteōs* in vv. 7, 9. *Ex ergōn nomou* occurs three times in 2:16, as well as in 3:2, 5. In the last two cases it is contrasted with *ex akoēs pisteōs*. The phrase also occurs in Rom 3:20, 28. In Rom 9:12, 32 Paul employs *ex ergōn* as does Eph 2:9. In Ephesians the shorter phrase envisions a legalistic attitude, but in Galatians *ex ergōn nomou* refers primarily to circumcision, dietary laws, and Jewish festival observances. This is the only occurrence of *katara* ("curse") in the Pauline writings (3:10, 13). Paul is clearly

establishing a contrast between the blessing of Abraham and the curse of the Law.

for it is written, "Cursed be everyone who does not persevere in doing everything written in the Book of the Law": The quotation is taken from Deut 27:26 and, except for a few changes, follows the LXX which reads "Cursed be every *human* who does not persevere in doing all the *words of this law*." The quotation is the last of twelve curses which were part of a covenant ceremony that the Israelites were to perform upon entering the Promised Land. The Levites were to declare a series of commands, each one bearing a curse for those who disobeyed it. After each command the people were to respond "Amen." R. Yates ("Saint Paul and the Law in Galatians," 111) notes that "Whereas the M. T. and the LXX speak of 'this Torah,' meaning the section of the twelve curses, Paul broadens its meaning to 'the book of the law' as such, meaning the entire pentateuchal corpus, with its 613 prescriptions." In the Greek text *tou poiēsai auta* ("to do them") is in an emphatic position at the end of the sentence.

11. *It is clear that no one is justified before God by the Law*: "By the Law," translates *en nomō* which is capable of a locative or instrumental sense ("in the Law," "by the Law"). "Before God" indicates that although a person may appear to be just in the sight of humans, this is not necessarily the case before God. See Phil 3:6 where Paul boasts of his former righteousness according to the Law.

because "the just one will live from faith": The quotation comes from Hab 2:4 and is also employed in Rom 1:17. However, it differs from both the LXX and the MT. The LXX reads, "But the righteous shall live by *my* faith," and the MT, "But the righteous shall live by *his* faith." By omitting the possessive pronouns, Paul leaves the quotation ambiguous. The Greek text can mean that the one made righteous by faith will live, or that the just one will live by faith. The second interpretation has been chosen here because Paul has been developing the theme of Christ's faith. He employs the passage from Habakkuk to show that the just person lives from or by the faith of Jesus Christ in whom he or she believes. Cosgrove (*The Cross and the Spirit*, 56–59) and Hays (*The Faith of Jesus Christ*, 207) argue that the early Church applied the passage to the Messiah with the understanding that the just one is Jesus.

12. *But the Law is not based on faith*: "Based on faith" translates *ek pisteōs* which refers to the faith of Christ on the basis of which one believes in Christ.

rather "the one who does them will live by them": The quotation comes from Lev 18:5 and differs slightly from the LXX and MT which read: "You shall keep my statutes and my ordinances: *by doing so one shall live*. I am the Lord." The quotation belongs to a larger section of Leviticus (18:1-20) which enumerates twelve sexual prohibitions. While Leviticus emphasizes that one will receive life by doing the Law, Paul focuses upon the aspect of doing which attends the Law. This quotation, like Hab 2:4, contains the word *zēsetai* ("will live") which allows Paul to bring the two texts together and compare them.

13. *Christ redeemed us from the curse of the Law*: *Exagorazein* ("to redeem") occurs twice in the undisputed Pauline writings. In both instances it is used in refer-

ence to the Law. Christ redeems humanity from the Law's curse (Gal 3:13), and God sends his Son to redeem those under the Law (Gal 4:5). Paul views "being under the Law" as a kind of slavery from which one must be ransomed. The pronoun *hēmas* ("us") refers to Jewish believers who have lived under the curse of the Law. The redemption of the Jew precedes that of the Gentile. See T. L. Donaldson, "The 'Curse of the Law' and the Inclusion of the Gentiles: Galatians 3:13-14."

becoming a curse on our behalf: Paul envisions a divine interchange: Christ assumes humanity's situation so that humanity can assume his situation. See 2 Cor 5:21, "For our sake he made him to be sin who knew no sin," and Rom 8:3, "sending his own Son in the likeness of sinful flesh."

for it is written, "cursed be everyone hanged on a tree": The quotation comes from Deut 21:23 which, in the LXX, reads *hoti kekatēramenos hypo theou pas kremamenos epi zylou* "because *cursed by God* is everyone hung on a tree." Deut 21:23 originally referred to the practice of hanging the corpse of a deceased criminal on a tree in order to disgrace it. The corpse, however, had to be removed before nightfall lest it defile the land. By the NT period the expression "to hang on a tree" was understood as crucifixion (Acts 5:30). Jesus, therefore, died under a curse because he was crucified, i.e., hung on a tree. Paul applies the quotation to Jesus, omitting the phrase "cursed by God" to show that he died under the curse of the Law in order to free those under the curse of the Law (3:10).

14. *in order that the blessing of Abraham might be extended to the Gentiles in Christ Jesus*: This is the first of two purpose clauses which explain Christ's redemptive work. "The blessing of Abraham" is found in Gen 22:17-18, "I will indeed bless you, and I will make your offspring as numerous as the stars of heaven and as the sand that is on the seashore. And your offspring shall possess the gate of their enemies, and by your offspring shall all the nations of the earth gain blessing for themselves, because you have obeyed my voice." In Gen 28:4 Isaac refers to "the blessing of Abraham," saying to Jacob, "May he give you *the blessing of Abraham*, to you and your offspring with you, so that you may take possession of the land where you now live as an alien— land that God gave to Abraham." Paul sees the fulfilment of the blessing through the Spirit. Abraham has become the father of innumerable descendants because the gift of the Spirit has made the Gentiles his descendants.

and in order that we might receive the promised Spirit through the faith: Under the influence of *eulogia* in the previous clause, some manuscripts (P46, D*, F, G) replace *epaggelian* ("promise") with *eulogian* ("blessing"). This purpose clause is coordinated with the first, not subordinated to it. While the first clause clearly refers to the Gentiles, this one includes Jewish believers as well as Gentiles. Having been acquitted, Jew and Gentile receive the eschatological gift of the promised Spirit. This is the first occurrence of *epaggelia*, a theme which will become a leitmotif in what follows (3:16, 17, 18, 21, 22, 29; 4:23, 28). In Rom 4:13 Paul interprets the content of the promise in a more traditional sense: Abraham and his descendants will inherit the world. But here the promise refers to the gift of the Spirit, as it does in Acts 2:32. The promised

Spirit is mediated *dia tēs pisteōs* ("through the faith"). This faith is the faith of Jesus Christ in whom the Gentiles now believe.

INTERPRETATION

Thus far, Paul has argued that there is no need for the Galatians to take up legal works because they have already received the Spirit from the message about Christ's faith in which they have believed. Legal works cannot bring them anything that they do not already have. Furthermore, Paul has shown the Galatians that there is a similarity between their situation and that of Abraham: just as Abraham believed God's promise and was justified, so they believed the message of faith and received the Spirit. Having introduced Abraham into the discussion in the last unit, in this unit Paul takes up the question of Abraham's descendants. Who are Abraham's sons and daughters? Paul's answer is *hoi ek pisteōs* ("people of faith"). Such people have received the blessings of Abraham and the promised Spirit; they are Abraham's descendants in Christ.

The structure of this unit is clearly defined. *Hoi ek pisteōs* encloses vv. 7-9 which develop the theme of the blessing of Abraham, while *epikataratos* ("cursed") forms a bracket around vv. 10-13 which develop the theme of the curse of the Law from which Christ has redeemed us. Verse 14 draws out the logical conclusion from what Paul has been saying in vv. 1-13. The structure is as follows.

> vv. 7-9   the blessing of Abraham
> vv. 10-13   the curse of the Law
> v. 14   the blessing of Abraham and the promised Spirit

Except for the allegory of Hagar and Sarah (4:21-30), no other section of Galatians draws as extensively from Scripture as does this unit. In v. 8 Paul quotes from Gen 12:3; in v. 10 from Deut 27:26; in v. 11 from Hab 2:4; in v. 12 from Lev 18:5; and in v. 13 from Deut 21:23. The last four quotations are related to each other by a series of verbal contacts. Thus *epikataratos* ("cursed") occurs in Deut 27:26 and Deut 21:23, and *zēsetai* ("will live") in Hab 2:4 and Lev 18:5, allowing Paul to compare texts which share a common word. In a similar fashion, *poiein* ("to do") appears in Deut 27:26 and Lev 18:5 bringing these texts together as well. By relating one text to another, Paul is able to interpret Scripture by Scripture. Thus he interprets the curse of Deut 27:26 by the curse mentioned in Deut 21:23. On the basis of the verb "to live," he shows that God's justice operates on the principle of faith (Hab 2:5) while the Law is based on the principle of doing (Lev 18:5). The "doing" of Lev 18:5, in turn, is related to the curse, mentioned in Deut 26:27, that comes upon those who do not "do" the Law.

v. 10 *Cursed* be everyone who does not persevere in *doing* everything
       written in the Book of the Law.
v. 11 The just one *will live* from faith.
v. 12 The one who *does* them *will live* by them.
v. 13 *Cursed* be everyone hung on a tree.

One may ask how the Galatians, who were Gentiles, could be expected
to be familiar with such a variety of scriptural texts. The most probable
explanation is that the agitators, in their endeavor to persuade the Galatians to be circumcised, had already employed some of these texts as well
as the story of Abraham. (See C. Cosgrove *The Cross and the Spirit*, 87–118.)
Thus the agitators may have told the Galatians that they would attain
a fuller share in the life of the Spirit, and be numbered among Abraham's
descendants, if they did what Abraham did: observe the Law and certify
the covenant through circumcision (Sir 44:20; Gen 17:10). The texts of
Lev 18:5 ("the one who *does* them *will live* by them") and Deut 27:26
("Cursed be everyone who does not persevere in doing everything written in the Book of the Law") were probably employed by the agitators.
Thus the agitators would have told the Galatians that life comes from
doing the Law (Lev 18:5) while those who fail *to do* the Law are under
a curse (Deut 27:26). If this was the case, Paul countered the argument
of the agitators by showing that faith is the true source of life (Hab 2:4)
because Christ has freed us from the curse of the Law (Deut 21:23).

The contrast that Paul establishes between *hoi ek pisteōs* and *hosoi ex
ergōn* is important for understanding this unit. These expressions refer
to two categories of people (see notes). But who are they? Because Abraham plays such a prominent role in this passage, many assume that the
first expression refers to those who believe as opposed to those who rely
on the power of their own works. While this analysis is true, it does not
express the full truth. This commentary has already argued that Paul is
not primarily concerned with the problem of legalism, as if the agitators
or the Galatians thought that they could or had to earn their salvation.
Moreover, the analysis of 2:16 has shown that Christian faith is rooted
in the faith of Jesus Christ. Consequently, here Paul draws a contrast between two kinds of people. *Hoi ek pisteōs* are those who have been justified by the faith of Jesus Christ and now put their faith in him, e.g., Paul's
converts. *Hosoi ex ergōn*, by contrast, still seek their justification in Torah;
they are best represented by the agitators themselves. Paul will argue that
because the Galatians belong to the first group they share the blessing
of Abraham.

The Blessing of Abraham (vv. 7–9). This is the shorter of the two subunits,
but it establishes Paul's principal argument. In v. 7, he forcefully reminds
the Galatians that *hoi ek pisteōs* are Abraham's sons and daughters. The
emphatic manner by which the verse begins suggests that the agitators

have argued another position: those who are circumcised and practice legal works are Abraham's descendants.

In v. 8 Paul says that God had always intended to justify the Gentiles *ek pisteōs*, and for that reason the gospel was preached in advance to Abraham. This phrase, *ek pisteōs*, should be read in light of *ek pisteōs Christou* (2:16). Seen in this light, it carries a meaning that includes, but goes beyond, the faith of the believer: God intended to justify the Gentiles by the faith of Christ in whom the Gentiles would believe. The quotation which follows, "all the Gentiles will be blessed in you" (Gen 12:3), shows that Paul sees a relationship between the gospel and the salvation of the Gentiles. But what is this relationship? As the rest of this chapter will show, the Gentiles received the blessing of Abraham by being incorporated into Christ (3:29), Abraham's seed. When God promised Abraham that all the nations would be blessed in him, therefore, He was already announcing, albeit in a hidden way, the coming of Christ.

In v. 9 Paul draws his conclusion, "for this reason, people of faith are blessed with faithful Abraham." "For this reason" (*hōste*) refers to God's promise to Abraham. In other words, *hoi ek pisteōs* are blessed with Abraham because they are Abraham's promised descendants. Paul moves from faith to blessing in the following way.

v. 7 The Gentiles are Abraham's descendants because they are *hoi ek pisteōs*.

v. 8 God promised Abraham that all the Gentiles would be *blessed* in him.

v. 9 Therefore, the Gentiles are *blessed* with Abraham because they are *hoi ek pisteōs*.

To summarize, Paul argues that those who belong to the community of faith established on the basis of Christ-faith, and so believe in Christ, have received the blessing of Abraham.

The curse of the Law (vv. 10–13). Having shown the Galatians that they are blessed with Abraham, Paul focuses upon the curse pronounced against those who are *ex ergōn nomou*. The argument here consists of four scriptural quotations. Beginning with a text from Deut 27:26, Paul argues in v. 10 that all who are *ex ergōn nomou* are under a curse. The text of Deut 27:26 is the last of a series of twelve curses that were part of a covenant ceremony which the Israelites were to perform upon entering the Promised Land. This twelfth and final curse pronounced a curse against those who violated any of the previous eleven prescriptions (Deut 27:15-25). Paul, however, takes the text of Deut 27:26 in a broader sense by applying it to the prescriptions of the entire Mosaic Law. Moreover, Paul seems to imply that everyone under the Law is under this curse since no one perfectly fulfills all of the prescriptions of the Law. In v. 13 Paul will argue that Christ freed us from this curse, but before doing so he employs two other texts to demonstrate that life comes from Christ-faith, not legal observance.

In vv. 11–12 Paul contrasts the texts of Hab 2:4 ("The just one will live from faith") and Lev 18:5 ("the one who does them will live by them"). As noted above, the two texts are related to each other by the verb "to live." Leviticus promises life to those who *do* the Law while Habakuk proclaims that the just one lives *from faith*. Since no one, however, fulfills the Law perfectly, the true source of life must be faith. The just one lives *ek pisteōs*, that is, from the faith of Christ in whom the just one believes. Thus no one is justified before God by the Law because the Law is based upon the principle of doing, and no one perfectly fulfills the Law. Moreover, in 3:21 Paul will affirm that it was never the purpose of the Law to give life. Righteousness can only come *ek pisteōs*, from the faith of Christ on the basis of which one believes.

Having established that life comes from faith and not legal observance, Paul returns to the line of argument begun in v. 10, that those who are under the Law are under a curse. Here, employing the text of Deut 21:23, he argues that the purpose of Christ's death was to free us from the curse of the Law. Since all those under the Law are under a curse, Christ came to do what humanity could not do by legal observance. Dying upon a cross ("hung on a tree"), he assumed the curse of the Law on behalf of us. While the pronoun *hēmōn* ("us") could include Gentiles as well as Jews, Paul probably has only the Jews in mind since only they were under the Law. In other words, Paul argues that the Messiah came to redeem his own people from the curse of the Law. The implication, therefore, is that it would be foolish for the Galatians to assume the very curse from which the Messiah freed Israel by adopting the Law. In effect, Paul makes the following argument. "We Jews were under the curse of the Law. This Law could not bring us life because it operates on the principle of doing, not on the principle of Christ-faith, and no one perfectly fulfills the Law. The Christ in whom we believe, however, freed us from the Law's curse by assuming the curse of the Law for us. How foolish for you Galatians to place yourself under the very curse from which Christ came to set us free."

The blessings of Abraham and the promised Spirit (v. 14). In this verse, consisting of two purpose clauses, Paul draws out the implications of Christ's death for Gentile as well as Jew. The Messiah's work of redeeming Israel from the curse of the Law has redemptive benefits for the Gentiles as well. First, in Christ, the Gentiles now enjoy the blessings of Abraham. Second, all have received the promised Spirit *dia tēs pisteōs*, literally, "through *the* faith." This awkward expression indicates that Paul has more in mind than the act of believing. The Spirit comes through "the faith," that is, the faith of Christ on the basis of which both Gentile and Jew believe.

How has God fulfilled the promise to Abraham? The answer is "through the Spirit." Through the Spirit Abraham has gained innumerable children from among the Gentiles. The Gentiles have become Abraham's descendants through the Spirit which they have received on the basis of the faith of Jesus Christ in whom they believe.

FOR REFERENCE AND FURTHER STUDY

Cosgrove C. H. *The Cross and the Spirit.* Macon, GA.: Mercer, 1988.
Dahl, N. A. "Contradictions in Scripture." *Studies in Paul.* Minneapolis: Augsburg, 1977.
Donaldson, T. L. "The 'Curse of the Law' and the Inclusion of the Gentiles: 3:13-14." *NTS* 32 (1986) 94–112.
Dunn, J. D. G. "Works of the Law and Curse of the Law (Gal 3.10-14)." *NTS* 31 (1985) 523–42.
Hamerton-Kelly, R. G. "Sacred Violence and the Curse of the Law (Galatians 3:13): The Death of Christ as a Sacrificial Travesty." *NTS* 36 (1990) 98–118.
Hansen, G. W. *Abraham in Galatians: Epistolary and Rhetorical Contexts.* JSNTSS 29; Sheffield: JSOT Press, 1989.
Sanders, E. P. *Paul and the Law, and the Jewish People.* Philadelphia: Fortress, 1983.
Schreiner, T. R. "Is Perfect Obedience to the Law Possible? A Reexamination of Galatians 3:10." *JETS* 27 (1984) 151–160.
Schwartz, D. R. "Two Pauline Allusions to the Redemptive Mechanism of the Crucifixion." *JBL* 102 (1983) 259–268.
Stanley, C. D. " 'Under a Curse': A Fresh Reading of Galatians 3.10-14." *NTS* 36 (1990) 481–511.
Williams, S. K. "Justification and the Spirit in Galatians." *JSNT* 29 (1987) 91–100.
Williams, S. K. "Promise in Galatians: A Reading of Paul's Reading of Scripture." *JBL* 107 (1988) 709–720.

The Law Does Not Annul the Promise (3:15-20)

15. Brethren, I am speaking in a human fashion. No one annuls or adds to someone's legally ratified testament. 16. The promises were spoken to Abraham and to his seed. It does not say, "and to the seeds," as if to many, but as to one, "and to your seed," who is Christ. 17. This is what I am saying. The Law which came 430 years later does not annul the testament ratified beforehand by God so as to cancel the promise.

18. For if the inheritance is based on Law, it no longer derives from promise. But God graciously granted it to Abraham through promise. 19. Then why the Law? It was added for the sake of transgressions until the seed should come to whom the promise was made. It was promulgated through angels by the hand of a mediator. 20. A mediator is not a mediator of one, but God is one.

NOTES

15. *Brethren, I am speaking in a human fashion*: In 3:1 Paul called the Galatians "foolish." Now, for the first time since 1:11, he calls them *adelphoi* ("brethren"). Rhetorically, the term reminds the Galatians of their close relationship to the Apostle. Even though the Galatians have been unfaithful to the gospel preached by Paul, the profound bond of union which unites them with Paul in Christ has not yet been broken. *Adelphoi* is used again in 4:12, 28, 31; 5:11, 13; 6:1, 18. *Kata Anthrōpon* ("in a human fashion") can mean that Paul is employing an example from everyday life. Thus the REB reads "let me give you an illustration." C. H. Cosgrove, ("Arguing Like a Mere Human Being"), however, argues that the expression is not neutral but refers to something that is merely human (Rom 3:5; Gal 1:11; 1 Cor 3:3; 9:8). That is, Paul will express a merely human position which he attributes to the agitators: God annulled the promise that He made to Abraham by issuing the Law. Because this implies that God has been unfaithful to His word, Paul calls his speech at this point *kata anthrōpon*.

No one annuls or adds to someone's legally ratified testament: This is the only occurrence of *epidiatassomai* ("to add a codicil") in the NT. *Diathēkē* is translated as "testament." In the LXX it translates the Hebrew *bĕrît* ("covenant"). The LXX may have rendered *bĕrît* as *diathēkē* because the covenant, like a will, is the declaration of an individual, not a mutual agreement between two parties. Paul uses *diathēkē* in the sense of covenant in Rom 9:4; 11:27. In 1 Cor 11:25 and 2 Cor 3:6, he speaks of the *new* covenant, and in 2 Cor 3:14 of the *old* covenant. In this section he plays on the double meaning of *diathēkē*: God's testament to Abraham is the covenant made with him (v. 17). The precise background for Paul's thought is not known since Roman and Greek law allowed a testament to be changed before the death of the testator. E. Bammel ("Gottes *DIATHĒKĒ*") contends that Paul has in mind a Jewish institution called the *mattenat bari* which permitted a person to make an irrevocable testament. G. A. Taylor ("The Function of *Pistis Christou* in Galatians") argues for a Roman testamentary device called *fidei commissum*.

16. *The promises were spoken to Abraham and to his seed*: Here, and in 3:21, Paul employs the plural *epaggeliai* ("promises"), but in 3:14, 17, 18, 22, 29, 4:28) he uses the singular. Schlier (*Galaterbrief*, 143) suggests that the promises refer to the three promises found in Genesis 17:1-9: the fruitfulness of Abraham and his seed (Gen 17:2, 4, 5, 6); the eternal possession of the land (Gen 17:8); and the Lord's promise to be God to Abraham and his seed (17:7).

It does not say, "and to the seeds," as if to many, but as to one, "and to your seed": The Genesis accounts speak of Abraham's descendants as his *spermati* ("seed," Gen 12:7; 13:15; 17:7; 24:7). In Genesis the noun usually functions collectively making the plural *spermasin* ("seeds") unnecessary. In some instances, however, Abraham's seed is understood to apply primarily to Isaac (17:21; 22:16-17; 24:7). Paul's exegesis is radically new because it interprets the text in reference to Christ.

who is Christ: Christ is used as a proper name as in 2:19, 20; 4:19. But some manuscripts (D*) make it a title, "the Christ." This phrase functions like an interpretative formula: Christ is Abraham's seed.

17. *This is what I am saying. The Law which came 430 years later*: The Law (*nomos*) is the Mosaic Law given to the Israelites on Mount Sinai. Exod 12:40 says that the Israelites dwelt in Egypt 430 years, whereas Gen 15:13 and Acts 7:6 speak of a 400 year period. The rabbis resolved the difference by saying that the 400 years of Gen 15:13 are to be reckoned from Isaac's birth, and the 430 years of Exod 12:40 are to be reckoned from the day on which God spoke the promise (Str-B, 2:688). In 4:10 Paul accuses the Galatians of observing days, months, seasons, and years. Here, however, he uses calculations from the Law to demonstrate the inferiority of the Law to the promise. See D. Lührmann, "Die 430 Jahre zwischen den Verheissungen und dem Gesetz (Gal 3,17)."

does not annul the testament ratified beforehand by God: Some manuscripts (D, F, G) make explicit what is implicit in the text by adding *eis Christon* ("unto Christ") after "by God." *Diathēkē* ("testament") is used ten times in Gen 17:1-14 to speak of the covenant God established with Abraham. Genesis records two accounts of God's covenant with Abraham (15:1-21; 17:1-27). Although Paul does not distinguish between them, he probably has the account of Genesis 17, which explicitly mentions circumcision, in mind. It is significant that while Paul says that the testament was ratified by God, he does not speak of God as the author of the Law.

so as to cancel the promise: The promise is the testament made to Abraham. Thus *epaggelia* ("promise") and *diathēkē* ("testament") are interchangeable. The promise to Abraham, according to v. 14, finds its fulfillment in the Spirit.

18. *For if the inheritance is based on Law, it no longer derives from promise*: P46 has *dia nomou* ("through the Law") rather than *ek nomou* which is translated "based on the Law." Paul employs an unreal condition to establish his point. If the inheritance came from the Law, then it would follow that it does not come from the promise made to Abraham. But this cannot be since God graciously granted the inheritance by promise to Abraham. Here *ek nomou* and *ex epaggelias* ("from promise") are contrasted. See Rom 11:6 where a similar contrast occurs between grace and works. This is the only use of *klēronomia* in the undisputed Pauline writings. The inheritance is the promised Spirit mentioned in v. 14. See Eph 1:13-14 which speaks "of the promised Holy Spirit, the guarantee of our inheritance."

But God graciously granted it to Abraham through promise: The verb *kecharistai* ("granted"), in the perfect tense, points to the gracious and enduring aspect of God's promise to Abraham. The same verb is employed in 1 Cor 2:12: "Now we have received not the spirit of the world, but the Spirit that is from God, so that we might understand the gifts bestowed on us (*charisthenta*) by God."

19. *Then why the Law?*: The Greek can be translated, "Then *what* is the Law?" or "Then *why* the Law?" since *ti* can be taken as a pronoun ("what") or as an adverb ("why"). The context, however, indicates that Paul is referring to the function of the Law. This question is not the beginning of a new unit but the outcome of what Paul has said thus far. If the inheritance comes through the promise, what is the function of the Law?

It was added for the sake of transgressions: The unexpressed subject of *prosetethē* ("it was added") is God. God added the Law, but the Law was not part of the original promise to Abraham. This is the only occurrence of *prostithēmi* ("to add") in Paul's writings. D* reads "traditions" (*paradoseōn*) in place of "transgressions," others (F, G, P46) read "acts" (*praxeōn*). The preposition *charin* can have either a causal or telic sense: the Law was added because of transgressions, i.e., to control them; or the Law was added for the purpose of transgressions. The second interpretation, moreover, can be taken in two ways: for the purpose of provoking transgressions, or for the purpose of identifying or making transgressions known. The latter interpretation is adopted here. A transgression is the violation of a specific commandment; where there is no law there is no transgression (Rom 4:15). It was only through the Law that sin was made known (Rom 3:20; 5:13; 5:20; 7:7-8, 13).

until the seed should come to whom the promise was made: Achris ("until") indicates that the purpose of the Law ends with the coming of the Christ. Thus Paul views the Law as having a beginning (430 years after the promise) and an end (the coming of the promised seed). Jewish tradition, however, viewed the Law as eternal (Wis 18:4; 2 Esdr 9:37). The seed (*sperma*) is Christ already identified as Abraham's descendant (v. 16). The occurrence of *sperma* here indicates that this verse is part of the unit begun at v. 15. N. Dahl ("Contradictions in Scripture," 72) sees an allusion to Gen 49:10 here ("until he comes to whom it belongs"). "The promise was made" translates *epēggeltai* ("it was promised"), the unexpressed subject of which is God.

It was promulgated through angels: According to Exod 31:18 Moses received the Law from God; there is no mention of angels. Later tradition, however, spoke of angels present at the giving of the Law or as the ones through whom the Law was given. Deut 33:2 (LXX) speaks of a myriad of angels at the Lord's right when he came from Sinai as does Ps 68:17, and Josephus (*Ant* 15:136) says, "we have learned from God the most excellent of our doctrines, and the most holy part of our law, by angels or ambassadors. . . ." A similar line of thought is found in Acts 7:38, 53 and Heb 2:2. While these traditions understand the role of the angels as enhancing the Law, Paul employs them to show the inferiority of the Law to the promise. See the discussion by Schlier, *Galaterbrief*, 156–158.

by the hand of a mediator: The mediator is Moses. See Exod 19:7; 20:19; 24:3; Lev 26:46; Deut 4:14; 5:4-5.

20. *A mediator is not a mediator of one*: This translation supplies the word "mediator" a second time to make better sense of the text, as does the KJV, even though it only occurs once in the Greek *ho de mesitēs henos ouk estin* ("but the mediator is not of one"). The phrase suggests that only a group needs a mediator. The sense is captured by the NEB, "But a mediator is not needed for one party." The people of Israel needed Moses to mediate for them because they were many. By contrast, there was no need for a mediator between God and Abraham; the communication was direct.

but God is one: Where there is more than one, there is need for a mediator. Since God is one, there is no need for a mediator. The one God communicates directly with Abraham, and so to Abraham's one seed, Christ.

INTERPRETATION

Thus far, Paul has shown the Galatians that if they practice legal works they will be liable to the curse of the Law. The Galatians are Abraham's descendants because they are *hoi ek pisteōs*, people of faith. Having shown the Galatians that they are descendants of Abraham, apart from legal works, in this unit Paul discusses the relationship between God's promise to Abraham and the Law. Does the Law alter or abrogate God's promise? Since the Law was given after the promise, perhaps God requires something more from Abraham's descendants.

At first this unit seems to contradict what Paul has just said in 3:7-14. There he states that *hoi ek pisteōs* are Abraham's descendants, but here he argues that Abraham's sole descendant is Christ (3:16). If Christ is Abraham's sole descendant, then how can the Galatians be Abraham's descendants, even if they are *hoi ek pisteōs?* The contradiction is more apparent than real, however, since Paul will conclude in 3:29 that all who belong to Christ are Abraham's seed. In effect, Paul is further defining what he has already said and offering another argument why Abraham's descendants are *ek pisteōs* and not *ex nomou*. People of faith are Abraham's descendants because they have been incorporated into Christ who is Abraham's seed. By contrast, those who rely upon the Law are not Abraham's descendants because they have not been incorporated into Christ.

Many commentators and translators limit this unit to vv. 15–18 which make a comparison between a human will or testament (*diathēkē*) and the testament or covenant (*diathēkē*) that God made with Abraham. Verses, 19–20, however, are an integral part of the argument that Paul develops. Having shown that God's promissory testament to Abraham was directed toward a *single* seed (vv. 15–16), in vv. 19–20 Paul explains that the Law was given by angels to *many* by the hand of a mediator, thereby betraying its inferiority to the promise. And whereas the one God gave the promise *directly* to Abraham, the Law was given *indirectly* to many by the hand of a mediator. This unit can be divided into three parts, each of which begins with a direct address or a question: *adelphoi* ("brethren"); *touto de legō* " ("this is what I am saying"); *ti oun ho nomos* ("then why the Law?"):

vv. 15–16   The inviolability of a testament
vv. 17–18   The late arrival of the Law
vv. 19–20   The inferiority of the Law to the Promise

The inviolability of a testament (vv. 15–16). Paul begins by reasserting the relationship which still exists between himself and the Galatians. Even though the Galatians are at the point of abandoning the gospel, and even though Paul has called them foolish and bewitched, he can still address them as *adelphoi*. Paul and the Galatians are still united in Christ. When he says that he is speaking "in a human fashion" he does not simply mean that he is giving an example from everyday life (see notes). As Cosgrove has argued, Paul is employing this expression in an apologetic vein, knowing that what he is about to say could be interpreted as blasphemous: that God tried to annul the promissory testament made with Abraham. That, of course, is unthinkable, and it is not Paul's view. But, in his mind, it reflects the position of the agitators when their argument is drawn to its logical conclusion. If the Law is more important than the promise, then the Law has altered the promise; a capricious God has annulled the testament made to Abraham. But if a human testament cannot be changed or annulled, how much more true is this for the testament that God made with Abraham?

Paul's legal example is clear enough, even if its background is obscure. He argues that once a will has been legally ratified no one, not even the testator, can annul or alter it. While most wills or testaments can be changed during the lifetime of the testator, and while they only become effective with the death of the testator (Heb 9:16-17), Paul envisions a testament which cannot be altered, even by the testator. It is this aspect of the example which presents a problem since Roman and Greek law allowed a testator to change a will after it had been drawn up. According to E. Bammel, however, there was a Jewish practice, the *mattenat bari'*, by which a testator could make an unalterable testament to another while still maintaining a certain use of the property or goods during his (the testator's) lifetime. In effect, it was a testament that did not need the death of the testator to make it effective.

According to Paul, the Living God made an analogous testament (*diathēkē*) with Abraham; that is, God made an unalterable promise to Abraham and to his seed. This, of course, is the only kind of covenant that suits the situation since God cannot die. To speak of a covenant that would take effect with the death of the testator would make no sense in this instance. Moreover, to speak of a covenant that the testator could change or annul would make God capricious. Therefore, Paul supposes a covenant, made by the Living God, by which God binds Himself unalterably. The testament (*diathēkē*) which Paul has in mind is the covenant (*diathēkē*) God made with Abraham as recorded in Genesis 17:

> When Abram was ninety-nine years old, the Lord appeared to Abram, and said to him, "I am God almighty; walk before me, and be blameless. And I will make my covenant (*diathēkē*) between me and you, and will make you exceedingly numerous." Then Abram fell on his face; and God said to him, "As for me, this is my covenant (*diathēkē*) with you: You shall be the ancestor of a multitude of nations. No longer shall you be named Abram, but your name shall be Abraham; for I have made you the ancestor of a multitude of nations. I will make you exceedingly fruitful; and I will make nations of you, and kings shall come from you. I will establish my covenant (*diathēkē*) between me and you, and your offspring after you throughout their generations, for an everlasting covenant (*diathēkē*), to be God to you and to your offspring after you. And I will give to you, and to your offspring (*kai tō spermati sou*) after you, the land where you are now an alien, all the land of Canaan for a perpetual holding; and I will be their God (Gen 17:1-8).

The offspring envisioned in this covenant includes all of Abraham's ancestors who will be born through Isaac; thus Genesis employs the singular of the Greek word for "seed" (*spermati*) in a collective sense. Paul takes advantage of the singular and envisions a single ancestor, Christ. The living God made a testament to Abraham which had as its beneficiary Abraham's unique seed, Christ. This will, Paul supposes, is unalterable and cannot be annulled.

The late arrival of the Law (vv. 17–18). Thus far, Paul has not spoken about the Law. He has simply argued from the lesser to the greater: if a legally ratified testament cannot be altered, how much more unalterable is the promissory testament God made with Abraham? Now, however, the Apostle introduces the Law into the discussion. Given its importance, perhaps the Law functions as a codicil to the testament given to Abraham. Or, perhaps it even annulled it! It is doubtful that the agitators took this line of argumentation, but Paul implies that this is the logical outcome of their theology. By insisting upon the Mosaic Law, they are saying that God altered the testament made with Abraham, or perhaps even abolished it.

In this section, Paul equates testament (*diathēkē*) and promise (*epaggelia*). God's promise to Abraham, recorded in Genesis 17, is his will and testament. Thus, when God made His *diathēkē* with Abraham, He promised the Patriarch that he would be the ancestor of a multitude of nations (Gen 17:4), and that He would give Abraham and his offspring the land (Gen 17:8). In v. 18, therefore, Paul says that if the inheritance (*klēronomia*) is based on Law, it no longer derives from promise; that is, it no longer comes from the testament God granted to Abraham. Promise and testament are one, and together they stand in juxtaposition to the Law. When speaking of the Law, Paul does not say that God is its author, but when referring to the testament or promise, he does identify God as the one who legally ratified the testament and graciously extended the promise to Abraham. This foreshadows what Paul will imply in vv. 19–20: whereas the promise comes directly from God, the Law does not. Not only is the Law a latecomer, it came through intermediaries. As important as it is, therefore, it cannot change or supplant the promise.

It is inconceivable for Paul that the Law could annul the promise or act as a codicil to God's testament. If it did, then God would be capricious. If the Law annulled the promise, then God would be unfaithful to Himself, as well as to Abraham. No, the Law was a latecomer; it was given at Sinai 430 years after God legally ratified His testament with Abraham. As important and as holy as the Law is, therefore, it cannot add to or annul what God has already promised by solemn oath to Abraham; the Law has another purpose.

The subordination of the Law to the promise (vv. 19–20). Having shown that the inheritance comes through the promise God made to Abraham, Paul must now address the question of the Law. If the inheritance comes through the promise, then what is the purpose and nature of the Law? Paul provides three answers: the Law was added to make transgressions known; its role is temporary; and it is inferior to the promise because it was promulgated by angels, through the hand of a mediator.

When Paul writes that the Law was added for the sake of transgressions, he means that the Law was given in order to make transgressions known. Here, Paul relies upon a distinction which he explains in Romans: "where there is no law, neither is there violation" (Rom 4:15). This does not mean that the absence of the Law results in the absence of sin. See Rom 5:13 ("sin was indeed in the world before the law"). Rather, the presence of the Law, with its specific commandments, makes people aware that they are committing sin by transgressing God's Law. Consequently, Israel was in a privileged position *vis-à-vis* the Gentiles. Whereas the Gentiles violated God's Law but were unaware of their violations, the Law made Israel conscious of its transgressions. From Paul's point of view, therefore, the Law was not given as a remedy for sin but a means of making Israel aware of sin. Because Israel had the gift of the Law, the Jews, unlike the Gentiles, were aware that their sins transgressed God's Law. Since the just requirements of the Law can only be fulfilled through the power of God's Spirit (Rom 8:1-4), however, the Law could not grant the power to accomplish what it commanded (Rom 7:14-20).

Because the Law could only make sin known, but not provide a definitive remedy for it, Paul assigns it a temporary role "until the seed should come to whom the promise was made." Thus Paul clearly establishes the temporal parameters of the Law; it entered the scene 430 years after God's promise to Abraham, and its role ends with the coming of Christ. Whereas Paul states that the Law has a temporary function, however, the main current of biblical tradition views it as imperishable and enduring. The author of Wisdom writes: "For their enemies deserved to be deprived of light and imprisoned in darkness, those who had kept your children imprisoned, through whom *the imperishable light of the law* was to be given to the world" (Wis 18:4). Likewise, the Matthean Jesus proclaims the enduring quality of the Law: "For truly I tell you, until heaven and earth pass away, not one letter, not one stroke of a letter, will pass from the law until all is accomplished" (Matt 5:18, also Luke 16:17). Paul's heterodoxy is not based on a new exegesis of Scripture but upon the appearance of Abraham's seed; Christ has made him aware that the Law has completed the work it was intended to accomplish.

Throughout this section Paul has said that God made a testament with Abraham, but he has not explicitly said that God gave the Law to Moses or the Israelites. The reason for this becomes clear in v. 19b: the Law "was promulgated by angels through the hand of a mediator." While the Exodus account of the giving of the Law does not speak of angels, later tradition associated angels with the giving of the Law (see notes). In Acts 7:53, for example, Stephen says to his persecutors: "You are the ones that received the law *as ordained by angels*, and yet have not kept it." And the author of Hebrews, referring to the Law, writes: "For if the message *declared through angels* was valid. . . ." (Heb 2:2). While Acts and Hebrews view the role of the angels as enhancing the status of the Law, Paul employs these, or similar traditions, to draw another conclusion: the Law is inferior to the promise precisely because it was promulgated by angels!

Exactly what Paul means when he refers to the angels as mediating the Law is disputed. A. Vanhoye ("Un mediateur des anges en Gal 3, 19-20"), proposes an interesting interpretation. On the basis of Acts 7:38 ("He is the one who was in the congregation in the wilderness *with the angel who spoke to him* at Mount Sinai"), he suggests that Paul has two mediators in mind: a mediating angel who spoke on behalf of the angels, and Moses who spoke on behalf of the Israelites. The Law was promulgated through angels who employed a mediating angel to speak with Moses, the mediator for the Israelites. As a result, at the giving of the Law, communication between God and Israel was indirect.

THE LAW
GOD . . . ANGELS . . . ANGEL . . . MOSES . . . ISRAEL

By contrast God spoke the promise directly to Abraham, for there was no need for mediators.

THE PROMISE
GOD . . . ABRAHAM

The Law is not evil; it has played its proper role. But it is subordinate to the promise both temporally and in the way it was promulgated. It cannot annul or change God's testament to Abraham. The promised inheritance, the gift of the Spirit, comes through Abraham's seed, not through the Law.

For Reference and Further Study

Bammel, E. "Gottes *DIATHĒKĒ* (Gal. III. 15-17) und das judische Rechtsdenken." *NTS* 6 (1959-60) 313-319.

Callan, T. "Pauline Midrash: The Exegetical Background of Gal 3:19b." *JBL* 99 (1980) 549-567.

Cosgrove, C. H. "Arguing like a Mere Human Being: Galatians 3:15-19 in Rhetorical Perspective." *NTS* 34 (1988) 536-549.

Giblin, C. H. "Three Monotheistic Texts in Paul." *CBQ* 37 (1975) 527-547.

Lührmann, D. "Die 430 Jahre zwischen den Verheissungen und dem Gesetz (Gal 3, 17)." *ZAW* 100 (1988) 420-423.

Taylor, G. "The Function of *PISTIS CHRISTOU* in Galatians." *JBL* 85 (1966) 58-76.

Vanhoye, A. "Un mediateur des anges en Gal 3, 19-20." *Bib* 59 (1978) 403-411.

Wallace, D. B. "Galatians 3:19-20: A *Crux Interpretum* for Paul's view of the Law." *WTJ* 52 (1990) 225-245.

The Law Is Not Opposed to the Promise (3:21-25)

21. Then is the Law against the promises of God? Of course not! If a law had been given capable of providing life, righteousness would really have been from the Law. 22. But Scripture confined everything under Sin so that the promise, based on the faith of Jesus Christ, might be given to those who believe. 23. Before the faith came, we were guarded, confined under the Law for the faith destined to be revealed, 24. so that the Law was our disciplinarian until Christ in order that we might be justified from faith. 25. But since the faith has come, we are no longer under a disciplinarian.

NOTES

21. *Then is the Law against the promises of God? Of course not!*: The phrase "of God" is found in S, A, C, D, but is absent from P46. One manuscript (104) has the phrase "of Christ." "Of God" is appropriate, even if it is not a firm reading, since Paul has emphasized that the promise, unlike the Law, comes directly from God. *Oun* ("then") connects these verses to the previous unit which dealt with the Law and the promise. If the Law does not alter the promise, perhaps it works against the promise by providing an alternate way of righteousness. Paul's question and response here is similar to what is found in Rom 7:7: "What then shall we say? That the law is sin? By no means!"

If a law had been given capable of providing life: This is the first part of a conditional sentence that is contrary to fact. A law capable of giving life was not given, but if such a law had been given it would have produced righteousness. *Zōopoiein* ("to give life") means more than to transmit physical life; it envisions resurrection life. See Rom 8:11; 1 Cor 15:22, 45. In 2 Cor 3:6 Paul writes that it is the Spirit which gives life, and in Rom 7:10 he says that the commandment (*entolē*) intended to give life led to death.

righteousness would really have been from the Law: This is the final part of the conditional clause; it describes what would have happened if a law capable of providing life had been given. Some manuscripts (F, G) replace *ontōs* ("really") with *alētheia* ("truly"). Both readings suggest that the Law offers an apparent righteousness devoid of life. The thought is similar to 2:21; the Law was not intended to provide righteousness. That Paul envisions a life-giving righteousness indicates that this righteousness (*dikaiosynē*) effects a change and transformation within the believer.

22. *But Scripture confined everything under Sin*: Here, Scripture (*hē graphē*) is not a synonym for the Law. As in 3:8, it is a personification of God's will. In Rom 11:32 Paul makes a similar statement: "For God has imprisoned all in disobedience so that he may be merciful to all." Here, and in Rom 11:32, Paul employs the verb, *sygkleiein* ("to hem in," "to confine," "to imprison"). Confining all under Sin means that Scripture has declared that all are under the power of Sin. See Rom 3:9-18 for a chain of scriptural quotations which indicates the plight of human sinfulness. This is the third and final use of *hamartia* ("Sin") in Galatians (1:4; 2:17); as in Romans 5-8, Sin is personified as a power which enslaves humanity.

so that the promise, based on the faith of Jesus Christ, might be given to those who believe: This is a result clause introduced by *hina* ("so that") rather than a purpose clause. The conclusion to be drawn is that the promise is given to those who believe. "Based on the faith of Jesus Christ," is a translation of *ek pisteōs Iēsou Christou*. The phrase can also be rendered as an objective genitive, "based on faith in Jesus Christ." By employing the subjective genitive, however, the final phrase ("to those who believe") is no longer redundant. Moreover, the subjective genitive, "the faith of Jesus Christ," helps to interpret "the faith" mentioned in vv. 23-25 (see below).

23. *Before the faith came*: The Greek employs the definite article before *pistin* which indicates that Paul is not speaking about faith in general but a specific faith. The context, especially v. 22, suggests that he is referring to *the* faith of Jesus Christ.

we were guarded, confined under the Law: "We" refers to the Jews and their situation under the Law. The participle *sygkleiomenoi* ("confined") further describes the verb *ephrouroumetha* ("guarded"): we were guarded by being confined. This confinement can be taken in either a negative or positive sense: the Law was our jailer, or the Law placed us under protective custody. The latter interpretation is preferable in light of *paidagōgos* (see below). The Law was given the role of protecting the Jew from Sin, even if it did not have the power to grant righteousness. The phrase *hypo nomon* ("under the Law") occurs in Rom 6:14, 15 where it is opposed to *hypo charin* ("under grace"), as well as in Gal 4:4, 5, 21; 5:18. It should be related to other phrases governed by *hypo*: "under sin" (Rom 3:9; 7:14); "under a curse" (Gal 3:10); "under the elements of the universe" (Gal 4:3), phrases which denote a realm or sphere apart from God, from which humanity must be redeemed.

for the faith destined to be revealed: "For" translates *eis* which is used in a temporal sense: the Jews were under the Law until the appearance of this faith. An interesting parallel is found in 1 Pet 1:5. "Faith" is again governed by the definite article *tēn mellousan pistin* ("the faith destined to be") and is best interpreted as the faith of Jesus Christ. In 1:12 Paul says that his gospel came through a "revelation" (*apokalypseōs*) of Jesus Christ, and in 1:16 he writes that God "revealed" (*apokalypsai*) his Son to him. The use of *apokalyptein* ("to reveal") here suggests that the faith destined to be revealed is the faithfulness of Jesus Christ manifested in his life and death. See Rom 1:17, 18; 8:18; for other uses of this verb.

24. *so that the Law was our disciplinarian*: I have translated *paidagōgos* as "disciplinarian" as does the NAB and NRSV. Other translations are: "custodian" (RSV); "a kind of tutor in charge of us" (NEB); "the law was put in charge of us" (NEB), and "slave" (NJB). The *paidagōgos* was a household slave who led the young boy to school and generally supervised his conduct. Although not a teacher, he did serve as a kind of moral guide, protecting the youth from immoral influences. Paul's primary emphasis is upon the constraining aspect of the Law as *paidagōgos*. Just as the *paidagōgos* necessarily limited the freedom of the minor, so the Law necessarily constrained the freedom of those under it in order to protect them from Sin, even though it could not grant life-giving righteousness. Paul uses the same word in 1 Cor 4:15 ("For though you might have ten thousand *paidagōgous* in Christ, you do not have many fathers") where he views himself as the father-founder of the community.

until Christ: This translates *eis Christon* which can be construed in a telic (unto Christ) or temporal (until the coming of Christ) sense. In the first instance, the emphasis is upon the purpose of the Law: to lead us to Christ. In the second, it is upon the temporal limits of the Law: it ends when Christ comes. Given Paul's insistence in this section upon the temporal limits of the Law, the second sense is preferable.

in order that we might be justified from faith: The purpose clause explains why the Jews were under the Law: to be justified *ek pisteōs* ("by faith," "on the basis of faith"). This is the way that the Galatians are also to be justified. This faith is the faith of Jesus Christ in whom the Galatians have come to believe. See notes and commentary on 2:16.

25. *But since the faith has come, we are no longer under a disciplinarian*: The genitive absolute (*elthousēs de tēs pisteōs*) is translated in a causal sense ("since"). Again, "faith" is governed by the definite article indicating a distinctive kind of faith: the faith of Jesus Christ. *Hypo paidagōgon* ("under a disciplinarian") corresponds to *hypo nomon* ("under Law"). Since Christ has come, we are no longer under the Law.

INTERPRETATION

In the previous unit, Paul argued that the Law does not add to or annul the promissory testament that God made with Abraham. Rather, the Law was given for the purpose of exposing transgressions. In this regard, it provided the Jews with a certain advantage that the Gentiles did not have, namely: it made the Jews aware that they were violating God's Law. In this unit Paul raises another issue. If the Law cannot alter or annul the promise, and if it is subordinate to the promise, then perhaps it is somehow contrary to or opposed to the promise; perhaps it functions as a rival means of providing righteousness. Paul answers his own question with an emphatic "no" and explains that the Law had another role within salvation history, one that was not contrary to that of the promise. That role, however, was only temporary, and now that the Christ has come it is ended.

Although this commentary treats these verses as a unit, they should not be read in isolation. In 4:1-5, Paul will liken the situation of the Jews, under the Law, to that of an heir placed under the authority of guardians and stewards until the day appointed for his majority. In this unit, and in 4:1-5, Paul repeatedly employs the preposition *hypo* ("under"): 3:22 "under Sin;" 3:23 "under the Law;" 3:25 "under a custodian;" 4:2 "under guardians and stewards;" 4:3 "under the elements;" 4:4, 5 "under the Law." He argues that the period of the Law (from Moses to Christ) was a time of confinement and restraint, a period of minority that limited the freedom of those under it. In effect, those under the Law were no different from slaves. But when God sent his Son, this period of minority ended, and the God-given role of the Law was concluded.

This unit can be divided into two parts. In vv. 21-22 Paul explains why the Law is not opposed to the promise. In vv. 23-25, employing the image of the *paidagōgos*, he elaborates upon the situation of humanity described in v. 22. The text can be outlined in the following way.

v. 21a   *Thesis*: the Law is not opposed to the promise.
v. 21b   *Hypothetical situation*: what would have happened if the Law could give life.
v. 22   *Real situation*: humanity was confined *under Sin*.
v. 23   *Before* the appearance of "the faith" we were *under the Law*.
v. 24   The Law was our *paidagōgos*.
v. 25   *After* the appearance of "the faith" we are no longer *under a paidagōgos*.

The Law is not opposed to the promise (vv. 21–22). Throughout this section, one has the sense that Paul is writing for himself as much as for the Galatians. Are the Law and the promise opposed to each other? In Phil 3:6, looking back at his life as a Pharisee, Paul could write that "as to righteousness under the law" he was blameless. Moreover, he undoubtedly knew that Deut 30:15-20 portrayed the Law as life-giving. Thus in Deut 30:19, Moses says to the people of Israel: "I call heaven and earth to witness against you today that I have set before you life and death, blessings and curses. Choose life so that you and your descendants may live." Finally, in Gal 3:12 Paul quotes from Lev 18:5: "You shall keep my statutes and my ordinances; *by doing so one shall live*." Nonetheless, the Apostle has come to the conclusion that righteousness and life do not come from the Law. It is imperative, therefore, that he explain this conclusion and clarify the role of the Law *vis-à-vis* God's promise.

Paul's answer to his own question is twofold: a description of what would have happened if the Law could give life; and a description of the actual situation of humanity. If the Law could give life then the way to righteousness would be through the Law. The equation of life and righteousness here indicates that the righteousness Paul envisions is more than a juridical pronouncement. To be declared righteous by God is to receive the eschatological gift of the Spirit; it is to be changed and transformed. This transformation does not mean that the Christian is incapable of sinning, as Romans 6 makes clear, but it does mean the bestowal of the Spirit which enables believers to fulfill the just demands of the Law (see Romans 8). If the Law had been life-giving, therefore, this righteousness would be the actual situation of those under it; they would have received the eschatological gift of the Spirit. In effect, they would have found another way to righteousness, and the Law would be opposed to the promise.

But Paul proclaims that this is not the case. Humanity's real situation is that it is under the power of Sin (*hypo hamartian*). Paul does not explain how he arrives at this conclusion except to say that Scripture confined all things (*ta panta*) under Sin. This is not to say that Scripture has become humanity's "jailer"; rather, it means that Scripture declares what is the actual situation: humanity's bondage to Sin. In Romans Paul will develop this concept at greater length, and in Philippians he will look back at the righteousness that he attained under the Law and count it as so much loss because of the "surpassing value of knowing Christ Jesus" (Phil 3:8). Here, however, Paul moves from his experience of salvation to the plight of humanity: if Christ died for sins, *then* all must have been under the power of Sin; otherwise there was no reason for Christ to die (2:21).

Paul's conclusion is that the Law is not a rival to the promise. As a result, the promise comes *ek pisteōs Iēsou Christou*, from the faith of Jesus Christ in whom the Galatians believe. This promise is the testament to Abraham, the promised Spirit (3:14) which makes all who are in Christ descendants of Abraham. But if the Law does not give life-giving righteousness, and if it is not opposed to the promise, what was its role?

The Law was our paidagōgos (vv. 23-25). Paul has concluded that the Law does not annul or alter the promise (3:15-20), nor is it opposed to the promise (3:21-22). Now, by employing the metaphor of the *paidagōgos*, he explains the precise role that the Law played in the history of salvation.

In the ancient world a young boy was usually placed in the care of an older, household slave called the *paidagōgos* (literally, "boy-leader"). Although the word brings to mind the English derivative "pedagogue," the *paidagōgos* was not a tutor or teacher. Rather, his primary task was "preventive and protective" (N. H. Young, *"Paidagōgos: The Social Setting of a Pauline Metaphor,* 158). In this regard, the *paidagōgos* functioned as a kind of moral guide for the young boy, keeping him from misadventure and protecting him from others. The role of the *paidagōgos* began when the boy was seven and continued to late adolescence (Young, 156-157). During that period the *paidagōgos* was the constant companion of the boy, constraining and limiting his freedom. An example of how the *paidagōgos* was viewed, and how he functioned, can be seen in Plato's *Lysis* 208 c. There, Socrates asks the young Lysis if his parents allow him to rule himself. When Lysis responds negatively, Socrates asks who, then, governs him. Lysis points to his *paidagōgos*, and Socrates responds with dismay: "Not a slave"? Lysis explains that the slave belongs to the family, but Socrates continues to express surprise that a free man should be ruled by a slave. When Socrates asks how the *paidagōgos* exercises his authority, Lysis responds that the *paidagōgos* takes him to school.

Although the *paidagōgos* had complete control over the youth, his role ended when the boy came of age. Indeed, for a youth to remain under the control of a *paidagōgos* beyond the appointed age was a matter of concern, as it was in the case of the Roman emperor Claudius (Young, 169).

In vv. 23-25 Paul assigns the Law the role of *paidagōgos*. Before the appearance of "the faith," that is, the faith of Jesus Christ (see notes), the Jews ("we") were guarded under the Law, so that their freedom was confined and constrained. Like a young boy, they could not do what they wanted to do because the Law ruled over them. In saying this, Paul is remarkably close to the view of the Law found in Josephus's *Against Apion* and in the *Letter of Aristeas*. In the first work, Josephus explains that the God of Israel did not leave anything, however insignificant, to chance. God determined which meats his people should abstain from and which meats they could enjoy, what people they could associate with, and what times should be devoted to labor and to rest. Thus Israel would live under God as under a father and master and would not be guilty of any sin through wilfulness or ignorance (*Apion*, 3:173-174). In the latter work, the author says that God hedged Israel in on all sides with commandments concerning meat, drink, touch, hearing, and sight (*Aristeas*, 142).

Although Josephus and the author of the *Letter of Aristeas* present the Law as constraining, neither views its role as temporary or servile. To the contrary, they suppose that by constraining the Jews, the Law protects them from sinning. Paul, however, interprets the situation differently. Leaving aside the moral and educative value of the Law, he compares it to a *paidagōgos* who limits the freedom of the young boy because the youth is still in the period of his minority (4:1-5). Like the *paidagōgos*, however, the role of the Law is temporary, and this is the point Paul wishes to make. *Before* the destined faith was revealed (v. 23), the Jew was confined under the Law. *Until* the time of Christ, the Law functioned as a *paidagōgos* (v. 24). *After* the coming of this faith, the faith of Jesus Christ, there is no need for the *paidagōgos* (v. 25) since the time of majority has come (4:1-5).

To summarize, Paul assigns the Law a temporary function. In the period between Moses and Christ it guarded the Jews, restraining their freedom. In doing so, it made them aware of their transgressions, and this was a distinct advantage. The Law did not, however, have the power to bestow life-giving righteousness since that was reserved to Abraham's heir, the Christ. It could tell the Jews that they were transgressing God's commandments, but it did not enable them to follow those commandments. Only the Spirit can do that. This view of the Law is not how the Old Testament presents the Law. It is a Christological interpretation developed in light of the revelation of Jesus Christ. In light of that saving revelation, Paul sees the real plight of humanity, a plight which only the death of Christ, not the Law, can remedy.

FOR REFERENCE AND FURTHER STUDY

Barrett, C. K. *Freedom & Obligation: A Study of the Epistle to the Galatians*. Philadelphia: Westminster, 1985.

Belleville, L. L. " 'Under Law': Structural Analysis and the Pauline Concept of Law in Galatians 3.21-4.1." *JSNT* 26 (1986) 53-78.

Cosgrove, C. H. "The Mosaic Law Preaches Faith: A Study in Galatians 3." *WTJ* 41 (1978-79) 146-164.

Hanson, A. T. "The Origin of Paul's Use of *paidagōgos* for the Law." *JSNT* 34 (1988) 71-76.

Longenecker, R. N. "The Pedagogical Nature of the Law in Galatians 3:19-4:7." *JETS* 25 (1982) 53-61.

Lull, D. J. " 'The Law was our Pedagogue': A Study in Galatians 3:19-25." *JBL* 105 (1986) 481-498.

Martin, B. L. *Christ and the Law in Paul.* NovTSup 62; Leiden: Brill, 1989.

Thielman, F. *From Plight to Solution: A Jewish Framework for Understanding Paul's View of the Law in Galatians and Romans.* NovTSup 61; Leiden: Brill, 1989.

Yates, R. "Saint Paul and the Law in Galatians." *ITQ* 51 (1985) 105-124.

Young, N. H. "*PAIDAGŌGOS*: The Social Setting of a Pauline Metaphor." *NovT* 39 (1987) 150-176.

Those in Christ Are Abraham's Descendants (3:26-29)

26. For you are all sons of God, in Christ Jesus, through the faith. 27. For all of you who were baptized into Christ clothed yourself with Christ. 28. There is neither Jew nor Greek, there is neither slave nor free, there is neither male and female, for all of you are one person in Christ Jesus. 29. And if you belong to Christ, then you are Abraham's seed, heirs according to promise.

NOTES

26. *For you are all sons of God*: The Greek word *gar* ("for") indicates that this verse is providing the proof for Paul's statement in v. 25: believers are no longer under the custodianship of the Law *because* they are "sons of God" (*hyioi theou*). The expression includes women as well as men as v. 28 shows, but the translation "sons" is maintained because Paul is employing a metaphor of inheritance that has the male offspring in view. The "sons" described here are adult sons who have come of age, not the son of 4:1-2 who is still a minor (*nēpios*). The designation "sons of God" was the prerogative of Israel (Exod 4:22-23; Deut 14:1-2; Hos 11:1; Sir 36:17; 3 Macc 6:28; 4 Ezra 6:55-59; Pss Sol 17:26-27; Jub 1:22-25), and that is how Paul understands it here. The Gentiles now enjoy a title once reserved for Israel. See the extensive discussion in B. Byrne, *"Sons of God"—"Seed of Abraham."* This sonship results from the gift of the Spirit (4:6-7; Rom 8:14).

in Christ Jesus, through the faith: For the sake of clarity, the translation reverses the order of the Greek (*dia tēs pisteōs en Christǫ Iēsou*, ". . . through the faith in Christ Jesus"). *Dia tēs pisteōs* ("through the faith") can be taken with what follows ("in Christ"), or with what precedes ("sons of God"). In the first case, Christ is the object of faith: you are sons of God through faith *in* Christ Jesus. In the second, Christ is the sphere or locale in which one is a son of God *through* "the faith" understood as an objective reality, the faith of Jesus Christ: you are sons of God in the sphere of Christ through Christ's faith. The second interpretation fits Paul's thought best since he does not otherwise employ *en Christǫ* when speaking of faith in Christ. Moreover, throughout this chapter, the faith of Jesus Christ has been a major motif. The language of this phrase is awkward and probably accounts for the smoother reading of P46, *dia pisteōs Christou Iēsou* which can be translated as an objective or subjective genitive: "through faith in Christ Jesus," or "through the faith of Christ Jesus."

27. *For all of you who were baptized into Christ clothed yourself with Christ*: The preposition *gar* ("for") indicates that this verse explains the last phrase of the previous verse: believers are sons of God in Christ *because* they have been clothed with Christ in baptism. *Hosoi*, which can be translated "for as many as," is not restrictive and so is rendered as "all." This is the only mention of baptism in Galatians. In Rom 6:3 Paul describes baptism into Christ as baptism into his death, but here he employs the imagery of clothing oneself (*enedysasthe*) with Christ. Similar imagery is used in Rom 13:12-14 and 1 Thess 5:8 as part of an ethical exhortation. In 1 Cor 15:53-54 Paul writes of being clothed with the resurrection body. Eph 4:24 speaks of clothing oneself "with the new self (*ton kainon anthrōpon*), created according to the likeness of God in true righteousness and holiness," and Col 3:10 of clothing oneself with the new self (*ton neon ton anakainoumenon*) "which is being renewed in knowledge according to the image of its creator." The LXX also employs the verb used here (*enduein*): being clothed with salvation (2 Chr 6:41); being clothed with righteousness (Job 29:14; LXX Ps 131:9; Isa 59:17); being clothed with shame (LXX Ps 34:26).

28. *There is neither Jew nor Greek*: Similar formulas are found in 1 Cor 12:13 and Col 3:11. Also, see Gal 5:6; 6:15; 1 Cor 7:19 and Eph 2:15. This couplet indicates the racial division in the world from the point of view of the Jew. *Hellēn* ("Greek") means the uncircumcised, the Gentiles. Except for Rom 1:14, Jew and Gentile is a constant couplet in Paul (Rom 1:16; 2:9, 10; 3:9; 10:12; 1 Cor 1:22, 24; 10:32; 12:13; Col 3:11).

there is neither slave nor free: This couplet points to the social barrier in the Greco-Roman world. Other Pauline texts show that Paul and his successors lived, in light of the eschatological imperative, with the social institution of slavery (1 Cor 7:21-24; Eph 6:5-8; Col 3:22-25; Eph 6:5-8; Philemon).

there is neither male and female: This couplet points to the sexual barrier between human beings, thus the use of *arsen* ("male") and *thēlu* ("female"). Whereas the other couplets employ the formula "neither . . . nor," this one reads "neither . . . and." This change probably reflects the text of Gen 1:27

(LXX), *arsen kai thēlu epoiēsen autous* ("male *and* female he made them"). That Paul did not intend to abolish the gender roles between men and women is apparent from the discussion in 1 Cor 11:2-16.

For all of you are one person in Christ Jesus: Some manuscripts (P46, A) read "For all of you belong to Christ *(este Christou)*." Others (S*), "For you are all in Christ" *(este en Christou)*. Both variants are probably attempts to make the present reading clearer by eliminating *heis* ("one") which might give the impression that the differences mentioned above no longer exist in fact. The word "person" is not found in the Greek text; it has been added to make Paul's thought clearer. All the baptized form a single person in Christ: they are a new creation. See 6:15.

29. *And if you belong to Christ, then you are Abraham's seed*: The discussion about Abraham's seed began at 3:7, and in 3:16 Paul identified Christ as the unique seed of Abraham. The discussion is brought to a conclusion by explaining that all who are in the one seed, Christ, are Abraham's seed through participation. See Rom 9:7-12 for another discussion of Abraham's descendants.

    heirs according to promise: The promise is the testament made to Abraham (3:15-18); its content is the Spirit (3:14).

INTERPRETATION

In the previous unit, Paul argued that the Law played a temporary role in salvation history akin to that of a *paidagōgos*. With the coming of Christ-faith that role ended: those in Christ are no longer under the Law. In this unit Paul provides yet another reason why the Law no longer rules over believers, and brings the whole discussion begun in 3:7 to a conclusion. Believers are no longer under the Law because they are adult "sons" [see notes] who have come of age. As "sons of God," in Christ Jesus, they are Abraham's seed, heirs of the promised inheritance, i.e., the Spirit. Finally, in addition to concluding the main argument of chapter three, this unit prepares for an important theme of the next unit: God has sent the Spirit of his Son into the hearts of the Galatians because they are "sons of God" (4:6-7).

These verses are somewhat distracting because Paul switches from the first person plural in vv. 23–25 to the second person plural in vv. 26–29. Moreover, in 4:3-5 he reverts to the first person plural only to return to the second person plural in 4:6-10. These changes indicate that Paul has two groups in view. In 3:23-25 and 4:3-5 he employs "we" to describe the situation of those under the Law (3:23; 4:5); this suggests that he is referring to the Jews before the coming of Christ. In 3:26-29 and 4:6-10, the use of "you" indicates that he is addressing the Galatians. Because of the Messiah's work of redeeming his own people from the Law, the Galatians have received sonship and the gift of the Spirit. In effect, Paul makes use of a schema which is also found in Romans: "to the Jew first and also to the Greek" (Rom 1:16).

3:23-25	"we"	the Jews
3:26-29	"you"	the Galatians
4:3-5	"we"	the Jews
4:6-10	"you"	the Galatians

The outline of this text is determined by three uses of *gar* ("for"), each of which indicates that what follows is grounding what precedes it. Thus, the Galatians are not under a *paidagōgos* (v. 25) *because* they are "sons of God" in Christ Jesus (v. 26). They are in Christ Jesus (v. 26) *because* they have been baptized into Christ (v. 27). And there is neither Jew nor Greek, slave nor free, male and female (v. 28a) *because* the baptized form one person in Christ (28b). The word "all" (*pantes*) creates a bracket around vv. 26-28, and v. 29 provides a conclusion both to this unit and the argument begun in 3:7.

> v. 26 *For* you are all sons of God in Christ Jesus, through faith.
>
> v. 27 *For* all of you who were baptized in Christ clothed yourself with Christ
>
> v. 28 There is neither Jew nor Greek
> There is neither slave nor free
> There is neither male and female
> *for* all of you are one person in Christ.
>
> v. 29 And if you belong to Christ,
> then you are Abraham's seed,
> heirs according to the promise.

You are "sons of God" (v. 26). The appearance of "sons of God" comes somewhat unexpectedly and the contemporary reader immediately thinks of divine sonship. The designation "sons of God," however, was a prerogative of the Israel *vis-à-vis* the nations. It designated Israel as the people of God because of God's election and calling. (See B. Byrne, *"Sons of God"—"Seed of Abraham,"* on which much of what follows is based.) Although "sons of God" is not a frequent designation in the OT, it, or an equivalent usage, is found in important texts.

> Then you shall say to Pharaoh, "Thus says the Lord: Israel is my *first-born son*. I said to you, 'Let my *son* go that he may worship me.' " (Exod 4:22-23)
>
> You are children (*hyioi*) of the Lord your God. . . . For you are a people holy to the Lord your God; it is you the Lord has *chosen* out of all the peoples of the earth to be his people, his treasured possession. (Deut 14:1-2)
>
> When Israel was a child, I loved him, and out of Egypt I called my *son*. (Hos 11:1)

During the intertestamental period, "sons of God" occurred in a wide variety of writings (see notes), especially in eschatological contexts, "suggesting that it was an epithet felt to be particularly applicable to the ideal Israel of the end-time, the holy and purified people of God, the citizens of his eternal kingdom" (Byrne, 62–23). For example, in the Book of Jubilees, God tells Moses that Israel will return to the Lord in all uprightness. Then the Lord will circumcise the hearts of the Israelites and of their descendants, purifying them so that they will no longer turn away from the Lord. On that day, the Israelites will keep the commandments of God; so that God will be a father to them and they will be sons to God. Thus the Israelites will be called "sons of the living God" (Jub 1:23-25).

When Paul tells the Galatians that they are "sons of God," therefore, he is saying that they belong to the people of Israel; they are the seed of Abraham (v. 29). Whereas the historic people of Israel understood its sonship in light of God's promise to Abraham *and the covenant made at Sinai,* Paul contends that the Galatians have come to this sonship because they are "in Christ" through faith (*dia tēs pisteōs*). This faith includes, but is more than, the faith of the believer as the definite article indicates: it is Christ-faith, the faith of Jesus Christ who gave himself upon the cross and in whom the Galatians believe.

Because you are baptized into Christ (v. 27). In Galatians Paul does not speak in any detail of baptism as he does in Romans. He supposes that his audience knows what he means because they have been baptized. Paul views baptism as an act of being clothed in Christ. The concept of being clothed is found in several OT texts, some of which speak of being clothed with righteousness and salvation. For example, the prophet Isaiah writes: "I will greatly rejoice in the Lord, my whole being shall exult in my God; for he has clothed me with the garments of salvation, he has covered me with the robe of righteousness, as a bridegroom decks himself with a garland, and as a bride adorns herself with jewels" (Isa 61:10). Likewise, Job says, "I put on righteousness, and it clothed me; my justice was like a robe and a turban" (Job 29:14). Here Paul views baptism as the moment when Christ, like a garment, envelops the believer. Although he does not employ the term, Paul is describing the righteousness which is conferred upon believers. See 1 Cor 1:30 where he writes that Christ "became for us wisdom from God, *and righteousness* and sanctification and redemption."

Contemporary authors caution against viewing baptism in isolation from faith, thereby turning it into a sacral act which works independently of faith. While this caution is well taken, it owes more to Catholic-Protestant debates over the nature of the sacraments than it does to Paul's own thought. If the Apostle does not envision a sacrament that works independently of faith, neither does he envision a personal faith which

effects its own salvation. Faith is made possible by the faith of Jesus Christ
so that believers are saved by what Christ has done. Baptism is the means
by which believers associate themselves with Christ's faith, thereby becoming incorporated into Christ.

You are one person in Christ (v. 28). Many commentators suspect that
this verse represents an earlier tradition, perhaps even a baptismal tradition. This view is a distinct possibility since the Pauline corpus contains
two other texts which are similar in content and structure to this verse.

> For in the one Spirit we were all baptized into the one body—
>   Jews or Greeks,
>   slaves or free—
> and we were all made to drink of one Spirit (1 Cor 12:13).

> In that renewal there is no longer
>   Greek and Jew,
>   circumcised and uncircumcised,
>   barbarian, Scythian,
>   slave and free;
> but Christ is all in all! (Col 3:11)

While both of these texts have the couplets "Greek and Jew" and "slave
and free," the third couplet "male and female" is not found in them.
Two other texts of Galatians, however, shed interpretive light upon this
text.

> For in Christ Jesus
> neither circumcision nor uncircumcision
> counts for anything;
> the only thing that counts is faith working through love
> (5:6).

> For neither circumcision nor uncircumcision is anything;
> but a new creation is everything (6:15).

It is not any outward mark that distinguishes one before God—if ever
such marks did—but faith. Distinctions of race, class, and sex have been
dissolved by the new creation that has occurred in Christ. In Christ, believers form the new eschatological person that the author of Ephesians
describes.

> He [Christ] has abolished the law with its commandments and ordi-
> nances, that he might create in himself *one new humanity* in place of the
> two, thus making peace, and might reconcile both groups to God in one
> body through the cross, thus putting to death that hostility through it
> (Eph 2:15-16).

While latter Gnostic literature developed this notion further, especially
the abolition of sexual differences (Gospel of Thomas, 22), Paul under-

stood this statement in a more subtle way. In this world, racial, social and sexual differences painfully separate people from each other, but for those who form the new eschatological person they cannot deny one full access to God's people, for God is impartial.

You are Abraham's seed (v. 29). Paul's argument has now reached its conclusion. The Galatians are also Abraham's seed, not because of legal observance, but because of incorporation into Christ, Abraham's promised offspring (3:16). The tension between Paul's argument in 3:7-14 and 3:15-20 is now resolved. In 3:7-14 he maintained that people of faith enjoy the blessing of Abraham, and in 3:15-20 he argued that Christ alone is Abraham's seed. How then can the Gentiles enjoy the blessing of Abraham if the one offspring of the Patriarch is Christ? Paul's answer is "incorporation into Christ." All who are "in Christ" are Abraham's seed. The corollary of this argument is that the blessing of Abraham cannot come through the Law since the Law does not incorporate one into Christ. The choice for the Galatians is Christ or the Law; there is no middle ground.

Paul has not spoken extensively about righteousness in chapter 3, but what he has said clarifies his understanding of justification. Those who are justified are incorporated into Christ who, like a garment, envelops them. Given the promised Spirit, they receive the life which only God can give. More than the justification of the individual, righteousness leads to the creation of a people.

FOR REFERENCE AND FURTHER STUDY

Boucher, M. "Some Unexplored Parallels to 1 Cor 11,11-12 and Gal 3, 28: The New Testament on the Role of Women." *CBQ* 31 (1969) 50–58.

Byrne, B. *"Sons of God"—"Seed of Abraham"*: A Study of the Idea of the Sonship of God of All Christians in Paul Against the Jewish Background. AnBib 83. Rome: Biblical Institute Press, 1979.

Conrat, M. "Das Erbrecht im Galaterbrief (3,15-4,7)." *ZNW* 5 (1904) 204–27.

Paulsen, H. "Einheit und Freiheit der Söhne Gottes—Gal 3:26-29." *ZNW* 71 (1980) 74–95.

Scroggs, R. "Paul and the Eschatological Woman." *JAAR* 40 (1972) 283–303.

Witherington, B. "Rite and Rights for Women—Galatians 3.28." *NTS* 27 (1980–81) 593–604.

Do Not Return to the Period of Your Minority (4:1-11)

1. What I am saying is that as long as the heir is a minor, he is no different from a slave even though he is the owner of everything 2. but is under guardians and stewards until the time appointed by the father. 3. Thus even we, when we were minors, were enslaved under rudimentary principles. 4. But when the fullness of time came, God sent his Son, born of a woman, born under the Law, 5. in order that he might ransom those under the Law, that we might receive adoption. 6. Because you are sons God sent the Spirit of his Son into our hearts crying, "Abba," that is "Father." 7. So you are no longer a slave but a son, and if a son, even an heir through God. 8. But then, not knowing God, you were enslaved to things that by nature are not gods. 9. But now, knowing God—rather known by God—how is it that you are turning again to weak and impotent rudiments which you wish to serve again? 10. You are observing days, months, festal seasons, and years. 11. I am afraid for you lest somehow I have labored in vain for you.

NOTES

1. *What I am saying is that as long as the heir is a minor*: "What I am saying" (*legō de*) indicates that the thought of the previous section demands further explanation. The concept of the *paidagōgos*, introduced in 3:24, leads to a reflection upon the period of humanity's minority. In 3:29 Paul spoke of "heirs according to the promise" made to Abraham; here *klēronomos* is used in a neutral sense as part of a legal example: the heir of an estate. In 4:7 the word will take on a theological sense once more. *Nēpios* is translated as "minor" because it is being employed in a legal example. In Rom 2:20; 13:11; and 1 Thess 2:7 it refers to a child, and in 1 Cor 3:1 it carries the added sense of immaturity. The notion of immaturity is in the background here as well.

    he is no different from a slave even though he is the owner of everything: "Owner" translates *kyrios*. See Matt 20:8 for a similar usage. Paul probably envisions a situation in which the father has died. Because the heir is a minor, however, he is the owner only *in potentia*.

2. *but is under guardians and stewards*: The precise legal situation to which Paul refers is disputed. In Roman Law the minor was under a tutor until he was fourteen, and then under a curator until he was twenty-five. Since Paul envisions a situation in which the heir is simultaneously under the authority of *epitropoi* and *oikonomoi*, however, it is unlikely that he is drawing this example from the realm of Roman Law. The *epitropos* was a guardian appointed by the child's father. The power of guardians "extended fully over the person and property of their ward. They were responsible for his physical maintenance and upbringing. . . . They had to see him educated, and they acted as his legal representative in any kind of transaction or dispute" (D. R. Moore-Crispin, "The Use and Abuse of Parallels," 207). See 2 Macc 11:1; 13:2; 14:2

where Lysias is described as "the king's *guardian* and kinsman, who was in charge of the government" (2 Macc 11:1). In contrast to the *epitropos* who was normally a friend or relative of the father, the *oikonomos* was of low social standing, a slave. Nevertheless, he could attain considerable power and was often placed in charge of financial and administrative affairs. In the NT the term refers to one who manages the master's property (Luke 12:42; 16:1, 3, 8), a city treasurer (Rom 16:23), and is applied to those who administer divine things (1 Cor 4:1-2).

until the time appointed by the father: "The time appointed" translates *prothesmia*, a legal term, but found only here in the NT, referring to a day appointed before-hand "within which money was to be paid, actions brought, claims made, elections held, etc., and if this period was allowed to expire, no further proceedings were allowed" (Liddell & Scott). Normally the age was set by the government, but in this instance Paul envisions the father establishing it.

3. *Thus even we, when we were minors*: The first person plural is emphasized by *kai hēmeis* ("even we") and can be understood in either an exclusive sense ("we Jewish Christians") or an inclusive sense ("we Jewish and Gentile Christians"). While most commentators prefer the latter interpretation, Paul's use of "you" in v. 6 suggests that the "we" in this verse should be taken in an exclusive sense: we Jewish Christians. Thus Paul is talking about the situation of his kinsmen just as he does in 2:16 (*kai hēmeis*, "even we"); 3:13; and 3:23-24.

were enslaved under rudimentary principles: "Rudimentary principles" translates *ta stoicheia tou kosmou* ("the elements of the world," or "the rudiments of the world"). The precise meaning of the phrase has long been a point of dispute. Helpful surveys of the secondary literature and the attempts to solve the problem are found in J. Blinzler, "Lexikalisches zu dem Terminus *ta stoicheia tou kosmou* bei Paulus"; Burton, *Galatians*, 510–18; Delling, *TDNT*, VII:670-87, and Mussner, *Galaterbrief*, 293–304. Difficulty in interpreting the phrase arises, in part, because *stoicheion* has a wide range of meaning; Blinzler lists nine: (1) a single letter; (2) the letters of the alphabet; (3) the fundamental principles of a science, of art, of instruction, or of an institution; (4) rudiments or first principles; (5) the physical elements (air, fire, water, earth); (6) supports or pillars; (7) the stars or heavenly bodies; (8) elemental spirits; (9) demons or spirits. These different meanings have led to varying interpretations of *ta stoicheia tou kosmou*, the most prominent of which are given by Burton (*Galatians*, 515): (1) the physical elements of the world (earth, air, fire, and water); (2) the heavenly bodies, especially the stars; (3) the spirits associated with these heavenly bodies; (4) the rudimentary principles of religious knowledge. Wis 7:17; 19:18; 4 Macc 12:13; and 2 Pet 3:10, 12 use *stoicheion* in the first sense, while the early Church Fathers generally adopted the second. Evidence for the third interpretation does not appear until the second century; Heb 5:12 provides an example of the fourth sense. The phrase found here, *ta stoicheia tou kosmou*, appears to be a Pauline formulation since it is found only here and in Col 2:8,20. However, since Colossians may be Deutero-

Pauline it is best not to interpret the text of Galatians in light of it. What Paul intends by this puzzling phrase can only be determined in light of the entire passage (4:1-11). Betz (*Galatians*, 204) notes that "A large number of scholarly investigations have arrived at the conclusion that these 'elements of the world' represent demonic forces which constitute and control 'this evil aeon' (1:4)." As the translation adopted by this text suggests, however, this commentary follows the interpretation of older commentators such has Ramsay, Lightfoot, and Burton who interpret the phrase as the rudimentary principles of religious life apart from Christ. In any case, the significant point is that, according to Paul, the *stoicheia* held sway over the Jews as well as the Gentiles.

4. *But when the fullness of time came*: The concept expressed here, *to pleroma tou chronou*, is almost apocalyptic. A predetermined period must be completed before the appearance of salvation. For similar examples see Tobit 14:5; Mark 1:15; Eph 1:10. Understood in reference to God, the fullness of time is the time determined by God. Understood in reference to humanity, it is the time when humanity came of age (Lightfoot, *Galatians*, 167). The fullness of time here corresponds to the time set by the father (*prothesmia*).

God sent his Son: The only occurrences of *exapostellein* ("to send") in Paul's writings are here and in v. 6 where a similar phrase occurs, "God sent the Spirit of his Son." In both instances, the emphasis is upon the Father's initiative. The whole of v. 4 sounds like an earlier tradition adopted by Paul. Although the preexistence of Christ is not explicitly stated here, it is probably implied. For other texts that point in the direction of preexistence see Rom 8:3; 1 Cor 8:6; 2 Cor 8:9; Phil 2:6-8; and Col 1:15-16.

born of a woman, born under the Law: Both phrases indicate the human condition of God's Son. The first uses a phrase employed elsewhere to describe the human condition (Job 14:1; Matt 11:11); it neither implies nor denies the virgin birth. Although Paul may have known that the name of Jesus' mother was Mary, he does not refer to her by name in his writings. The second phrase points to Jesus' Jewish heritage: he was a son of the Law. The same phrase (*hypo nomon*) is used in 3:23 and 4:5 to describe the situation of humanity's enslavement and in 5:18 it is contrasted with being led by the Spirit. Its use here indicates that God's Son experienced the fullness of the human condition.

5. *in order that he might ransom those under the Law*: This is the first of two purpose clauses which explain why God sent his Son. The pronoun "he," which is the unexpressed subject of the verb *exagorasē* ("ransomed"), refers to Jesus. See 3:13 where the same verb is used in reference to Christ ransoming humanity from the curse of the Law. The object of the Son's ransoming activity is *tous hypo nomon* ("those under the Law"): the Jewish people. In 1 Cor 6:20; 7:23, however, Paul writes that the Corinthians (Gentiles) were "ransomed" at a great price. The imagery is that of a slave whose freedom has been purchased by another.

that we might receive adoption: This second purpose clause is coordinated with the first, not dependent upon it. The "we" now includes the Gentiles as v. 6 indicates. *Hyiothesia* was the legal term for adoption in the Greco-Roman world. This "process of adoption was often combined with making a will (*diatithēmi*)" (W. v Martitz, *TDNT*, VIII: 398). In the NT the term only occurs in the Pauline writings (Rom 8:15, 23; 9:4; Gal 4:5; Eph 1:5). In light of Graeco-Egyptian papyri, Moore-Crispin ("The Use and Abuse of Parallels," 216) draws the following conclusions about adoption: (1) the adopted son becomes the true son of his adopted father; (2) the father agrees to provide the necessities of food and clothing; (3) the adopted son cannot be repudiated; (4) the adopted son cannot be reduced to slavery; (5) the natural parents cannot reclaim the adopted son; (6) adoption leads to the right of inheritance.

6. *Because you are sons*: *Hoti de este hyioi* can be translated "the proof that you are sons" or "because you are sons." The first translation implies that sonship derives from the Spirit whereas the second suggests that the Spirit comes as a result of sonship. Rom 8:14-15 argues in favor of the first translation, but the more natural translation of *hoti* is "because." Moreover, v. 5 indicates that sonship results from the sending of God's Son. Paul, however, does not intend to describe a strict chronological process so that there is no need to press the order of sonship followed by the Spirit. *Hyios* and *hyiothesia* have been translated as "son" and "sonship" in order to be faithful to the example the Apostle employs. Paul's thought here, however, is not gender exclusive.

God sent the Spirit of his Son into our hearts: "God" is absent from some manuscripts (B, 1739). P46 does not have *tou hyiou* ("of the Son"). The omission of *tou hyiou* is understandable since "the Spirit *of his Son*" does not occur elsewhere in the NT, and elsewhere in Galatians Paul simply speaks of the Spirit. In 2 Cor 3:17, however, Paul writes of the "Spirit of the Lord," and in Phil 1:19 of the "Spirit of Jesus Christ." Moreover, in Rom 8:9-10 the phrases "Spirit of God," "Spirit of Christ," and "Christ is in you" refer to the same reality. In his discussion of this, Burton (*Galatians*, 222–23), notes that while Paul clearly distinguishes Christ from God the Father, he does not so clearly distinguish Christ and the Spirit. To experience the Spirit is to experience the Risen Lord (2 Cor 3:17).

crying, "Abba," that is "Father": The Aramaic "Abba" is found in Mark 14:36 and Rom 8:15. In each instance it is translated as *ho patēr* which is to be rendered as a vocative, "Father!" Jesus' unique form of address to God becomes available to all believers through the agency of the Spirit.

7. *So you are no longer a slave but a son*: "Son" is now used in a theological sense: a son of God. Compare 3:26 where "sons of God" was used as an epithet for the people of God. Here Paul's meaning is more individualized: the believer becomes an adopted son of God through Christ.

and if a son, even an heir through God: The final phrase *dia theou* ("through God") is unusual since God is usually portrayed as the source or origin and Christ as the mediator. This difficult reading has given rise to a series of variants: (1) "an heir of God," (2) "an heir on account of God," (3) "an heir through Christ," (4) "an heir through Jesus Christ," (5) "an heir of God through Jesus Christ," (6) "an heir through God in Jesus Christ," (7) "an heir of God and fellow heir with Christ." The reading "through God" expresses the graciousness of God's activity rather than mediation: the believer becomes an heir because of what God has done.

8. *But then, not knowing God*: *Alla* ("but") is a strong adversative which indicates that a new phase of the argument has begun. *Tote* ("then") stands in contrast to *nyn* ("now"), the first describing life before Christ's coming, the latter, life after Christ's coming. "Not knowing God" is a Jewish characterization of the Gentiles: people who are ignorant of the one God, the God of Israel. See Jer 10:25; Ps 79:6; 1 Thess 4:5; 2 Thess 1:8.

you were enslaved to things that by nature are not gods: The phrase *tois physei mē ousin theois* can also be translated "to gods who are not gods at all" (REB). So translated, *physei mē ousin* is construed as an adjectival phrase limiting *theois*. (See 1 Cor 8:5 where Paul seems to concede the existence of such gods.) The translation adopted here takes the participle *ousin* substantively and *theoi* as its predicate. *Ousin* can be translated as "beings" (RSV, NRSV, NEB) or as "things" (NAB, NJB). The latter translation is adopted here because of what Paul says in v. 10. In sum, he describes the former conduct of the Galatians as an enslavement to things that have the appearance of being gods but in fact are not. See 1 Cor 8-10 where Paul describes the former conduct of the Corinthians who worshipped such gods by their participation at sacred meals.

9. *But now, knowing God*: *Nyn* ("now") forms a contrast with *tote* ("then") in v. 8. The God the Galatians know is the God of Israel revealed in Jesus Christ.

rather known by God: The phrase limits the former assertion lest the Galatians mistakenly think that the act of knowing begins with them. Knowledge of God results from having been known by God. See Rom 8:28-30; 1 Cor 13:12.

how is it that you are turning again to weak and impotent rudiments which you wish to serve again: *Palin* ("again") and *palin anōthen douleuein* ("to serve again") indicate that the weak and impotent rudiments (*asthenē kai ptōcha stoicheia*) are the non-gods mentioned in v. 8. By referring to these non-gods as *stoicheia* Paul relates them to the *stoicheia tou kosmou* mentioned in v. 3. Jews were under the *stoicheia tou kosmou*, understood as the rudimentary principles of religion apart from Christ, when they were under the Law. The Gentiles were under the *asthenē kai ptōcha stocheia*, understood as elementary principles of religion, when they served false gods. By turning to circumcision the Galatians trade one rudimentary form of religion for another.

10. *You are observing days, months, festal seasons, and years*: Although the Galatians have not yet accepted circumcision (5:2), the present tense of the verb *paratēreisthe* ("observing") suggests that they have begun to adopt Jewish calendar practices. Compare the list here with Col 2:16: *heortēs* ("festivals"), *neomēnias* ("new moon"), *sabbatōn* ("Sabbaths"). *Hēmeras* ("days") probably refers to the Sabbath, as well as other Jewish festivals. See Rom 14:5. The only use of *sabbatōn* in the Pauline writings is 1 Cor 16:2 and Col 2:16. *Mēnas* ("months") is probably used in reference to the new moon which begins each month. Num 10:10 mentions the festival of the new moon, and Num 28:11

lists the offerings to be brought on that day. In 2 Kings 4:23 the new moon and the Sabbath are mentioned together. *Kairous* ("times") refers to a fixed time such as a festal season. In Exod 23:14, 17 and Lev 23:4 the word is employed in conjunction with Israel's three great feasts: Passover, Pentecost, and Tabernacles. *Eniautous* ("years") could be the Jubilee year or the beginning of the new year.

11. *I am afraid for you lest somehow I have labored in vain for you*: Paul concludes this section with a statement, similar to that found in 4:20, of his emotional state. But see 5:10 where he expresses greater confidence in the community.

INTERPRETATION

In 3:1-29 Paul developed a series of arguments to show the Galatians that they are Abraham's descendants because they have been incorporated into Abraham's one seed, Jesus Christ. Although Paul's argument takes many twists and turns in chapter three, it is nonetheless a single, sustained argument which comes to its conclusion in 3:29, "if you belong to Christ, then you are Abraham's seed, heirs according to promise." In 4:1–5:12, however, Paul's strategy takes a rhetorical turn. To be sure, the Apostle continues to argue, in various ways, that the Galatians are children of the promise. But from this point forward, his rhetoric assumes a more personal tone as he rebukes the Galatians and makes a series of appeals and requests to them. Thus in this unit (4:1-11) he rebukes the Galatians for returning to the period of their minority by placing themselves under the Law. In 4:12-20 the rebuke becomes more personal as he appeals to the Galatians to become as he is: free from the Law. In 4:21-31, Paul returns to the question of Abraham's descendants. He rebukes the Galatians for misinterpreting the Law and appeals to them to cast out the slave woman and her son, that is, the agitators. Finally, in 5:1-12 Paul makes his most direct appeal to the Galatians, warning them that if they accept circumcision they will cut themselves off from Christ. In effect, by rebuking the Galatians and appealing to them not to place themselves under the Law, this section (4:1–5:12) supports and develops the argument made in 3:1-29 that the Galatians are the children of the promise.

The material of this unit (4:1-11) is clearly connected with what has preceded and prepares for what will follow. In 3:23-25, Paul introduced the theme of the *paidagōgos*, in order to show that the time of the Law was a period of servitude and immaturity, and in 3:26-29 he developed the themes of sonship and inheritance. All of these themes reappear in 4:1-11. Finally, Paul's statement of perplexity in 4:11 prepares for the next unit (4:12-19) in which he makes the most personal and emotional appeal of this letter. The material of this unit falls into a clearly defined outline. In vv. 1–2 Paul employs an example from the legal realm as he did in 3:15. Next, in vv. 3–7 he applies the example to those under the Law. Finally in vv. 8–11, with the example still in mind, he rebukes the Galatians for returning to the weak and impotent rudiments of religion.

vv. 1–2   a legal example
vv. 3–7   application
vv. 8–11   rebuke and appeal

A legal example (vv. 1–2). The manner in which Paul opens this unit ("What I am saying. . . .") suggests that he is not completely satisfied with his argument thus far. He has shown the Galatians that they are Abraham's seed in Christ, that is, "sons of God." Moreover, he has explained the temporary role of the Law which functioned as a *paidagōgos*. However, lest the Galatians still regard the Law as something which completes and perfects their faith in Christ (see 3:3), Paul now explains that the Law belongs to a period of spiritual minority. To make his point, he draws a comparison between the situation of an heir who is under (*hypo*) the authority of guardians (*epitropoi*) and stewards (*oikonomoi*), and the situation of those under (*hypo*) the Law.

An heir (*klēronomos*) is placed under the authority of guardians (*epitropoi*) and stewards (*oikonomoi*) until a date (*prothesmia*) determined by the father. While the guardian was a friend or relative of the father, responsible for the heir's education and well-being, the steward was a slave charged with the daily running of the estate (see notes). By this arrangement, written in the father's will, the father could assure himself that the son-heir would be under guidance and care until a time which he, the father, had determined. Paul's example seems to presuppose that the father has already died. The son, therefore, is the owner of the entire estate. Nonetheless, because he is a minor (*nēpios*), he is no different from a slave since he is under the power of guardians and stewards until the day set by the father for his majority.

While the authority of the guardians and stewards brings to mind that of the *paidagōgos* mentioned in 3:23–25, Paul introduces a new element here. In the case of the *paidagōgos* the primary focus was upon the restricting power of the *paidagōgos* over his charge. Here, in addition to the restricting power of the guardians and stewards, Paul highlights the minority (*nēpios*) of the heir. The heir is under the restrictive power of guardians and stewards because he is a minor. Only when the day set by the father arrives will the heir attain his majority and inherit his father's estate, free from guardians and stewards.

Application of the example (vv. 3–7). Paul now applies his example, "Thus, *even we*, when *we* were minors (*nēpioi*), were enslaved under rudimentary principles (*hypo ta stoicheia tou kosmou*)." But to whom is Paul referring? Jewish Christians like himself? His Gentiles converts, especially the Galatians? Or both Jewish and Gentile believers? While Paul's example ultimately has both Jews and Gentiles in mind, here he focuses primarily upon Jewish Christians like himself. Thus he says in v. 4 that God sent his son in order to redeem those "under the Law." There is, he implies, a correspondence between the situation of the heir and that of those under the Law. Just as the heir apparent is under guardians and stewards, so those under the Law were under the *stoicheia tou kosmou*, and just as the heir came to his majority on the day (*prothesmia*) set by the father, so "we" came to our majority in the fullness of time (*to plērōma tou chronou*) when God sent His Son to redeem those under the Law. The analogy Paul establishes is as follows.

heir . . . under guardians and stewards . . . until the time appointed
we . . . under *stoicheia tou kosmou* . . .   until the fullness of time.

What Paul means by *ta stoicheia tou kosmou* has been, and probably will remain, a point of dispute (see notes). Several solutions have been proposed, but most fall into one of two categories: (1) the *stoicheia* are the powers or beings associated with the elements, especially the heavenly bodies; (2) the *stoicheia* are the first principles or rudiments of learning. By translating the phrase "the elemental spirits" of the universe, or of the world the NEB, REB, and NRSV favor the first interpretation, while the rendition of the NIV, "the basic principles of the world," leans toward the second. The NAB, by contrast, leaves both options open with its translation, "the elemental powers of the world." Schlier (*Galaterbrief*, 191), argues that the context demands that the *stoicheia* be understood as personal beings since they are likened to guardians, stewards (4:1), and gods (4:8). But the emphasis in this unit upon the period of humanity's minority supports the translation adopted here, "rudimentary principles." Before the fullness of time, those under the Law were in their spiritual minority; they lived under the rudimentary principles of religion because Christ-faith had not yet made its appearance (3:23). But with the appearance of Christ-faith the period of minority ended. Those who have believed on the basis of the faith of Christ are freed from the rudimentary principles of the Law as expressed in circumcision, dietary rules, and calendar observances.

In referring to the *stoicheia tou kosmou*, Paul is undoubtedly adopting a concept familiar to the Galatians and applying it to the situation of his Jewish co-religionists. In effect, he says to the Galatians: "Even we Jews were under the powers which you call the *stoicheia tou kosmou*. But whereas you experienced the *stoicheia* by worshipping false gods (4:8), we experienced them by living under the Law; especially its legal works of circumcision, dietary regulations, and calendar observances, all of which set us apart from the Gentile world. But now that the fullness of time has come, we have been freed from those rudimentary principles." Just as the minority of the heir ended on the day appointed by the father, so the minority of those under the Law ended when God sent his Son, "in order that he might ransom those under the Law, that we might receive adoption (*hyiothesia*)."

The introduction of the adoption theme is somewhat disruptive since Paul's example presupposes that the heir is a son or daughter even though he does not explicitly say so. The disruption, however, is only apparent. In vv. 3–5a, Paul has been focusing upon those under the Law, Israelites like himself who could already claim the honor of sonship (Rom 9:4), even though they were only minors under the Law. But now Paul's thought shifts to the Gentiles since God's redemptive act on behalf of Israel has implications for them as well. While the sending of the Son redeemed those under the Law (4:5a), it also resulted in adoption for the Gentiles (4:5b). Consequently the Galatians can call God "Abba," just as Jesus did (Mark 14:36) because the coming of Christ has made them sons and daughters. Moreover, like all sons and daughters they are heirs (*klēronomoi*), but heirs whose period of minority has ended.

The power to call God "Abba" comes from the Spirit. By reminding the Galatians that the Spirit of Christ dwells in them, Paul recalls the argument already made in 3:1-6. There he reminded the Galatians that they received the Spirit from the message of faith (*ex akoēs pisteōs*), not from legal works (*ex ergōn nomou*). Here he tells them that God has sent (*exapesteilen*) the Spirit of his Son into their hearts because (*hoti*) they are sons and daughters. The gift of the Spirit and their adoption does not depend upon legal works but upon God's act of sending his Son (*exapesteilen*), born under the Law, to redeem those under the Law (cf. 3:13, "Christ redeemed us from the curse of the Law becoming a curse on our behalf"). Consequently, being under the Law does not result in the completion and perfection of faith (3:2) but in a state of servitude and minority.

Rebuke and appeal (vv. 8–11). Having set forth his example and applied it to the situation of Jewish Christians like himself, Paul turns his attention to the Galatians with an appeal that is, in fact, a sharp rebuke. He reminds the Galatians that at one time (*tote*), prior to their faith in Christ, they were enslaved (*edouleusate*) "to things that by nature are not gods." But now (*nyn*), when they should know better, they are turning again to the weak and impotent *stoicheia* to which they want to be enslaved (*douleusein*) again; they are already submitting to calendar observances required by the Law. Paul wonders if his preaching, which centered on the death of Christ, has been in vain.

The situation of the Galatians, prior to their conversion, was marked by ignorance because they did not know the God of Israel. Like other Gentiles, they worshipped things which they thought were gods, but in fact were not. See 1 Thess 1:9 ("how you turned to God from idols, to serve a living and true God"), and 1 Cor 8:5-6 ("even though there are many so-called gods in heaven or on earth . . . yet for us there is one God"). But with the coming of Christ-faith, the time of ignorance ended and the time of knowledge began. The Galatians came to know the one God because they were "known by God." This last expression, which also occurs in 1 Cor 8:3 and 13:12, is a reference to God's elective love (Rom 8:29; 11:2; Phil 3:12; 2 Tim 2:19). Just as Israel knew the one God because God chose her from all the nations of the earth (Amos 3:2, "You only have I known of all the families of the earth"), so the Galatians now know God because they belong to God's chosen people. They are "sons of God" (3:26) because of the adoption (*hyiothesia*) they received when God sent his Son (4:5).

During this period of ignorance the Galatians were enslaved to the weak and impotent *stoicheia*, the same *stoicheia* mentioned in 4:3. But whereas in 4:3 Paul spoke of the *stoicheia tou kosmou* in reference to Israel, here he speaks of them in reference to the Galatians who are Gentiles. Israel and the Gentiles were enslaved to the *stoicheia*, but in different ways. For Israel the enslavement meant being under the Law with its legal practices of circumcision, dietary regulations, and calendar observances. For the Gentiles the enslavement came from a rudimentary form of religion which led them to the worship of things which by their very nature were not gods. Paul warns the Galatians that by placing themselves under the Law, they are returning to the house of the *stoicheia* by another door!

The mention of days, months, festal seasons, and years undoubtedly refers to calendar observances of the Law required of those who accept circumcision; e.g., Sabbaths, new moons, and annual feasts. In and of itself there is nothing wrong with the observance of such days. In 1 Cor 16:8, for example, Paul says that he wants to stay in Ephesus until Pentecost, and in Rom 14:5-6 he writes, "Some judge one day to be better than another, while others judge all days to be alike. Let all be fully convinced in their own minds. Those who observe the day, observe it in honor of the Lord." But in the case of the Galatians Paul sees these calendar observances as part of a wider pattern. The Galatians believe that by doing these legal works they will complete and perfect their faith (3:3). In effect, they call into question the sufficiency of Christ-faith by acting as if legal observances are necessary to make them Abraham's seed and "sons of God." Paul's counter-argument is simple: the Galatians are returning to the rudimentary form of religion from which they have so recently been converted.

It is difficult to say to what extent the Galatians were actually observing Jewish feasts. While the present tense suggests that they were already engaging in such practices, 5:2-11 indicates that the majority of Galatians had not yet accepted circumcision. In all likelihood, therefore, the observance of Jewish feasts had only begun. Paul, however, seizes upon this point because it allows him to introduce the *stoicheia tou kosmou* which he relates to the Law. If the Messiah came to redeem his own people from the Law, and if the Law was a way of being under the *stoicheia*, then why are the Galatians returning to the very *stoicheia*, from which they have so recently escaped, by placing themselves under the Law? Paul's perplexity about the Galatians leads him to ask if he has labored in vain. In the next section he will develop the personal sentiments expressed in v. 11 in greater detail.

For Reference and Further Study

Belleville, " 'Under Law' Structural Analysis and the Pauline Concept of Law in Galatians 3.21-4.11." *JSNT* 26 (1986) 53–78.

Blinzler, J. "Lexikalisches zu dem Terminus *ta stoicheia tou kosmou* bei Paulus." *Studiorum Paulinorum Congressus Internationalis Catholicus*. AnBib 17–18, vol. 2; Rome: Pontifical Institute, 1963, 429–42.

Delling, G. *Stoicheō, TDNT*, VII.

Howard, G. *Paul: Crisis in Galatia*. SNTSMS 35; Cambridge University Press, 1979.

Moore-Crispin, D. R. "Galatians 4:1-9: The Use and Abuse of Parallels." *EvQ* 60 (1989) 203–223.

Reicke, B. "The Law and This World according to Paul: Some Thoughts Concerning Gal 4:1-11." *JBL* 70 (1951) 259–276.

Robinson, D. W. B. "The Distinction between Jewish and Gentile Believers in Galatians." *AusBR* 13 (1965) 29–48.

Schweizer, E. "Slaves of the Elements and Worshipers of Angels: Gal 4:3, 9 and Col 2:8, 18, 20." *JBL* 107 (1988) 455–494.

Taubenschlag, R. *The Law of Greco-Roman Egypt in the Light of the Papyri 332 B.C. to 640 A.D.* New York: Herald Square Press, 1944.

Become as I Am (4:12-20)

12. Brethren, I am asking you, become as I am because I have become as you are. You did me no wrong; 13. you know that it was because of a bodily ailment that I first preached the gospel to you. 14. You neither despised nor disdained the trial which my physical condition caused you, but you welcomed me as an angel of God, as Christ Jesus. 15.

Where, then, is that happiness of yours? For I can testify to you that if possible you would have torn out your eyes and given them to me. 16. So, have I become your enemy by telling you the truth? 17. They court your favor, not in a way which is commendable, but they want to isolate you in order that you might court their favor. 18. It is always good to be courted in what is good, and not only when I am present among you, 19. my children for whom I am suffering the pangs of birth until Christ be formed in you. 20. I would like to be present to you now and change my tone because I am at a loss about you.

Notes

12. *Brethren, I am asking you, become as I am because I have become as you are*: Paul has become like the Galatians inasmuch as he has set aside those practices of the Law which separate Jew from Gentile (2:15-16), the very practices that the Galatians want to assume. Therefore, he asks them to become as he is: one who lives by Christ rather than by the Mosaic Law. In 1 Cor 9:21 Paul says that although he became *anomos* ("outside of the Law") to those outside of the Law, he is *ennomos Christou* ("under Christ's Law"). In Phil 3:8-9 he says that he set aside his righteousness, gained under the Law, in order to gain Christ. For texts in which Paul is presented as an example to be imitated, see 1 Cor 4:16; 11:1; Phil 3:17; 1 Thess 1:6; 2 Thess 3:7, 9.

    You did me no wrong: The verb *adikein* can mean to injure someone physically, or to treat someone unjustly; the latter makes better sense here as the following verses will show. The Galatians did not treat Paul unjustly when he first visited them. But now, by subscribing to circumcision, they are implying that his gospel was deficient. So, in v. 16 Paul will ask if he has become their enemy. Compare 2 Cor 2:5; 7:12 where Paul refers to an incident in which a member of the Corinthian community caused him pain and wronged him.

13. *you know that it was because of a bodily ailment*: "Because of a bodily ailment" translates *di' astheneian tēs sarkos* (literally, "through weakness of the flesh"). In Rom 6:19; 8:26; 1 Cor 2:3; 2 Cor 11:30 *astheneia* refers to human weakness, but here it has the sense of illness. The preposition *dia* ("because") suggests that the bodily ailment was the cause of Paul's preaching to the Galatians. Ramsay (*Galatians*, 417–422) suggests that a fever forced Paul, during the course of his first missionary journey (Acts 13:4–14:26), to leave the low country of Pamphylia for the high country of Antioch in Pisidia located in the Province of Galatia (Acts 13:13-14). This suggestion, however, is dependent upon the historical reliability of Acts and assumes the South Galatian hypothesis. The nature of Paul's illness remains a point of conjecture: fever-headache, epilepsy, eye disease. Verse 15 could indicate an eye ailment, but that verse need not be interpreted in this fashion. Perhaps the ailment is related to the "thorn in the flesh" mentioned in 2 Cor 12:7.

    that I first preached the gospel to you: *To proteron* can be construed as "the first time" (a second time being implied), or as "originally," "formerly," "first."

If the first translation is adopted, Paul is referring to the first of two visits to Galatia. According to *BDF*, no. 62, Hellenistic Greek did not necessarily employ *to proteron* in its strict classical sense, "the first of two." Turner (*Grammar of New Testament Greek*, III, Syntax, 30), however, states that the comparative sense, "the first time," is possible. Proponents of the South Galatian hypothesis, e.g., Ramsay, argue that the first visit was that of Acts 13:3–14:26 and the second that of Acts 16:1-6. This results in an early dating of the letter. Proponents of the North Galatian hypothesis contend that the two visits are those of Acts 16:6; 18:23, which results in a later dating of the letter. Both hypotheses, of course, suppose the historical reliability of Paul's missionary journeys as recounted in Acts. See the introduction of this commentary for an alternate view.

14. *You neither despised nor disdained the trial which my physical condition caused you*: This translation attempts to overcome the difficulties caused by an awkward Greek phrase: *kai ton peirasmon hymōn* ("and your trial"). A smoother but less reliable reading is found in S², 81, 104, 326 which omit the possessive pronoun. P46 reads *mou* instead of *hymon* and omits *oude exeptysate* ("nor disdained") so that the text reads "You did not despise *my* trial in my flesh." The more difficult reading, which is adopted here, is attested by a series of good and widespread witnesses (S*, A, B, C², D*, F, G, 33). The sense of the passage is that although Paul's physical ailment was a *peirasmon* ("trial") to the Galatians, they did not ridicule him. The literal meaning of *ekptyein* which here is translated as "disdain" is "to spit out," as a defense against sickness and other demonic threats (*TDNT*: II, 448–449); this is the only occurrence of the word in the NT. *Exouthenein* ("to despise") is a common word in Paul's writings (Rom 4:3, 10; 1 Cor 1:28; 6:4; 16:11; 2 Cor 10:10; 1 Thess 5:20).

but you welcomed me as an angel of God, as Christ Jesus: *Aggelon* can be translated as "messenger" or as "angel." But since *hōs aggelon theou* is coordinated with *hōs Christon Iēsoun*, the latter translation has been adopted. See 1:8 where the same word is used. The willingness of the Galatians to receive Paul as if he were Christ recalls Jesus' words in Matt 10:40.

15. *Where, then, is that happiness of yours?*: *Ho makarismos hymon* can be interpreted as an objective or subjective genitive. In the first instance, it means the happiness or blessedness Paul ascribed to the Galatians for the way in which they received him. In the second, adopted here, it refers to the happiness or good fortune that the Galatians ascribed to themselves that Paul fortuitously preached the gospel to them. Since Paul is speaking of the Galatians' former attitude toward him, the latter choice seems preferable.

For I can testify to you that if possible you would have torn out your eyes and given them to me: This phrase has suggested to some that the ailment mentioned in v. 13 was an affliction of the eye. However, the phrase may simply be an indication of the esteem with which the Galatians once held Paul, the eye being one of the most prized members of the body.

16. *So, have I become your enemy by telling you the truth?*: Except for Eph 4:15, this is the only occurrence of the verb *alētheuein* ("to speak the truth") in the NT. In 2:5, 14 Paul refers to the "truth of the gospel," and in 5:7 he asks the Galatians who hindered them from obeying the truth. Speaking the truth to the Galatians means proclaiming the truth of the gospel: righteousness through Christ-faith, apart from the Law. *Echthros* ("enemy") can be understood in a passive sense (hated by the Galatians) or active sense (hostile to the Galatians). The latter seems preferable since the Galatians view Paul as someone who has become hostile to them. See Paul's usage of the word in Rom 5:10; 11:28; 12:20; 1 Cor 15:25, 26; Phil 3:18.

17. *They court your favor, not in a way which is commendable*: "They court your favor" translates *zēlousin* which occurs three times in vv. 17–18. The unexpressed subject, "they," refers to the agitators. The verb can be used in a negative sense ("be filled with jealousy toward someone") or a positive sense ("desire," "be deeply concerned about someone"). The positive sense is intended here. The agitators are courting the favor of the Galatians, "but in a way that is not commendable" (*ou kalōs*) because they want them to adopt legal works.

    but they want to isolate you: *Ekkleiein* has the sense of excluding someone by withdrawing fellowship. It is not stated from whom the Galatians will be excluded. Paul may mean exclusion from fellowship with Law-free believers like himself, or from fellowship with Christ (5:4).

    in order that you might court their favor: Paul plays on the verb *zēloun*. Once the Galatians have accepted the position of the Judaizers they will be dependent upon them as teachers. A few manuscripts (D*, F, G) read, "but seek the better gifts," which is probably assimilated from 1 Cor 12:31.

18. *It is always good to be courted in what is good, and not only when I am present among you*: Paul continues to play on the verb *zēloun*, but this time he employs the passive infinitive. Others may court the favor of the Galatians, provided it is *en kalŏ* ("in what is good"). The phrase is not explained but it suggests that Paul is referring to the realm of Christ apart from the Law. In 2 Cor 7:7 Paul writes that Titus told him of the Corinthians' zeal for him (*ton hymōn zēlon hyper emou*).

19. *my children for whom I am suffering the pangs of birth until Christ be formed in you*: Verse 19 can be construed as the conclusion of v. 18 or as the beginning of a new sentence. Here it is taken as the conclusion of v. 18 rather than as the beginning of a new sentence. Verse 20, with the particle *de*, is clearly the beginning of a new sentence. The Galatians are Paul's *tekna* ("children") because he is the founder of the community. See 1 Cor 4:14-15; 1 Thess 2:7; Phlm 10 for similar usage. Except for 4:27 and Rev 12:2, this is the only use of *odinein* ("suffer birth pangs"). B. Gaventa ("The Maternity of Paul") notes that "*Odinein* . . . never refers to the mere *fact* of a birth, but always to the accompanying anguish" (192–93). She argues that "Paul's anguish, his travail, is not simply a personal matter or a literary convention . . . but reflects the anguish of the whole created order as it awaits the fulfillment of God's action in Jesus Christ" (194). The adverb *palin* ("again") suggests that he

suffered the pangs of childbirth when he first founded the community. Because the community has strayed from the truth, he must endure these pains once more until *morphōthę̄ Christos en hymin* ("Christ may be formed in you"). This is the only use of the verb *morphoun* in the NT. It means to take shape or form, like an embryo in a womb. The text could mean (1) that Christ is formed in the Galatians so that he lives in them as he lives in Paul (2:20) or (2) that Christ is formed within the community in its life and ministry as its guiding spirit. See Phil 3:10 where Paul speaks of being conformed (*symmorphizomenos*) to Christ's death.

20. *I would like to be present to you now*: Galatians is different from Paul's other correspondence inasmuch as it makes no reference to an impending visit. See Rom 15:14-33; 1 Cor 4:14-21; 2 Cor 12:14–13:13; Phil 2:19-24; 1 Thess 2:17–3:13; Phlm 21-22. This may indicate that Paul is not in a position to visit the Galatians even though the crisis is acute. If Paul is writing from Ephesus, perhaps he is in the midst of his difficulties with the Corinthian Church.

and change my tone: The phrase refers to Paul's harsh tone in this letter. See 1:6.

because I am at a loss about you: The verb *aporein* ("to be at a loss," "to be in doubt," "to be uncertain") is used often in the NT to emphasize that people simply cannot fathom a particular situation (Mark 6:20; Luke 24:4; John 13:22; Acts 25:20; 2 Cor 4:8). That Paul cannot understand the behavior of the Galatians could imply that he does not fully comprehend the situation at Galatia.

INTERPRETATION

Thus far, Paul has employed a number of theologically sophisticated arguments to persuade the Galatians that there is no need for them to adopt circumcision and works of the Law. This section, with its strong personal and emotional appeal, therefore, comes as a surprise to the reader, just as it must have surprised the Galatians. Suddenly, and somewhat unexpectedly, Paul leaves the lofty heights of theological argumentation and appeals to the strong ties which once united him and the Galatians. If his theological arguments do not persuade them, perhaps a recollection of the Galatians' former affection for him as the founder of their community will deter them from their disastrous course.

H. D. Betz is correct when he notes, "All commentators point out that the section 4:12-20 presents considerable difficulties" (*Galatians*, 220). While most commentators attribute Paul's erratic style here to his emotional state at the time of writing the letter, Betz argues that the rhetorical character of the passage has not been fully appreciated. In his view (*Galatians*, 221), Paul is offering "a string of topoi belonging to the theme of 'friendship' (*peri philias*)." This appeal to friendship, Betz contends, conforms with Hellenistic style "which calls for change between heavy and light sections and which would require an emotional and personal approach to offset the impression of mere abstractions'' (*Galatians*, 221). Betz's last point is well taken. After the dense argumentation of chapter three, this section provides a welcome relief. It is debatable, however, that Paul is presenting a series of topoi belonging to the theme of friendship. While Paul appeals to the former relationship that existed between himself and the Galatians, he does not describe it as a relationship between friends. Rather, he reminds the Galatians that he is the founder of the community whom they once received as an angel of God (v. 14).

Why, then, has Paul introduced this personal appeal? First, from a rhetorical point of view, a personal appeal provides the Galatians with some relief from the intricacies of Paul's exegetical thought which has dominated chapter three and the first part of this chapter. Realizing that he must afford the Galatians an opportunity to absorb what he has said, Paul turns to a more concrete and personal line of argumentation. As in 1:13–2:21, he employs autobiographical material to support his case: there was a time when the Galatians viewed him as God's own messenger. Second, at different points in the letter thus far, Paul has written somewhat harshly to the Galatians. In 1:6, for example, he accused them of abandoning the one who called them, and in 3:1 he portrayed them as senseless people who allowed others to bewitch them. The personal appeal of this section allows Paul to express genuine concern for the Galatians enabling him to reaffirm the bond of unity that still exists between him and them. Finally, this appeal is related to what Paul will say about the Galatians in the moral exhortation of chapters five and six. From that moral exhortation, it is evident that the crisis at Galatia resulted in a serious division within the Galatian churches; the teaching of the agitators proved divisive. Here, by harkening back to an earlier period in the community's history, Paul reminds the Galatians of that period of peace and harmony when they were united because they accepted his Torah-free gospel. To regain that unity the Galatians must return to the generosity of that earlier period, as described here.

This section is of special interest, then, because of what it says about the founding of the Galatian churches and about Paul's relationship to them. The Apostle portrays himself as a guide worthy of imitation (v. 12a), and as the founder and parent of the community (v. 19). At one time the Galatians esteemed him as an angel of God (v. 14), but now they view him as their enemy (v. 16). Not even Paul understands why this has happened. The text can be outlined in the following way.

v. 12a   An appeal to imitate Paul.
vv. 12b-15 A reminder of a better time.
vv. 16-17   A warning about the agitators.
vv. 18-20   An expression of parental concern.

An appeal to imitate Paul (v. 12a). Paul appeals to the Galatians to imitate him because he has become like them. But if Paul has become like the Galatians, why should they imitate him? What does the Apostle mean when he says that he has become like them? And what, in his demeanor, are the Galatians to imitate? The most obvious answer to the first question is found in Paul's behavior at Antioch where he freely associated, and enjoyed table fellowship, with Gentile Christians. There, he became like a Gentile, living as though he were outside of the Law. In other words, when Paul was in the presence of Gentiles, he no longer felt constrained by those legal works that once formed a boundary between Gentiles and Jews. He became like the Galatians inasmuch as he lived outside of the Law (*anomos*, 1 Cor 9:21). This should not be construed to mean that Paul became an antinomian. To the contrary, in 1 Cor 9:21 Paul insists that although he became as one outside of the Law to those outside of the Law, he was under Christ's Law (*ennomos Christou*). Rather, Paul's point is that he no longer relies upon the Law, especially in the outward manifestation of its legal works. Whereas his life formerly centered upon the Law (Phil 3:5-6), now it focuses upon the Christ who lives in him (2:20). Paul is asking the Galatians, therefore, to imitate his life inasmuch as he has died to the Law and associated himself with the crucified Christ (2:19). Christ, not the Law, must become the focal point of their lives.

A reminder of a better time (vv. 12b-15). This section provides the most explicit statement in the letter about the founding of the Galatian community. A serious illness (*di'astheneian tēs sarkos*) became the occasion for Paul to preach the gospel among the Galatians. Since illness was perceived by some as a sign of weakness, and even of sin (John 9:2), Paul's illness could have provided the Galatians with an excuse to reject him. For example, one of the complaints leveled against him at Corinth was, "His letters are weighty and strong, but his bodily presence is weak, and his speech contemptible" (2 Cor 10:10). In Corinth certain members of that congregation were inclined to reject Paul in favor of other apostles because, in their view, his physical weakness contradicted the powerful message of salvation which he proclaimed. The remarkable aspect of Paul's preaching at Galatia, then, was the manner in which the community welcomed him. Although his sickness was a temptation (*peirasmon hymōn*) for the Galatians to reject him, they accepted Paul as God's own messenger (*aggelon*), as if he were Christ himself. More than that, they counted it sheer good fortune on their part (*makarismos*) that this sickness brought Paul to them. If Paul had not been sick, then they would never have heard the gospel! Because of this they were willing to sacrifice what was most precious to them for the sake of their founder-Apostle.

Despite this valuable information about the establishment of the Galatian congregations, many questions remain unanswered. For example, what was the nature of the sickness that afflicted Paul? A fever headache? Epilepsy? An eye disease? How did this illness become the reason for him to preach the gospel at Galatia? Finally, when and where did all of this take place? Is Paul referring to a visit made to the churches of Antioch in Pisidia, Iconium, Lystra, and Derbe (Acts 13:3–14:28), all of which were in the Roman province of Galatia? Or is he alluding to a visit made to the churches in the territory of Galatia, around the cities of Ancyra, Tavium, and Pessinus, as suggested by Acts 16:6; 18:23? (See the notes, and the introduction to this commentary.)

Paul recalls these events in order to remind the Galatians of the kindness they once extended to him. In doing so, he introduces another theme which becomes more explicit in his Corinthian correspondence. There, Paul tells the Corinthians that he came to them "in weakness and in fear and in much trembling" with the result that their faith rests "not on human wisdom but on the power of God" (1 Cor 2:3, 5). In 2 Cor 12:9 he writes that he will boast of his weakness "so that the power of Christ may dwell in me." By welcoming the infirm Apostle the Galatians, without realizing it, confirmed the maxim that God's power is made perfect in weakness (2 Cor 12:9). Paul came to them infirm and weak, and yet they accepted his message. Consequently, it was not because of his power that the gospel flourished but because of the power of the Spirit (3:1-5).

A warning about the agitators (vv. 16–17). Despite the original reception that he received from the Galatians, the situation has radically changed, causing Paul to ask if the Galatians now perceive him as their enemy. Paul knows that the changed situation has occurred because of outsiders who have come to Galatia with a version of the gospel that requires circumcision and legal works in addition to Christ-faith. The agitators have told the Galatians that, as well as believing in Christ, they must be circumcised in order to participate in the blessings of Abraham. Even if the agitators did not say that Paul deceived the Galatians, they must have implied that his gospel was defective. Consequently, Paul ironically attributes the Galatians' changed attitude toward him to his own preaching of the gospel. The Galatians now consider him their enemy because he, unlike the agitators, told them the truth; that is, "the truth of the gospel" (2:5, 14): salvation comes, apart from the Law, through the faith of Jesus Christ in whom the Galatians have believed.

Verse 16 provides Paul with an occasion to say something about the agitators. Employing a play on words, he warns the Galatians that the agitators are only "courting" their favor so that the Galatians will eventually "court" their favor. By paying attention to the Galatians now, the agitators hope to make them dependent upon them as authentic teachers of the gospel. Their true motive, however, is to isolate and exclude the Galatians from the wider fellowship of believers who live by the Torah-free gospel. By accepting circumcision and legal works the Galatians will no longer be able to associate with Gentile believers who do not observe such practices and customs. In Paul's view, this Torah-centered gospel will eventually exclude the Galatians from fellowship with Christ (5:4).

Just how much Paul knew about the agitators is debatable. He clearly assigned malevolent motives to their preaching, just as he did to the false brethren in Jerusalem (2:4). He judged the agitators harshly because they intruded upon his missionary territory and disturbed the congregations that he founded. Perhaps it was this divisive situation within the Galatian community, resulting from the preaching of the agitators, that led Paul to attribute a selfish motivation to them. It is possible, however, that the agitators viewed their Torah-centered gospel as an authentic corrective to Paul's own preaching. In that case, this letter presents us with a clash between missionaries equally zealous for the truth of the gospel. Only time would show, however, that Paul, not the agitators, understood the full significance of the Christ event and its implication for Gentile believers.

An expression of parental concern (vv. 18–20). Paul places himself in the role of the gracious missionary. Even though the Galatians are his children, he is not jealous if others should court their favor, provided that it is for the good of the community. In other words, Paul does not begrudge others the privilege of preaching to his children as long as they preach the truth of the gospel: justification, apart from Law, on the basis of Christ-faith. Any other preaching, such as a Torah-centered gospel, will only lead to the disintegration of the community which Paul has parented.

Having made his point, Paul once more places himself in the role of the community's founder. The Galatians are his children because he is the founder of the community. More than a "friend," he is like a parent to them, like a mother. The maternal imagery employed here, however, is complex. Instead of saying that he gave birth to the community, Paul tells the Galatians that he is again suffering the pangs of birth (*ōdinō*) until Christ is formed in or among them (*en hymin*). Thus Christ, like an embryo, takes shape among the Galatians, but Paul suffers the pains of childbirth; as the apostolic founder of the community, he suffers for the Galatians. The adverb *palin* ("again") suggests that Paul endured such travails when he first founded the community. The disruption caused by the preaching of the agitators, however, has made it necessary to reestablish the community on the basis of Christ alone. Christ must be formed in the Galatians once more, i.e., the Galatians must be conformed to the crucified Christ (2:19-20). While the modern reader thinks of Christ being formed in the individual, it is more likely that Paul has the entire community, as a corporate body, in mind. Christ must take shape in the life and ministry of the Galatian churches as they conform themselves to the Crucified One.

In most of Paul's other letters, the Apostle announces that he will visit the congregation soon (Rom 15:14-33; 2 Cor 12:14; 13:1-4). The announcement of the apostolic visitation adds authority to the letter by notifying the community that Paul will come to see if his directives have been fulfilled. In Galatians, however, there is no mention of an apostolic visitation. To the contrary, Paul expresses his frustration that he cannot visit the community, and his inability to do so adds to his distress about his children's behavior. While v. 20 has a rhetorical flourish ("I am at a loss about you"), it may well express an important aspect of the Galatian crisis: Paul did not know the details of the situation.

Where is Paul writing from? If this letter is dated in the mid-fifties, Paul would be based in Ephesus. In that case, his controversy with the Corinthian Church may have made it impossible for him to visit Galatia. Or, Paul may have already left Ephesus for Macedonia, making a return to Galatia difficult, if not impossible. In either case, for reasons that are not specified, the Apostle cannot come to Galatia, nor is he sending one of his trusted co-workers, Timothy or Titus, in his stead. If the conflict is to be resolved, it will be on the basis of this letter.

FOR REFERENCE AND FURTHER STUDY

Betz, H. D. *Galatians: A Commentary on Paul's Letter to the Churches in Galatia.* Philadelphia: Fortress, 1979, 220–237.

Gaventa, B. R. "The Maternity of Paul: An Exegetical Study of Galatians 4:19." *The Conversation Continues: Studies in Paul and John in Honor of J. Louis Martyn.* R. T. Fortna and B. Gaventa, eds. Nashville: Abingdon, 1990, 189–201.

Martyn, J. L. "A Law-Observant Mission to the Gentiles: The Background of Galatians." *SJT* 38 (1985) 307–324.

Refoulé, F. "Date de l'épître aux Galates." *RB* 95 (1988) 161–183.

Expel the Children of the Slave Woman! (4:21-31)

21. Tell me, you who want to be under the Law, do you not understand the Law? 22. It is written that Abraham had two sons, one by the slave woman and another by the free woman. 23. But the one by the slave woman was begotten according to the flesh, and the one by the free woman was begotten through promise. 24. These things are spoken allegorically, for these women represent two covenants, one from Mount Sinai is begetting children into slavery: this is Hagar. 25. "Hagar" stands

for Mount Sinai in Arabia, but she corresponds to the present Jerusalem, for she is enslaved with her children. 26. But the Jerusalem which is above is free; she is our mother. 27. For it is written:

> Rejoice, O barren one who did not give birth,
> Break forth and cry out, you who did not suffer the pangs of birth,
> Because many are the children of the barren one,
> More than of her who has a husband.

28. You brethren are children of the promise in the line of Isaac. 29. But just as formerly the one begotten according to the flesh persecuted the one begotten according to the Spirit, so it is even now. 30. But what does Scripture say?

> Cast out the slave woman and her son,
> for the son of the slave woman will not inherit with the son of the free woman.

31. For this reason, brethren, we are not children of the slave woman but of the free woman.

NOTES

21. *Tell me, you who want to be under the Law*: *Legete moi* ("tell me") marks an abrupt change of tone when compared to the previous section (4:12-20). *Hypo nomon* (literally, "under Law") is also found in 3:23; 4:4, 5; 5:18. Paul employs the expression to indicate a situation of slavery under the Law. The participial phrase *hoi . . . thelontes* ("you who want to be") indicates that the Galatians have not yet adopted the practice of the Law in earnest. Compare 5:3 which might suggest that the Galatians do not realize that being under the Law requires that they keep all of the commandments of the Law. Also, see 4:9 where Paul speaks of the Galatians *wanting* to enslave themselves (*douleuein thelete*) to the *stoicheia* once more.

   do you not understand the Law?: Some manuscripts (D, F, G, 104, 1175) replace *akouete* ("understand") with *anaginoskete* ("read"), suggesting that it is the Law which the Galatians read in the worshipping assembly that they do not understand. Thus Paul is using Law in the sense of *haggada*, narrative, e.g., the story of Sarah and Hagar.

22. *It is written that Abraham had two sons, one by the slave woman and another by the free woman*: *Hena . . . kai hena* is used for *hena . . . heteron* ("one . . . another"). The reference is to Abraham's sons Ishmael and Isaac. Paul does not mention Abraham's six sons by Keturah (Gen 25:1-2), his wife after Sarah's death. The birth of Ishmael is recounted in Gen 16:1-7, the birth of Isaac in Gen 21:1-7. The slave woman is Hagar and the free woman Sarah. *Paidiskē* is the diminutive of *pais* ("girl") but normally refers to someone who is a servant or slave (Acts 12:13; 16:16). The adjective *eleuthera* ("free") serves

to introduce the theme of freedom (*eleutheria*) which is developed in chapter five (5:1, 13).

23. *But the one by the slave woman was begotten according to the flesh, and the one by the free woman was begotten through promise*: Kata sarka ("according to the flesh") and *di'epaggelias* ("through promise") contrast the ways in which the two children were born. According to Gen 16:1-2, Abraham had relations with his maid servant Hagar at the behest of Sarah. By contrast, Isaac was born when Abraham was a hundred years old and Sarah ninety. The birth was the result of God's power and fulfilled the promise (Gen 15:4; 17:19; 18:10; 14). While the Lord did provide for Hagar and Ishmael (Gen 16:7-14; 21:15-21), God established his everlasting covenant with Isaac rather than with Ishmael (Gen 17:19).

24. *These things are spoken allegorically*: Atina ("these things") is employed instead of the simple relative pronoun and refers to everything that Paul has said in vv. 22–23. The verb *allēgorein* comes from two words *allos* ("other") and *agoreuein* ("to speak"). Its basic meaning is "to say something other," something other than the apparent meaning of the words. Used as an exegetical tool, allegory views the persons, places, and events within the narrative as pointing to, or corresponding to, another reality which has a deeper, religious meaning. Although there are other allegories in the NT, and in Paul's writings (Rom 11:17-24; 1 Cor 5:6-8; 9:8-10; 10:1-11), this is the only use of the verb in the NT.

for these women represent two covenants: Only one of the two covenants (*diathēkai*) is identified: God's covenant with Israel at Sinai at which the Law was given. In Rom 9:4 Paul speaks favorably of the covenants that God made with Israel. In 1 Cor 11:25 he speaks of the new covenant in the context of the Eucharist, and in 2 Cor 3:6, 14 he contrasts the new and the old covenant (the Mosaic covenant). Although Paul does not identify the second covenant, he probably has in mind the promise made to Abraham which he discussed in 3:15-17 and which finds its fulfillment in Abraham's seed, Christ.

one from Mount Sinai is begetting children into slavery: this is Hagar: Mia ("one") refers to the first covenant and is identified as the Sinai covenant. This covenant begets children into slavery (*eis douleian*) because it places them under the Law. It is this covenant that Hagar, identified for the first time, symbolizes. J. L. Martyn ("The Covenant of Hagar and Sarah," 177) calls attention to the present tense of the participle *gennōsa* ("is begetting") which indicates that this covenant is continuing to give birth to children. *Hē tis*, although translated as "this," can be taken as a simple relative pronoun.

25. *"Hagar" stands for Mount Sinai in Arabia*: This phrase presents a complicated textual problem. The reading adopted here is that of A, B, D, *de Hagar Sina* ("and Hagar is Mount Sinai"). Some manuscripts, however, read *gar* ("for") in place of the simple connective *de* ("and"), while others omit either Hagar or Sinai.

> *for* Hagar is Mount Sinai in Arabia (K, P);
> *and* Mount Sinai is in Arabia (P46);

for Hagar is a mountain in Arabia (it);
for Mount Sinai is in Arabia (S, C, G).

C. K. Barrett ("The Allegory of Abraham, Sarah, and Hagar," 163-64) notes that "a decisive consideration in favor of the long text is that the omission of Hagar leaves a bare piece of geographical information of little interest to the readers or relevance to the context." In the Greek text, Hagar is governed by the neuter article *to* (literally, "the Hagar") which is not translated in English. The article indicates that it is not Hagar the person that Paul has in mind but the word "Hagar" which is in the text; for this reason Hagar is placed in quotation marks. Paul may have associated Hagar with Mount Sinai because Sinai is located in Arabia, the land of Hagar's descendants through Ishmael. See Ps 83:6 which speaks of the "Hagrites." It is less likely that Paul is dependent upon the linguistic similarity between the Arabic word *hajar* ("rock" or "cliff") and certain place names of the Sinai peninsula.

but she corresponds to the present Jerusalem: *De* is translated as "but," giving the sense that *even though* Sinai is in the land of Arabia, it corresponds to Jerusalem which is not. This is the only instance of *systoichein* in the NT. It means to stand in the same line or column, e.g., like soldiers. Here, Paul is establishing two columns which he is also contrasting. "Hagar" (the unexpressed subject of the verb) stands in the same line or column as does the present Jerusalem, the opposite of which is the Jerusalem above. The present Jerusalem is the home of the agitators, the center of Jewish Christianity.

for she is enslaved with her children: "She," that is, the present Jerusalem, is enslaved (*douleuei*) because she is under the Law which Paul has already described as a *paidagōgos*. Her children (*tekna*) are the converts of the agitators; see commentary. Thus there is a correspondence between Hagar's child who was born into slavery and the present Jerusalem whose children are born into the slavery of the Law; they stand in the same column.

26. *But the Jerusalem which is above is free*: Instead of continuing the temporal imagery and speaking of the future Jerusalem, Paul switches to a spatial image, *hē anō Ierousalēm* ("the Jerusalem which is above"). Hebrews 12:22 speaks of the heavenly Jerusalem (*Ierousalēm epouraniō*) and Rev 3:12; 21:2, 10 of the new or holy Jerusalem that descends from heaven; but here there is no indication that the Jerusalem above will descend from heaven to earth. Other examples of the heavenly Jerusalem can be found in 4 Ezra 7:26; 8:52; 13:36; and 2 Bar 4:2-3. In the text from Baruch it is said of the city, "It is not in your midst now; it is that which will be revealed, with me, that was already prepared from the moment that I decided to create Paradise. And I showed it to Adam before he sinned." (Quoted from *The Old Testament Pseudepigrapha*, vol. 1, ed. J. H. Charlesworth.) This Jerusalem is free (*eleuthera*) from the Law. For a full discussion of the heavenly Jerusalem, see A. T. Lincoln, *Paradise Now and Not Yet*, 9-32.

she is our mother: The thought of Ps 86:5 (LXX) may lie behind this expression (*Mēter Sion, erei anthrōpos*: "A man shall say, 'Zion is my mother' "). If the agitators employed the expression, "Jerusalem is our mother," as a slogan, it is possible that Paul is countering them here. Some manuscripts (S², A,

C³) insert *pantōn* before *hēmōn* resulting in the reading, "she is the mother of us all." While this leads to a more universal application, it "obscures Paul's distinction between the 'chosen ones' and the 'sons of Hagar' " (B. Metzger, *A Textual Commentary on the Greek New Testament*, 596).

27. *For it is written: "Rejoice, O barren one who did not give birth, break forth and cry out, you who did not suffer the pangs of birth, because many are the children of the barren one, more than of her who has a husband"*: The quotation is a precise rendering of Isa 54:1 according to the LXX. The words were spoken in the context of the exile and promised the restoration of Jerusalem. Paul applies the text to the Jerusalem which is above, the mother of his Gentile converts. She will have more children than the present Jerusalem, the home of the agitators.

28. *You brethren are children of the promise in the line of Isaac*: Some manuscripts (S, A, C, D²) read "we are" in place of "you are" in order to coordinate this verse with vv. 26 and 31 which employ the first person plural. "In the line of Isaac" translates *kata Isaak*. The Galatians are children of the promise (*epaggelias tekna*) because, like Isaac, they were begotten in extraordinary circumstances. See Rom 9:8 for a similar expression (*ta tekna tēs epaggelias*).

29. *But just as formerly the one begotten according to the flesh persecuted the one begotten according to the Spirit*: This verse alludes to the story in Gen 21:8-14 in which Sarah demands that Abraham cast out Hagar and her child because Ishmael was "playing" with Isaac. The Hebrew text employs the participle *mṣḥq* ("playing") which is rendered by *paizonta* in the LXX. While *paizein* means "to play" or "to amuse oneself," it can also mean "to jest" or "to make sport of." But even if Paul read the LXX with the last meaning in mind, he has gone beyond the LXX by speaking of persecution (*ediōken*), an important word in this letter (1:13, 23; 5:11; 6:12). Nonetheless, it is interesting that Josephus says that although Sarah first loved Ishmael, she was not willing for him to be brought up with Isaac since he was too old for Isaac and was capable of doing him harm after Abraham had died (*Ant.* 1:215). Earlier, Paul spoke of Isaac being begotten "through promise" (v. 23); here Paul writes "begotten according to the Spirit," thereby equating promise and Spirit.

so it is even now: Paul points to a contemporary experience, but he does not explicitly say who is doing the persecuting. Cosgrove (*The Cross and the Spirit*, 84) argues that the verb *diōkein* ("to persecute") is never used in the NT of internal strife within the Church, and therefore it must refer to persecution from the synagogue. But the situation at Galatia suggests that Paul is referring to the agitators, not to Jews who are not Christians. See commentary.

30. *But what does Scripture say? "Cast out the slave woman and her son, for the son of the slave woman will not inherit with the son of the free woman"*: This is a quotation from Gen 21:10 which reads, according to the LXX, "Cast out *this* slave woman and her son, for the son of *this* slave woman will not inherit with *my son Isaac*." Paul replaces "my son Isaac" with "the son of the free woman" in order to emphasize the theme of freedom that he is developing here, and which he will develop further in chapter five.

31. *For this reason, brethren, we are not children of the slave woman but of the free woman*:

Dio ("for this reason") is replaced by *ara* ("then") by P46, by *ara oun* ("therefore, then") by F, G, and by *hēmeis de* ("and we") by A, C, P. The use of "we" rather than "you" (v. 28) associates Paul and other Jewish believers with the Galatians.

INTERPRETATION

This is, without doubt, one of the most puzzling and disturbing passages in the whole of Galatians. On the one hand, the very location of these verses within the argument of Galatians is puzzling. In 3:1-29, Paul argued that the Galatians are the descendants of Abraham because they have been incorporated into Abraham's one descendant, the Christ. Following this argument Paul appealed to the Galatians not to return to the period of their minority (4:1-11) and to become imitators of him (4:12-20). In neither of these passages was there any reference to Abraham. The Galatians might reasonably conclude, therefore, that Paul had said all that was necessary about their relationship to the great Patriarch. Somewhat unexpectedly, however, Paul returns to the story of Abraham. It is not surprising, therefore, that so influential a commentator as Burton calls this a "supplemental argument," and writes: "Before leaving the subject of the seed of Abraham it occurs to the apostle, *apparently as an afterthought* [emphasis mine], that he might make his thought clearer and more persuasive by an allegorical interpretation of the story of Abraham and his two sons, Ishmael and Isaac, the one born in the course of nature only, the other in fulfillment of divine promise" (*Galatians*, 251). Burton's comment is important because it expresses the sentiments of many commentators: why has Paul returned to the story of Abraham? Surely it would have made better sense to introduce this argument immediately after 3:1-29.

On the other hand, the passage is disturbing. While Burton suggests that Paul introduced the allegory in order to make his thought clearer and more persuasive, a great company of exegetes protests that this is one of the most confusing passages of the New Testament. Even the general reader immediately notices that Paul's allegorical interpretation goes against the plain and literal sense of the Book of Genesis by apparently associating the descendants of Hagar with the Sinai covenant. Moreover, Paul's reading of Genesis 17 completely neglects the fact that the eternal covenant which God established with Abraham was a covenant of circumcision (Gen 17:10). It is not surprising, then, that a commentator so sympathetic to Paul as Calvin should write about this passage, "As an argument it is not very strong; as confirmation of his earlier vigorous reasoning, it is not to be despised" (*Galatians*, 84). Every commentator, therefore, must face the following questions: why has Paul introduced this passage at this point in the letter, and what is the meaning of this allegorical exegesis?

The placement of this passage has been problematic because most commentators view it as another "argument" that the Galatians are authentic children of Abraham. Recently, however, G. W. Hansen has argued that this passage is a "biblical appeal" to the Galatians, with its punch line in 4:30, to expel the agitators from their midst (*Abraham and Galatians*, 145). Consequently, while this passage enjoys a certain value as a scriptural argument, it must also be understood as an appeal or request to the Galatians. Put another way, the genre of this passage is mixed, enjoying elements of appeal as well as of persuasion. Viewed in this way, the passage is not out of place since it occurs in that portion of the letter which has already been identified as "Rebuke and Appeal" (4:1–5:12). Moreover, the themes of freedom and slavery, which play such a central role in this passage, prepare the Galatians for chapter five where these two themes are developed further.

There is, however, an important connection between this passage and Paul's personal appeal in 4:12-20 as J.L. Martyn, drawing on the work of B. Gaventa, has shown ("The Covenant of Hagar and Sarah," 160–192). At the conclusion of his personal appeal in 4:12-20, Paul calls the Galatians his children (*tekna mou*) and laments that he must once more endure the pains of childbirth until Christ is formed in them (4:19). In this passage, the word *teknon* ("child") occurs four times (4:25, 27, 28, 31) in reference to the children of the slave women and the free woman who are identified as the children of the present Jerusalem and the children of the heavenly Jerusalem, respectively. While the majority of commentators identify the children of the present Jerusalem with Judaism, and the children of the heavenly Jerusalem with Christianity, Martyn suggests that Hagar and the present Jerusalem refer to the children being born by the Law-observant mission of the agitators (called "the Teachers" by Martyn) while the children of the heavenly Jerusalem are the recipients of Paul's Torah-free mission. Understood in this way, the placement of this passage is not so puzzling. Having lamented that he must once more suffer the pangs of childbirth for his children (*tekna*) (4:19), Paul talks about the children of two different apostolates: his circumcision-free apostolate and the circumcision-apostolate of the agitators.

An important aspect of this approach is Martyn's insight that Paul is not referring to the religions of Judaism and Christianity in the Hagar-Sarah allegory but to Jewish Christians who insist upon the Law and Gentile Christians of a Pauline persuasion who do not. In other words, this passage reflects a struggle between two factions of early Christianity rather than opposition between Christianity and Judaism. If this exegesis is accurate, it has important implications for Jewish-Christian relations since it implies that Paul was not polemicizing against Judaism but against a certain expression of early Christianity that insisted upon judaizing its Gentile converts.

The passage may be outlined in the following way.

v. 21	Introduction
vv. 22–27	Allegory and interpretation
	vv. 22–23 allegory
	vv. 24–27 interpretation
vv. 28–31	Application and appeal
	v. 28 identification of the Galatians
	v. 29 persecution by Ishmael's descendants
	v. 30 expel the agitators!
	v. 31 identification of the Galatians

As the outline shows, the passage is divided into two major sections. The first (vv. 22–27) is enclosed by the expression *gegraptai gar* ("for it is written") which occurs in vv. 22 and 27 and introduces scriptural texts important for Paul's argument (Gen 16:15; 21:2; Isa 54:1). The second section is enclosed by two references to the Galatians as children of the promise (v. 28) and children of the free woman (v. 31). But whereas v. 28 addresses the Galatians directly ("you"), in v. 31 Paul includes himself with his audience ("we").

Introduction (v. 21). There is a challenging tone in this opening remark. Paul implies that the Galatians do not understand the Law which they want to assume. But why does Paul begin with this question? C. K. Barrett (*Essays on Paul*, 154–170) provides a solution when he suggests that the agitators were the first to make use of the Hagar-Sarah story. Indeed, the story is so eminently suited to the position of the agitators that it is difficult to understand why Paul would have employed it if the agitators had not. Thus the Galatians "heard the Law" from the agitators who told them that Abraham had two sons. Ishmael, begotten by Hagar, was the ancestor of Gentiles like the Galatians, while Isaac, begotten by Sarah, was the ancestor of Israel. Moreover, when Abraham said to God, "O that Ishmael might live in your sight," the Lord replied, "No, but your wife Sarah shall bear you a son, and you shall name him Isaac, I will establish my covenant with him as *an everlasting covenant* for his offspring after him" (Gen 17:18-19). Since the sign of this covenant was circumcision (Gen 17:10), it is not difficult to imagine the line of argumentation that the agitators brought to Galatia: "The real descendants of Abraham are those who accept the covenant of circumcision that God made with Abraham. You believe in the Christ and that is commendable. But now you must complete your conversion by becoming Abraham's descendants in the line of Isaac, for true Israelites, including the Messiah, belong to this line."

On face value, the agitators had a strong scriptural argument that Paul could not counter with a literal reading of the Genesis text. Consequently, he appeals to an allegorical interpretation to show the Galatians that, although they heard the Law from the agitators, neither they nor the agitators understand the deeper meaning of the Law, a meaning revealed in Christ. Thus v. 21 might be paraphrased, "Tell me you who want to accept circumcision, you have heard the story of Abraham's two sons from the agitators; but do you know the real meaning of the story when read in light of the Christ?"

Abraham had two sons (vv. 22–23). Paul begins this section *gegraptai gar* ("for it is written") but does not quote any specific text. Instead, he refers to the birth accounts of Ishmael and Isaac found in Gen 16:1-16; 21:1-7. According to the first, Ishmael was born to Abraham's Egyptian slave girl, Hagar, when Abraham was eighty-six years old. Abraham had relations with Hagar at the behest of Sarah, for Sarah had born him no children and clearly did not expect to do so. The birth of Ishmael was *kata sarka* ("according to the flesh"), then, because it took place in an ordinary way: a woman who was not barren gave birth to a child. According to the second account, Abraham's wife, Sarah, a free woman, conceived and bore a son to Abraham, even though she was barren and Abraham was a hundred years old. This second birth was *di'epaggelias* ("through promise") because it fulfilled God's promise to Abraham (Gen 17:19; 18:10, 14). The Galatians must have been familiar with this story because, at the outset, Paul does not identify either the mothers or their children. Indeed, he never identifies Sarah or Ishmael by name. Thus the Galatians probably heard the same story from the agitators who employed it in their attempt to persuade them to be circumcised. The Hagar-Sarah story, therefore, is common ground for Paul, the Galatians, and the agitators.

These women are two covenants (vv. 24–27). Having established common ground with the Galatians, Paul introduces a reading of the Genesis stories in light of the Christ. If the Galatians want to know the true meaning of this story, then they must realize that the narrative is to be interpreted allegorically; that is, there is a meaning that goes beyond the plain, literal sense since the characters of the story represent deeper realities. Paul does not explain the criteria that he employs in his allegorical exegesis; he simply interprets the text. Each woman represents a covenant (*diathēkē*), but he only identifies one of the covenants: the one associated with Hagar. Within this story, "Hagar" stands for Mount Sinai which, although it is in Arabia, corresponds to the present Jerusalem. The distinguishing mark of this covenant and the children which it produces is slavery. The other covenant is not identified. While several commentators relate it with the new covenant (2 Cor 3:6), it is more likely that Paul has in mind the *diathēkē* God made with Abraham (3:15-16). Nevertheless, it is important to remember that Paul does not explicitly say this. Instead of contrasting the two covenants, he contrasts the present Jerusalem with the Jerusalem which is above whose children are free. Thus Paul establishes two tables.

SLAVE WOMAN	FREE WOMAN
Hagar	_____
Mount Sinai	_____
Present Jerusalem	Jerusalem above
Slave children	Free children

A glance at the two columns reveals that Paul does not explicitly identify what or who corresponds to Hagar or Mount Sinai. Rather, in v. 27 he introduces a quotation from Isa 54:1 to prove that the children of the Jerusalem above have become more numerous than the children of the present Jerusalem. That quotation, moreover, employs the same verb that Paul used in 4:19 when he spoke of the birth pains that he must endure until Christ is once more formed among the Galatians.

> 4:19 my children for whom I am suffering the pangs of birth (*ōdinō*) until Christ be formed in you.
> 4:27 Break forth and cry out, you who did not suffer the pangs of birth (*ōdinousa*).

In vv. 28 and 31 Paul will identify the Galatians as the children of the promise and the children of the free woman. But who are the children of the slave women? The majority of commentators identify the children of the slave women with Judaism, understood as Israel which does not believe in Jesus as the Messiah. Thus Betz writes: "he [Paul] wants to create a dualistic polarity between "Judaism" and "Christianity," in order to discredit his Jewish-Christian opposition" (*Galatians*, 246). And Lagrange, identifying Hagar with Judaism and Sarah with the Church notes: "Même l'Église, longtemps sterile, est aujourd'hui féconde et assurée des bénédictions. Le judaïsme est une religion de crainte, une religion d'esclaves" (*Galates*, 121).

While this exegetical tradition has a long history and is espoused by a host of commentators, there are reasons to call it into question. First, the interpretation is anachronistic. When Paul wrote Galatians, Christianity was not yet perceived as a religion distinct from Judaism. Rather, faith in Christ was a way of living within the covenant people of Israel. What was new was Paul's assertion that Gentiles could participate in the life of the covenant people apart from circumcision and Law. Second, although Paul disagreed with those Jews who did not believe in Christ, in the present instance his disagreement was with Jewish Christians, not with Jews in general. Third, if the agitators, who were Jewish Christians, used the story of Hagar and Sarah in order to discredit Paul's position, then it is more likely that Paul employed an allegorical interpretation of the same story to discredit them rather than Judaism or Jews in general.

The present Jerusalem, therefore, refers to the city of Jerusalem mentioned in chs. 1-2, the center of Jewish Christianity. There, Jewish Christians not only believed in Christ, they also practiced the Law; Jerusalem was their "mother." There is no reason, however, to assume that Paul was opposed to a Jewish Christianity *provided that* it was not imposed upon Gentiles as a condition for entering the covenant community. Jewish Christians could and should continue to practice the Law as long as they realized that Christ, not the Law, was the source of their justification. A Judaizing mission to the Gentiles, however, was contrary to the agreement established at Jerusalem (2:9), and by coming to Galatia the agitators were infringing upon Paul's missionary territory. Because of this, Paul views the agitators with hostility. They have told the Galatians that Jerusalem is their mother and that they are the true descendants of Abraham through Isaac. The truth, according to Paul, is precisely the opposite. The agitators belong to the line of Hagar who stands for Sinai (see notes), which represents the Law, which represents slavery (3:21-4:11), which represents Jerusalem. In effect, Paul has turned the scriptural argument of the agitators against them. He has employed the Law to condemn those who would put the Galatians under the Law. This reversal can be diagramed in the following way.

ARGUMENT OF THE AGITATORS

Hagar/Ishmael = Gentiles	Sarah/Isaac = Jewish Christians

PAUL'S ALLEGORICAL EXEGESIS

Hagar/Ishmael = Sinai = Present Jerusalem = Slavery = the Agitators.	Sarah/Isaac = Galatians and Torah-free Christians

To use language that Paul employed earlier in 3:9-10, those who are descended from the slave woman are *hoi ex ergōn* ("those from works"), and those who are descended from the free woman are *hoi ek pisteōs* ("those from faith").

Expel the agitators (vv. 28-31). Having countered the argument of the agitators by placing them in the column of the slave woman and the Gala-

tians in the column of the free woman, Paul now employs the Law to
appeal to the Galatians. Since they know what the Law really says, they
should expel the agitators. This section begins with Paul calling the Galatians *adelphoi* ("brethren") and telling them that they are the children of
the promise according to the line of Isaac (the only time Isaac is named).
It concludes in a similar way. Paul calls the Galatians *adelphoi*, but this
time he says that "we" are children of the free women. In vv. 29–30 Paul
returns to the story of Hagar and Sarah as told in Gen 21:8-14. According to that account, "Sarah saw the son of Hagar the Egyptian slave
whom she had borne to Abraham, *playing* with her son Isaac. So she said
to Abraham, 'Cast out this slave woman with her son; for the son of this
slave woman shall not inherit along with my son Isaac' " (Gen 21:9-10).
Paul makes two important changes in the story. First, he interprets
Ishmael's playing with Isaac as persecution (*ediōken*). Second, whereas
Gen 21:10 reads "my son Isaac," Paul says "the son of the free women."
By these alterations Paul actualizes the story for the Galatians. Just as
the one born *kata sarka* ("according to the flesh") formerly persecuted
the one born *kata pneuma* ("according to the Spirit"), so the same is hap-
pening today.

But who is persecuting whom? The answer here depends upon the
choice one makes earlier in regard to the Sarah-Hagar allegory. If the children of Hagar are the Jews, then Paul is referring to the persecution of
Christians by Jews. But if the children of Hagar are the agitators, then
Paul is referring to their activity within the Galatian community. This second choice makes eminent sense within the context of Galatians. While
the Galatians clearly did not perceive the activity of the agitators as persecution, that is how Paul interpreted it. Indeed, this accords with his warning in 4:17, "They court your favor, not in a way which is commendable,
but they want to isolate you in order that you might court their favor."
The agitators are persecuting the Galatians because they seek to deprive
them of their freedom by enslaving them under the Law.

The full force of Paul's quotation from Gen 21:9 now becomes apparent. When the Apostle writes, "Cast out the slave woman and her son,"
he is not simply recalling the judgment of Scripture upon the historical
Hagar and Ishmael. Rather, he is making the text contemporary for the
Galatians. It is a direct command to expel the agitators from their midst.
The agitators are the descendants of the slave woman and her son inasmuch as they rely upon the Law. Their fate, therefore, should be no less
than that experienced by Hagar and Ishmael. Paul is not talking about
Jewish people in general, nor is this a prophetic declaration that the
Church will and must expel Judaism. Rather, in the context of the Galatian crisis, the text reflects an intra-church dispute between the Pauline
circle and the agitators. Moreover, Paul's argument is not with Jewish

Christians as such, but with a particular faction of Jewish Christians, the agitators at Galatia who have violated the Jerusalem agreement.

For Reference and Further Study

Barrett, C. K. "The Allegory of Abraham, Sarah, and Hagar in the Argument of Galatians." *Essays on Paul.* Philadelphia: Westminster, 1982, 154–170.

Cosgrove C. H. "The Law Has Given Sarah No Children (Gal. 4:21-30)." *NovTest* 29 (1987) 219–235.

Gaston, L. "Israel's Enemies in Pauline Theology." *Paul and the Torah.* Vancouver: University of British Columbia, 1987, 80–99.

Hansen, G. W. *Abraham in Galatians: Epistolary and Rhetorical Contexts.* JSNTSS 29; Sheffield: JSOT, 1989, 141–154.

Lincoln, A. T. *Paradise Now and Not Yet: Studies in the Role of the Heavenly Dimension in Paul's Thought with Special Reference to His Eschatology.* SNTSMS 43; Cambridge University Press, 1981, 9–32.

Martyn, J. L. "The Covenants of Hagar and Sarah." *Faith and History: Essays in Honor of Paul W. Meyer.* J. T. Carroll *et al* (eds). Atlanta: Scholars Press, 1990, 160–192.

Robinson, D. W. B. "The Distinction between Jewish and Gentile Believers in Galatians." *AusBR* 13 (1965) 29–48.

Steinhauser, M. G. "Gal 4, 25a: Evidence of Targumic Tradition in Gal 4, 21-31?" *Bib* 70 (1989) 234–240.

Avoid Circumcision! (5:1-12)

1. For freedom Christ has set us free. Stand firm then, and do not be subjected again to a yoke of slavery. 2. See, I Paul am telling you that if you allow yourselves to be circumcised Christ will be of no benefit to you. 3. Again, I testify to every man who allows himself to be circumcised that he is obligated to do the entire Law. 4. You are cut off from Christ, you who are seeking to be justified by Law; you have fallen from grace. 5. For by the Spirit, on the basis of faith, we eagerly await the hope of righteousness. 6. For in Christ Jesus neither circumcision nor uncircumcision means anything but faith expressing itself through love. 7. You were running so well. Who hindered you from obeying the truth? 8. This persuasion is not from the one calling you. 9. A little yeast leavens the entire lump. 10. I have confidence in you, in the Lord, that you will not take a different view; the one disturbing you will bear the judgment, whoever he is. 11. But if I, brethren, am still preaching circumcision, why am I still being persecuted? Then the scandal of the cross is abolished. 12. Would that those disturbing you might castrate themselves!

Notes

1. *For freedom Christ has set us free*: This verse presents three problems: (1) a series of complicated textual variants; (2) the relationship of this verse to what precedes and follows; (3) and the meaning of the dative *tē̜ eleutheria̜* ("freedom"). First, some manuscripts introduce *oun* ("then") after *tē̜ eleutheria̜* ("freedom"). Still others introduce the relative *hē̜* ("which"), some before, some after, *eleutheria̜*. These variants are attempts to effect a smoother, less abrupt reading, e.g., "Therefore, with the freedom by which Christ freed us, stand fast." The text adopted here has the support of S*, A, B. These variants, in turn, highlight the second problem: what is the relationship of this verse to what precedes and follows? Is 5:1 the conclusion of 4:21-31, the beginning of a new section, or a transitional verse? On the one hand, the opening words of 5:2 appear to be the forceful beginning of a new section and suggest that this verse (5:1) belongs to the previous section. On the other hand, 5:1 lacks a connecting particle joining it to the previous section. It is probably best, therefore, to view 5:1, rather than 5:2, as the beginning of a new section. Third, *tē̜ eleutheria̜* can be understood as a dative of instrument ("by freedom," "with freedom") in which case the sense is: by freeing us from the Law, Christ set us free. Or it can be understood as a dative of purpose ("for freedom"), i.e., Christ set us free for the purpose of being free from the Law. This view is adopted here and by many modern translations (RSV, NAB, NEB, REB), and it is supported by what has just been said in the Hagar-Sarah allegory: the Galatians have been called to the line of Sarah. Furthermore, in 5:13 *eleutheria̜* clearly has the sense of purpose. In 5:13, however, Paul uses the noun with a preposition, *ep eleutheria̜* ("to freedom"), and in Rom 8:21 he writes *eis tēn eleutherian* ("for freedom"). The freedom Paul intends is freedom from the Law. Paul employs the noun "freedom" in Rom 8:21; 1 Cor 10:29; 2 Cor 3:17; Gal 2:4; 5:1, 13 (twice); the verb "to free" in Rom 6:18, 22; 8:2, 21; Gal 5:1; and the adjective "free" in Rom 6:30; 7:30; 1 Cor 7:21, 22; 9:1; 12:13; Gal 3:28; 4:22, 23, 26, 30, 31.

Stand firm then, and do not be subjected again to a yoke of slavery: Some manuscripts omit the adverb "then" (*oun*) or place it after the word "freedom" (see above). *Stēkete* ("stand firm") is "virtually confined to Paul" (*BDF*, 73) and mostly in the imperative. The sense is either "do not give in," or, "remain constant in the freedom you have received." In favor of the latter is Paul's usage elsewhere where Christians are encouraged to remain steadfast in something (1 Cor 16:13; Phil 4:1; 1 Thess 3:8). The passive of *enechein* ("be subjected to") has the sense of being loaded down with or entangled with something. Thus in 3 Macc 6:10, "Even if our lives have become *entangled* in impieties . . . ." *Zygō̜ douleias* ("a yoke of slavery") points to the Law which the Galatians want to embrace, while *palin* ("again") recalls their former slavery to the *stoicheia* (4:9). See Acts 15:10 where the Law is viewed as a yoke, and 1 Tim 6:1 which speaks of the "yoke of slavery." In Matt 11:29-30, "yoke" is used favorably in reference to Jesus' teaching, contrasting the yoke of Jesus with the yoke which the religious leaders have placed upon the people by their interpretation of the Law.

2. *See, I Paul am telling you*: The expression underlines Paul's apostolic authority. A similar interjection is found in 6:11 and 2 Cor 10:1. In 2 Corinthians it is clearly the beginning of a new section. For other instances of "I, Paul," see 1 Thess 2:18; Eph 3:1; Col 1:23.

that if you allow yourselves to be circumcised: This is the first time that Paul explicitly mentions the problem of circumcision in reference to the Galatians. The passive, *peritemnēsthe* ("to be circumcised"), has the sense, "allow oneself to be" (*BDF*, 314); the present tense indicates that the Galatians have not yet accepted circumcision.

Christ will be of no benefit to you: For other uses of *ōphelein* ("be of benefit to") see Rom 2:25; 1 Cor 13:3; 14:6. The first of these is interesting because Paul writes: "Circumcision indeed *is of value* if you obey the law; but if you break the law, your circumcision becomes uncircumcision." This text however, has the Jew in mind while the text of Galatians clearly has Gentiles in view.

3. *Again, I testify to every man who allows himself to be circumcised*: Some manuscripts (D*, F, G) omit *palin* ("again"), thereby obviating a problem, namely; is Paul recalling something that he said to the Galatians on the occasion of an earlier visit, e.g., when he spoke the truth to them (4:16)? Or is he merely emphasizing what he has just said in v. 2? A similar problem occurs in 1:9. If the former option is chosen, then Paul already taught the Galatians that there is no need for circumcision, and it is difficult to understand how the Judaizers have made such inroads. Thus the use of *palin* is a rhetorical device which emphasizes v. 2. The present participle, *peritemnomenọ̄*, ("to be circumcised") indicates that the Galatians have not yet accepted circumcision.

that he is obligated to do the entire Law: The phrase *holon ton nomon poiēsai* ("to do the entire Law") stands in contrast to *ho pas nomos peplērōtai* ("the whole Law is fulfilled") in 5:14. In 5:3 the adjective ("entire") is in the predicate position and Paul employs the verb *poiein* ("to do"). In 5:14 the adjective ("whole") is in the attributive position and Paul employs the verb *plēroun* ("to fulfill"). H. Hübner writes, "The attributive position of *pas* does indeed emphasise (sic!) the totality of the Law as contrasted with the individual pronouncements of the Law" (*Law in Paul's Thought*, 37). And H. Räisänen (*Paul and the Law*, 63) notes, "there is a polemical correspondence between Gal 5:3 and 5:14. Whoever accepts the Torah, must fulfil it *in its totality*; as for Christians the same law *in its totality* is fulfilled in the love command." Those who accept circumcision, therefore, must *do* all of the commandments of the Law. See Rom 2:25, "Circumcision is indeed of value if you obey (*prassēs*) the Law; but if you break (*parabatēs*) the Law, your circumcision becomes uncircumcision." Also, Matt 5:19, and especially Jas 2:10 where the phrase *holon ton nomon* is again found: "For whoever keeps the whole law (*holon ton nomon*) but fails in one point has become accountable for all of it." The verb *poiein* ("to do") has already been used in 3:10, 12, in reference to the Law, where Paul opposes "doing" and "faith." In 6:13 Paul says that "even those who receive circumcision do not themselves keep (*phylassousin*) the Law." E.P. Sanders (*Paul, The Law, And the Jewish People*, 29) interprets this text differently; he writes, "Paul may very well simply have been reminding his converts that, if they accept circumcision, the consequence would be that they would have to begin living their lives according to a new set of rules for daily living." It appears, however, that Paul's point is more forceful: the Galatians must do *all* of the commandments of the Law.

4. *You are cut off from Christ, you who are seeking to be justified by Law*: *Katārgein* ("to cut off") is a distinctive Pauline word. Of its twenty-seven occurrences in the NT, twenty-five are found in writings attributed to Paul, three in Galatians (3:17; 5:4, 11). Its literal meaning is to make something ineffective, e.g., Luke 13:7, a tree which wastes the ground in which it is planted. In the passive it has the sense of being parted from or released from something. So a woman is "released" from the Law when her husband dies (Rom 7:2). If the Galatians practice circumcision, they will "be parted from" or "released from" Christ. The aorist is used in a proleptic sense; this has not yet taken place, but it will if they allow themselves to be circumcised. "To be justified" (*dikaiousthe*) means to stand in the correct relationship to God by means of legal works. *En nomǭ* can be taken in a locutive sense, "in the realm of the Law," or an instrumental sense, "by means of the Law." The latter best fits the context.

you have fallen from grace: The literal sense of *ekpiptein* is to fall to the ground, like a flower (Jas 1:11). Here, as in 2 Pet 3:17, the verb is used figuratively, "to lose something." The Galatians will lose God's favor if they allow themselves to be circumcised.

5. *For by the Spirit, on the basis of faith*: In the phrase *pneumati ek pisteōs, pneuma* ("Spirit") is not governed by the definite pronoun. Nevertheless, it most likely refers to the Spirit of Christ and God. See 3:3; 5:16, 18, 25 for other instances where the article is not used. The dative case is to be understood as instrumental, by means of the power of the Spirit. *Ek pisteōs* (2:16; 3:8, 9, 11, 12, 22, 24) also has an instrumental sense. The phrase should be read in light of 2:16, *ek pisteōs Christou*.

we eagerly await the hope of righteousness: The pronoun *hēmeis* ("we"), placed at the beginning of this phrase, is emphatic and distinguishes those who rely on faith from those who are trying to be justified by the Law. The hope of righteousness (*elpida dikaiosynēs*) can be understood as an objective genitive (a hope which has righteousness as its object), or as a subjective genitive (the hope which righteousness produces, the hope which derives from righteousness). The majority of commentators take the phrase in the first sense, but Paul normally speaks of being justified as a present reality (Rom 5:1, 9) and of salvation as a future reality (Rom 5:9). Furthermore, Gal 2:21; 3:21 seem to suppose that righteousness is a present reality. Thus the sense of the phrase is "we eagerly await the hoped for reality that righteousness brings." See the excellent discussion by Fung (*Galatians*, 224–227). In Rom 8:19, 23, 25; 1 Cor 1:7; Phil 3:20 the verb *apekdoxomai* ("to eagerly await") is used in the sense of eschatological expectation.

6. *For in Christ Jesus*: Vaticanus (B) omits "Jesus," but the name is well attested otherwise. Christ Jesus is the sphere or the realm in which the believer dwells.

Burton says that it is similar to the modern phrase "in Christianity" (*Galatians*, 279).

neither circumcision nor uncircumcision means anything: A like phrase occurs in 6:15 and 1 Cor 7:19. The thought is similar to that of 3:28: in the realm of Christ external differences are not important—not even the lack of circumcision; in the light of Christ both are indifferent.

but faith expressing itself through love: This translates *alla pistis di agapēs energoumenē*. The participle *energoumenē* can be taken as a middle ("working") or as a passive ("made effective"). In an effort to safeguard the integrity of faith, most commentators take the phrase in the first sense: faith working through love. Many patristic writers, however, adopted the second sense: faith is made effective through love, love understood as God's love or Christ's love. Paul, however, probably has the love of neighbor in mind here (see 5:14; 6:10). Thus the first interpretation is adopted: faith working through love. Compare 1 Cor 7:19, "Circumcision is nothing, and uncircumcision is nothing *but obeying the commandments of God* (*alla tērēsis entolōn theou*) is everything." For other uses of the noun "love," see 5:13, 22. For the use of the verb "to love," see 5:14. The supreme example of love is Christ who handed himself over for our sake (2:20), thereby expressing his faith through love.

7. *You were running so well*: Paul uses the athletic imagery of a race to describe the Christian life. The believer is like a runner in a race striving to reach the finish line. See 1 Cor 9:24, 26; Gal 2:2; Phil 2:16; Heb 12:1. The agitators, however, have impeded the progress of the Galatians by cutting them off from their goal.

Who hindered you from obeying the truth: *Tis* ("who") appears to refer to an individual agitator as does *hostis* ("whoever") in v. 10 which creates a certain tension with 1:7 and 5:12 which refer to the agitators (plural). The singular, however, is to be taken in a generic sense, "anyone," e.g. "anyone who hinders you." The general meaning of *egkoptein* is to hinder, but given the imagery of a race, the sense is that of one runner cutting off or blocking another from the finish line. Paul uses the same word in Rom 15:22 ("I have so often been hindered from coming to you") and 1 Thess 2:18 ("but Satan blocked me"). The verb has the same root as *apokoptein* ("to castrate") in 5:12. The agitators are hindering the Galatians by urging circumcision. Some important manuscripts (S*, A, B) do not have the definite article before *alētheia* ("truth"), but it is found in P46, S², C, D, F, G. The truth is "the truth of the gospel" (2:5, 14) that Paul spoke to the Galatians (4:16).

8. *This persuasion is not from the one calling you*: A few manuscripts (F, G) insert "Do not be persuaded by anyone (*mēdeni peithesthe*) before this verse. D* omits the negative *ouk*, giving the sense, "This persuasion (*peismonē*) is from the one who calls you." But the negative is found in the majority of manuscripts. *Peismonē* refers to the rhetorical arguments of the agitators intended to persuade the Galatians to their point of view. As in 1:6, the one calling the Galatians is God.

9. *A little yeast leavens the entire lump*: D* and some Latin manuscripts replace *zymoi* ("leavens") with *doloi* ("adulterates"). A similar change is found in 1 Cor 5:6. This saying is a proverb comparable to, "one bad apple spoils the whole barrel." Leaven is usually used figuratively as a sign of hypocrisy or false teaching (Matt 16:6; Mark 8:15; Luke 12:1), but it is employed in a positive sense in Matt 13:33. Here it symbolizes the agitators, their teaching or both.

10. *I have confidence in you, in the Lord*: "In the Lord," is not found in Vaticanus (B), but is present in the majority of manuscripts. "Lord" refers to Christ, not to God. See Burton, *Galatians*, 284–85. The second perfect, *pepoitha* ("have confidence"), is used with a present meaning. Despite the situation at Galatia, Paul remains confident because he relies on the Lord.

   that you will not take a different view: The different view is that proposed by the agitators. *Phronein* ("to think," "to take a view") is a common Pauline word. It occurs twenty-six times in the NT, twenty-three in the writings attributed to Paul.

   the one disturbing you will bear the judgment, whoever he is: Ho tarassōn ("the one disturbing") is the same participle used in 1:7, but in 1:7 it is employed in the plural. The use of the singular here, and in the phrase *hostis ean ē* ("whoever he is"), is to be taken as a generic singular. Paul is not referring to a particular individual but to a hypothetical situation: anyone who troubles the Galatians will be held responsible, whoever he is. This interpretation, adopted by Burton (*Galatians*, 285), provides a plausible explanation for the tension which arises between the use of the plural in 1:7 and the singular here. Paul uses *bastazein* in reference to bearing weaknesses or burdens (Rom 15:1; Gal 6:2, 5), and in reference to the marks of Christ (6:17) which he bears. But here he means that anyone who troubles the Galatians will bear the *krima*: the final judgment before the Lord.

11. *But if I, brethren, am still preaching circumcision*: D*, F, G omit *eti* ("still"), thereby eliminating the problem: to what period in his life is Paul referring? The period before his call? The period after his call? According to Acts 16:3, Paul circumcised Timothy since it was known that Timothy's father was a Greek. But in 1 Cor 7:18 Paul writes, "Was anyone at the time of his call uncircumcised? Let him not seek circumcision." There is no evidence that Paul, the Christian, advocated circumcision in his preaching to Gentiles. The reference here, therefore, is probably to Paul's pre-Christian period. The agitators, however, may have misinterpreted Paul's indifference to circumcision (1 Cor 7:18-19) as meaning that the Gentiles should be circumcised.

   why am I still being persecuted?: Eti ("still") refers to Paul's present circumstances: the proclamation of his Torah-free gospel has resulted in persecution. In 2 Cor 11:23-29 he refers to dangers (*kindunoi*) from his own people, from Gentiles, and from false brethren (2 Cor 11:26). The persecution to which he refers here probably comes from false brethren as well, i.e., the agitators. See 4:29 and the comments there. In Gal 6:12 Paul accuses the Judaizers of compelling circumcision in order to avoid persecution.

Then the scandal of the cross is abolished: *Ara* is used as an inferential particle ("so," "then," "consequently"). It points to what would happen if Paul preached circumcision. According to 1 Cor 1:23 "Christ crucified" is a *skandalon* ("scandal," "stumbling block") to Jews. Here, the cross is identified as the *skandalon*. The scandal is that the one upon whom the Law (Deut 21:23) pronounced a curse (3:13) is the source of salvation.

12. *Would that those disturbing you might castrate themselves*: The verb *apokopsontai* is the future middle of *apokoptein*. The literal meaning is, "would that they would *cut themselves off*." But since the time of Chrysostom and Ambriosiaster, it has been interpreted in the sense of castrate oneself, make oneself a eunuch. If Paul has Deut 23:1 in mind ("No one whose testicles are crushed or whose penis is cut off shall be admitted to the assembly of the Lord"), then he may intend a pun: may they cut themselves off from the community of Israel by castrating themselves! See Phil 3:2 where Paul calls circumcision mutilation (*tēn katatomēn*).

INTERPRETATION

Commentators, in their outlines of Galatians, disagree about the placement of this unit within the broader context of the letter. Burton, Lightfoot, Bonnard, Betz, and Bruce, for example, view it as the beginning of a new section that consists primarily of moral exhortation (parenesis). But Lagrange, Schlier, Mussner, Fung, and Longenecker treat it as the conclusion of the material which has preceded. Moreover, although the majority of commentators agree that this unit consists of vv. 1–12, Lightfoot, Bruce, and Fung contend that v. 1 is the conclusion of the Sarah-Hagar allegory so that this unit consists of vv. 2–12. There are good arguments for these various positions since many of the themes found in this unit are also present in the material which precedes and follows it. For example, the theme of freedom, so boldly proclaimed in 5:1, recalls the Sarah-Hagar allegory which proclaimed that the Galatians are the children of the free woman (4:31). But this same theme also foreshadows Paul's warning in 5:13 that the Galatians should not allow their freedom to be abused by the flesh. Likewise, the theme of the Spirit in 5:5 recalls what Paul said about the Spirit (3:2, 3, 5, 14; 4:6, 29) as well as what he will write about the Spirit (5:16, 17, 18, 22, 25; 6:1, 8). Finally, references to the agitators (5:10, 12) recall what has been said in 1:7; 4:17 and prepare for Paul's remarks in 6:12-13. In a word, this section recalls what has preceded and foreshadows what will come.

In addition to the themes listed above, one can point to other relationships between this unit and what precedes or follows. For example, R. Longenecker (*Galatians*, 221–222) contends that structurally 1:6-10 and 5:1-12 form an *inclusio*. He points to (1) "the sustained severity" found in both units; (2) the reference to "the one who called you" found in 1:6 and 5:8; (3) the expressions, "the grace of Christ" in 1:6 and "fallen away from grace" in 5:4; (4) the use of *palin* ("again") in 1:9 and 5:3; and (5) the anathemas of 1:8-9 which are paralleled by the threat of judgment in 5:10b. In addition to these parallels, moreover, one can point to another set of parallels between this unit and 6:10-17. In both units there are the following parallels: doing and keeping the Law (5:3; 6:13a); neither circumcision nor the lack of it is important (5:6; 5:15); and the relationship between circumcision and persecution (5:11; 6:12).

Since this unit contains material which recalls what precedes as well as foreshadows what will come, it is clearly something of a transitional piece which summarizes past arguments and introduces a new phase of the argument. Within the outline of Galatians developed for this commentary, however, this unit is viewed as the conclusion of the section which precedes it, for the following reasons. First, the material which follows, especially 5:13–6:10, is clearly parenetic in nature; that is, it functions as moral exhortation. In this unit, however, Paul appeals to the Galatians to avoid circumcision (5:1-6) and rebukes them for falling prey to the agitators (5:7-12). Second, since ch. 3 Paul has argued that the Galatians are Abraham's descendants by incorporation into Christ, but Paul has not explicitly mentioned the main issue: circumcision. In 5:1-12 he explicitly introduces the issue of circumcision for the first time. In effect, this unit provides the necessary conclusion to the argument begun in 3:1. Having reminded the Galatians that they received the Spirit apart from legal works, and that they are Abraham's descendants by incorporation into Christ, now Paul can explicitly say, "avoid circumcision!" Consequently, while this unit is transitional in nature, it functions as the conclusion of the argument begun in 3:1. The material can be outlined in the following way.

v. 1   A call to freedom
vv. 2–6   The consequences of circumcision
    v. 2   No benefit from Christ
    v. 3   The need to do the whole Law
    v. 4   A fall from grace
      v. 5 because the justified wait in hope
      v. 6 because faith expresses itself through love
vv. 7–12   Rebuke and judgment
    v. 7   A rebuking question
    v. 8   A rebuking statement
    v. 9   A proverb
    v. 10a A statement of confidence
    v. 10b A statement of judgment
    v. 11   A response to an accusation
    v. 12   A final judgment

After an initial call to freedom (v. 1), in vv. 2–4 Paul focuses upon the consequences of circumcision. Verses 5–6 provide supporting reasons for the statement in v. 4 that those who seek justification by the Law are cut off from grace. In vv. 7–12, Paul's tone becomes one of rebuke and judgment as he turns to the agitators as well as to the Galatians. Verses 7–10a are related to each other by the words *peithein* ("to persuade") and *peismonē* ("persuasion"). In v. 7, Paul asks who hindered the Galatians from obeying (*peithesthai*) the truth. In v. 8 he says that this persuasion (*peismonē*) is not from God, and in v. 10a he states his confidence (*pepoitha*) in the Galatians. Finally, in vv. 10b–12 Paul responds to an accusation of the agitators and pronounces his judgment against them.

Christ has set us free (v. 1). Paul begins with a ringing statement of freedom. Associating himself with the Galatians, he proclaims that Christ has set *us* free. Therefore, the Galatians must take care lest they entangle themselves again in a yoke of slavery. In reference to the Galatians, the adverb "again" recalls their slavery under the *stoicheia*, the weak and impotent rudiments of religion which they once served by paying tribute to things that, by their very nature, are not gods. Now, however, the Galatians are in danger of accepting another form of slavery, the yoke of the Law.

Since the notion of the Law as an oppressive yoke of slavery was foreign to the Judaism of his day, Paul's thought here can only be understood within the context of his own writings. In light of the Damascus road event, he discovered that the role of the Law was temporary and subordinate to the promise which God made to Abraham. Moreover, even though Paul was blameless "as to righteousness under the Law" (Phil 3:6), he now understands that the Law was never intended to give righteousness or life (2:21; 3:21). Rather, it was given so that those under it would know that they were transgressing God's command (3:19). It was a *paidagōgos* that restricted and limited freedom because those under it had not yet attained their majority (3:23-25). In Paul's view, then, to submit to the Law is to submit to a yoke of slavery. To be sure, this yoke is different in kind from that of the *stoicheia*, but it is a yoke nonetheless. Paul's view here is contrary not only to the religious thought of his day but to that of the modern mind as well. While the contemporary religious person sees law as a safeguard from sin, Paul argues that being under the Mosaic Law is a form of slavery since it makes the violation of particular commandments possible (Rom 7:7). By contrast, freed from the Law, those in Christ fulfill the Law through love (5:14).

The consequences of circumcision (vv. 2-6). Having admonished the Galatians to maintain their freedom and to avoid the yoke of slavery, in these verses Paul draws out the consequences the Galatians will face if they submit to circumcision: (1) Christ will be of no benefit to them; (2) they will be obliged to *do* all of the prescriptions of the Law and; (3) they will fall from grace. Therefore, the Galatians must choose either Christ or the Law. To understand Paul's logic at this point, it is important to recall that his remarks are directed to Gentiles, and that he is opposing Christ and the Law as two means of salvation. Paul is *not* arguing that Jewish Christians are cut off from Christ because they are circumcised. Nor is he suggesting that Jews who have believed in Christ must abandon their observance of the Law. Indeed, Jews in general, and Jewish Christians in particular, are not Paul's concern at this point. Moreover, one can suppose that Paul did not object when Jewish Christians continued to practice the Mosaic Law *provided that* they understood that Christ, not the Law, was the source of their righteousness. But in the case of the Galatians, and Gentiles generally, Paul's approach was different. If the Galatians allow themselves to be circumcised Christ will be of no benefit to them. Why? Because by submitting to circumcision the Galatians will imply that what God accomplished in Christ was insufficient: not only must they believe in Christ, they must also be circumcised and accept the Law. It is the "also," the implicit admission that the death of Christ is insufficient, that is at the core of Paul's argument. In light of Christ, Paul argues that incorporation into Christ is the God-established means for Gentiles to become descendants of Abraham and receive the promised Spirit. Christ gave himself for sins to free all from the present evil age (1:4). If the Law could have accomplished this, it would not have been necessary for Christ to die (2:21). The acceptance of circumcision by the Galatians, therefore, will be paramount to denying the salvific power of Christ's death.

Did those Galatians who were about to accept circumcision understand all of this? Did the agitators tell them that the Christ event was insufficient? Although the agitators insisted upon circumcision, they probably did not establish the sharp dichotomy between Christ and the Law that Paul did. Moreover, the Galatians undoubtedly thought that by circumcision they were completing and perfecting their faith in Christ rather than denying it. But in light of the Damascus road event, Paul saw a deeper dimension to the Christ event than did either the agitators or the Galatians. Through incorporation into Christ, God provided a way for the Gentiles to become Abraham's descendants, apart from the Law. The Christ event was sufficient for salvation.

To impress upon the Galatians the consequences of circumcision, Paul insists that if they are circumcised they will be obliged to do the whole Law, that is, the individual commandments and prescriptions of the Law. Were the Galatians ignorant of the relationship between circumcision and the Law? Did the agitators neglect to teach them the full implications of circumcision? Some commentators, on the basis of 5:3, respond affirmatively to these questions. It seems unlikely, however, that Jewish-Christian missionaries would have made such a sharp dichotomy between circumcision and Law observance. Moreover, it appears that the Galatians were already observing some prescriptions of the Law (4:10). A more probable explanation is that Paul is merely reminding the Galatians of the full implications of circumcision, with an emphasis upon the aspect of *doing* all of the prescriptions of the Law.

The circumcised place themselves under the obligation of doing all that is written in the Book of the Law (3:10 quoting Deut 27:26). They try to find life by doing the commandments (3:12 quoting Lev 18:5). Circumcision is not merely an entrance rite, it is a solemn commitment to a Jewish way of life which is characterized by nomistic service, i.e., doing the Law. But in the light of Christ, Paul argues that the Law does not give righteousness (2:21), and was not intended to give life (3:21). Therefore, *even if* the Galatians do all of the prescriptions of the Law, it will be of no avail to them. Rather, they will find themselves in the curious position of trying to be justified by the Law. Trying to be justified by the Law, they will implicitly be admitting that there is no need for Christ. Having made Christ superfluous, they will have fallen from grace. The statement that circumcision demands total observance of the Law, therefore, is not an assault upon a superstitious understanding of the power of circumcision; it is a way of recalling Paul's arguments in 2:21; 3:10-14; 3:21. Circumcision involves doing the Law, but doing the Law does not bring life. What is needed is an alternate principle of salvation, Christ, through whom the Law can be *fulfilled* (5:14). Incorporated into Christ, believers fulfill the Law through faith that expresses itself through love.

In order to ground his statement in v. 4, that those seeking to be justified by the Law are cut off from grace, Paul reminds the Galatians who they are (v. 5) and what is really important (v. 6). While the agitators and those attracted to them seek to be justified by nomistic service as well as by faith in Christ, Paul and those associated with him are people who already enjoy a righteousness which has been given by Christ. On the basis of this righteousness, they wait in confidence for the eschatological gifts for which they hope. Moreover, what really matters is a faith capable of expressing itself in love, a faith analogous to the faith of the Son of God who gave himself for us because he loved us (2:20). By contrast the physical mark of circumcision, or the lack of it, means nothing.

To summarize, Paul warns the Galatians that, for Gentiles like themselves, circumcision has dire consequences. More than a rite of initiation, it is the first step in a life of nomistic service by which an individual seeks to be justified by the Law. Justification by the Law, however, excludes justification by Christ. Those Galatians who embrace circumcision will gain no profit from Christ. Instead, they will cut themselves off from the grace of Christ.

Rebuke and judgment (vv. 7–12). Having warned the Galatians of the consequences of accepting circumcision, in these verses Paul turns his attention to the agitators and the havoc they have wrought, pronouncing judgment upon them and rebuking the Galatians. As in 3:1 Paul employs graphic imagery to ask the Galatians who interfered with their first obedience. Who bewitched them (3:1)? Who impeded them in the race for the finish line (5:7)? Paul, of course, knows who the agitators are, but he does not enhance their status by identifying them. Rather, he compares them and their teaching to yeast. Just as a small amount of yeast causes a large amount of dough to rise, so a few people and their teaching have infected the Galatian community for the worse, throwing it into confusion and disorder. Despite the present circumstances, Paul says that he remains confident in the community, a surprising statement in light of his earlier remark (4:20). This confidence, however, is not an expression of the apostle's belief in his power to dissuade the Galatians from their course; rather it is confidence in the Lord. Thus, although Paul finds it difficult to understand the present frame of mind of the Galatians, he trusts that the situation will be favorably resolved since the truth of the gospel he preaches comes from Christ. As for the agitators, they will face a stern judgment from God at the appropriate time (cf. 1 Cor 3:10-17). The reference in v. 10b to the one disturbing the Galatians does not mean that Paul is speaking about an individual, e.g., a ringleader of the disturbance. Rather it should be understood in a generic sense (see notes): *anyone* who disturbs the Galatians will stand in judgment before the Lord, no matter who he is.

Paul's statement in v. 11 suggests that he has been accused of "preaching circumcision." The very thought, of course, is absurd since Paul preaches "Christ crucified." But the Apostle must deal with it, and he does so with two arguments. First, if he "preaches circumcision" why is he being persecuted? Here, persecution should be understood as persecution from the agitators, not persecution from Jews. The agitators "persecute" Paul by opposing the circumcision-free Gospel he preaches to the Gentiles, just as the false brethren did at Jerusalem (2:4-5). If Paul "preached circumcision," then the agitators would certainly not have opposed his missionary activity among the Gentiles. But in fact, they do. Second, if Paul "preaches circumcision" then he has made the scandal of the cross ineffective. The scandal of the cross, of course, is the offer of salvation on the basis of faith in the crucified Messiah rather than on the basis of the observance of the Mosaic Law. By "preaching circumcision" Paul would remove the offense of a crucified Christ, but in fact he does not.

But how did the charge that Paul preached circumcision arise? If this is what the agitators were telling the Galatians, what was their basis in fact for saying so? There is nothing in Paul's writings which suggests that he ever, as a Christian, required Gentile Christians to accept circumcision. It is possible, however, that the agitators misunderstood or twisted certain events or words from Paul's life, e.g., the circumcision of Timothy (Acts 16:3), the incident concerning Titus (2:3), remarks such as 5:6; 6:15; 1 Cor 7:19 that neither circumcision nor the lack of it is important. Whatever the case, it appears that the agitators told the Galatians that Paul does, in other circumstances, preach circumcision. If the agitators told this to the Galatians, it is small wonder that the latter were prepared to accept circumcision.

Some have argued that the agitators were fundamentally benevolent toward Paul, and that they merely tried to complement his missionary activity. Paul's final, rather crude, remark belies this, at least as Paul saw it. His wish that those who require circumcision should castrate themselves shows that he, at least, views the agitators as dangerous opponents. Even if Paul overstated his case, the relationship between him and the agitators was anything but cordial.

FOR REFERENCE AND FURTHER STUDY

Hübner, H. *Law in Paul's Thought.* Edinburgh: T & T Clark: 1984, 36–42.

Matera, F. J. "The Culmination of Paul's Argument to the Galatians: Gal 5:1–6:17." *JSNT* 32 (1988) 79–91.

McEleney, N. J. "Conversion, Circumcision, and the Law." *NTS* 20 (1973–74) 319–341.

Merk, O. "Der Beginn der Paränese im Galaterbrief." *ZNW* 60 (1969) 83–104.

Räisänen, H. *Paul and the Law.* Philadelphia: Fortress, 1986, 62–73.

Sanders, E. P. *Paul, the Law, and the Jewish People.* Philadelphia: Fortress, 1983, 27–29.

III: LIVING BY THE SPIRIT (5:13–6:10)

Love Fulfills the Law (5:13-15)

13. You were called to freedom, brethren, only do not let your freedom
become an occasion for the flesh, but through love be enslaved to one
another. 14. For the whole Law is fulfilled in one word, "love your neighbor as yourself." 15. If you bite and tear each other to pieces, watch out
lest you are consumed by one another.

NOTES

13. *You were called to freedom, brethren*: This verse is connected to the previous
unit by *gar* ("for"), which has been left untranslated. *Gar* indicates that the
theme of freedom introduced in 5:1-12 is being taken up again, but from a
different vantage point. As in 1:6; 5:8, God is the one who called (*eklēthete*,
"you were called") the Galatians. The pronoun *hymas* ("you") is emphatic
and serves to distinguish the Galatians from those who are disturbing them
(v. 12); while the agitators urge circumcision, the Galatians were called to
freedom. The preposition *epi (ep' eleutheria*, "to freedom") indicates the goal
and purpose of the Galatians' calling. See 5:1 and the discussion there. This
freedom is redemption from the Law and its curse (3:13; 4:5). For other Pauline uses of freedom, see Rom 8:21; 1 Cor 10:29; 2 Cor 3:17. In 2 Cor 3:17 Paul
makes a connection between freedom and the Spirit. However, see Jas 1:25;
2:12 which equates Law and freedom. For admonitions similar to this one
in Galatians, see 1 Cor 8:9; 1 Pet 2:16. For a warning against a false promise
of freedom, see 2 Pet 2:19.

only do not let your freedom become an occasion for the flesh: The Greek reads,
monon mē tēn eleutherian eis aphormēn tē̦ sarki, literally, "only not the freedom
an occasion for the flesh," making it necessary to supply the verb "become."
"An occasion" translates *aphormēn* whose literal meaning is "the starting-
point or base of operations for an expedition" (*BAG*). It is used here in the
sense of "occasion," "pretext," "opportunity," as it is in Rom 7:8, 11 (in
regard to sin) and 2 Cor 5:12; 11:12; 1 Tim 5:14. *Sarx* ("flesh") has several
meanings in Paul's writings. In Galatians it is employed in the following ways:
(1) that which covers the bones of a human being, 3:3; 6:13; (2) the body,
4:13-14; (3) the human person, flesh and blood, 1:16; 2:16; (4) human descent, 4:23; (5) earthly existence, 2:20; (6) the external and outward side of
life, that which is natural and earthly, 6:12; (7) human nature which opposes
itself to God through self-seeking, 5:13, 16, 17, 19, 24; 6:8. Thus far in Galatians, *sarx* has been employed in a neutral sense, but from this point forward
it takes on an ethical tone.

but through love be enslaved to one another: The word love is preceded by the definite article in Greek (*tēs agapēs*), suggesting that Paul has a special kind of love in view. Some manuscripts (D, F, G, 104) read *dia tē agapē tou pneumatos* ("through the love of the Spirit"), which is an attempt to make the nature of this love explicit. *Dia agapēs* recalls a similar phrase in 5:6. The verb *douleuete* is translated "be enslaved" rather than "serve" since Paul is contrasting two kinds of slavery: slavery to the Law (5:1), and slavery to the neighbor through love. See 4:8, 9, 25 where the verb is also used in the sense of slavery, especially to the *stoicheia*.

14. *For the whole Law is fulfilled in one word, "love your neighbor as yourself"*: The text of Marcion reads, "For the whole Law is fulfilled *among you*. . . ." Other manuscripts (D*, F, G) read "For the whole Law is fulfilled among you in one word. . . ." These readings are later alterations intended to make Paul's thought more explicit. "The whole Law" (*ho pas nomos*) is the Law viewed as a unity, the Law in its totality. Compare 5:3 which speaks of *holon ton nomon*, the entire Law viewed in light of its multiple precepts. The circumcised must do the many precepts of the Law, whereas the one justified by faith fulfills the Law through the love commandment. *Peplērōtai* ("is fulfilled") is in the perfect tense and could be translated, "the whole Law has found its full expression . . ." (*BAG*). The phrase "in one word" (*en eni logō*) employs logos in the sense of "commandment," much as does the Hebrew *dabar*. The commandment is Lev 19:18. It is also employed in Matt 5:43; 19:19; 22:39; Mark 12:31; 12:33; Luke 10:27; Rom 13:9 and Jas 2:8. In Rom 13:8-10 Paul says that he who loves his neighbor has fulfilled the Law (*nomon peplērōken*), that the other commandments are summed up (*anakephalaioutai*) in the love commandment, and that love is the fulfilling (*plērōma*) of the Law.

15. *If you bite and tear each other to pieces, watch out lest you are consumed by one another*: *Daknein* means "to bite" as in the case of the serpents which bit the Israelites in the wilderness (Num 21:6; Barn 12:5). Here it has the figurative sense of offend or nettle. *Katesthiein* means "to eat up," "to consume," "to devour." Here it has the figurative sense of destroy. *Analiskein* means "to consume." The imagery is that of wild animals, and it clearly progresses from biting to eating to consuming. As the following verses show, Paul is referring to party strife and contention at Galatia.

INTERPRETATION

In the first part of this letter (1:11–2:21), Paul reminded the Galatians that the truth of his Torah-free Gospel is founded upon his call: the revelation of Jesus Christ that he received from God. In part two (3:1–5:12), he drew out the implications of the truth of the gospel that he preaches: the Galatians are Abraham's descendants because they are in Christ (3:1-29). Consequently, they must not return to the period of their minority (4:1-11); they must become as Paul is (4:12-20); they must expel the agitators (4:21-31); and they must avoid circumcision (5:1-12). With this unit (5:13-15), Paul begins the third and final part of his letter, "Living by the Spirit" (5:13–6:10).

While the majority of commentators agree that the third part of the letter consists of parenetic material, that is, moral exhortation, there is little agreement about how this material functions within the whole of Galatians. Paul has argued that to be under the Law is to be under a curse (3:10-14); that the Law functioned as a *paidagōgos* (3:23-25); that Christ came to redeem those under the Law (4:4-5); and that the Galatians must not allow themselves to be enslaved by the yoke of the Law (5:1-5). In effect, he has told them that they are free from the Law. But in the third part of this letter (5:13–6:10), it appears that the Apostle contradicts what he has already said. Having argued that the Galatians are not under the Law, in 5:14 Paul proclaims that the Law is "fulfilled" in the commandment to love one's neighbor, and in 6:2 he writes that bearing one another's burdens fulfills the Law of Christ. Moreover, this part of the letter consists of rules, regulations, and exhortations to do good, e.g., 6:1-10. What, then, is the relationship of this part of the letter to what Paul has already said, especially his critique of the Law in 3:1–5:12?

John Barclay (*Obeying the Truth*, 9–23) has summarized the major attempts to respond to this question. On the one hand, he notes that a number of commentators argue that this section (5:13–6:10) is "wholly or largely unrelated" to what has preceded it. The position has been developed in four ways. (1) J. C. O'Neill (*The Recovery of Paul's Letter to the Galatians*) finds it strange that Paul should suddenly warn his readers against antinomianism. In his view there is nothing specifically Pauline in this section. Consequently, he proposes that the material found in 5:13–6:10 was interpolated by a later editor "because an epistle meant for building up the Church at large would need to have its own ethical section" (71). (2) A less radical position is taken by M. Dibelius who, in contrast to O'Neill, acknowledges that Paul is the author of the parenetic material but contends that the material is not conditioned by the particular circumstances of this letter. Thus, although the parenesis provides moral exhortation, it is unrelated to the letter's argument. (3) Other commentators view this section as "a defense against possible objections or misunderstandings" (*Obeying the Truth*, 12). Burton, for example, writes, "In this paragraph the apostle deals with a new phase of the subject, connected, indeed, with the main theme of the letter, but not previously touched upon. Aware that on the one side it will probably be urged against his doctrine of freedom from law that it removes the restraints that keep men from immorality, and certainly on the other that those who accept it are in danger of misinterpreting it as if this were the case, he fervently exhorts the Galatians not to fall into this error, but, instead, through love to serve one another" (*Galatians*, 290). While this approach sees this section as "connected" to what has preceded, it tends to reduce the parenesis to "an apologetic appendix" (*Obeying the Truth*, 12). (4) Finally, W. Lütgert (*Gesetz und Geist*) and J. H. Ropes (*The Singular Problem*) have argued that Paul had to deal with two different groups at Galatia: legalists who wanted to adopt the Law and spiritualistic radicals whose freedom from the Law led to antinomianism. According to this view, 5:12–6:10 is directed against this antinomian front.

On the other hand, Barclay notes that many commentators have attempted to integrate 5:13–6:10 into the whole of Galatians. (1) W. Schmithals ("Die Häretiker in Galatien"), for example, contends that Paul's opponents at Galatia were Jewish Gnostics who combined circumcision with a libertine style of life. The agitators were not serious about observing the Law (see, 5:3; 6:13); nonetheless they advocated circumcision and veneration of the *stoicheia*. In effect, Schmithals combines the two parties of Lütgert's two front hypothesis into a single opposition group. (2) Still others argue that Paul employs parenesis to dispel the Galatians' moral confusion. H. D. Betz (*Galatians*, 273), for instance, argues that "flagrant misconduct" was a major problem at Galatia. In the absence of a code of Law, the Galatians asked how they were to act. Realizing that they needed help, and that in the Law the agitators offered a concrete solution, Paul provides the Galatians with a new definition of the ethical task, one founded upon love. (3) Finally, others (D. Lull, B. H. Brinsmead, G. Howard) see this section as "a continuation of Paul's ironical polemic against the law" (*Obeying the Truth*, 22). Thus Howard (*Crisis in Galatia*, 12) views Paul's words "as an attack on his opponents," while Brinsmead (*Dialogical Response*, 190) sees this section as "a rhetorical *refutatio*, the final argument against the intruding theology."

Barclay's own conclusions are prudent and, for the most part, are adopted in this commentary. He argues (1) that Paul's exhortation is a development and conclusion of his earlier arguments (216); (2) that this section is a specific response to the crisis at Galatia (217); (3) that Paul is fighting only on one front and is primarily concerned with the status of Gentile believers (218); and (4) that 5:13–6:10 is an appeal to the Galatians to let their lives be guided by the Spirit since the Spirit can provide the necessary moral guidance that they seek. Thus this moral exhortation operates as a warning against moral danger, defined here as "the flesh" (219). The moral exhortation of 5:13–6:10, therefore, is integral to the argument which Paul has developed thus far. Indeed, if Paul cannot establish a relationship between his Torah-free gospel and the moral life, his argument in the first four chapters of this letter loses its force. Galatians 5:13–6:10, however, is the culmination of Paul's argument. Not only does it show that those who have been freed from the Law can live a moral life; more importantly, it establishes that those who are led by the Spirit, and follow the Spirit's lead, fulfill the Law. In other words, Paul employs moral exhortation to establish, on a practical level, the argument he so carefully develops in the first four chapters of this letter. The material in this unit can be outlined in the following way.

> v. 13a A reminder that the Galatians were called to freedom
> v. 13b A warning regarding the flesh
> v. 13c Love: a remedy for the flesh
> v. 14   A reason for serving each other through love
> v. 15   A warning about community division.

Freedom, flesh, and love (v. 13). The beginning of this unit clearly recalls the opening verse of the previous unit: "for freedom Christ has set us free" (5:1). However, whereas Paul made use of the first person plural in 5:1, here he employs the second person plural, making it clear that what he is about to say applies directly to the Galatians. God called them to freedom, just as He called Paul through his grace (1:15). This freedom, of course, is freedom from the Mosaic Law; the Galatians are not under the Law. The concept of freedom from the Law, however, can be misinterpreted to mean license, e.g., free from the Law, the Galatians can do whatever they want. Consequently, Paul warns them that they should not allow their freedom to become an occasion for the flesh.

Here flesh (*sarx*) refers to the inclination and tendency in the human person to live an existence completely and totally centered on the self. While this inclination can express itself in carnal disorders, that is not Paul's primary concern in this passage, as the context makes clear (see v. 15). The flesh is a power and force opposed to the Spirit of God. Controlled by the flesh, human beings seek their own advantage at the expense of others. Controlled by the flesh, human beings live self-centered lives at the expense of others. Controlled by the flesh, one's primary and exclusive concern is to live for oneself. Consequently, when the flesh takes control of people, there is dissension and party strife, and people no longer live in community for the sake of each other as God intended. The real problem, then, is the flesh, not freedom from the Law. Seizing upon freedom, the flesh seduces the human person by perverting freedom into license. Aware of this, Paul cautions the Galatians not to let their freedom become a base of operations from which the flesh can make an assault upon them. If the Galatians are to preserve their freedom, they must, paradoxically, become enslaved to each other through love (*dia tēs agapēs*). The love which Paul has in view, however, is not simply a human virtue; it is the fruit of the Holy Spirit (5:22). By being enslaved to each other, the Galatians will neutralize the flesh's power to abuse their freedom. Serving one another in love, there will be no occasion for them to live only for themselves.

Fulfilling the Law (v. 14). There is a fundamental reason why Paul exhorts the Galatians to serve each other through love; the Law is fulfilled in the commandment: "Love your neighbor as yourself." Consequently, Paul distinguishes between *doing* the Law and *fulfilling the Law.* Whereas the circumcised are obligated to do the Law, those who are in Christ fulfill the Law through the love commandment. Thus, in Galatians, when Paul speaks about the Jewish observance of the Law, he employs the verbs "to do" (*poiein*; 3:10, 12; 5:3), and "to obey" (*phylassein*; Gal 6:13). But when he speaks of those who are in Christ and their relationship to the Law, he uses the verb "to fulfill" (*plēroūn* or *anaplēroun*; Gal 5:14; 6:2). This contrast is especially striking in the last two chapters of Galatians.

5:3   Those who are circumcised must do (*poiēsai*) the whole Law.
5:14 The Law is fulfilled (*peplērōtai*) by the love commandment.
6:2   If you bear one another's burdens you will fulfill (*anaplērōsete*) the Law of Christ.
6:13 Even the circumcised do not obey (*phylassousin*) the Law.

Moreover, in Rom 2:25 Paul employs similar language. He writes, "Circumcision indeed is of value if you obey (*prāssēs*) the Law; but if you break the Law, your circumcision has become uncircumcision." But in Rom 8:3-4 he notes that God sent his Son, "so that the just requirements of the Law might be fulfilled (*plērōthȩ̄*) in us." And in Rom 13:8-10 writes:

Owe no one anything, except to love one another; for the one who loves another has fulfilled (*peplērōken*) the Law. The commandments, "You shall not commit adultery; You shall not murder; You shall not steal; You shall not covet;" and any other commandment, are summed up (*anakephalaioutai*) in this word, "Love your neighbor as yourself." Love does no wrong to a neighbor; therefore, love is the fulfilling (*plērōma*) of the Law.

By "fulfilling the Law," Paul clearly has something more in mind than "doing" the several prescriptions of the Law, even if these are done perfectly. To fulfill the Law "implies that the obedience offered *completely satisfies* what is required" (S. Westerholm, "On Fulfilling the Whole Law," 234). By contrast, doing the Law does not result in fulfilling the Law, because the works of the Law are not radical enough. As D. Lull (*Spirit in Galatia*, 129) notes, they do not "go to the root of the problem, which is the flesh's domination of the center of human existence." By contrast, the fruit of the Spirit, *agapē*, is exercised in the sphere of Christ. Love completely satisfies the requirements of the Law because it is a gift of the Spirit, accomplished in Christ. Consequently, although the Galatians are not under the Law, they fulfill the Law through love. Their freedom from the Law, properly understood, does not lead to license.

A warning about community division (v. 15). Paul's final warning indicates that the Galatians have already allowed the flesh to use their freedom as an opportunity for misconduct. The language in this verse compares the Galatians to wild beasts who begin by biting one another, but finish by tearing each other apart, and even consuming one another. The problem of the flesh at Galatia is social and communal rather than carnal. The Galatians are deeply divided and at odds with each other. Each one is more concerned with his or her own welfare than with the needs of the community. If the Galatians are to overcome the flesh and fulfill the Law of Christ (6:2), they must bear one another's burdens.

FOR REFERENCE AND FURTHER STUDY

Barclay, J. M. G. *Obeying the Truth: A Study of Paul's Ethics in Galatians.* Edinburgh: T. & T. Clark, 1988.

Barrett, C. K. *Freedom and Obligation: A Study of the Epistle to the Galatians.* Philadelphia: Westminster, 1985, 53–90.

Brinsmead, B. H. *Galatians—Dialogical Response to Opponents.* SBLDS 65; Scholars Press, 1982, 163–185.

Howard, G. *Paul: Crisis in Galatia.* SSNTMS 35; Cambridge University Press, 1979, 11–19.

Lull, D. J. *The Spirit in Galatia: Paul's Interpretation of Pneuma as Divine Power.* SBLDS 49; Scholars Press, 1980, 113–130.

O'Neill, J. C. *The Recovery of Paul's Letter to the Galatians.* London: SPCK, 1972.

Ropes, J. H. *The Singular Problem of the Epistle to the Galatians.* HTS 14; Harvard University Press, 1929.

Westerholm, S. "Letter and Spirit: The Foundation of Pauline Ethics." *NTS* 30 (1984) 229–248.

Westerholm, S. "On Fulfilling the Whole Law (Gal 5:14)." *SEA* (1987) 229–237.

Walk by the Spirit (5:16-26)

16. This is what I mean, walk by the Spirit and there is no likelihood of carrying out the craving of the flesh. 17. For the flesh has longings at odds with the Spirit, and the Spirit is at odds with the flesh; for they are opposed to each other, so that you cannot do whatever you want. 18. If you are led by the Spirit, you are not under the Law. 19. The works of the flesh are plain. These are fornication, immorality, sensuality, 20.

idolatry, sorcery, enmity, strife, jealousy, outbursts of anger, selfish ambition, dissensions, factions, 21. envy, drinking bouts, carousing, and things like these. I warn you about such things, as I warned you before, those who do such things will not inherit the Kingdom of God. 22. But the fruit of the Spirit is love, joy, peace, patience, kindness, goodness, faith, 23. gentleness, self-control. Against such things there is no Law. 24. Those who belong to Christ [Jesus] have crucified the flesh with its passions and desires. 25. If we live by the Spirit, let us also follow the Spirit. 26. Let us not be conceited, provoking one another, being envious of one another.

NOTES

16. *This is what I mean, walk by the Spirit and there is no likelihood of carrying out the craving of the flesh*: *Legō de* ("This is what I mean") adds emphasis to what Paul is about to say and marks the beginning of a new section. See 3:17; 4:1; 5:2. "And there is no likelihood of carrying out" translates *ou mē telesēte* which could also be taken as a negative imperative ("do not carry out"). The context, however, suggests the future since Paul is assuring the Galatians that they will overcome the flesh if they follow the Spirit. The Spirit (*pneumati*) refers to the Spirit of God and is contrasted with the *epithymian sarkos* ("craving of the flesh") which manifests itself in the "works of the flesh" listed in vv. 19–21a. *Epithymia* ("craving," "desire") can have a good sense as in Phil 1:23 and 1 Thess 2:17. Here, and in other instances, it has a negative connotation: a desire for something which is forbidden (Rom 1:24; 6:12; 1 Thess 4:5). *Peripatein* ("to walk") is a common word in Paul's writings and is usually employed in a figurative sense: to conduct oneself in a particular way (Rom 6:4; 8:4; 13:13; 14:15. Also, Eph 2:2, 10; 5:2, 8, 15; Col 3:7). In this section the verb is elucidated by vv. 18 and 25 where Paul speaks of being "led" by the Spirit and "living" by the Spirit.

17. *For the flesh has longings at odds with the Spirit, and the Spirit is at odds with the flesh*: A literal translation of the Greek is: "For the flesh desires against the Spirit and the Spirit against the flesh." The Spirit is the Spirit of God, not the human spirit. The flesh is unredeemed humanity which seeks its own self. Exactly what the flesh and Spirit desire is described in the two lists of vv. 19–23.

for they are opposed to each other: Flesh and Spirit are opposed to each other because they belong to different realms. To dwell in the realm of the Spirit is to be in Christ. To dwell in the realm of the flesh is to live in the realm of unredeemed humanity.

so that you cannot do whatever you want: This is a translation of *hina mē ha ean thelēte tauta poiēte* which is best taken as a result clause. Other translations are: "to prevent you from doing what you would" (RSV); "to prevent you from doing what you want" (NRSV); "so that you may not do what you want" (NAB); "so that what you will do you cannot do" (NEB); "so that you cannot do what you want" (REB). Here one must determine what *ha ean thelēte* refers to: (1) the desires of the flesh, (2) the desires of the Spirit, (3) the desires of the flesh and the Spirit, and why the Galatians cannot do what they want to: (1) because the Spirit holds the flesh in check, (2) because the flesh frustrates the Spirit, (3) because flesh and Spirit hold each other in check. This commentary argues for a fourth interpretation. The Galatians cannot do whatever they want because "flesh" and "Spirit" represent two totally different ways of living. The Galatians must choose one or the other; they cannot choose both.

18. *If you are led by the Spirit, you are not under the Law*: *Pneumati agesthe* ("led by the Spirit") expresses a thought similar to that found in v. 16, "walk by the Spirit." This verse, however, shows that walking or conducting one's life according to the Spirit is not the result of personal effort alone: proper ethical conduct comes from willingly following the lead of the Spirit. See Rom 8:14 where Paul says that those led by the Spirit are children of God, and 1 Cor 12:2 which describes the former condition of the Corinthians when they were heathen (*ethnē*): "you were enticed and led astray to idols that could not speak."

19. *The works of the flesh are plain*: This is the only occurrence of *ta erga tēs sarkos* ("the works of the flesh") in Paul's writings. However, a similar expression is found in Rom 13:12 where he speaks of *ta erga tou skotous* ("the works of darkness") which are opposed to *ha hopla tou phōtos* ("the armor of light"). *Ta erga tou sarkos* also recalls *ta erga tou nomou* (2:16; 3:2, 5, 10). The two expressions, though different, are related to each other by the concept of "doing."

These are fornication: Some manuscripts (S*, D, F, G) begin this list with *moicheia* ("adultery"), probably because the next work is fornication. By doing so, they increase the number of works to sixteen. *Porneia* ("fornication") indicates illicit sexual activity such as prostitution and fornication. In the OT, where the relationship between God and Israel was viewed as a marriage, Israel's idolatry was called *porneia* ("harlotry"). See Hos 6:10. In Acts 15:20, 29; 21:25, the Gentiles are asked to avoid *porneia*. The meaning of *porneia* in Acts and Matt 5:32; 19:9, however, is disputed. Some see it as a form of unchastity, others an illicit marriage union between kinfolk such as is prohibited by Lev 18:6-18. In Paul's writings, *porneia* describes the kind of unlawful sexual activity that, from the Jewish point of view, characterizes Gentiles, and to which new converts are especially susceptible (1 Cor 5:1; 6:13, 18; 7:2; 1 Thess 4:3). In 2 Cor 12:21 Paul couples *porneia* with *akatharsia* and *aselgeia*, the next two works of this list. In Eph 5:3 and Col 3:5 *porneia* is coupled with *akatharsia*.

immorality: *Akatharsia* denotes impurity or uncleanness. In 2 Cor 12:21, Eph 5:3, and Col 3:5 it is associated with *porneia*, suggesting that it is the kind of uncleanness which derives from sexual immorality. In 1 Thess 4:7 it is opposed to *hagiasmos* ("holiness"). In Rom 1:24 (6:19) Paul says that God delivered humanity to *akatharsia*, which Paul explains by pointing to sexual immorality.

sensuality: The precise meaning of *aselgeia* is difficult to define: licentiousness, debauchery, sensuality. In Rom 13:13, because of its relationship to *kōmois* and *methais* (reveling and debauchery), it seems to have the sense of debauchery. But its relationship to *porneia* and *akatharsia* here, and in 2 Cor 12:21, favors the meaning of sensuality with a view to sexual misconduct.

20. *idolatry*: In 1 Cor 10:14, after a discussion of meat sacrificed to idols, Paul warns the Corinthians to flee *eidōlolatria*. In Col 3:5, *eidōlolatria* is identified with greed (*pleonexia*). In 1 Pet 4:3 it is the last of six vices used to characterize Gentile behavior (licentiousness, passions, drunkenness, revels, carousing *and* idolatry).

sorcery: The only other occurrence of *pharmakeia* in the NT is in Rev 18:23. The word does occur in the LXX: in Exod 7:11, 22; 8:7, 18 in reference to Pharaoh's magicians; in Isa 47:9, 12 in regard to magic as practiced by Israel; and in Wis 12:4; 18:13 in regard to the magic of the Canaanites and Egyptians.

enmity: *Echthra* is related to the adjective (*echthros*) and the noun *echthra*. Rom 8:7 and Jas 4:4 speak of enmity toward God. See Eph 2:14,16 which describes the enmity between Jew and Gentile as well as between God and humanity. The nature of the enmity here is defined by the following works which are characterized by community dissension.

strife: In the NT all nine occurrences of *eris* are found in writings attributed to Paul. In Rom 1:29; 13:13; 2 Cor 12:20; 1 Tim 6:4; and Titus 3:9 the word occurs in lists of vices. In 1 Cor 1:11; 3:3 it refers to the concrete problems of the Corinthian community. In Phil 1:15 it points to the false motivation from which some preach the gospel.

jealousy: Some manuscripts (S, C, D*, F, G) read the plural *zēloi* rather than the singular *zēlos*. The word can have a positive sense such as zeal or ardor, but here it means jealousy within the context of community, see Rom 13:13; 1 Cor 3:3; 2 Cor 12:20. In the last two passages, *zēlos* is coordinated with *eris*, and Paul says that the two are signs that the Corinthians are still *sarkinoi* ("carnal"), walking or behaving in merely a human fashion. In Jas 3:14 *zēlos* is used with *eritheia* ("dissensions") which is also found in this list. In Sir 30:24; 40:5 *zēlos* is used with *thymos*, the next work of this list.

outbursts of anger: *Thymos* is used most frequently in Revelation (ten times, often in terms of God's anger). In Eph 4:31 and Col 3:8 it is coupled with *orgē* ("wrath"). In 2 Cor 12:20 it is part of a list in which *zēlos* and *eritheia* (the next work of this list) occur.

selfish ambition: In Aristotle, *eritheia* denotes "a self-seeking pursuit of political office by unfair means" (BAG). But its meaning in the NT is less sure. Except for Jas 3:14, 16 all occurrences are found in Paul's letters (Rom 2:8; 2 Cor 12:20; Phil 1:17; 2:3) where the sense of selfish ambition seems to fit well.

dissensions: The only other occurrence of *dichostasia* in the NT is Rom 16:17 where it is coupled with *skandala* and is opposed "to the teaching you have learned."

factions: *Hairesis* can refer to sects or parties as in Acts 5:17; 24:5. But here, and in 1 Cor 11:19 it has the sense of dissension or faction (cf. 2 Pet 2:1).

21. *envy*: *Pthonos* is also found in Rom 1:29 and Phil 1:15. In the first it is part of a list of vices which includes *eris*. In the second, Paul says that some preach the gospel *dia phthonon kai erin* ("through envy and rivalry"). For other uses, see 1 Tim 6:4; Titus 3:3; 1 Pet 2:1. In 1 Tim 6:4 it is coupled with *eris*.

drinking-bouts: The only other occurrences of *methē* in the NT are Luke 21:34 and Rom 13:13. In Rom 13:13 it is coupled with *kōmos,* the next work on this list. *Methē* means drunkenness, but its use with *kōmos* ("carousing," "revelry") suggests drinking-bouts (BAG).

carousing: *Kōmos* originally referred to a festal procession in honor of Dionysus, then to a joyous meal or banquet (BAG). But in Wis 14:23; 2 Macc 6:4 and the NT (Rom 13:13; 1 Pet 4:3) it is used in the sense of excessive feasting.

and things like these: This indicates that this list of works is not exhaustive.

I warn you about such things, as I warned you before: Some manuscripts (S*, A, C, D) introduce *kai* after *kathōs* to emphasize the comparison between *prolegō* and *proeipon*: "I warn you . . . *even* as I warned you." "About such things" translates the relative pronoun *ha*. *Prolegein* can mean "to predict" or "to tell beforehand" as it does in Rom 9:29 and 1 Thess 3:4, but here there is the added sense of warning as the next phrase indicates. Paul appears to refer to an earlier visit to Galatia.

those who do such things will not inherit the Kingdom of God: *Ta toiauta* "such things" refers to the list of works just enumerated. Similar phrases with the verb *prassein* ("to do") are found in Rom 1:32; 2:2-3. The verb *prassein* is often used in a sense similar to *poiein* ("to do"). Although the kingdom of God is a major theme in the Synoptic gospels, its role is less prominent in Paul's writings and those attributed to him. The kingdom of God, or the kingdom, occurs eight times in the undisputed Pauline correspondence (Rom 14:17; 1 Cor 4:20; 6:9, 10; 15:24, 50; Gal 5:21; 1 Thess 2:12) and five times in the Deutero-Pauline writings (Eph 5:5; Col 1:13; 2 Thess 1:5; 2 Tim 4:1, 18). In 1 Cor 6:9, 10; 15:50 the verb *klēronomein* ("to inherit") is coupled with the phrase, as it is here. Eph 5:5 employs the noun "inheritance." While Paul uses the phrase *basileia theou* without the definite article here, in Rom 14:17; 1 Cor 4:20; 15:24, he employs the article (*hē basileia tou theou*). The absence of the article here does not appear to be significant. For Paul the kingdom is an eschatological reality (1 Cor 15:24, 50), but it impinges upon the lives of people here and now (Rom 14:17; 1 Cor 4:20). While it is preeminently God's gift (1 Thess 2:12; Col 1:13), it demands appropriate ethical conduct (1 Cor 6:9, 10; Gal 5:21).

22. *But the fruit of the Spirit is*: In contrast to the flesh, which produces "works," the Spirit generates "fruit" (*karpos*). *Karpos* is a major ethical concept in the Gospel of Matthew (3:8, 10; 7:16, 17, 18, 19; 12:33; 21:43). In Paul's writings, this is the only place that *karpos tou pneumatos* ("fruit of the Spirit") occurs. In Rom 6:22 he employs *karpos* with *hagiasmos* ("holiness"), and in Phil 1:11 he speaks of *karpos dikaiosynēs* ("fruit of righteousness"). Also, see Eph 5:9. The word *karpos* shows that the ethical life of the Christian is the singular fruit of the Spirit rather than the attainment of a series of virtues. This *karpos*

should be distinguished from the gifts (*charismata*) of the Spirit which are given for the sake of the community (1 Cor 12:4-31).

love: Agapē is a major concept in Paul's writings. It occurs nine times in Romans, fourteen times in 1 Corinthians, nine times in 2 Corinthians, three times in Galatians, four times in Philippians, five times in 1 Thessalonians, three times in Philemon, and twenty-eight times in other writings attributed to him. The concept can be understood from two vantage points: 1) the love of humans for each other and for God; 2) God's own love. In regard to the first, Paul speaks of faith expressing itself through love (5:6) and of serving one another through love (5:13). In Rom 13:10 he says that love of neighbor is the fulfillment of the Law. In 1 Cor 8:1 he proclaims that love builds up the community, and in 1 Thess 1:3; 3:6, 12 he points to the love of the Thessalonians. Finally, in 1 Cor 13:1-13, he gives a detailed description of *agapē* which he calls the highest and greatest gift (12:31; 13:13). In several instances, Paul speaks of *agapē* in relationship to God (2 Cor 13:11), Christ (2 Cor 5:14), and the Spirit (Rom 15:30). God's love has been poured into our hearts (Rom 5:5). God has proven his love for us (Rom 5:8). Nothing will separate us from the love of Christ or God (Rom 8:35, 39). This usage indicates that *agapē* is not merely a virtue by which one person loves another, or even God. It derives from God, Christ, and the Spirit, and enables the believer to love others and God in return. Thus it is a manifestation of the fruit of the Spirit.

joy: Paul often speaks of his own *chara* (Rom 15:32; 2 Cor 2:3; Phil 1:4; 2:2; 4:1; 1 Thess 2:19). But this joy has its root and origin in the Spirit (Rom 14:17; 1 Thess 1:6), in God (Rom 15:13), and in faith (Phil 1:25).

peace: Eirēnē, along with *charis* ("grace"), is part of the greeting found in Paul's letters (Rom 1:7; 1 Cor 1:3; 2 Cor 1:2; Gal 1:3; Phil 1:2; 1 Thess 1:1; Phlm 3). Like love and joy, this peace and grace come from God and Christ. God is the God of peace (Rom 15:33; 16:20; Phil 4:9) and has called us in peace (1 Cor 7:15). The kingdom of God is a matter of righteousness, peace and joy (Rom 14:17). As a result of being justified humanity is at peace with God (Rom 5:1). This peace is the new relationship between God and humanity because of what God has done in Christ.

patience: In Rom 2:4; 9:22; 1 Pet 3:20 *makrothymia* is applied to God: God's patience and forbearance. In 2 Cor 6:6 it is applied to Paul, and in Eph 4:2; Col 1:11; 3:12 it is viewed as a virtue for which to strive. While practiced by humans, *makrothymia* is rooted in the divine forbearance.

kindness: Chrēstotēs ("goodness," "kindness," "generosity") is predicated of Paul in 2 Cor 6:6 where *makrothymia* ("patience") is also listed. It is also applied to God (Ps 30:20; Rom 2:4; 11:22; Eph 2:7; Titus 3:4). In Col 3:12 it is listed as one of the virtues, along with *makrothymia* and *prautēs*, that should clothe a Christian.

goodness: In the NT, *agathōsynē* ("goodness," "uprightness," "generosity") is only found in writings attributed to Paul (Rom 15:14; Eph 5:9; 2 Thess 1:11), and is predicated of human beings.

faith: *Pistis* is best understood in the context of this letter, and of Paul's writings, as trust in God which is founded on God's faithfulness as manifested in the faith of Jesus Christ.

23. *gentleness*: *Prautēs* ("gentleness," "humility," "consideration," "meekness") is predicated of human beings (1 Cor 4:21; 2 Cor 10:1; Gal 6:1; Col 3:12; 2 Tim 2:25; Titus 3:2). Jesus is also described as meek (*praus*; Matt 11:29; 21:5), and according to Matt 5:5 the meek will inherit the earth. There is no description of God as meek.

self-control: *Egkrateia* (self-control, especially as regards sexuality) plays an important role in Hellenistic ethics and was highly esteemed by Philo and the Essenes, but this is its only occurrence in Paul's writings. See Acts 24:25; 2 Pet 1:6 for other uses. Its minor role in the NT may derive from the fact that NT ethics focuses upon the aspect of gift rather than self-mastery. In 1 Clem 38:2, where *egkrateia* is mentioned, the author reminds the audience that it is bestowed by God. At the end of this list some manuscripts (D*, F, G) add *agneia* ("chastity").

Against such things there is no Law: This statement secures Paul's main point. The Law and the Spirit belong to different realms. The fruit of the Spirit derives from the Spirit, not from a Law which prescribes it as something to be accomplished.

24. *Those who belong to Christ [Jesus] have crucified the flesh*: Some manuscripts (P46, D, F, G) omit "Jesus" but it is found in manuscripts of good quality (S, A, B, C, P). The phrase "those who belong to Christ" (*hoi tou Christou Iēsou*) means more than possession. It indicates participation in the life of Christ. In this sense *sarx* ("flesh") is used figuratively for unredeemed humanity. Thus, in Rom 6:6 Paul says, "We know that our old self (*ho palaios hēmōn anthrōpos*) was crucified with him . . . ." And in Gal 2:19 Paul says that he was crucified with Christ.

with its passions and desires: *Pathēma* usually refers to suffering and misfortune, e.g., the sufferings of Christ (2 Cor 1:5). But here it denotes the passions which in Rom 7:5 are called sinful. *Epithymia* ("desire") can have a good sense as in Phil 1:23, but here it refers to the desires manifested by the works of the flesh. See Rom 1:24; 6:12; 13:14; Gal 5:16; and 1 Thess 4:5.

25. *If we live by the Spirit*: The dative (*pneumati*) indicates that the believer lives by means of the Spirit, by the power of the Spirit. The phrase recalls vv. 16, 18.

let us also follow the Spirit: Some manuscripts (P46, F, G) omit *kai* ("also"), others (2495) place it after *pneumati* in order to obtain a smoother reading, "and let us follow the Spirit." *Stoichein* means "to be in line with" or "to stand beside someone." Here it has the sense of "follow," as in Rom 4:12 (". . . but also follow the example of faith that our ancestor Abraham had before he was circumcised"). This meaning fits the context since Paul has been speaking of walking with the Spirit (v. 16) and being led by the Spirit (v. 18).

26. *Let us not be conceited, provoking one another, being envious of one another*: This is the only occurrence of *kenodoxos* ("conceited," "boastful") in the NT. The

two participles which follow explain the kind of conceit Paul has in mind: provoking and challenging other members of the community (*prokaloumenoi*); being envious of other members of the community (*phthonontes*). Envy is one of the works listed above (v. 21), and it is found in other lists as well (Rom 1:29; 1 Tim 6:4; Titus 3:3; 1 Pet 2:1).

INTERPRETATION

Paul's moral exhortation began in the previous unit (5:13-15). Reminding the Galatians that they have been called to freedom, he warned them that if they do not serve one another in love, their freedom will become an opportunity for the flesh (understood as a power or force) to abuse their freedom. Free from the Law, the Galatians will fulfill the Law if they love one another. Here (5:16-26), Paul's parenesis becomes more explicit. Having warned the Galatians not to abuse their freedom, and having exhorted them to serve one another in love, he describes the works of the flesh that abuse freedom, and the fruit of the Spirit which fulfills the Law. Paul explains how the Galatians, who are not under the Law, can lead a good and moral life. His answer is disarmingly simple, and perhaps naive. If the Galatians "walk" by the Spirit, are "led" by the Spirit, and "follow" the Spirit, the Spirit will produce its fruit within them. Conversely, if they succumb to the urging of the flesh, they will do the works of the flesh. In order to illustrate what he means by "the works of the flesh" and "the fruit of the Spirit," Paul provides the Galatians with two lists. The first contains fifteen examples of the works of the flesh, while the second enumerates nine manifestations of the fruit of the Spirit. For Paul, Christian morality is a matter of living in the correct realm. Those who dwell in the realm of the flesh will inevitably do the works of the flesh, while those who live in the realm of the Spirit—and obey the urging of the Spirit—will enjoy the fruit of the Spirit. This unit can be outlined in the following way.

> Flesh and Spirit are opposed to each other (vv. 16-18)
> > v. 16   how to overcome the craving of the flesh
> > v. 17   why the Galatians cannot do whatever they want
> > v. 18   the consequences of being led by the Spirit
> Works of the flesh and fruit of the Spirit (vv. 19-23)
> > vv. 19-21a   the works of the flesh
> > v. 21b   who will not inherit the kingdom of God
> > vv. 22-23   the fruit of the Spirit
> Three conclusions (vv. 24-26)
> > v. 24   those in Christ have crucified the flesh
> > v. 25   let us follow the Spirit
> > v. 26   let us avoid provoking one another

The flesh and the Spirit are opposed to each other (vv. 16–18). In these verses Paul establishes the major contrast of this unit: the Spirit and the flesh. This contrast, however, is not to be understood in terms of body and soul. The Spirit (*pneuma*) is the Spirit of God while the flesh (*sarx*) refers to unredeemed humanity: humanity turned in and upon itself. Those who have been incorporated into Christ have received the Spirit; they are spiritual (*pneumatikoi*) because they dwell in the realm of the Spirit. Conversely, those who have not been incorporated into Christ have not received the Spirit; they are carnal (*sarkinoi*) because they dwell in the realm of the flesh, i.e., unredeemed humanity. Consequently, the whole person (body and soul) is either spiritual or carnal depending upon the realm in which he or she dwells. Thoughts as well as actions can be carnal if they do not proceed from the Spirit. Conversely, the most material activity can be spiritual if it proceeds from the Spirit.

Paul's initial advice is that the Galatians should "walk" by the Spirit, that is, conduct themselves in a manner that accords with the Spirit. The expression "to walk" in the Spirit is related to the OT idea of walking (Hebrew: *halak*) in the commandments of the Lord. It implies conducting one's life in a particular manner. Thus in Deut 5:33 Moses says, "You shall *walk* in all the way which the Lord your God has commanded you, that you may live, and that it may go well with you." And the Psalmist writes, "Blessed is the man who *walks* not in the counsel of the wicked, nor stands in the way of sinners, nor sits in the seat of scoffers, but delights in the Law of the Lord" (Ps 1:1-2). For other examples see Lev 26:3; Deut 11:22; 26:17; 28:9; Pss 81:13; 86:11. To walk in the Spirit, then, means to conduct one's life in a particular way, a way which excludes opposing conduct. Thus Paul can assure the Galatians that if they walk in the Spirit, they will not fulfill the craving of the flesh.

In Paul's theology Spirit and flesh are two realms which stand in total and utter opposition to each other. Whereas the flesh seeks to please itself, the Spirit seeks to please God. These two realms cannot peacefully coexist, nor can there be any compromise between them. They are opposed to each other so that the Galatians cannot do whatever they want.

The final phrase of v. 17 ("so that you cannot do whatever you want") has been interpreted in several ways. (1) Some have understood it to mean that the Galatians cannot do what they want (fulfill the urging of the Spirit) because the flesh frustrates them. (2) Others have taken the phrase to mean that the Galatians cannot do what they want (fulfill the urging of the flesh) because the Spirit wars against the flesh. (3) Still others have argued that Paul is describing a situation in which both Spirit and flesh hold each other in check. As a result, the Galatians find themselves caught between two great powers which prevent them from acting one way or the other. The thrust of this passage, however, is that the Galatians will

not fulfill the craving of the flesh if they walk by the Spirit. It seems unlikely, therefore, that Paul is speaking of the flesh frustrating the Spirit
(no. 1) or of a stalemate between the two (no. 3). Moreover, while the
suggestion that Spirit frustrates the desires of the flesh (no. 2) fits the
context, it does not explain why Paul emphasizes the mutual opposition
between Spirit and flesh. A suggestion proposed by Barclay (*Obeying the
Truth*, 115), however, is helpful. He contends that Paul is assuring the
Galatians that they are not in the dangerous position of libertinism, doing
whatever they want, because "they are caught up into a warfare which
determines their moral choices." The result of this warfare between Spirit
and flesh is that the Galatians *must* align themselves with the Spirit or
with the flesh; they cannot do battle for both, i.e., they cannot do whatever they want.

In addition to walking by the Spirit, the Galatians must also allow
themselves to be led by the Spirit (v. 18). While "being led" by the Spirit
essentially repeats the idea of "walking by" the Spirit, the imagery of
being led suggests an element of submission and obedience which is freely
given. The believer must actively choose to follow the prompting of the
Spirit. But just as one cannot simultaneously belong to the realm of the
Spirit and to the realm of the flesh, so one cannot simultaneously be led
by the Spirit and be under the Law. Being under the Law and being led
by the Spirit refer to two different realms. In Galatians, "being under
the Law" refers to a period of minority and slavery, the time previous
to the coming of Christ-faith. While the Law itself does not belong to the
realm of the flesh (Rom 7:12), those who are "under the Law" are still
in the realm of the flesh since they are not yet in Christ. Those who are
led by the Spirit, however, have been incorporated into the realm of
Christ. They are not "under the Law" because they are in Christ, and
because they are in Christ they fulfill the Law through the love command.

The works of the flesh and the fruit of the Spirit (vv. 19–23). Having
described the opposition between flesh and Spirit, Paul now provides
the Galatians with two lists which catalogue the works of the flesh and
the fruit of the Spirit. These lists are often referred to as catalogues of
vices and virtues. And it is generally assumed that here Paul draws upon
the popular traditions of moral philosophers, e.g., the Stoic philosophers,
who made use of virtue and vice lists to provide their audiences with
concrete examples of virtues to be imitated and vices to be avoided. Thus
many commentators would agree with the words of B. S. Easton written
more than sixty years ago: "It is now generally recognized that the catalogues of virtues and vices in the New Testament are derived ultimately
from the ethical teaching of the Stoa" ("New Testament Ethical Lists," 1).

There are, however, significant differences between the popular moral
philosophers who employed these lists and Paul. First, the moral phi-

losophers presupposed that knowledge is the source of virtue, and they viewed themselves as doctors of the soul whose work it was to dispel ignorance and error. Therefore, vices were frequently listed first in order "to depict the diseased soul in moral slavery from which philosophy would rescue it" (Malherbe, *Moral Exhortation*, 138). In Paul's writings, however, the problem is the power of sin (*hamartia*) which can only be overcome by the Spirit. For Paul the solution to humanity's plight is not knowledge derived from moral philosophy but transference to the realm of the Spirit.

Second, moral philosophers employed virtue and vice lists to assist students in the development of character by showing them what to emulate and what to avoid. While Paul was also concerned with proper ethical behavior, his lists are usually set within an eschatological context. For example, in 1 Cor 6:10 and Gal 5:21, after listing "vices" to be avoided, he warns his audience that those who do such things will not inherit the kingdom of God. Likewise, the list of vices in Rom 1:29-31 is found in a section whose major theme is the revelation of God's eschatological wrath (Rom 1:18). Even Paul's successors placed their vice lists within the context of an eschatological warning: "Be sure of this, that no fornicator or impure person, or one who is greedy (that is, an idolater), has any inheritance in the kingdom of Christ and of God" (Eph 5:5).

To summarize, although the lists of virtues and vices found in Paul's writings share the form of the virtue and vice lists of the popular moral philosophers, Gal 5:19-23 should not simply be viewed as a Hellenistic catalogue of virtues and vices. Nor should Paul's ethics be understood as an expression of popular moral philosophy. For Paul the issue is sin and grace rather than virtue and vice.

A more helpful model for understanding Gal 5:19-23 is found in the Dead Sea Scrolls, the *Manual of Discipline* (*1QS* 3:13–4:26). *1QS* is an example of the genre of the Two Ways, a genre also found in early Christian literature of the second century (*Didache* 1-5, *The Letter of Barnabas* 18-20, and *The Shepherd of Hermes*, Mandate 6, 2). According to *1QS*, God provided two spirits by which humanity "walks" until the day of God's eschatological visitation: the spirit of truth which springs from a fountain of light, and a spirit of falsehood which springs from a source of darkness. While the spirit of truth leads to "a spirit of humility, patience, abundant charity, unending goodness, understanding, and intelligence" (*1QS* 4:3), the ways of the spirit of falsehood are "greed, and slackness in the search for righteousness, wickedness and lies, haughtiness and pride, falseness and deceit, cruelty and abundant evil" (*1QS* 4:9, 11, quoted from *The Dead Sea Scrolls in English*, ed. G. Vermes. Sheffield: JSOT Press, 1987).

A comparison reveals that there are important similarities between *1QS*

3:13-4:26 and Gal 5:19-23. First, both view good and evil in terms of two forces which are opposed to each other. *1QS* speaks of the spirits of truth and falsehood, Galatians of the Spirit and the flesh. Second, both view the moral life within an eschatological context. According to *1QS* the struggle between good and evil will continue until the day of God's eschatological visitation, according to Galatians the eschatological goal is the kingdom of God. Third, both documents view the moral life in terms of walking in a particular way. In *1QS* humanity walks according to one of two spirits, in Galatians one is called to walk by the Spirit, to be led by the Spirit, and to follow the Spirit's lead. Finally, according to S. Wibbing (*Die Tügend-und Lästerkataloge*, 104–106), six of the nine manifestations of the fruit of the Spirit in the Galatian catalogue are found in the list of *1QS* that describes the way of the righteous: *prautēs* ("gentleness"), *makrothymia* ("patience"), *agathōsynē* ("goodness"), *chrēstotēs* ("kindness"), *pistis* ("faith"), and *eirēnē* ("peace"). These similarities suggest that it is no longer sufficient to say with Easton that "the catalogs of virtues and vices in the New Testament are derived ultimately from the ethical teaching of the Stoa." To be sure, the list of Gal 5:19-23 shares in the genre of the Stoic virtue and vice catalogs, but this section of Galatians also shares in the genre of the Two Ways with its emphasis upon walking in the proper way until the day of God's eschatological visitation. Paul is not talking about "virtues" and "vices" but about two ways of life, each of which is determined by a power or force: the way of the flesh and the way of the Spirit. Pauline morality is not about character development but about participation in the life of the Spirit.

According to Paul the works of the flesh (*ta erga tēs sarkos*) are evident for all to see. He does not really need to list them, and the catalogue that he does draw up is not intended to be exhaustive. These works proceed from the power of the flesh and have one element in common: concern for one's self at the expense of one's neighbor. The works of the flesh are a manifestation of humanity turned in upon itself.

In vv. 19–21a Paul lists fifteen works of the flesh which can be separated into four categories: (1) *works of sensuality* (fornication, immorality, sensuality); (2) *works of idolatry* (idolatry, sorcery); (3) *works of community dissension* (enmity, strife, jealousy, outbursts of anger, selfish ambition, dissensions, factions); and (4) *works of self-indulgence* (drinking bouts, carousing). The list begins with *porneia* ("fornication"), a work especially characteristic of Gentiles who, by their very birth, are sinners because they are deprived of Torah. From *porneia* comes immorality and sensuality. Like *porneia*, idolatry is also characteristic of the Gentiles who do not know the true God because they are ignorant of Torah.

The works of community dissension, however, dominate this list (seven of the fifteen works). Moreover, while many of these works are found in other NT vice catalogs, three of them appear only here, and are not found in the vice lists of the popular moral philosophers: *dichostasia* ("dissension"), *hairesis* ("faction"), and *echthra* ("enmity"). (See *Die Tügend-und Lästerkataloge*, 97.) The introduction of these three works and the emphasis upon community dissension in this section, suggest that Paul is addressing a specific problem in the Galatian congregation. In other words, even if Paul is drawing upon traditional material at this point, he has chosen and introduced material which focuses upon the situation at Galatia. The Galatian congregation is afflicted by community dissension, a situation also suggested by Paul's remarks in 5:15 and 5:26. The works in the final section of this list, those of self-indulgence, reinforce what has preceded. Dissension breeds self-indulgence.

Before describing the fruit of the Spirit, Paul introduces a note of warning. Those who "do" the works of the flesh will not inherit the kingdom of God. This warning indicates that 5:19-21a is more than a list of vices which are contrary to good character. The works of the flesh will call down God's eschatological judgment: exclusion from the kingdom of God.

One might expect that Paul would entitle his second list, "the works of the Spirit." Instead the Apostle speaks of the singular fruit of the Spirit (*ho karpos tou pneumatos*) which manifests itself in different ways. The change of language is significant. The expression, "fruit of the Spirit" reveals that what follows derives from the Spirit rather than from human effort. The image, however, should not be interpreted to mean that the moral life of the believer is automatic or divinely determined. In 6:9 Paul exhorts the Galatians not to tire of doing good (*to de kalon poiountes mē egakakōmen*), and in 6:10 he writes, "let us do good to all" (*ergazōmetha to agathon pros pantas*). In other words, Paul is not averse to speaking of "doing good" and he is quite aware that the moral life of the Christian requires work and effort. The context within which doing good is accomplished, however, is the sphere of the Spirit. Consequently, the good deeds done by the Christian are the fruit of the Spirit.

Unlike the first list which purposely gives a sense of disorder and confusion, this list consists of three triads which give a sense of order and harmony:

> love, joy, peace
> patience, kindness, goodness
> faith, gentleness, self-control

Except for *egkrateia* ("self-control") the "virtues" listed here have their background in the literature of the Bible. *Agapē* ("love") heads the list and is the source of all that follows. Without it everything else is meaningless (1 Cor 13:1-3). *Agapē* stands in sharp contrast to *porneia*, the first of the works of the flesh. Paul has already spoken of *agapē* in 5:6 ("faith expressing itself through love") and 5:13 ("through love be enslaved to one another"). "Joy" and "peace," often associated with each other (Rom 14:17; 15:13), complete the first triad.

The remaining triads present "virtues" which stand in sharp contrast to the works of the flesh which produce community dissension. Patience, kindness, goodness, faith, and gentleness are the antidote to enmity, strife, jealousy, outbursts of anger, selfish ambition, dissensions, and factions, while self-control is the remedy for drinking bouts and carousing. In other words, the craving of the flesh and the craving of the Spirit are diametrically opposed (5:17). Whereas the former seeks only itself and leads to community dissension, the latter desires the good of others and results in unity and harmony.

Paul concludes this list by saying "against such things there is no Law." There is no Law against these things because they belong to the realm of the Spirit. As Paul writes in 5:18, "If you are led by the Spirit, you are not under the Law." Thus if the Galatians are led by the Spirit, they will find themselves in a realm free from the Law, but not opposed to the Law. They will find themselves in a realm that does not command them to "do this" or "avoid that" because God's own Spirit, the Spirit of Christ, will lead and guide them. The fruit of the Spirit is not a list of virtues in the sense that moral philosophy understands the term "virtue." The items of this list are manifestations of the singular fruit of the Spirit which is accessible to those who dwell in the realm of the Spirit.

Three conclusions (v. 24). Having clarified the difference between the works of the flesh and the fruit of the Spirit, Paul draws three conclusions. First, those who are in Christ have crucified the flesh with its passions and desires. This strange expression recalls what the Apostle said in 2:19 ("I am crucified with Christ"). Here, however, the verb is in the active voice which indicates a decision on the part of Christians. By their association with the crucified Christ, they have put the power of the flesh to death. The flesh, with its desires and passions, is no longer a viable option for them because believers have been transferred to the realm of the Spirit.

The second conclusion is in the form of an exhortation. If the Galatians live by the Spirit, then they should follow the Spirit's lead. Here the language recalls what Paul has already said in 5:16 ("walk by the Spirit") thereby forming an inclusio. It also recalls what Paul wrote in 3:1-6 when he asked the Galatians if they received the Spirit from the works of the Law or from the message of faith. The Galatians already enjoy the life of the Spirit because of what God has done in the Christ event. But if one remains passive, living by the Spirit is not enough; one must also follow the Spirit's lead; one must make an active decision to be led by the Spirit (5:18).

Paul's third and final conclusion addresses the situation of the Galatian community: "Let us not be conceited, provoking one another, being envious of one another." This verse as well as 5:15 and 5:19-21a (the works of the flesh), refers to the situation at Galatia. The Galatians have received the Spirit, they are living in the Spirit, and yet the power of the flesh is still at work among them. It is imperative, therefore, that the Galatians walk by and follow the Spirit's lead. Only then will they overcome the works of the flesh. Christian morality is not automatic or magical; the fruit of the Spirit calls for the active participation of the believer.

For Reference and Further Study

Barclay, J. M. G. *Obeying the Truth: A Study of Paul's Ethics in Galatians.* Edinburgh: T. & T. Clark, 1988.

Easton, B. S. "New Testament Ethical Lists." *JBL* 51 (1932) 1–12.

Lutjens, R. " 'You Do Not Do What You Want': What Does Galatians 5:17 Really Mean?" *Presbyterion* 16 (1990) 103–118.

Malherbe, A. *Moral Exhortation, A Greco-Roman Sourcebook.* Philadelphia: Westminster, 1986.

Martinez Peque, M. "Unidad de Forma Y Contenido en Gal 5, 16-26." *EstBib* 45 (1987) 105–125.

Suggs, M. J. "The Christian Two Ways Tradition: Its Antiquity, Form, and Function." *Studies in New Testament and Early Christian Literature: Essays in Honor of Allen P. Wikgren.* D. E. Aune, ed. NovTSup 33; Leiden: Brill, 1972, 60–74.

Vermes, G. *The Dead Sea Scrolls in English.* Sheffield: JSOT Press, 1987.

Wibbing, S. *Die Tügend-und Lästerkataloge im Neuen Testament und ihre Traditionsgeschichte unter besonderer Beruchsichtigug der Qumran-Texte.* BZNW 25; Berlin: Alfred Töpelmann, 1959.

Fulfill the Law of Christ (6:1-10)

1. Brethren, even if a person is detected in some transgression, you who are spiritual, restore such a one in a spirit of gentleness, watching yourself lest even you be tempted. 2. Bear one another's burdens and thus you will fulfill the Law of Christ. 3. If someone thinks that he is something, although he is not, he is deceiving himself. 4. Let each one test his own work, and then he will have a boast toward himself alone and not as regards another, 5. for each one will bear his own load. 6. But let the one who is instructed in the word share all good things with the one who instructs. 7. Do not be deceived. God is not to be treated with contempt, for whatever a person sows, this he will reap. 8. The one who

sows to his own flesh will reap corruption from the flesh, and the one who sows to the Spirit will reap eternal life from the Spirit. 9. Let us not grow weary of doing what is good, for in due time we will reap the harvest if we do not grow faint. 10. Therefore, while we have the time, let us do what is good toward all, especially to those who belong to the household of faith.

NOTES

1. *Brethren, even if a person is detected in some transgression*: Some manuscripts read *anthropos ek hymon* or *tis ek hymōn* ("a person from among you," or "someone from among you") in place of *anthrōpos* ("person"). Although these readings are undoubtedly later additions, they interpret the text correctly: Paul is not speaking of just anyone but of a community member. The verb *prolambanein* ("to detect") has the sense of overtaking or surprising someone, see Wis 17:17. The meaning here is that a believer is unexpectedly caught in the midst of unbecoming conduct. *Kai* ("even") emphasizes that this injunction must be obeyed even if the person has begun to carry out the deed. *Paraptōma* occurs with some frequency in Romans (4:25; 5:15, 16, 17, 18, 20; 11:11, 12), but this is its only occurrence in Galatians. It refers to a false step, a transgression, or sin. The idea of a false step fits this context because Paul has spoken of walking with, and being led by, the Spirit (5:16, 18).

you who are spiritual: The pronoun *hymeis* refers to all of the Galatians, not to a special group, and emphasizes their status as *pneumatikoi* (spiritual persons). This is the only occurrence of *pneumatikos* in Galatians, but the word is found three times in Romans and several times in 1 & 2 Corinthians. Thus the Law is spiritual (Rom 7:14); teaching and persons are spiritual (1 Cor 2:13, 15); there are spiritual gifts (1 Cor 12:1); and there is a spiritual body (1 Cor 15:44, 46, 47). In all of these cases, persons or things are viewed as spiritual because they belong to the realm of God or have been transformed by the power of the Spirit. In 1 Cor 2:15 the person who is *pneumatikos* stands in contrast to the *psychikos anthrōpos* (1 Cor 2:14). "The latter is a person who has nothing more than an ordinary human soul; the former possesses the divine *pneuma*, not beside his natural human soul, but in place of it; this enables him to penetrate the divine mysteries" (BAG).

restore such a one: The verb *katartizein* denotes the restoration of someone or something to its former condition; see 2 Cor 13:11 ("put things in order") and Matt 4:21 ("mending their nets"). Here the transgressor must be restored to the community and the life of the Spirit.

in a spirit of gentleness: Pneumati ("in a spirit") could refer to the divine Spirit or to the human spirit. The latter is suggested by the context here. Because they are spiritual people, the Galatians are to correct one another in a spirit characterized by *prautēs* ("gentleness"), which is one of the gifts of the Spirit listed above (5:23).

watching yourself lest even you be tempted: Paul switches from the second person plural to the second person singular thereby making his injunction more personal. Although he does not explain what he means by being tempted (*peirasthēs*), there are at least two possibilities: (1) the one correcting the transgressor may be tempted to do the same thing or, (2) the act of correction may become an occasion for conceit (*kenodoxos*, 5:26). The latter best fits the context. In Phil 2:4 Paul also uses the verb *skopein* ("to watch"), admonishing the Philippians to look after the interests of others as well as their own.

2. *Bear one another's burdens*: This is the only time that Paul uses *baros* ("burden") in this sense (cf. 2 Cor 4:17; 1 Thess 2:7). He does not explain what these burdens are, but the context suggests temptations to sin. In Rom 15:1 Paul encourages the strong "to bear (*bastazein*) with the failings (*ta asthenēmata*) of the weak," and in Gal 6:5 he says that each one "will have to bear (*bastasei*) his own load (*phortion*)."

   and thus you will fulfill the Law of Christ: Some rather good manuscripts (S, A, C, D) read *anaplērōsate* ("fulfill," aorist imperative) rather than *anaplērōseto* ("you will fulfill," future indicative). This may be an attempt to conform the text to the imperatives in v. 1 (*katartizete*) and v. 2 (*bastazete*). See Metzger, *A Textual Commentary of the New Testament*, 598. The verb *anaplērōsete* recalls what Paul said in 5:14 ("the entire Law is fulfilled in one word"). There, however, Paul used the simpler form of the verb (*peplērōtai*). The prefix *ana*, as in Matt 13:14, is probably intended to give the verb added force. The expression "the Law of Christ" (*ton nomon tou Christou*) does not occur elsewhere. A similar phrase is found in 1 Cor 9:21 where Paul says of himself, "though I am not free from God's law but am under Christ's law (*ennomos Christou*)." In Rom 3:27 he speaks of the "Law of faith" (*nomou pisteōs*) and in Rom 8:2 of "the Law of the Spirit of life in Christ Jesus." Later Christian literature continues this tradition. Jas 1:25 says, "But those who look into the perfect law (*nomon teleion*), the law of liberty, and persevere, being not hearers who forget but doers who act—they will be blessed in their doing." And in 2:8, James writes "You do well if you really fulfill the royal Law (*nomon teleite basilikon*), according to the scripture, 'You shall love your neighbor as yourself.'" The final phrase indicates that James relates this royal Law to the love commandment. *Barnabas* 2:6 says, "These things then he abolished in order that the new Law (*ho kainos nomos*) of our Lord Jesus Christ, which is without the yoke of necessity might have its oblation not made by man." Finally, in the *Shepherd of Hermes* (Sim 5, 6, 3) the author writes, "When, therefore, he had cleansed the sins of the people, he showed them the ways of life, and gave them the Law which he 'received from his Father.'" While these later writings do not interpret Paul's thought, they indicate how "the Law of Christ" was being understood. For a fuller discussion of this concept, see the commentary on this section.

3. *If someone thinks that he is something, although he is not, he is deceiving himself*: Paul does not explain why a person might think that he or she is something, but the context suggests a sense of pride after restoring a fellow believer, or a sense of immunity from a similar failure in one's own life. The expression

dokei tis einai ("that he is something") also occurs in 2:6 in regard to the pillar apostles. The participial phrase *mēden ōn* ("although he is not") is concessive. It could indicate the general condition of humanity: no one is in a position to regard him or herself as beyond transgression. Or, it could indicate the particular situation of individuals who think that they are more important than they are. This is the only occurrence of *phrenapataoun* ("to deceive") in the NT.

4. *Let each one test his own work*: In this letter Paul has employed *ergon* ("work") in conjunction with the Law (2:16; 3:2, 5) and the flesh (5:19). Here, *ergon* could be interpreted collectively to denote a person's deeds. See Heb 6:10; Rev 22:12. Each person must test the deeds he or she has done. Barclay (*Obeying the Truth*, 161), however, suggests that "his own work" refers "to the basic character of a person's existence." For other exhortations to examine oneself, see 1 Cor 11:28; 2 Cor 13:5. Also, see 1 Cor 3:10-15 (the work of everyone will be tested) and 1 Thess 5:21 (test everything).

and then he will have a boast toward himself alone and not as regards another: This is the only occurrence of the noun *kauchēma* ("boast") in Galatians. The verb occurs in Gal 6:13, 14 and frequently in Romans and 1 & 2 Corinthians where it usually carries a negative connotation (1 Cor 1:29). Here the sense is less theologically charged. One's ground for boasting is not in the failures of another but in the measure of one's own work.

5. *for each one will bear his own load*: Barclay (*Obeying the Truth*, 161) notes: "This verse neatly sums up what Paul has been saying about personal accountability." Paul employs *phortion* ("load") rather than *baros* (v. 2). Here "load" refers primarily to one's weaknesses and failures. The future tense ("will bear") suggests that Paul has the last judgment in view.

6. *But let the one who is instructed in the word share all good things with the one who instructs*: The participles *katēchoumenos* and *katēchounti* come from *katēchein* which means "to inform," "to teach," or "to instruct." In the NT this always refers to religious instruction (Luke 1:4; Acts 18:25; Rom 2:18; 1 Cor 14:19). In 2 Clem 17:1 it denotes instruction given to one who has been converted. Here the participles refer to teacher and student, respectively. The teacher imparts *ton logon* ("the word"); that is, the Christian message (see Phil 1:14; 1 Thess 1:6; Col 4:3) while the student must share (*koinōneitō*) all good things (*en pasin agathois*). The last phrase could be construed to mean that student and teacher should share in whatever is mutually good, but it is usually understood to mean financial support. For other instances where Paul says that those who have received the faith are indebted to others, or that the teacher or preacher is entitled to remuneration, see Rom 15:27 and 1 Cor 9:11, 14. In Rom 15:27 Paul uses the same verb he employs here, *koinōnein* ("to share"), and in Phil 4:15 he says that the Philippians entered into partnership (*ekoinōnēsen*) with him, giving and receiving.

7. *Do not be deceived. God is not to be treated with contempt*: For other examples of this phrase (*mē planasthe*) in Paul's writings, see 1 Cor 6:9; 15:33. The emphasis here is upon self-deception rather than upon the teaching of the agi-

tators. This is the only occurrence of *myktērizein* in the NT. The word means
"to turn up one's nose at," "to treat with contempt." It is employed in reference to God and means "to mock," "to treat with contempt," or perhaps
"to outwit" (BAG). The Galatians must not delude themselves into thinking
that they can outwit God; they will reap what they sow.

for whatever a person sows, this he will reap: Some manuscripts (P46) have the
plural *ha* and *tauta* ("what things . . . these things") in place of the singular
ho and *touto* ("whatever . . . this"). This phrase explains why God cannot
be treated with contempt: one cannot reap a harvest different from what one
has planted. Similar sayings are found in Job 4:8 and Prov 22:8. In 2 Cor 9:6
Paul writes, "the one who sows sparingly will also reap sparingly, and he
who sows bountifully will also reap bountifully." But in Paul's discussion
of the resurrection body, this rule of sowing no longer applies (1 Cor 15:42-44):
one sows the mortal body but the body which is raised is incorruptible.

8. *The one who sows to his own flesh will reap corruption from the flesh, and the one
who sows to the Spirit will reap eternal life from the Spirit*: This is a neatly balanced
verse which contrasts two kinds of sowing and two kinds of harvests. Somewhat similar balanced phrases can be found in Rom 8:6, 13. The first kind
of sowing is to one's own flesh (*eis tēn sarka heautou*). The addition of *heautou*
("one's own") indicates that in this instance *sarx* refers to the human body
as in 2 Cor 7:1. Understood in this way, sowing to one's own flesh probably
means relying upon the physical mark of circumcision (see 6:13). The second
kind of sowing is sowing to the Spirit (*eis to pneuma*). Here the Holy Spirit,
rather than the human spirit, is intended. Such sowing entails relying upon
the power of the Spirit rather than upon the power of circumcision and the
Law (see the discussion of 3:1-5). Corresponding to sowing to one's own flesh
is the harvest of corruption (*phthoran*). In 1 Cor 15:42, 50, in a discussion of
the mortal and the resurrection bodies, Paul contrasts *phthora* ("corruption")
and *aphtharsia* ("incorruption"). While the first is the state of the mortal body,
the latter is the condition of the resurrection body. The harvest of corruption, then, is eternal death, the opposite of resurrection life. Corresponding
to sowing to the Spirit is the harvest of eternal life (*zōēn aiōnion*, see Rom 2:7;
5:21; 6:22-23) which is attained through resurrection from the dead.

9. *Let us not grow weary of doing what is good*: The phrase *to de kalon poiountes*
("doing what is good") may seem out of place in a letter which has contrasted
the faith of Christ with doing the works of the Law unless one recalls that
doing good results from the power of the Spirit. Similar phrases can be found
in Rom 7:21; 13:3; 2 Cor 13:7. In 1 Thess 5:21 *kalon* ("good") is used as a
term for what is morally good, and in 2 Thess 3:13 there is a phrase very
similar to this *mē egkakēsēte kalopoiountes* ("do not be weary in doing what is
right").

for in due time we will reap the harvest if we do not grow faint: The phrase *kairǫ
idiǫ* ("due time") indicates that there is an appointed time for the harvest.
Somewhat similar phrases are found in 1 Tim 2:6; 6:15, but in both instances
kairos is in the plural. The verb *ekluomai* ("to grow weary") is also used in
Matt 15:31 and Mark 8:3: the crowd of people will *faint* on the way if Jesus

dismisses them without feeding them. See Heb 12:3, 5. The sense in Galatians is that since the time of harvest is still distant, there is a danger of becoming weary of doing good on a regular basis.

10. *Therefore, while we have the time, let us do what is good toward all*: In exhorting the Galatians to do good, Paul employs the verb *ergazomai*. He uses a similar phrase in Rom 2:10, "glory and honor and peace for everyone *who does good*." Here and in Romans, Paul is referring to moral conduct. The phrase *pros pantas* ("toward all") includes non-believers as well as believers as the next phrase indicates.

especially to those who belong to the household of faith: This is the only occurrence of *tous oikeious tēs pisteōs* ("the household of faith") in Paul's undisputed correspondence. Eph 2:19 describes the Church as the household of God; there is probably a similar meaning intended here. The phrase indicates that while Christians have an obligation to do good toward all, they have a special obligation to one another.

INTERPRETATION

Thus far in his moral exhortation, Paul has told the Galatians that the Law is fulfilled in the love commandment (5:14), and that they will not fulfill the desires of the flesh if they walk according to the Spirit (5:16). Except for the extended lists of "virtues" and "vices" in 5:18-23, however, Paul has not provided the Galatians with a great deal of practical advice. Thus the Galatians might well ask, "what does it mean to love my neighbor in the concrete circumstances of life?" Or, "what does it mean to walk by the Spirit and to follow the Spirit's lead?" In this unit (6:1-10), therefore, Paul provides the Galatians with a moral exhortation that is precise, concrete, and practical.

The internal structure of this material presents a problem. While it is apparent that this unit contains a number of maxims, it is not clear how or if these maxims are related to each other. Recognizing the problem, H. D. Betz suggests that 5:25–6:10 is a collection of *sententiae*, "in the Cynic-Stoic diatribe tradition" (292). According to Betz, the *sententiae* are arranged as a series, the sequence being "neither uncoordinated nor overly systematized" (292). While Betz has made an important contribution toward identifying the form of these maxims, J. Barclay (*Obeying the Truth*, 149–150) has provided a helpful suggestion concerning the internal structure of the unit. Taking 5:24-26 as the heading for the maxims of this unit, he distinguishes between those which emphasize the corporate responsibility of the Galatians (A) and those which highlight the individual's accountability before God (B). This distinction is clearer in the Greek text than in translation since contemporary English no longer differentiates between singular and plural in the use of the pronoun "you."

6:1a   (A) Corporate responsibility to correct a sinning Church member
6:1b   (B) Individual accountability to look to oneself
6:2   (A) Corporate responsibility to bear burdens
6:3-5   (B) Individual accountability to test one's work and bear one's own burden
6:6   (A) Corporate responsibility to support teachers
6:7-8   (B) Individual accountability: sowing and reaping
6:9-10 (A) Corporate responsibility to do good

Correcting the sinner (v. 1). The opening verse of this unit points to the corporate responsibility of the Church to restore a member who has gone astray, and concludes with a warning that each individual is accountable for his or her own behavior. Paul addresses the Galatians as *adelphoi* ("brethren"), an indication that despite the troubles at Galatia, the bond of unity between him and the congregation is still intact. Moreover, when he refers to the *pneumatikoi* ("you who are spiritual"), he has the entire Galatian community in mind, not a small or elite group within the congregation. The Galatians are Paul's *adelphoi* and they are *pneumatikoi* because, with Paul, they are "in Christ."

As *adelphoi* and *pneumatikoi*, however, the Galatians have important corporate responsibilities to restore a sinful member to the community. The responsibility of correcting a sinful member, however, must be done in a manner that manifests the fruit of the Spirit. Consequently, the *pneumatikoi* must restore the sinner in a spirit of *prautēs* ("gentleness," see the fruit of the Spirit in 5:23). Although the advice here does not refer to a specific situation (cf. 1 Cor 5:1-5), it undoubtedly has the Galatian community, riddled by dissension, in view (see, 5:15, 18-21, 26).

Having addressed the community, in the last half of this verse Paul unexpectedly turns to the individual. While the community has the responsibility of restoring sinful members, each individual must take care that the moment of correction does not become the moment of temptation. The temptation Paul has in mind could be a temptation to commit a similar sin, but in light of what the Apostle has just said in 5:26, it is more probable that he is warning his converts of the danger, inherent in fraternal correction, of being conceited (*kenodoxos*) and of provoking one another. The one who has not sinned can easily succumb to a sense of superiority, thereby provoking the one being corrected. In addition to restoring the sinner in a spirit of gentleness, therefore, individual members of the community must guard against being conceited, lest they provoke those whom they are trying to restore.

The Law of Christ (v. 2). Having apprised the Galatians of their corporate responsibility to restore the community member who has sinned, and having warned individual members of their personal accountability,

Paul returns to the theme of corporate responsibility. The members of the community must bear (*bastazete*, plural imperative) one another's burdens if they hope to fulfill the Law of Christ. While some authors, most notably J. G. Strelan, have argued that Paul has financial burdens in view, the context suggests that he is referring to the faults and failures of community members. In addition to restoring sinful members of the Church, the Galatians have a corporate responsibility to render moral support to one another. In this way they will follow the example of Christ. Far from viewing life in the Spirit as immunity from moral weakness or failure, therefore, Paul shows himself to be a realist. He fully understands that even the *pneumatikoi* are capable of sinning; incorporation into Christ does not eliminate moral weakness or failure. Nevertheless, those who are in Christ enjoy the advantage of living within a community where others are, or should be, supportive of them in their weaker moments. Thus, not only must the community restore those members who have fallen away, it must also sustain its faithful members so that they will not fall into sin. By doing so, the community will fulfill the Law of Christ.

The precise meaning of *ho nomos tou Christou* has been and remains a point of dispute among commentators. Among the more important interpretations are the following.

(1) *A Messianic Law*. In different ways, C. H. Dodd, W. D. Davies, and P. Stuhlmacher have argued that the Law of Christ refers to the teaching of Jesus or to a messianic Torah. Dodd and Davies, for example, contend that the essential content of the Law of Christ comes from a body of traditional ethical teaching that derives from Jesus. Thus, while he does not want to confine the Law of Christ to a restricted body of Jesus' sayings, Dodd writes, "it appears that even for Paul, with his strong sense of the immediate governance of Christ through his Spirit in the Church, that which the Lord 'commanded' and 'ordained' remains the solid, historical and creative nucleus of the whole" (*Ennomos Christou*, 148). And in a similar vein, Davies says, "Paul had access to the tradition of the words of Jesus. This he had 'received' and this he 'transmitted' . . . so that this tradition constituted for him part of the 'law of Christ' " (*The Setting of the Sermon*, 366). The approach of Stuhlmacher remains within this general category, but clearly goes beyond that of Dodd and Davies. For Stuhlmacher, the Law of Christ "is the Zion Torah inaugurated by Christ through his obedient death" ("The Law as a Topic," 126). By "Zion Torah" Stuhlmacher means the Law which is the eschatological fulfillment of the Mosaic Law, a Law for all nations, a Law promised in texts such as Mic 4:1-4; Isa 2:2-4; 25:7-9; Jer 31:31-34; and Ezek 20; 36:22-28; 40-48 (114). It is the Law of the messianic age. While the positions of Dodd, Davies, and Stuhlmacher are attractive, they have not found broad-based support for two reasons. First, it is difficult to isolate a coherent body

of Jesus' ethical teachings in Paul's writings. Second, there is scant evidence to support the notion of a new, Messianic Law, distinct from the Mosaic Law (see P. Schäfer, "Die Torah der messianischen Zeit," and Davies, *The Setting of the Sermon*, 183–190).

(2) *The Love Commandment.* Somewhat in reaction to the position described above, others have argued that the Law of Christ is nothing less than the love commandment. Thus V. Furnish writes that Paul "is directing attention to a concrete way in which God's gift and demand of love revealed in Christ may be expressed in the Christian life" (*Theology and Ethics*, 65). And C. K. Barrett affirms that the Law of Christ mentioned in 6:2 "is virtually indistinguishable from the law of love in 5:14" (*Freedom and Obligation*, 83). This approach is correct in drawing a relationship between 6:2 and 5:14, and it takes the context of Galatians seriously, but is too general to be satisfying.

(3) *A Paradigm of the Christian Life.* R. Hays and H. Schürmann interpret the Law of Christ in light of Christ's example of sacrificial self-giving. Thus Hays writes that "Christ's example of burden-bearing (2:20; 3:13; 4:4-5) establishes a normative pattern (*nomos*) which all who are in Christ are called to 'fulfill' in their relationship with others" ("Christology and Ethics," 287), and Schürmann sees the Law of Christ exemplified in the behavior of the pre-existent Son of God who showed his love not only in the incarnation and crucifixion but also in his earthly life ("Das Gesetz," 286). While this position has the advantage of taking into account the story of Jesus' sacrificial love, especially as it is related in Galatians, it makes too great a separation between the Law of Moses and the Law of Christ.

(4) *The Law redefined by Christ.* Drawing attention to the relationship between the Law of Christ mentioned in 6:2, and the fulfillment of the Law by the love commandment in 5:14, Barclay argues that when Paul speaks of the Law of Christ the word "Law" still refers to the Mosaic Law. Thus, fulfilling the Law of Christ is another reference to fulfilling the Mosaic Law (*Obeying the Truth*, 132). The Law *of Christ* means the Law in its relationship to Christ, the Law of Moses as "redefined and fulfilled by Christ in love" (134). To bring this into sharper focus it is helpful to compare two other texts in which Paul employs a number of phrases to describe the Law.

Rom 3:27
Then what becomes of boasting? It is excluded. By what law? By that of works (*dia poiou nomou; tōn ergōn*)? No, but by the law of faith (*alla dia nomou pisteōs*).

Rom 8:2
For the law of the Spirit of life in Christ Jesus (*ho gar nomos tou pneumatos tēs zōēs en Christō*) has set you free from the law of sin and death (*apo tou nomou tēs hamartias kai tou thanatou*).

In these texts, Paul employs a series of expressions (in the genitive case in the Greek text) to describe the Law. On the one hand, the Law is characterized by works, sin, and death; on the other hand, by faith and the Spirit of life. Paul, however, is not referring to two different laws but to the Mosaic Law and its relationship to Christ. Apart from Christ, the Mosaic Law (good and holy in itself) is characterized by works. As such it exposes sin which leads to death. In Christ, the same Law is characterized by faith and God's life-giving Spirit. The Law *of Christ*, therefore, refers to the Law in its relationship to Christ; it is the Law in the realm of Christ. Thus in 1 Cor 9:21 Paul can say that although he is not under the Law (*hypo nomou*) he is not *anomos* ("lawless"), but *ennomos Christou* ("subject to" or "in Christ's Law"). When Paul speaks of the Law of Christ, then, he is referring to the Mosaic Law understood in relationship to Christ. The Law of Christ is the Law *as interpreted and lived by Jesus*. It is the Mosaic Law interpreted through the love commandment and exemplified by Jesus' life of self-giving love on behalf of others (1:4; 2:20).

Testing oneself (vv. 3–5). Having called the members of the Galatian community to bear one another's burdens, Paul returns to the theme of personal accountability. Those who correct others and bear their burdens can easily overestimate their importance. Therefore, Paul warns the Galatians that anyone who thinks that he is important is deceiving himself. The phrase employed here (*ei gar dokei tis einai ti*) recalls Paul's earlier description of the pillar apostles in 2:6 as *tōn dokountōn einai ti* ("those considered to be influential"). Someone may consider himself to be important, or be considered important by others, but God shows no partiality. Consequently, Paul warns the Galatians that restoring other members of the community and bearing their burdens should not lead one to overestimate his or her importance.

The antidote to self-deception is to test oneself. Therefore, Paul exhorts each of the Galatians to test (*dokimazetō*) his or her own work. Similar exhortations to self-examination are found in the Corinthian correspondence: "Examine (*dokimazetō*) yourselves, and only then eat of the bread and drink of the cup" (1 Cor 11:28); "Examine yourselves to see whether you are living in the faith. Test (*dokimazete*) yourselves" (2 Cor 13:5). When Paul says that each of the Galatians should examine his or her own work (*ergon heautou*), he is referring to the work or project of the Christian life. Those who restore others to the Christian community and bear their burdens must constantly examine their own lives, lest they themselves fail. Thus, bearing the burdens of others will not become an occasion to boast to another. Rather, those who test themselves will know the frailty of human nature and the limited value of boasting, even to oneself.

This subunit, and indeed the first six verses, concludes with a reminder that each of the Galatians will have his or her own burden to bear (*phortion bastasei*). The language employed here recalls the injunction of v. 2 ("Bear one another's burdens") and seems to contradict it. But if the verse is understood in terms of the final judgment, the contradiction is more apparent than real. Thus Calvin (*Galatians*, 111) writes, "To destroy our sloth and pride he brings before us the judgment of God, in which each man for himself and without comparison will render an account of his life." Some modern commentators deny this eschatological interpretation. For example, Betz (*Galatians*, 304) writes, "The future tense is gnomic ('one must bear'), not eschatological." But the broader context of Paul's moral exhortation to the Galatians (see 5:21; 6:8-10) favors an eschatological interpretation. Understood in an eschatological sense, this final verse provides the Galatians with yet another reason for bearing one another's burdens. They should support the weaknesses and frailties of others because everyone has weaknesses and failures that will be brought to the judgment seat of God.

Support for teachers of the Word (v. 6). Once again Paul returns to the corporate responsibility of the Galatian community: those who have been instructed in the gospel must share all good things with their teachers. While some commentators argue that Paul has spiritual goods and a spiritual communion in mind, the majority explain the phrase *en pasin agathois* ("in all good things") as financial support. Those instructed in the gospel must support their teachers. If this verse reflects something of the actual situation of the Galatian community, it suggests that some members of the community devoted much of their time to the instruction of others and were dependent upon offerings from others for their livelihood.

Sowing and reaping (vv. 7-8). Again, Paul calls each member of the community to personal accountability: each one will reap what he or she has sown. Those who sow to the flesh will reap corruption, while those who sow to the Spirit will reap eternal life. Although most modern commentators read these verses independently of v. 6, some older commentators read them in light of v. 6. For example, in his paraphrase of Galatians, Erasmus applied these verses to the teachers mentioned in v. 6. "Wherefore I warn you to teach honestly, for God is not mocked. But whatever seed one sows, such also is the harvest he will reap. One who hands down a carnal teaching will reap, for his carnal seed, a fruit which will perish. But one who imparts a spiritual teaching will gain from the spiritual and heavenly teaching a like reward, namely, eternal life" (*Collected Works of Erasmus*, 128). Calvin, however, applied these verses to those who were taught by the teachers. Those who sow sparingly in the support of their teachers will reap a harvest which corresponds to their sowing. This older line of interpretation has the advantage of relating these verses to v. 6.

Moreover, Calvin's exegesis finds some support from 2 Cor 9:6 which employs the metaphor of sowing and reaping to encourage the Corinthians to give liberally to the Jerusalem collection. The eschatological coloring of Gal 6:7-8 ("corruption," "eternal life"), however, suggests that these verses have more than v. 6 in view. If the Galatians sow to their own flesh, that is, rely upon the mark of circumcision, they will reap corruption. But if they sow to the Spirit by relying upon Christ, they will reap eternal life.

A responsibility to do good (vv. 9-10). In these final verses Paul returns to the theme of corporate responsibility and an eschatological horizon controls his ethical reflection. The Galatians must not tire of doing good (*kalon poiountes*) since they will reap a harvest in the proper time. And while they have time, they must do good (*ergazōmetha to agathon*) to all, but especially to the household of faith. This is the first time that Paul has spoken about "doing" good, and undoubtedly his language sounds strange in a letter which emphasizes justification by faith. But as the parenesis of this letter demonstrates, Paul is not an antinomian, and his Torah-free gospel makes the strictest demands upon its adherents. The Pauline notion of doing good must be understood in light of the fruit of the Spirit which includes *agathōsynē* ("goodness"). Christians do good because they live in the realm of the Spirit. As they live in the realm of the Spirit, the Spirit is at work within them, allowing and encouraging them to do good.

The time for doing good, however, is limited by the eschatological horizon of the coming harvest. Therefore, while there is still time, Christians must act. Paul's reference to the household of faith reminds the Galatians that although they must do good toward all, the members of the Church have a special claim upon their charity. Thus this unit concludes where it began, with an exhortation to assist members of the Church who have gone astray and to bear one another's burdens.

FOR REFERENCE AND FURTHER STUDY

Barclay, J. M. G. *Obeying the Truth: A Study of Paul's Ethics in Galatians.* Edinburgh: T. & T. Clark, 1988, 126-142.

Davies, W. D. *Paul and Rabbinic Judaism: Some Rabbinic Elements in Pauline Theology.* 4th ed. Philadelphia: Fortress, 1980, 142-146.

Davies, W. D. *The Setting of the Sermon on the Mount.* Cambridge University Press, 1964, 109-190, 341-366.

Dodd, C. H. *"Ennomos Christou."* More New Testament Studies. Grand Rapids: Eerdmans, 1968, 134-148.

Furnish, V. P. *Theology and Ethics in Paul.* Nashville: Abingdon, 1968, 59-65.

Hays, R. "Christology and Ethics in Galatians." *CBQ* 49 (1987) 268-290.

Räisänen, H. *Paul and the Law.* Philadelphia: Fortress, 1983, 77-82.

Schäfer P. "Die Torah der messianischen Zeit." *ZNW* 65 (1974) 27–42.

Schürmann, H. " 'Das Gesetz des Christus' (Gal 6, 2). Jesu Verhalten und Wort als letzgültige sittliche Norm nach Paulus." *Neues Testament und Kirche: Für Rudolf Schnackenburg.* J. Gnika, ed. Freiburg: Herder, 1974, 282–300.

Strelan, J. G. "Burden-Bearing and the Law of Christ: A Re-Examination of Galatians 6:2." *JBL* 94 (1975) 266–276.

Stuhlmacher, P. "The Law as a Topic of Biblical Theology." *Reconciliation, Law, Righteousness: Essays in Biblical Theology.* Philadelphia: Fortress, 1986.

THE CONCLUSION (6:11-18)

The Conclusion (6:11-18)

11. See with what large letters I am writing to you, by my own hand. 12. Those who want to make a good showing in the flesh, these are trying to compel you to be circumcised, only that they might not be persecuted for the Cross of Christ. 13. Not even those who are circumcised keep the Law, but they want you to be circumcised so that they can boast in your flesh. 14. But far be it from me to boast except in the Cross of our Lord Jesus Christ, through which the world has been crucified to me, and I to the world. 15. Neither circumcision nor uncircumcision is anything, but a new creation. 16. Peace and mercy upon those who conduct themselves by this rule, and upon the Israel of God. 17. Henceforth let no one trouble me, for I bear the marks of Jesus on my body. 18. The grace of our Lord Jesus Christ be with your spirit, brethren. Amen.

NOTES

11. *See with what large letters I am writing to you, by my own hand*: Some manuscripts (P46, B*, 33) read *ēlikois* in place of *pēlikois* ("what large"); the meaning, however, is essentially the same. Still others (642) read *poikilois* ("diversified," "manifold"). The verb *egrapsa* ("I am writing") employs the epistolary aorist: Paul's action of writing the letter is present, but when the letter reaches the Galatians, they will view his action as past. This verse indicates that Paul employed a secretary for the composition of this letter. From what Paul says here, it appears that he wrote the remainder of the letter in large letters, perhaps to emphasize and recapitulate the main points he has made. For other indications that Paul employed a secretary in his letter writing see Rom 16:22;

1 Cor 16:21; and Phlm 19. Also, see Col 4:18 and 2 Thess 3:17 which, however, are of doubtful Pauline origin.

12. *Those who want to make a good showing in the flesh, these are trying to compel you to be circumcised*: The subject of the action is the agitators. Although Paul has already warned the Galatians not to be circumcised (5:2-6), this is his first explicit statement that the agitators are trying to compel the Galatians to be circumcised. The agitators will appear in a good light to other Jewish Christians, and to their Jewish compatriots who are not Christians, if they can convince Paul's Gentile converts to be circumcised. This is the only occurrence of *euprosōpein* ("to make a good showing," "to make a fair appearance") in the NT. Here, *sarx* ("flesh") is to be taken literally: the flesh marked by circumcision. The verb *anagkazein* ("to compel") is used in a conative sense and is the same verb employed in 2:3, 14. Just as the false brethren tried to compel Titus to be circumcised, and just as Peter tried to compel the Gentiles to judaize, so the agitators are trying to compel the Galatians to accept circumcision.

only that they might not be persecuted for the Cross of Christ: Some manuscripts (P46, B, K) read "Christ Jesus." This purpose clause explains the motivation of the agitators: they want to avoid persecution. The verb *diōkōntai* ("persecuted") recalls Paul's question in 5:11: if he is still preaching circumcision, why is he being persecuted? It is difficult, however, to explain why the agitators would be persecuted if Paul's Galatian converts remain uncircumcised. Perhaps Paul is applying his personal experience to the agitators: if they preach a Torah-free gospel they, like him, will experience persecution from fellow Jewish Christians. In Phil 3:18 Paul refers to those who are disturbing the Philippians as "enemies of the Cross of Christ." Here, and perhaps in Philippians, the Cross (*stauros*) stands for what God has done in Christ: the Cross is the content of Paul's Law-free Gospel.

13. *Not even those who are circumcised keep the Law*: Some manuscripts (P46, B, F, G, L) read *peritemēmenoi* (perfect tense, "have been circumcised") in place of the present participle. The perfect tense suggests that the circumcised are Jews in general. The present participle, which is the better reading, can be taken as a middle or passive. Taken as a middle, it could refer to those Galatians who are accepting circumcision: "those who receive circumcision" (see Munck, "The Judaizing Gentile Christians"). Taken as a passive, it could mean the circumcised in general, or the agitators. The phrase which follows ("that they can glory in your flesh"), however, suggests that Paul is referring to the agitators. Although they preach circumcision, not even they observe all of the commandments of the Law (cf. 5:3).

but they want you to be circumcised so that they can boast in your flesh: The purpose clause explains the motivation of the agitators: they wish to glory or boast (*kauchēsōntai*) in the flesh of the Galatians (*en tē hymeterą sarki*). Here, "flesh" refers to the external mark of circumcision. Thus in 2 Cor 11:18, Paul speaks of "super apostles" who boast *kata sarka*; that is, of their accomplishments and their Jewish heritage. And in Phil 3:4, after he ironically claims confidence *en sarki* ("in the flesh"), Paul speaks of his Jewish heritage, beginning with his circumcision on the eighth day.

14. *But far be it from me to boast except in the Cross of our Lord Jesus Christ*: In contrast to the agitators who boast in the mark of circumcision, Paul boasts in the Cross. Boasting (*kauchaomai*) is an important theme in Paul's writings. Humanity is tempted to boast or glory in its own accomplishments. Paul excludes such boasting (1 Cor 1:29; 3:21). Those who boast must boast in the Lord (1 Cor 1:21; 2 Cor 10:17; Phil 3:3), or in their weakness (2 Cor 11:30; 12:5,9) which serves to manifest God's power. Authentic boasting glories in the crucified Christ (1 Cor 2:2).

    through which the world has been crucified to me, and I to the world: Kosmos ("world") denotes the present age which is hostile to God, enslaved to sin, and at odds with what belongs to the realm of God. Jew and Gentile were enslaved to the *stoicheia tou kosmou* (4:1-11), but Christ died to deliver humanity from the present evil age (1:4). *Di'hou* ("through which") could also be translated "through whom," but the antecedent appears to be the Cross of Christ rather than Christ. By being crucified with Christ (2:19-20), Paul has died to the present age, and the present age no longer has a claim upon him. See Rom 6:1-11, especially v. 11, "So you also must consider yourselves dead to sin and alive to God in Christ Jesus."

15. *Neither circumcision nor uncircumcision is anything, but a new creation*: Some manuscripts (S, A, C, D, F, G) begin this verse *en gar Christọ Iesou oute* ("for in Christ Jesus neither. . . ."), but this reading probably derives from 5:6 which begins in the same way. In 5:6 Paul says that "faith working through love," not circumcision nor the lack of it, is important. In 1 Cor 7:19 he writes that what matters is "obeying the commandments of God," not circumcision nor the lack of it. Here, Paul refers to "a new creation" (*kainē ktisis*), an expression he employs in 2 Cor 5:17 ("So if anyone is in Christ, there is a new creation: everything old has passed away; see, everything has become new"). In 2 Cor 5:18-19, Paul explains that the new creation is the result of God's work of reconciliation in Christ. Here, in Galatians, the new creation refers to what God has done in Christ by tearing down the barriers of race, class, and sexuality (3:28) that formerly separated people. This new creation results from being in Christ.

16. *Peace and mercy upon those who conduct themselves by this rule, and upon the Israel of God*: The verb *stoichēsousin* ("conduct themselves") is future indicative, but some manuscripts (P46) read the subjunctive, others (A, C*, D, F, G) the present indicative. It is the same verb employed in 5:25 ("let us follow the Spirit"). Understood literally, *kanōn* refers to a straight rod or bar such as is used by a carpenter for measurement. Here the word is employed metaphorically and means a "rule" or "standard" by which believers can measure their lives. This rule or standard is the new creation which God has brought about in Christ. As a result of this new creation there is neither Jew nor Gentile, slave nor free, male nor female. This verse seems to draw upon Psalms 124:5 (LXX) and 127:6 (LXX) which conclude, *eirēnē epi ton Israel* ("peace upon Israel").

Paul, however, alters the phrase in two ways. First he includes *eleos* ("mercy") within the blessing. Second, he writes "the Israel of God" rather than "Israel." In the Greek text the phrase "the Israel of God" is introduced by the conjunction *kai* ("and the Israel of God"). If the *kai* is epexegetic, "the Israel of God" is simply a further explanation of "those who conduct themselves by this rule," and the *kai* need not be translated, see REB. But if the *kai* is taken as a copulative, the *kai* must be translated and "the Israel" of God is distinct, in some way, from "those who conduct themselves by this rule." The several interpretations of this phrase, and a solution for understanding it, are proposed in the commentary on this section.

17. *Henceforth let no one trouble me*: *Tou loipou* can be used adverbially in relationship to the matter under discussion ("as far as the rest is concerned"), or in relationship to time ("henceforth"). The latter fits the context better. Those who have troubled Paul are the agitators and those who have aligned themselves with them.

for I bear the marks of Jesus on my body: The agitators have no claim upon Paul because he bears, on his body (*en tǫ sōmati*), the *stigmata tou Iesou*. At this point there are different manuscript readings: "the marks of Christ," "the marks of the Lord Jesus," "the marks of our Lord." *Stigma* denotes a mark, such as a tatoo or a brand. In the ancient world masters placed a *stigma* on their slaves. Moreover, persons devoted to the service of a particular temple often carried a distinguishing brand mark. Here the context suggests that Paul is using the term metaphorically: the *stigmata* are the wounds and scars which he has received in the service of the crucified Christ. See 2 Cor 4:10 where Paul speaks of carrying in his body "the death of Jesus," and 2 Cor 6:4-6; 11:23-29 where he lists his apostolic sufferings. Those who preach circumcision avoid persecution and the *stigma* which accompany it. This metaphor fits Paul's conception of himself as the *doulos* ("slave") of Christ (Rom 1:1; Gal 1:10; Phil 1:1). These scars mark him as a slave of Christ.

18. *The grace of our Lord Jesus Christ be with your spirit, brethren. Amen*: Some manuscripts (S, P) omit "our." Similar blessings can be found in Phil 4:23; 2 Tim 4:22; Phlm 25. Several manuscripts contain subscriptions at the end of the letter: "to the Galatians" (S, A, B*, C, D, F, G); "I have written from Rome" (B¹). Here, "spirit" refers to the inner spirit of the Galatians rather than to the Holy Spirit. Paul extends a blessing of salvation ("grace") to the Galatians which is meant to touch their innermost being. He concludes by calling the Galatians *adelphoi* ("brothers"), indicating that the bond of unity remains between him and them. Like the opening of this letter (1:5), the farewell of this letter concludes with "amen."

INTERPRETATION

Hellenistic letters usually closed with (1) a wish on the part of the sender for the good health of the recipient, and (2) a word of farewell (*errōse*). Thus a typical, Hellenistic letter ends in this fashion, "I pray for your health continually together with that of your children. Farewell" (quoted from Stowers, *Letter Writing*, 61). W. Doty (*Letters*, 39) notes, however, that "Pauline and other primitive Christian letters are less bound to the closing conventions of the Hellenistic letters than to any other formulaic portion." Instead of the usual wish for good health and a word of farewell, the following elements can be found in the conclusions of the seven letters which most agree come from Paul's hand.

(1) The commendation of particular individuals to the Church: Rom 16:1-2; 1 Cor 16:15-18.

(2) A letter signature which indicates that the letter comes from Paul: 1 Cor 16:21-22; 2 Cor 13:13; Gal 6:11.

(3) Greetings to particular individuals within the Church and, or, greetings from those with Paul to the Church: Rom 16:3-15, 21-23; 1 Cor 16:19-20a; 2 Cor 13:12b; Phil 4:21-22; Phlm 23-24. Moreover, in conjunction with the greeting, there is often an exhortation to extend a "holy kiss" to one another: Rom 16:16; 1 Cor 16:20b; 2 Cor 13:12a.

(4) An exhortation, warning, or summary of Paul's argument: Rom 16:17-20a; 1 Cor 16:13-14; 2 Cor 13:11; Gal 6:12-17.

(5) A doxology: Rom 16:24-27.

(6) A request that the letter be read to all: 1 Thess 5:27.

(7) A closing benediction or grace: Rom 16:20b; 1 Cor 16:23-24; Phil 4:23; 1 Thess 5:28; Phlm 25; Gal 6:18.

No one letter has all of these elements. Galatians, for example, contains only three of the elements noted above: a signature device; a final exhortation or warning which serves as a summary of Paul's argument; and a closing grace. Unlike many of Paul's other letter closings, however, Galatians lacks any commendation of particular individuals, greetings to particular members of the Church, greetings from those with Paul, or an instruction to greet one another with a holy kiss. The absence of these elements points to the strained relationship between Paul and the Galatians, as does the replacement of the traditional letter thanksgiving with a statement of rebuke (1:6-10).

The letter closing of Galatians is polite but formal. Instead of greeting other members of the Church, or extending greetings from the Pauline circle to the Galatians, Paul takes the opportunity of the letter closing to summarize important elements of his argument. Thus in his commentary on Galatians, John Chrysostom in his comment on 6:10 notes, "Paul, after a short moral discourse, returns again to that former subject which chiefly disturbed his mind." And H. D. Betz (*Galatians*, 313) comments that this section "contains the interpretive clues to the understanding of Paul's major concerns in the letter as a whole and should be employed as the hermeneutical key to the intentions of the Apostle.'' While Betz's remark, that the letter closing is the ''hermeneutical key'' to the Apostle's intention, may be an overstatement, he has correctly highlighted the importance of these final verses. More than any other Pauline letter closing, the conclusion of Galatians summarizes important points of Paul's argument. The unit can be outlined in the following way.

v. 11	letter signature
vv. 12-17	a summary of Paul's argument
	vv. 12-13 a final warning about the agitators
	vv. 14-17 a final statement of Paul's position
v. 18	closing grace

A letter from Paul's own hands (v. 11). In the ancient world, authors often employed secretaries or scribes to assist them in the process of letter writing. Cicero, for example, employed the scribe Tiro, and in the composition of Romans, Paul utilized a scribe by the name of Tertius (Rom 16:22). From this verse, it is clear that Paul also made use of a scribe or secretary in the writing of Galatians. The exact role of this scribe, however, is not so clear since scribes or secretaries were used in at least three different ways. (1) In some instances, the author dictated the letter to the scribe, syllable by syllable, word for word. (2) In other cases, the author instructed the scribe about the sense of the letter, but left the exact formulation of the letter to the scribe. (3) In still other situations, authors commissioned scribes to write letters in their name without defining, in a specific manner, the letter content.

It is probably impossible to determine what method Paul employed in the composition of his own letters. Moreover, if the Apostle made use of different scribes, it is probable that he utilized them differently, depending upon their abilities and the nature of the letter to be written. In the case of Galatians, however, given the severity of the crisis, it seems unlikely that Paul would have commissioned anyone to write in his name without first defining the content of the letter to be written. Moreover, given the highly theological nature of the argument, and the emotional tone of this letter, it seems most probable that Paul took an active role in the composition of Galatians, perhaps dictating it word-for-word.

While a great number of Greek and Latin Fathers thought that Paul personally wrote the whole letter, most commentators, following Theodore of Mopsuestia and Jerome, contend that he only wrote the conclusion of this letter with his own hand. Moreover, there is general agreement among commentators that the reference to Paul's large letters does not refer to their misshapen appearance, as Chrysostom thought, but simply to their size. By employing such large letters, Paul adds emphasis to the content of this unit. It is as if the Apostle said, "these letters are so large that even you will not miss the point."

The nature and motivation of the agitators (vv. 12–13). At different moments in this letter, Paul has written about the agitators and their motivation; the most specific references are 1:7; 4:17; 5:10, 12. But now, in this final unit, Paul produces the most extended passage in the whole of Galatians about those who have been troubling the Church. In doing so, the Apostle exposes the true nature of his opponents and calls into question their motivation. His accusations against the agitators can be summarized in four points which are somewhat chiastically arranged:

v. 12a   they want to make a good showing *in the flesh;*
v. 12b   *they urge circumcision* in order to avoid persecution;
v. 13a   they themselves do not keep the law;
v. 13b   *they urge circumcision* in order that they can boast *in the flesh* of
         the Galatians.

The two questions which arise most often in connection with these verses are: (1) What is the nature of the persecution that the agitators seek to avert? (2) What does Paul mean when he says that the agitators themselves do not keep the Law? In regard to the first question, many have followed the lead of R. Jewett ("The Agitators," 205) who argues "that Jewish Christians in Judea were stimulated by Zealotic pressure into a nomistic campaign among their fellow Christians in the late forties and early fifties. Their goal was to avert the suspicion that they were in communion with lawless Gentiles." By circumcising Paul's converts, the agitators would prove to the zealots that those who believed in Jesus as the Messiah, and even their Gentile converts, were faithful to the laws and practices of Torah. In doing so, they would avoid Zealot persecution. But what sense does it make for Jewish Christians in Judea to travel hundreds of miles to North, or even South Galatia? Would it not be more important to insure that Gentile proselytes, in and around Jerusalem, were circumcised? It is unlikely that the agitators traveled hundreds of miles to circumcise Gentile converts in order to avoid the persecution of zealots in and around Jerusalem. Rather, Paul is simply applying the experience of his own life to the agitators. In effect, he says that he has experienced persecution from Jews, and Jewish Christians like the agitators, because he preaches a Torah-free gospel. Thus far the agitators have not experienced such persecution, but if they preach a Torah-free gospel they will suffer persecution from Jews, and from Jewish Christians like themselves.

In regard to the second point, it has been argued that the agitators do not keep (*phylassousin*) the Law because (1) it is impossible to observe; or because (2) the agitators were sycretists whose only concern was the outward manifestations of the Law, not the observance of its precepts and commandments. Here, however, Paul's intention is to expose the nature and motivation of the agitators. In all likelihood, the agitators encouraged the Galatians to observe the Law, but, from Paul's perspective, the agitators did not keep the Law. Again, in Paul's view, they are a hypocritical lot, primarily concerned with making a good appearance in, and boasting in, the flesh.

The essential points of Paul's argument (vv. 14–17). Having exposed the motivation of the agitators, Paul takes the opportunity of these final verses to summarize the essential points of his argument: (1) he boasts in the Cross of Jesus Christ; (2) Christ has brought about a new creation which destroys the walls of division that scarred the old creation; (3) Paul bears the marks of Christ.

Paul's first point emphasizes the difference between him and the agitators. Whereas they boast in the physical mark of circumcision, the Apostle boasts in the Cross of Christ. While boasting in the Cross of Christ has become a hallmark of Christianity, modern readers must continually remind themselves of how shocking Paul's words must have sounded two thousand years ago. Crucifixion was usually reserved for slaves, violent criminals, and political rebels. It was, in the Greco-Roman world, the most humiliating and degrading form of punishment, a sign of weakness and defeat. Despite this cultural aversion to the cross, Paul boasts in the cross as the sign of God's power and salvation. Moreover, he proclaims that through the cross he has been crucified to the world, and the world has been crucified to him. This phrase is a striking way of saying that this age, which stands in sharp opposition to God, no longer has any real existence for Paul; nor does this age want anything to do with the Apostle. Paul and this world are dead to each other, because Paul, unlike this world, has willingly embraced the Cross of Christ.

Paul's second point is a summary of his doctrine of justification. Because the Christ event has brought about a new creation, neither circumcision nor the lack of it means anything. The statement that neither circumcision nor the lack of it means anything recalls what Paul wrote in 5:6. But whereas there he said that in Christ neither circumcision nor the lack of it means anything, but faith expressing itself through love, here he proclaims that the determining factor is the new creation. What that new creation is, Paul explains in 2 Cor 5:17: "if anyone is in Christ, there is a new creation." Incorporation into Christ, then, is incorporation into a new creation where there is neither Jew nor Greek, slave nor free, male nor female (3:28). Put another way, it does not matter if the Galatians remain uncircumcised; nor does it matter if Jewish Christians are circumcised, in Christ both are one. In the language of Ephesians, "He has abolished the law with its commandments and ordinances, that he might create in himself one new humanity in place of the two, thus making peace'' (2:15).

For Paul, this new creation is a rule (*kanōn*) of conduct by which the Galatians must lead their lives: they must live in Christ as a new creation. Thus Paul writes, ''Peace and mercy upon those who conduct themselves by this rule, and upon the Israel of God.'' The final phrase of this verse has given rise to a multitude of interpretations. If the conjunction *kai* (''and'') is merely explanatory, then ''the Israel of God'' is ''those who conduct themselves by this rule.'' Put another way, the Galatians are ''the Israel of God.'' But if, as most commentators believe, the *kai* is not merely explanatory, then ''the Israel of God'' refers to a group that is, in some way, distinct from ''those who conduct themselves by this rule.'' This is the view of most commentators, and it has produced a number of suggestions. (1) The Israel of God is the historic Israel upon whom Paul now calls God's mercy. Thus Burton (*Galatians*, 347) punctuates the text to read, ''. . . and mercy upon the Israel of God.'' (2) The Israel of God is a portion of Israel within all of Israel, God's own Israel. (3) The Israel of God is the whole of Israel which, in accordance with Rom 11:26, will be saved at the eschaton. (4) The Israel of God consists of those Jewish Christians who, unlike the agitators, do not judaize Gentiles. (5) The Israel of God is the Church which consists of Gentiles and Jews. (6) The Israel of God consists of Jewish and Gentile Christians who conduct themselves by this rule.

Given the argument of this letter, it is difficult to accept those solutions which draw a sharp contrast between the Galatians ''who conduct themselves by this rule'' and the Israel of God (nos. 1–4). In ch. 3, Paul argued that the Galatians are Abraham's descendants because they are in Christ; they are part of the promised inheritance. Moreover, it is clear from ch. 3 that Paul does not view the Church as a new Israel (no. 5). Rather, those who are ''in Christ,'' Gentile as well as Jew, are Abraham's descendants. Consequently, the Israel of God refers to those Gentile and Jewish believers who walk according to the new creation established by God's act in Christ. In this verse, then, ''the Israel of God'' includes the Galatians, yet goes beyond them. Paul extends a greeting of peace and mercy to the Galatians, and then to all of those who, like them, conduct themselves according to the rule of the new creation.

Paul's third and final point is to remind the Galatians that he has suffered for the Torah-free gospel that he has preached to them. Unlike the agitators, he has been ''branded'' by the sufferings of his apostolic ministry. For an extended list of those sufferings see 2 Cor 11:23-29. The sufferings that Paul has endured in his apostolate are the outward manifestation of his co-crucifixion with Christ. He, unlike the agitators, has a right to boast because he has suffered for the gospel.

The closing grace (v. 18). Paul concludes his letter to the Galatians with a brief benediction. This closing grace is similar to many others found in Paul's correspondence (Rom 16:20b; 1 Cor 16:23-24; Phil 4:23; 1 Thess 5:28; Phlm 25), except for the last two words, *adelphoi, amēn*. Despite the harsh tone of this letter, there is still a strong bond of union between Paul and the Galatian community. And although the Galatians have been tempted to abandon the Torah-free gospel, Paul still refers to them as *adelphoi*, a relationship rooted in Christ. Thus the letter concludes with a note of hope that this relationship will weather the storm of this disagreeable incident. The Apostle proclaims his "amen" as if to say, here is the truth of the gospel, there is no other! Amen.

FOR REFERENCE AND FURTHER STUDY

Bahr, G. J. "Paul and Letter Writing in the Fifth (*sic*) Century." *CBQ* 28 (465–477).

Bahr, G. J. "The Subscriptions in Pauline Letters." *JBL* 87 (1968) 27–41.

Clark, K. W. "The Israel of God." *Studies in the New Testament and Early Christian Literature.* D. E. Aune, ed. Leiden: E. J. Brill, 1972, 161–169.

Davies, W. D. "Paul and the People of Israel." *Jewish and Pauline Studies.* Philadelphia: Fortress, 1984, 123–152.

Doty, W. G. *Letters in Primitive Christianity.* Philadelphia: Fortress, 1973, 39–42.

Jewett, R. "The Agitators And the Galatian Congregation." *NTS* 17 (1971) 198–212.

Martyn, J. L. "Apocalyptic Antinomies in Paul's Letter to the Galatians." *NTS* 31 (1985) 410–424.

Munck, J. "The Judaizing Gentile Christians." *Paul and the Salvation of Mankind.* Atlanta: John Knox, 1959, 87–134.

Stowers, S. K. *Letter Writing in Greco-Roman Antiquity.* Philadelphia: Westminster, 1986.

INDEXES

SELECTED SCRIPTURAL QUOTATIONS

OTHER LITERATURE

INDEX OF AUTHORS

INDEX OF SUBJECTS